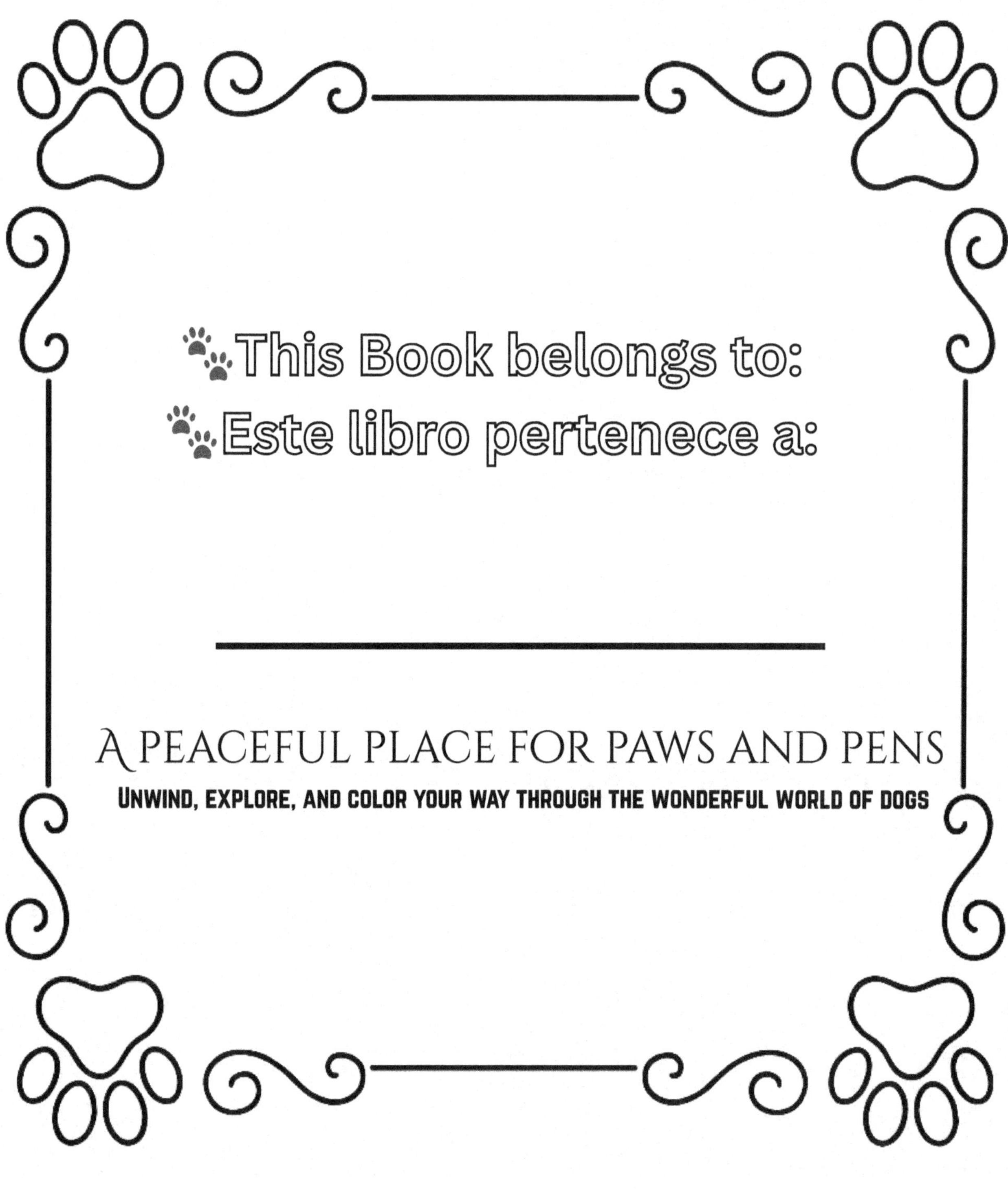

This Book belongs to:
Este libro pertenece a:

A PEACEFUL PLACE FOR PAWS AND PENS
Unwind, explore, and color your way through the wonderful world of dogs

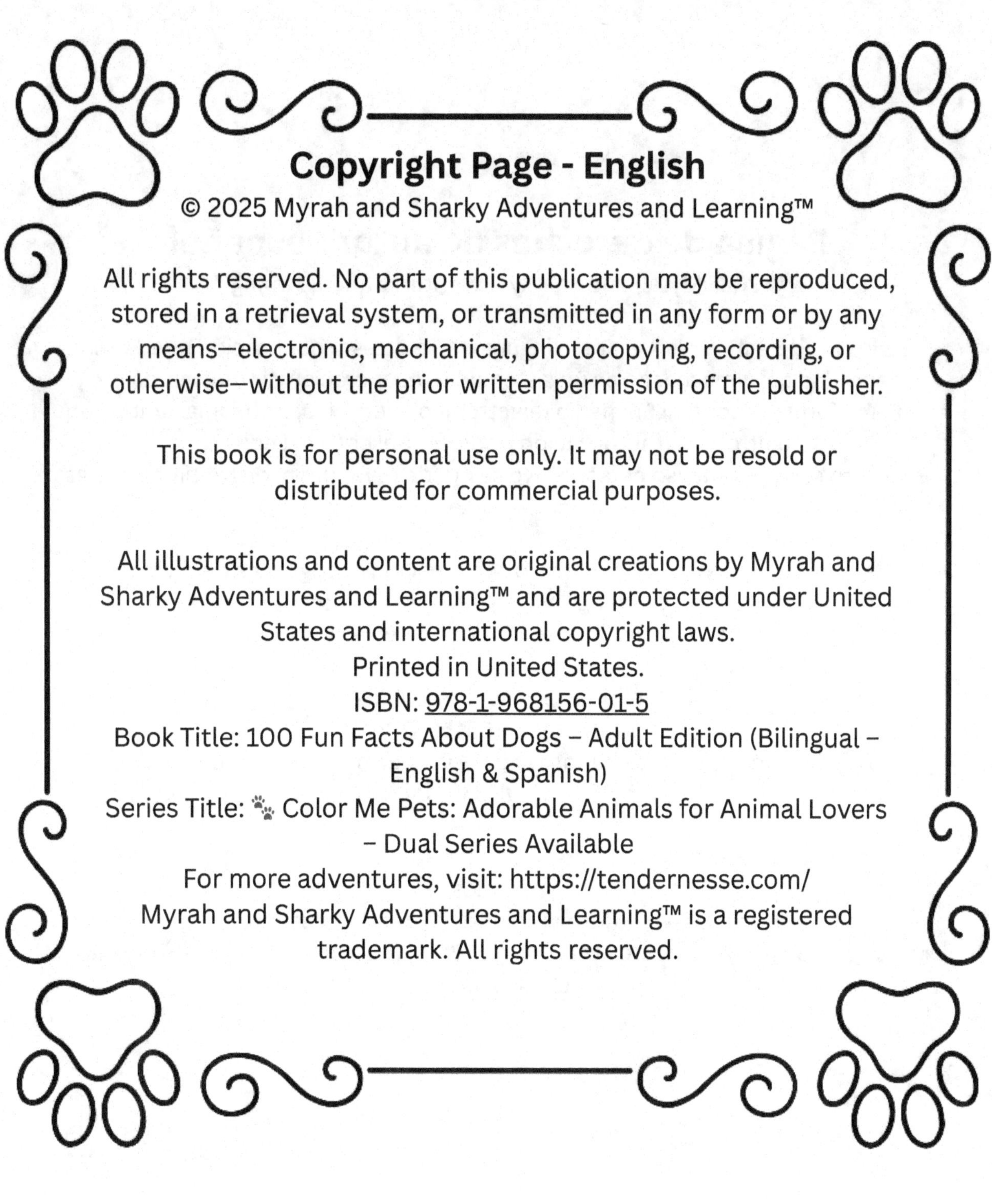

Copyright Page - English

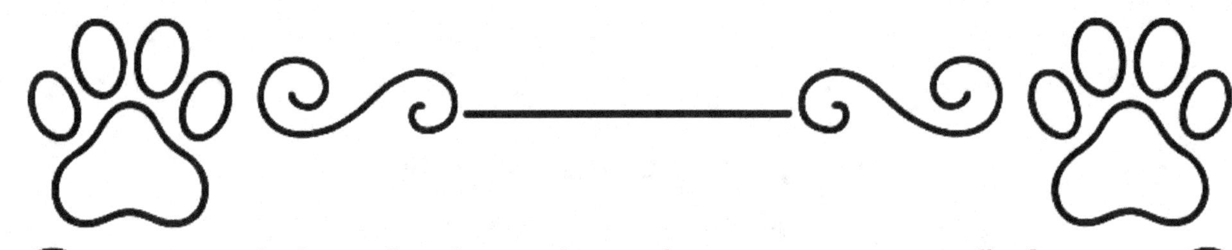

Página de derechos de autor - español

© 2025 Myrah and Sharky Adventures and Learning™

Impreso en Estados Unidos.
ISBN: 978-1-968156-00-8
Título del libro: 100 datos curiosos sobre los perros – Edición para adultos (bilingüe: inglés y español)

Título de la serie: Color Me Pets: Animales adorables para amantes de los animales
Para más aventuras, visita: https://tendernesse.com/
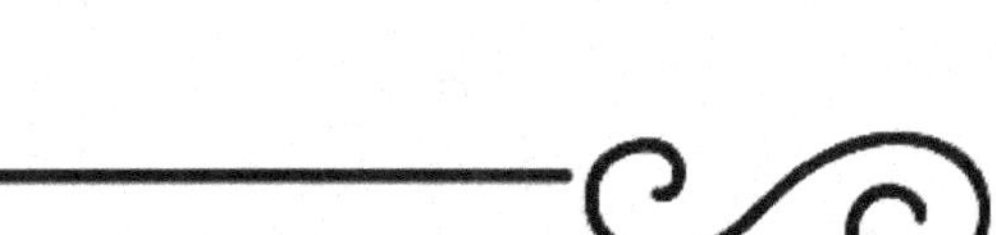

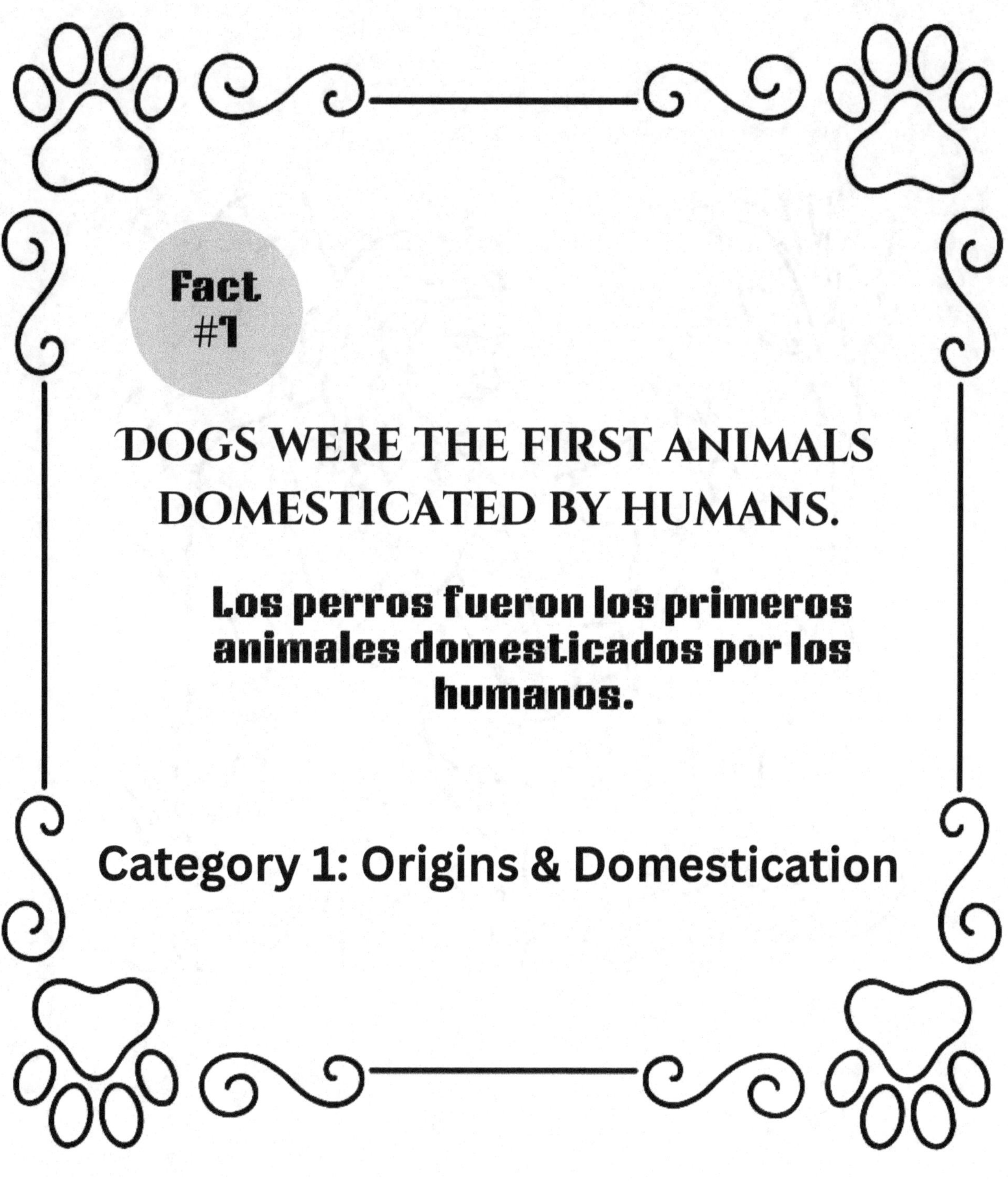

Fact #1

DOGS WERE THE FIRST ANIMALS DOMESTICATED BY HUMANS.

Los perros fueron los primeros animales domesticados por los humanos.

Category 1: Origins & Domestication

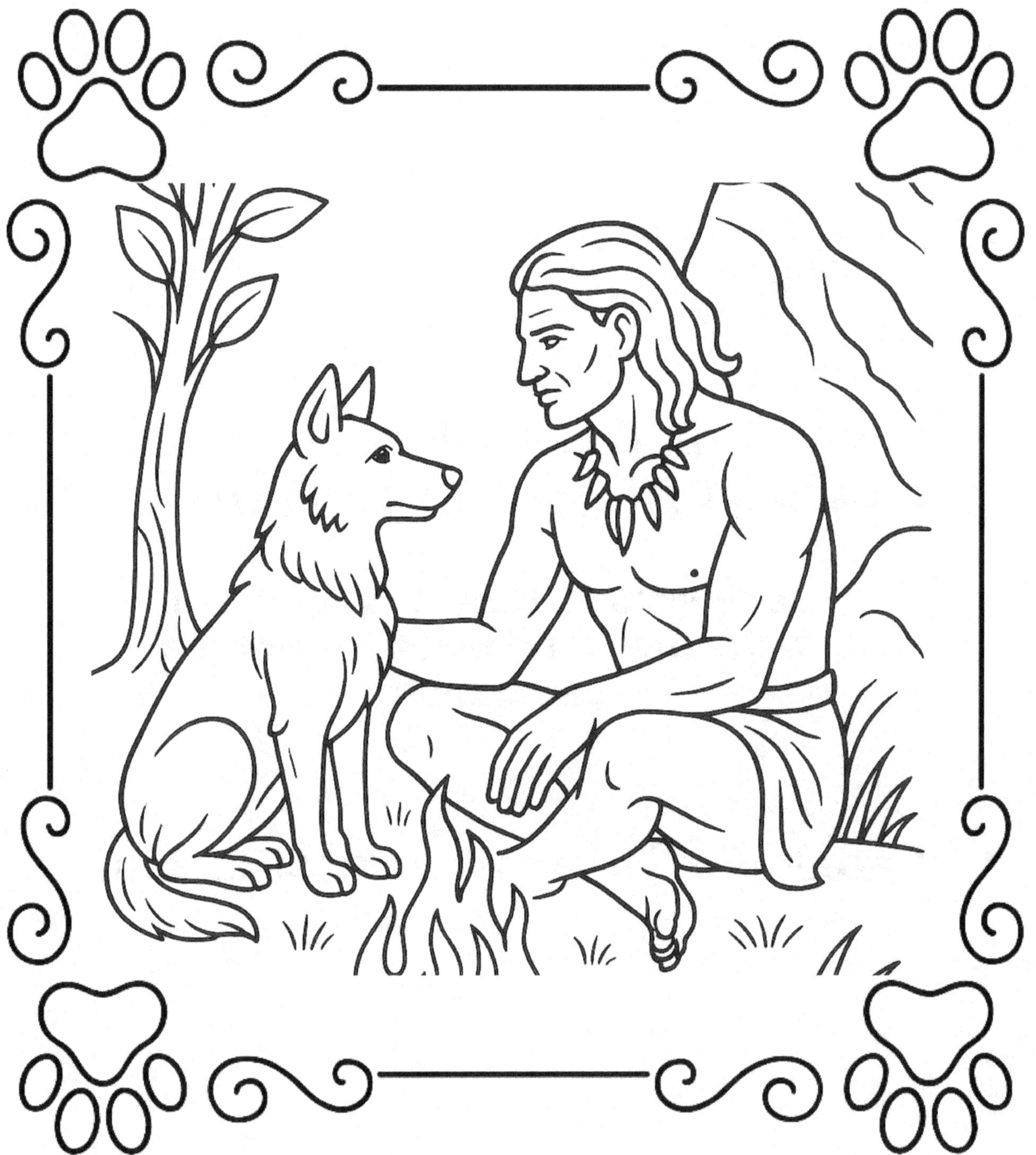

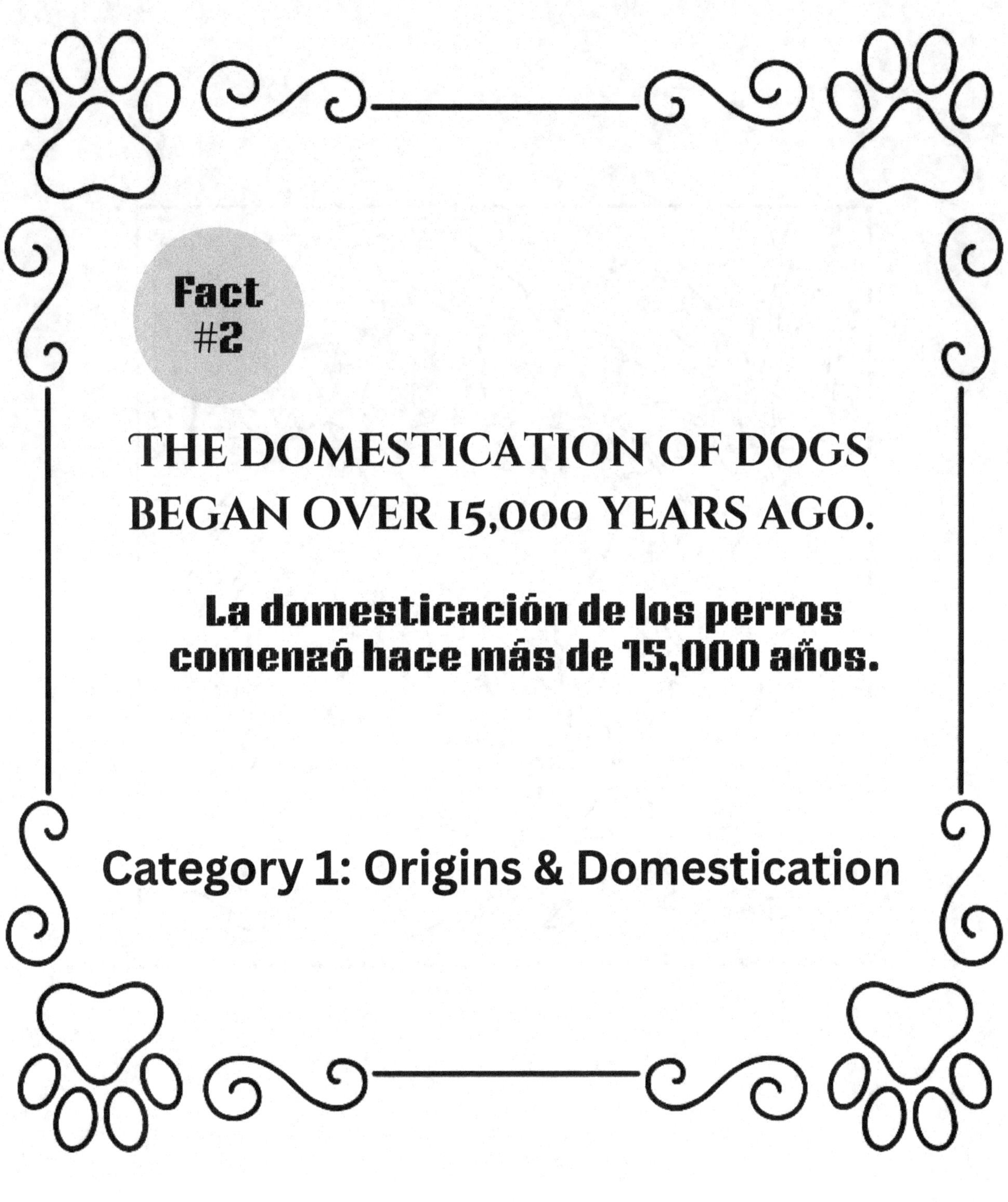

Fact #2

THE DOMESTICATION OF DOGS BEGAN OVER 15,000 YEARS AGO.

La domesticación de los perros comenzó hace más de 15,000 años.

Category 1: Origins & Domestication

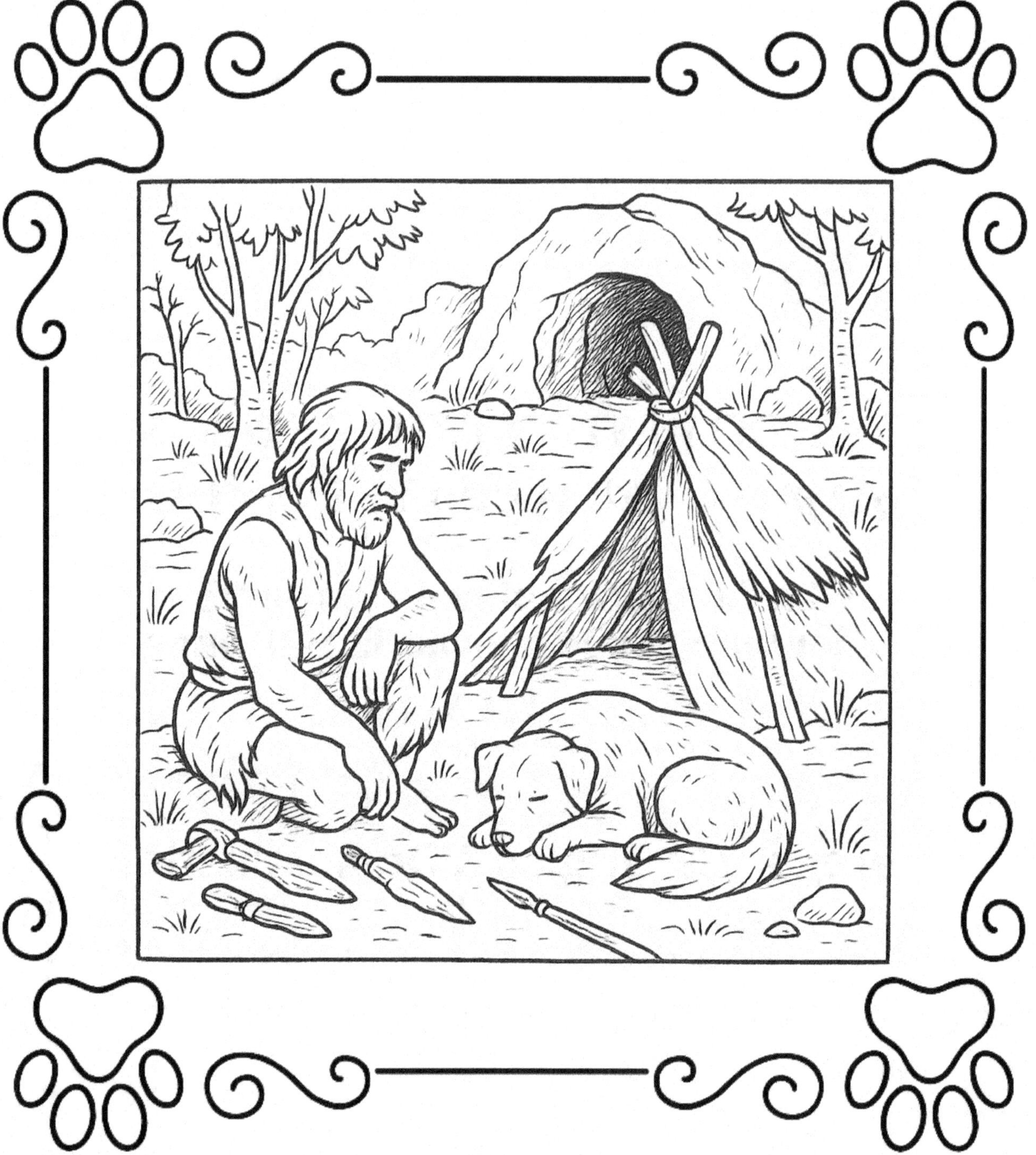

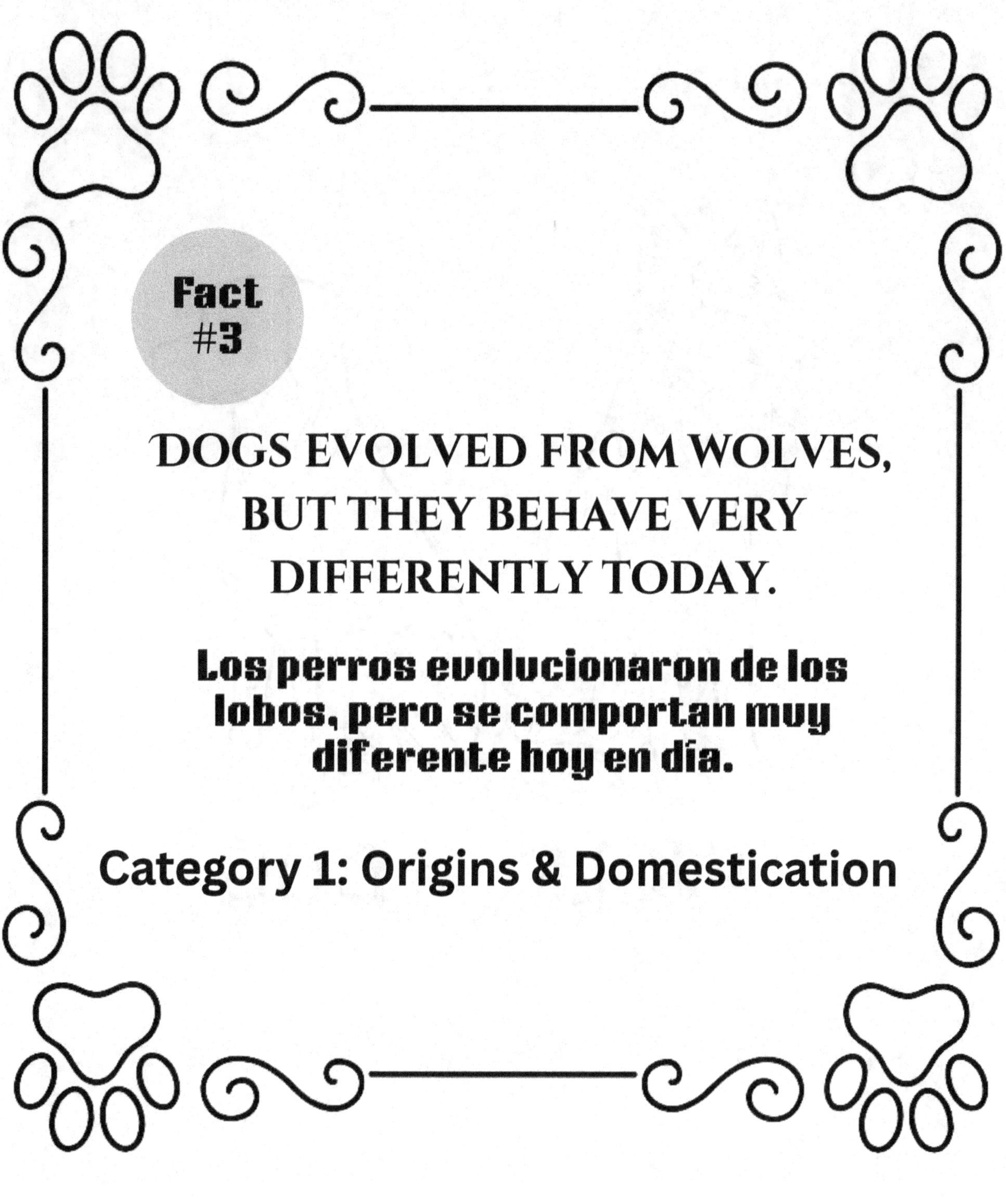

Fact #3

DOGS EVOLVED FROM WOLVES, BUT THEY BEHAVE VERY DIFFERENTLY TODAY.

Los perros evolucionaron de los lobos, pero se comportan muy diferente hoy en día.

Category 1: Origins & Domestication

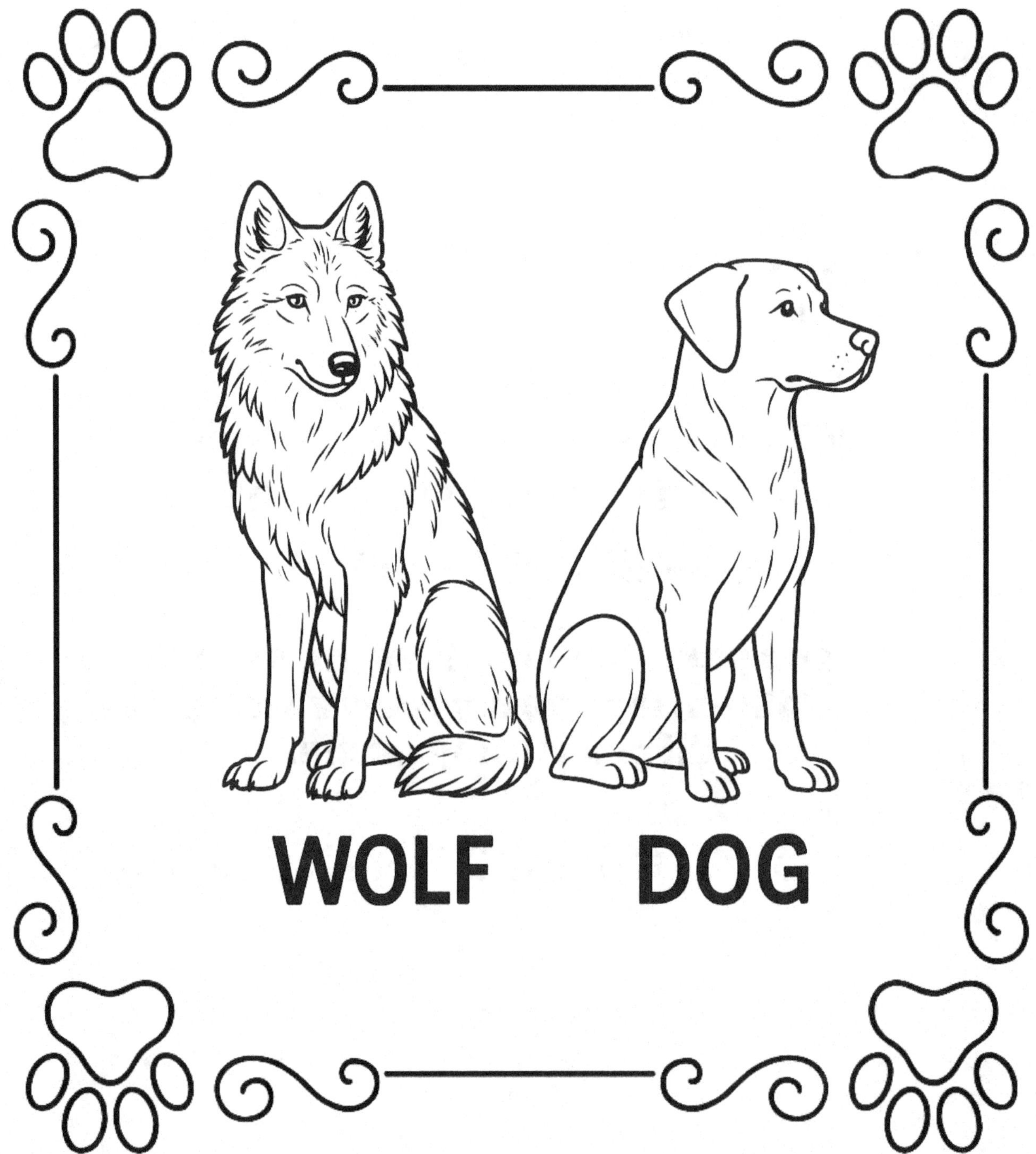

WOLF
DOG

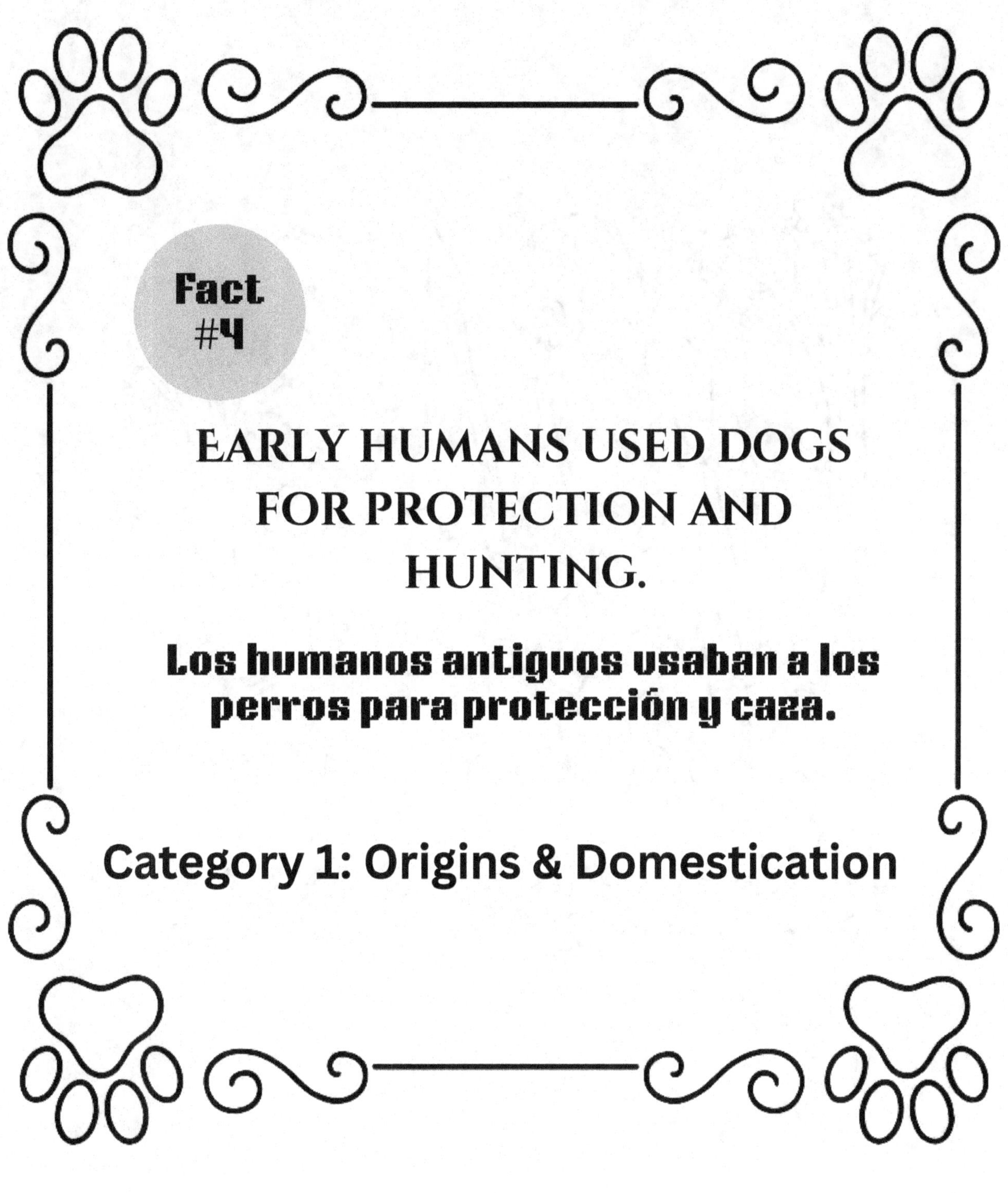

Fact
#4

EARLY HUMANS USED DOGS
FOR PROTECTION AND
HUNTING.

Los humanos antiguos usaban a los
perros para protección y caza.

Category 1: Origins & Domestication

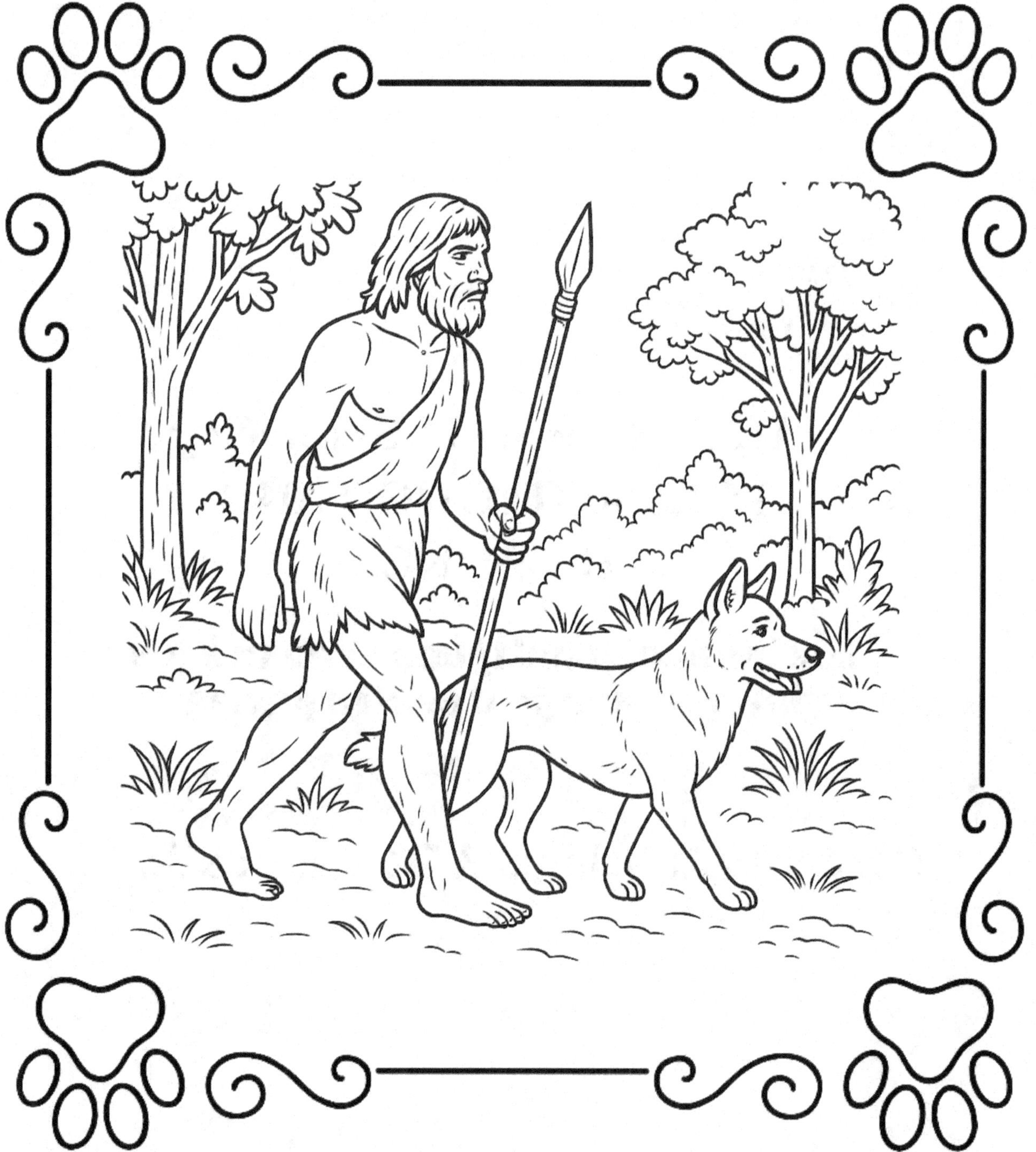

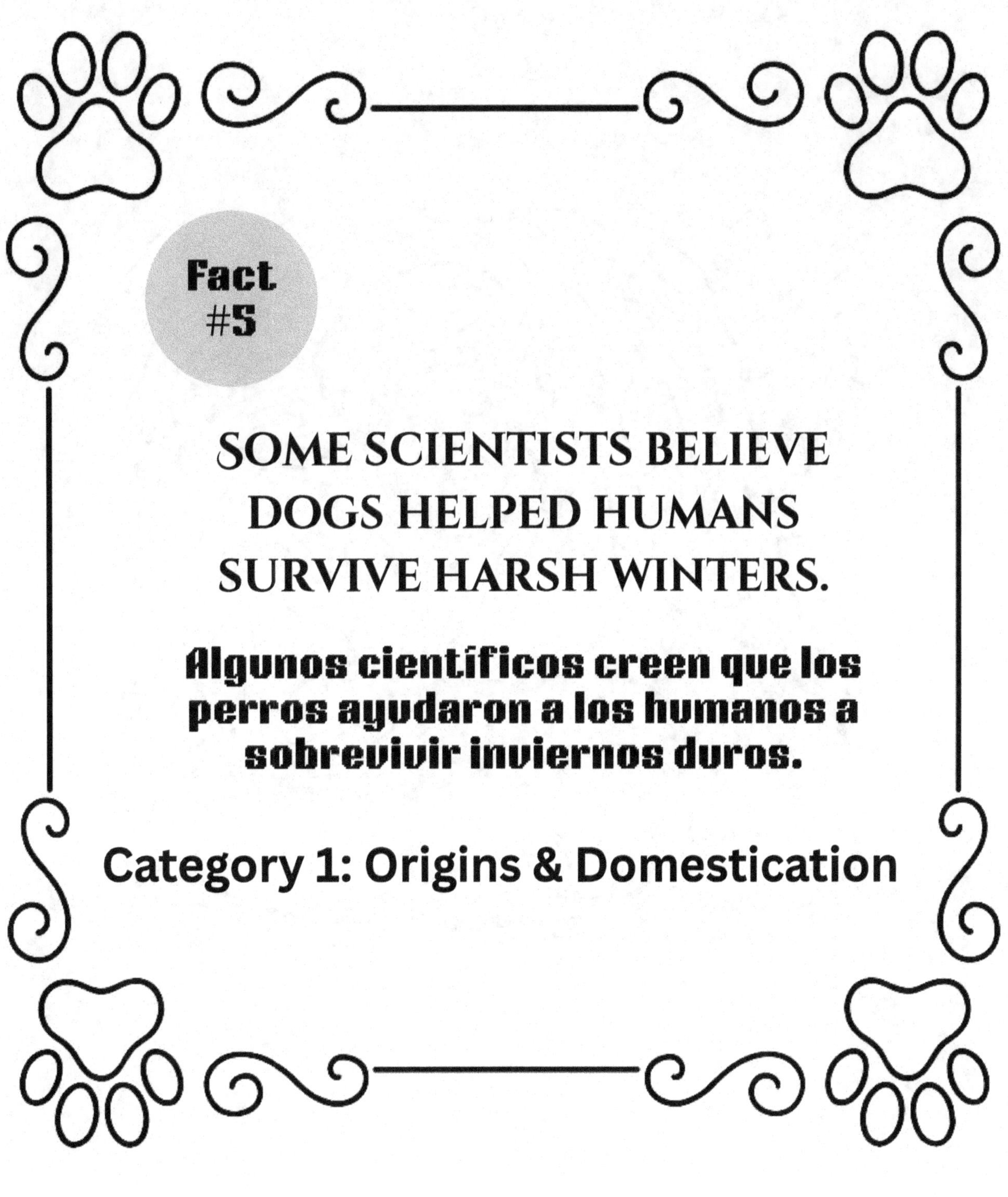

Fact #5
SOME SCIENTISTS BELIEVE DOGS HELPED HUMANS SURVIVE HARSH WINTERS.
Algunos científicos creen que los perros ayudaron a los humanos a sobrevivir inviernos duros.
Category 1: Origins & Domestication

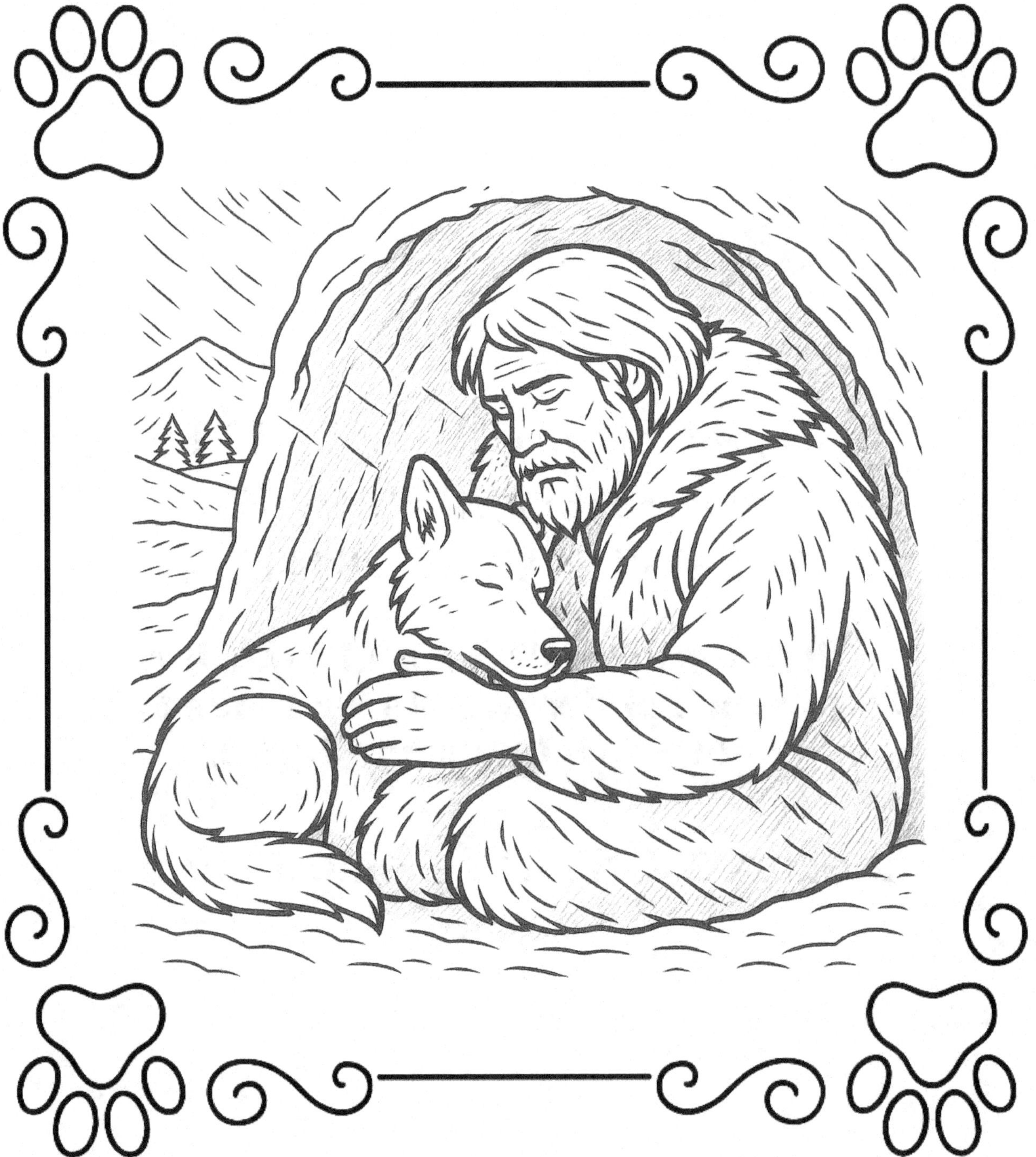

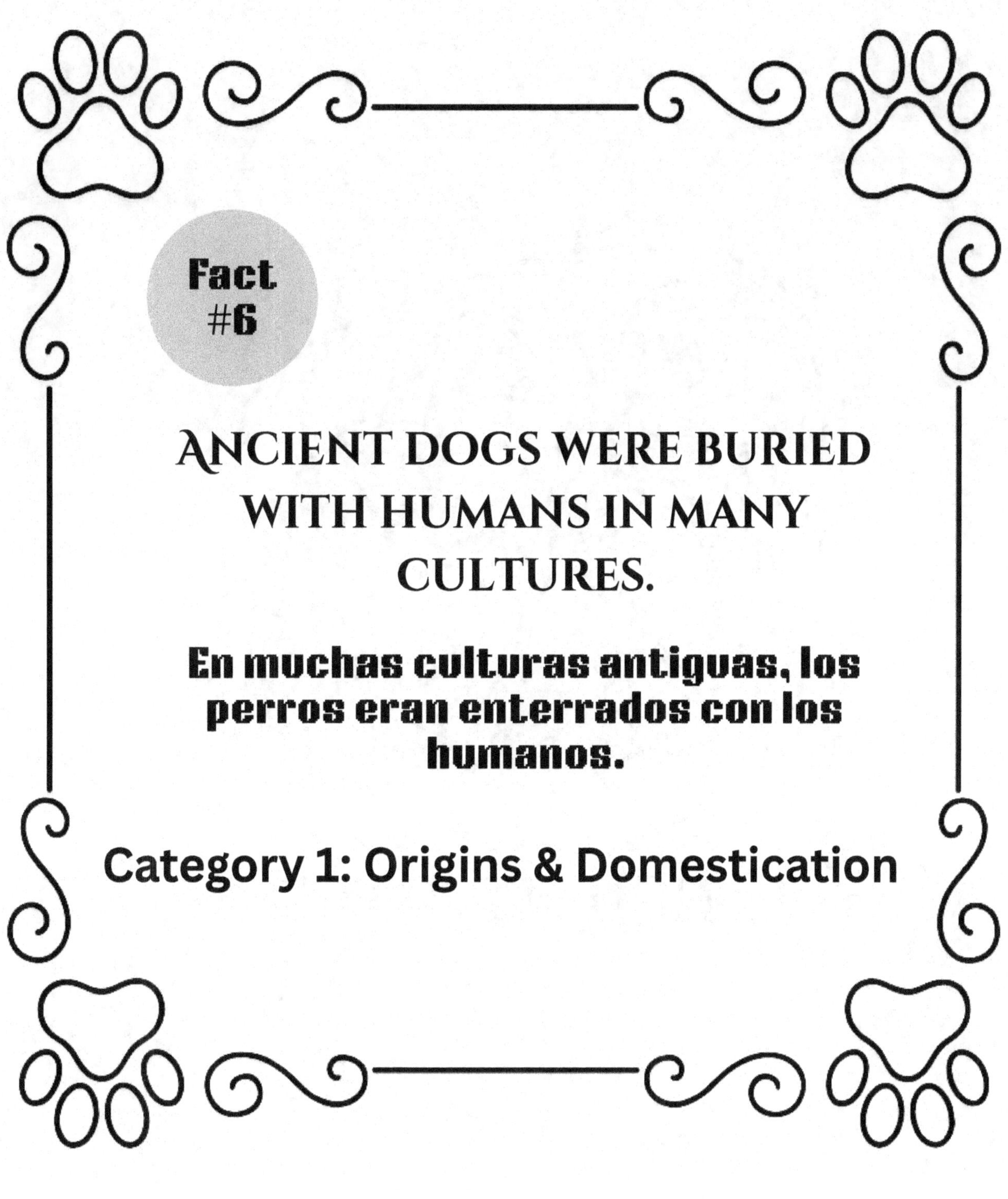

Fact #6

ANCIENT DOGS WERE BURIED WITH HUMANS IN MANY CULTURES.

En muchas culturas antiguas, los perros eran enterrados con los humanos.

Category 1: Origins & Domestication

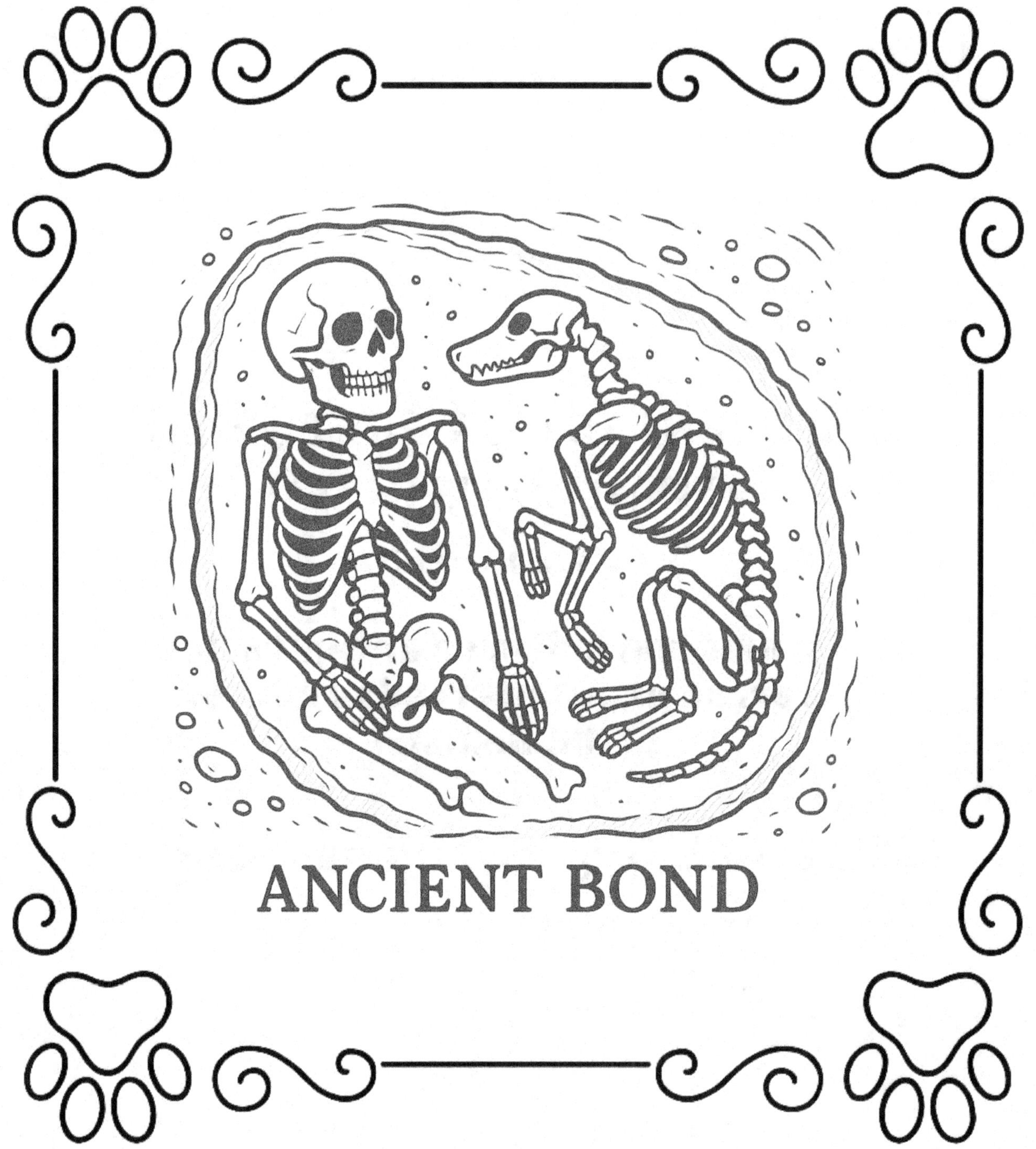

ANCIENT BOND

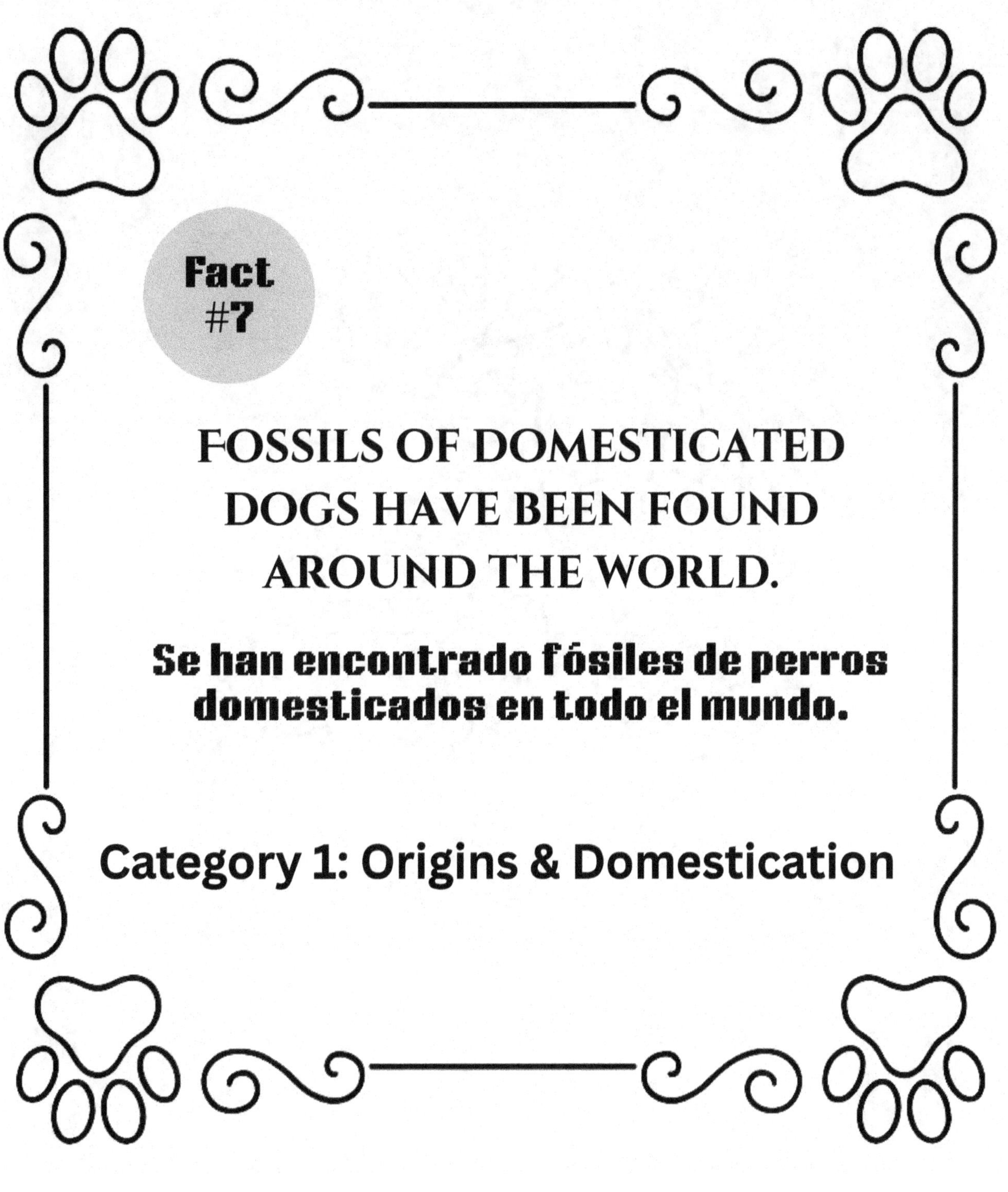

Fact #7

FOSSILS OF DOMESTICATED DOGS HAVE BEEN FOUND AROUND THE WORLD.

Se han encontrado fósiles de perros domesticados en todo el mundo.

Category 1: Origins & Domestication

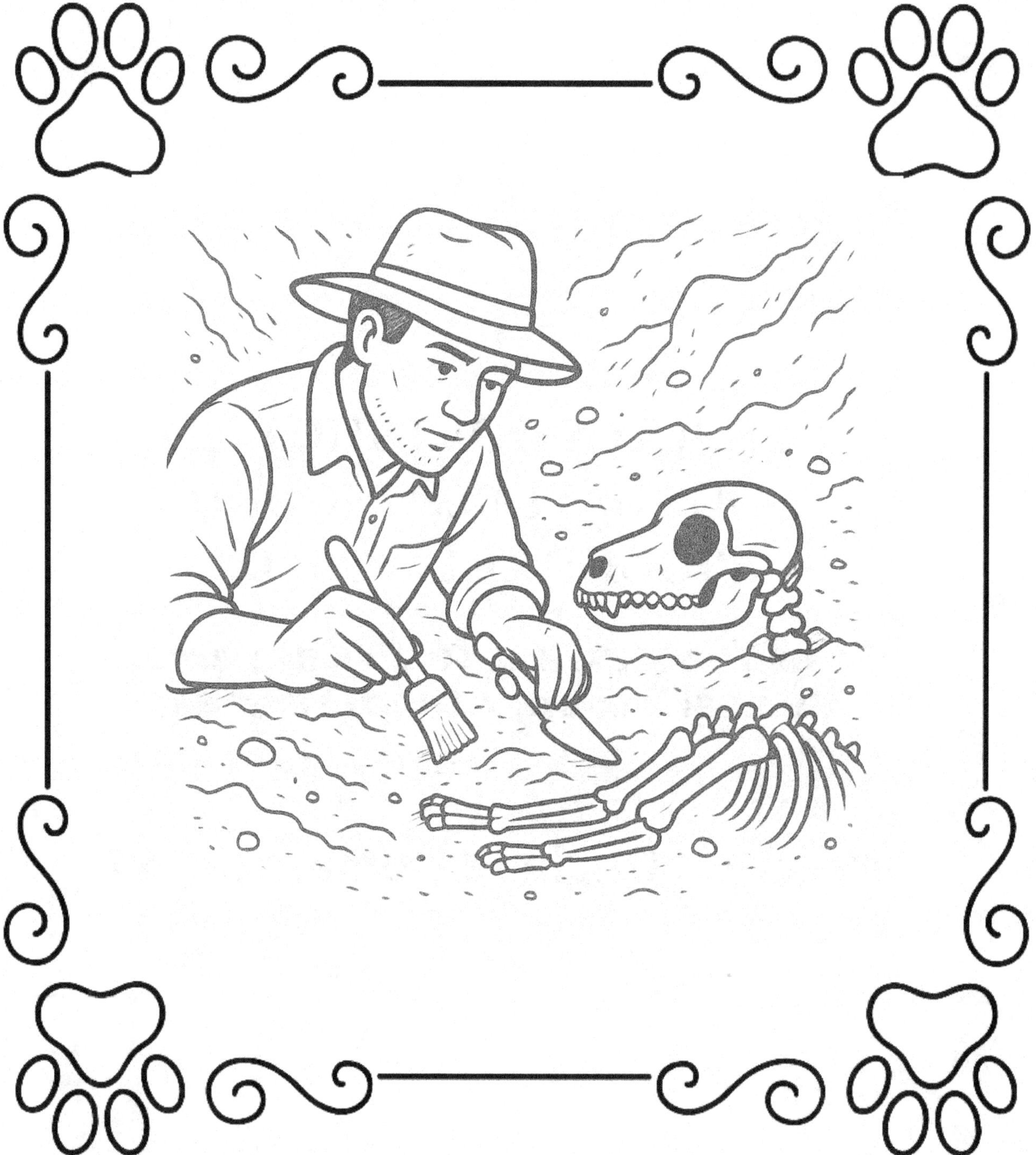

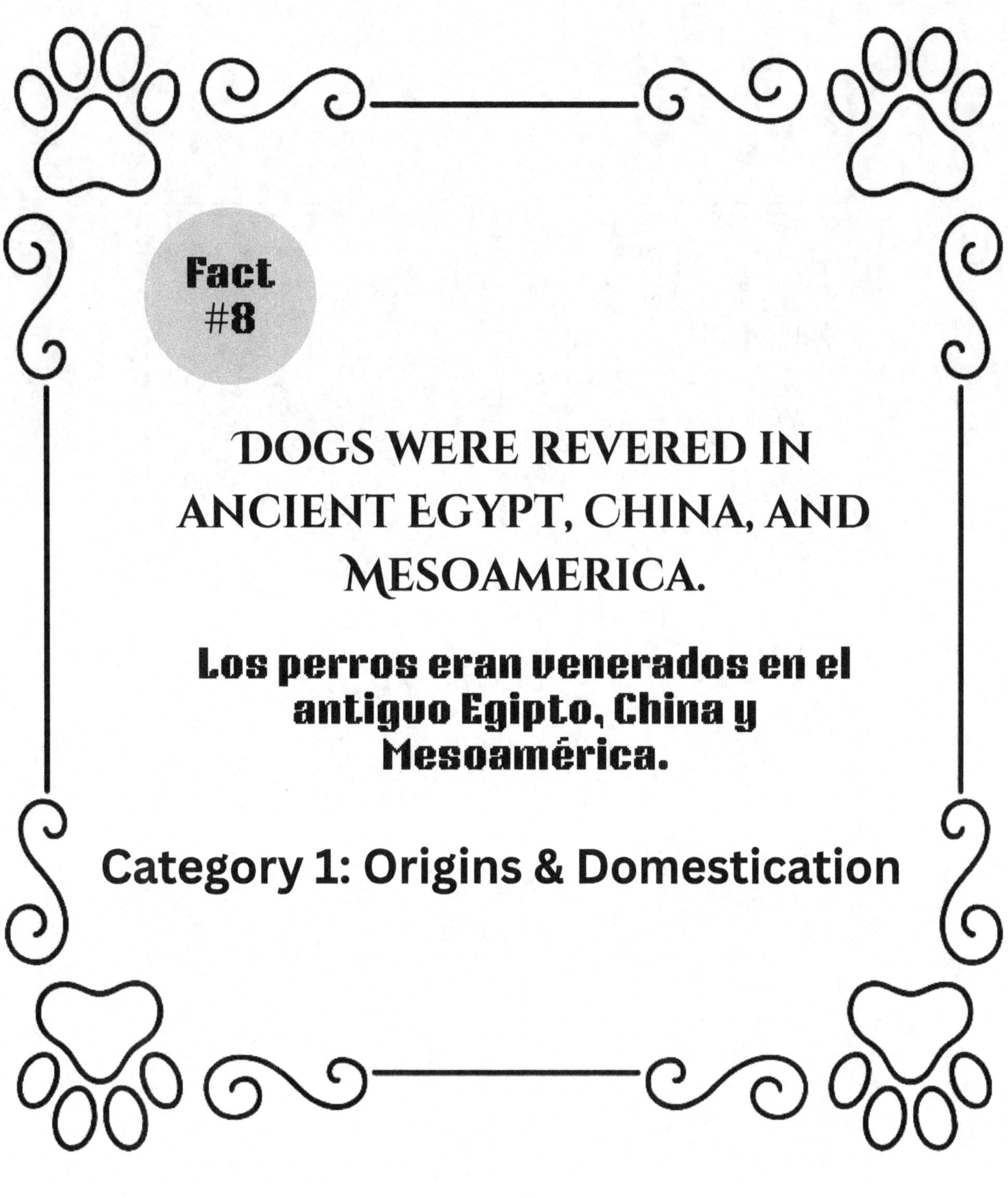

Fact
#8

DOGS WERE REVERED IN
ANCIENT EGYPT, CHINA, AND
MESOAMERICA.

Los perros eran venerados en el
antiguo Egipto, China y
Mesoamérica.

Category 1: Origins & Domestication

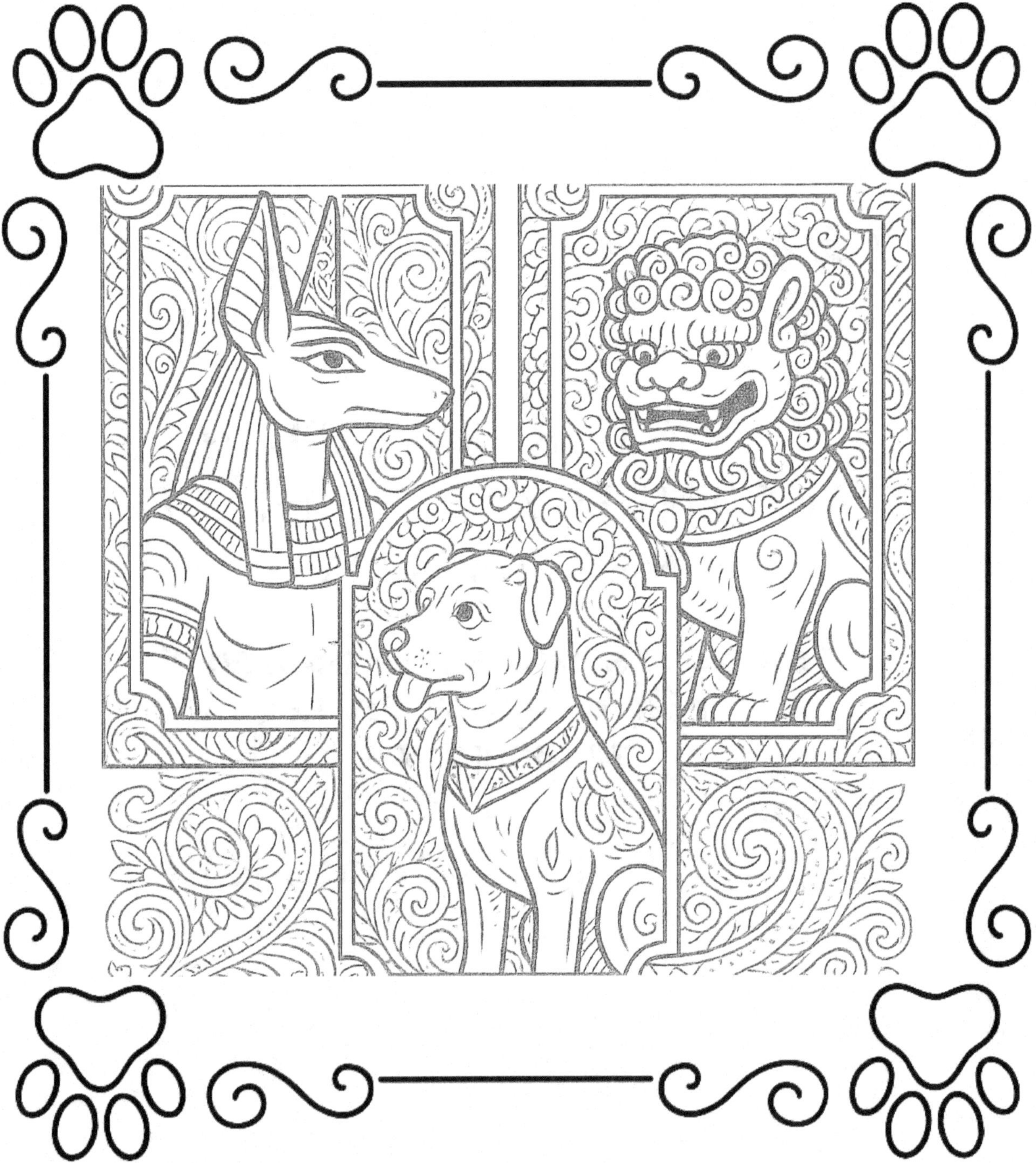

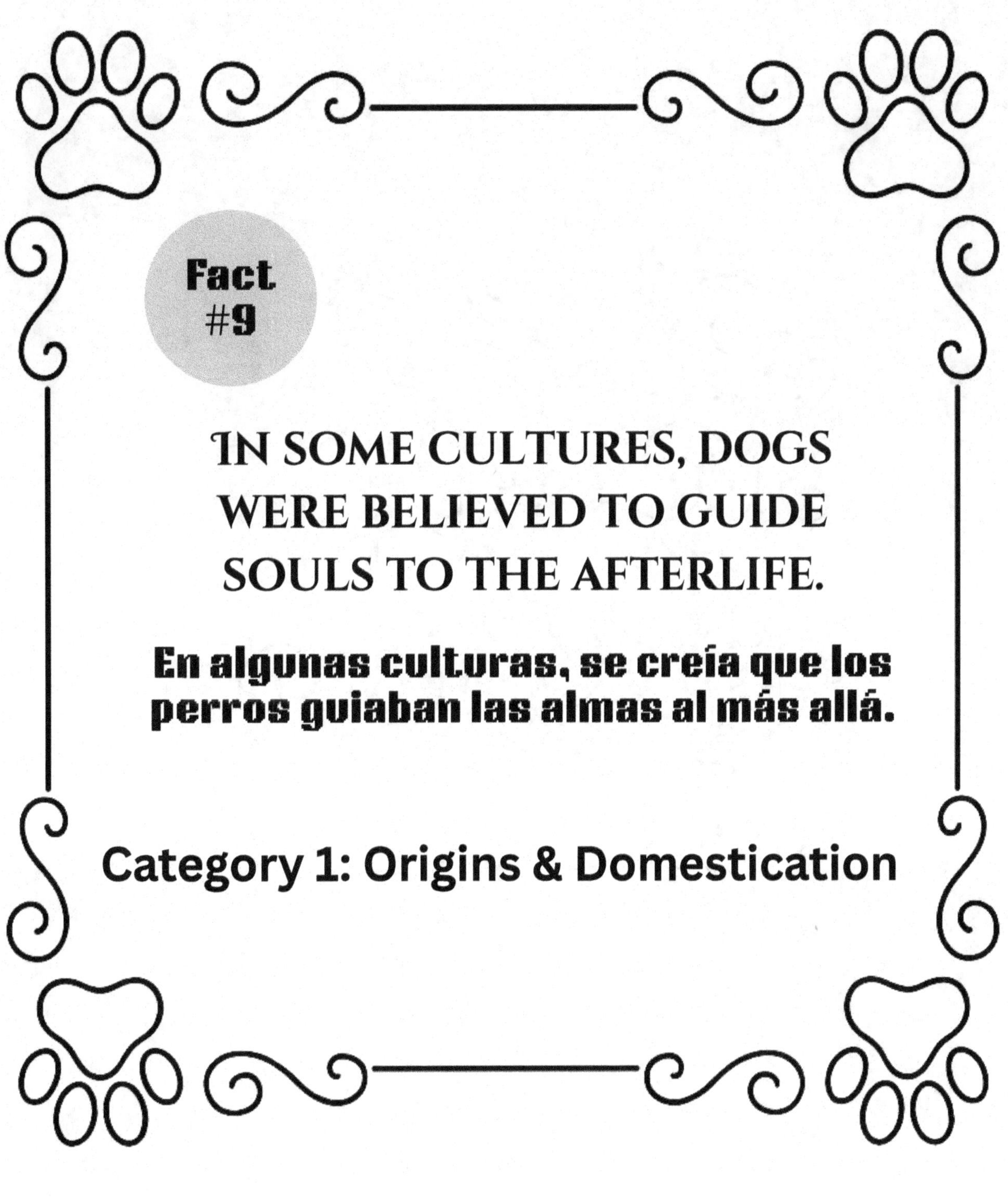

Fact #9

IN SOME CULTURES, DOGS WERE BELIEVED TO GUIDE SOULS TO THE AFTERLIFE.

En algunas culturas, se creía que los perros guiaban las almas al más allá.

Category 1: Origins & Domestication

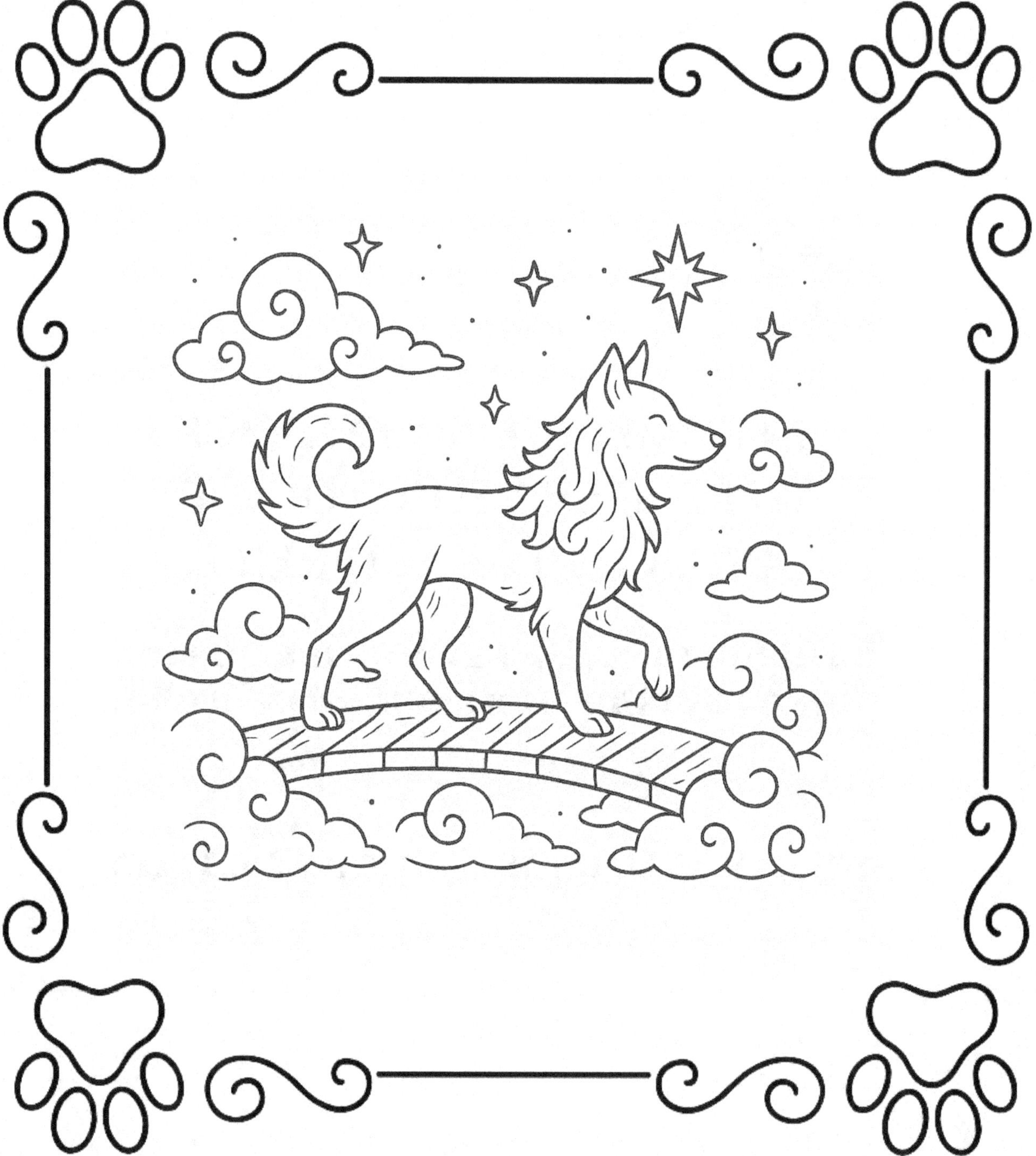

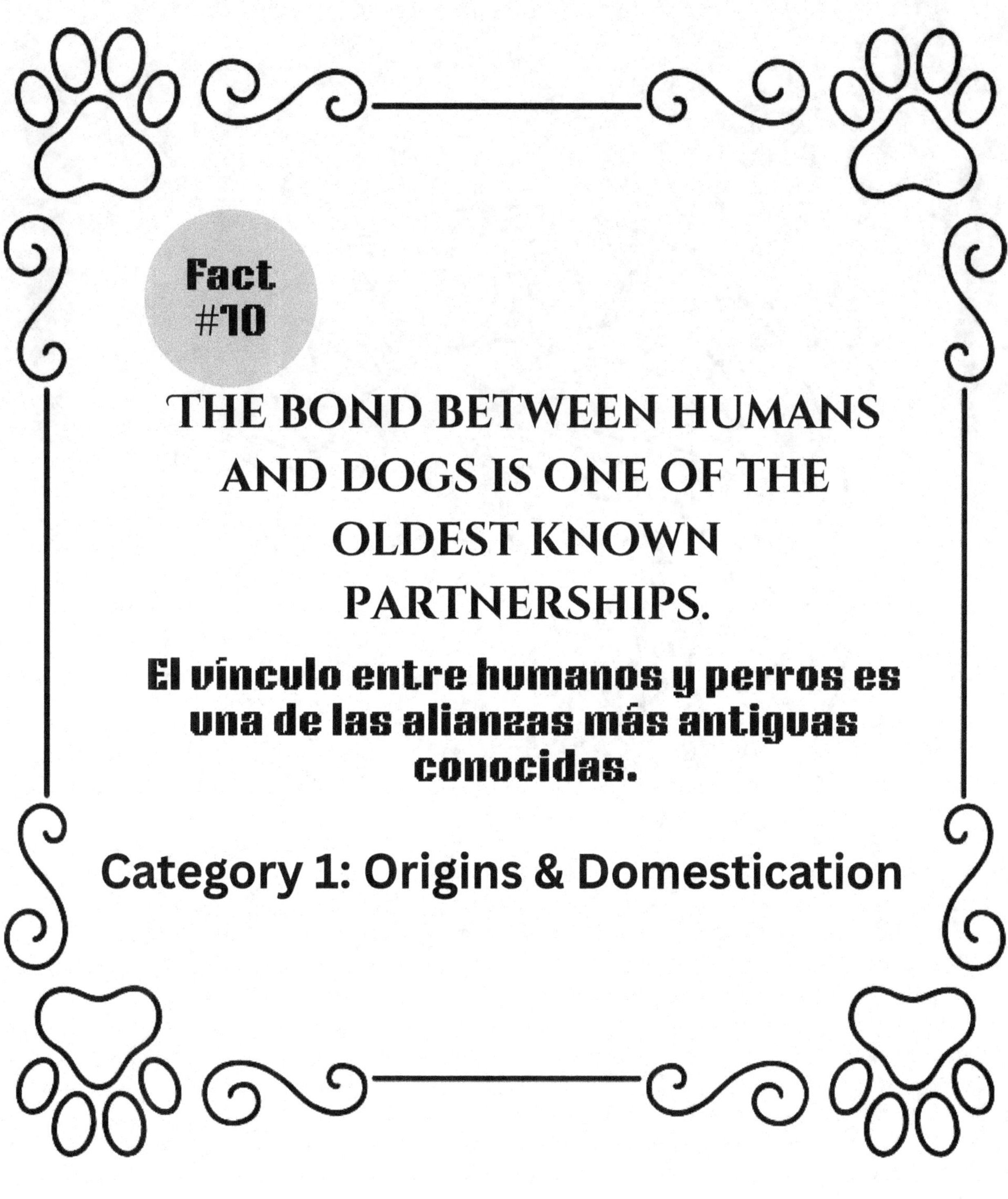

Fact #10

THE BOND BETWEEN HUMANS AND DOGS IS ONE OF THE OLDEST KNOWN PARTNERSHIPS.

El vínculo entre humanos y perros es una de las alianzas más antiguas conocidas.

Category 1: Origins & Domestication

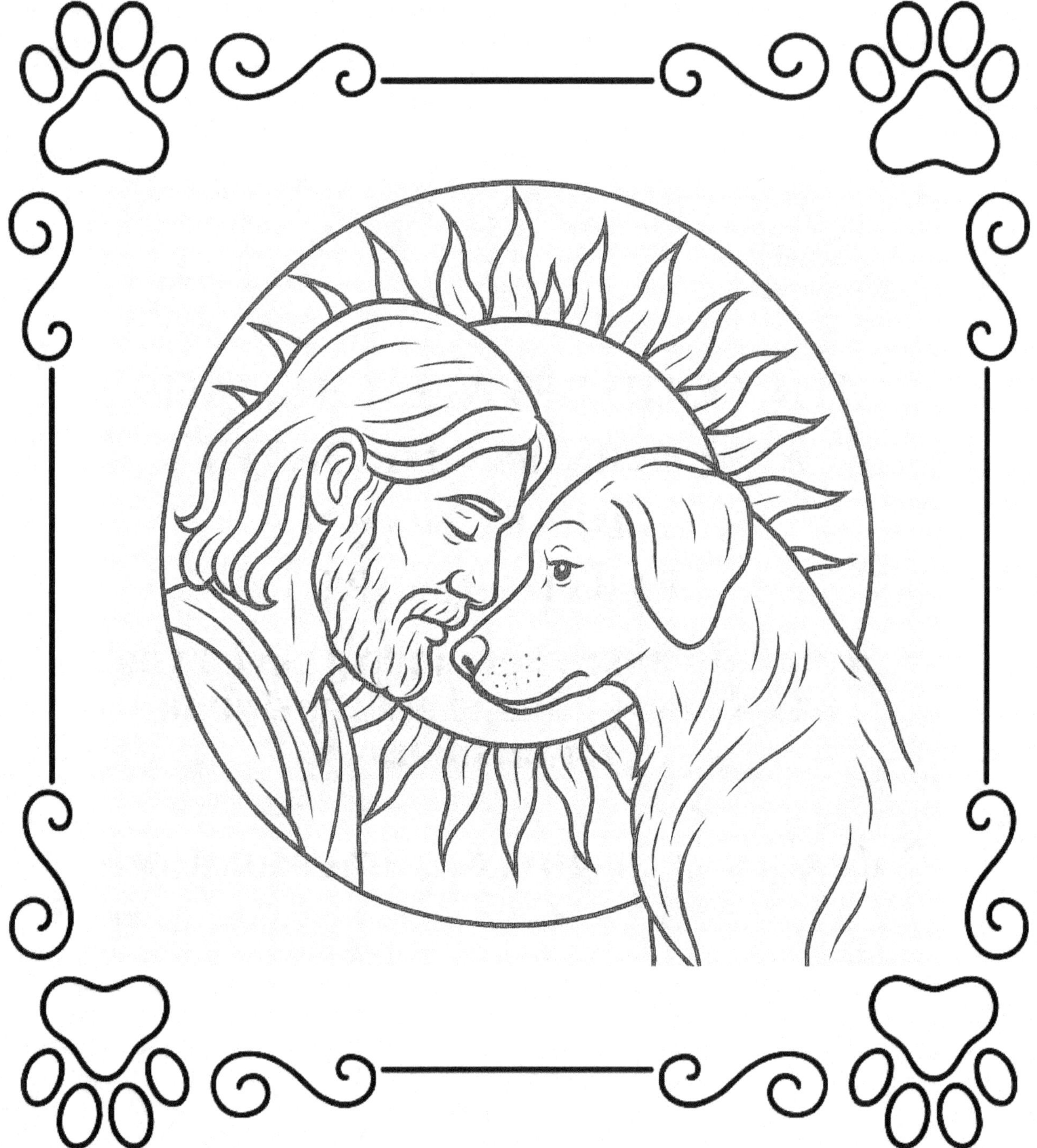

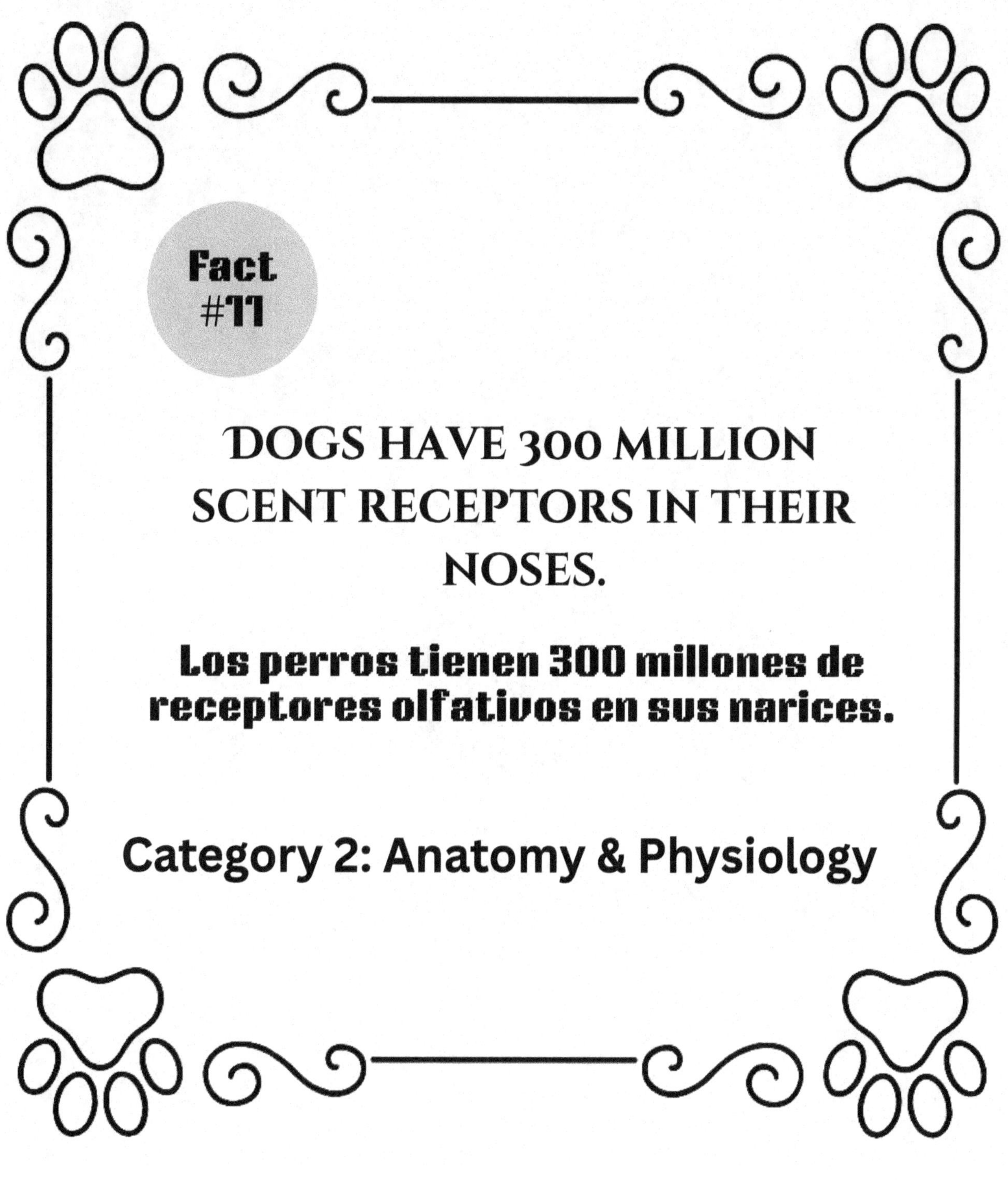

Fact
#11

DOGS HAVE 300 MILLION SCENT RECEPTORS IN THEIR NOSES.

Los perros tienen 300 millones de receptores olfativos en sus narices.

Category 2: Anatomy & Physiology

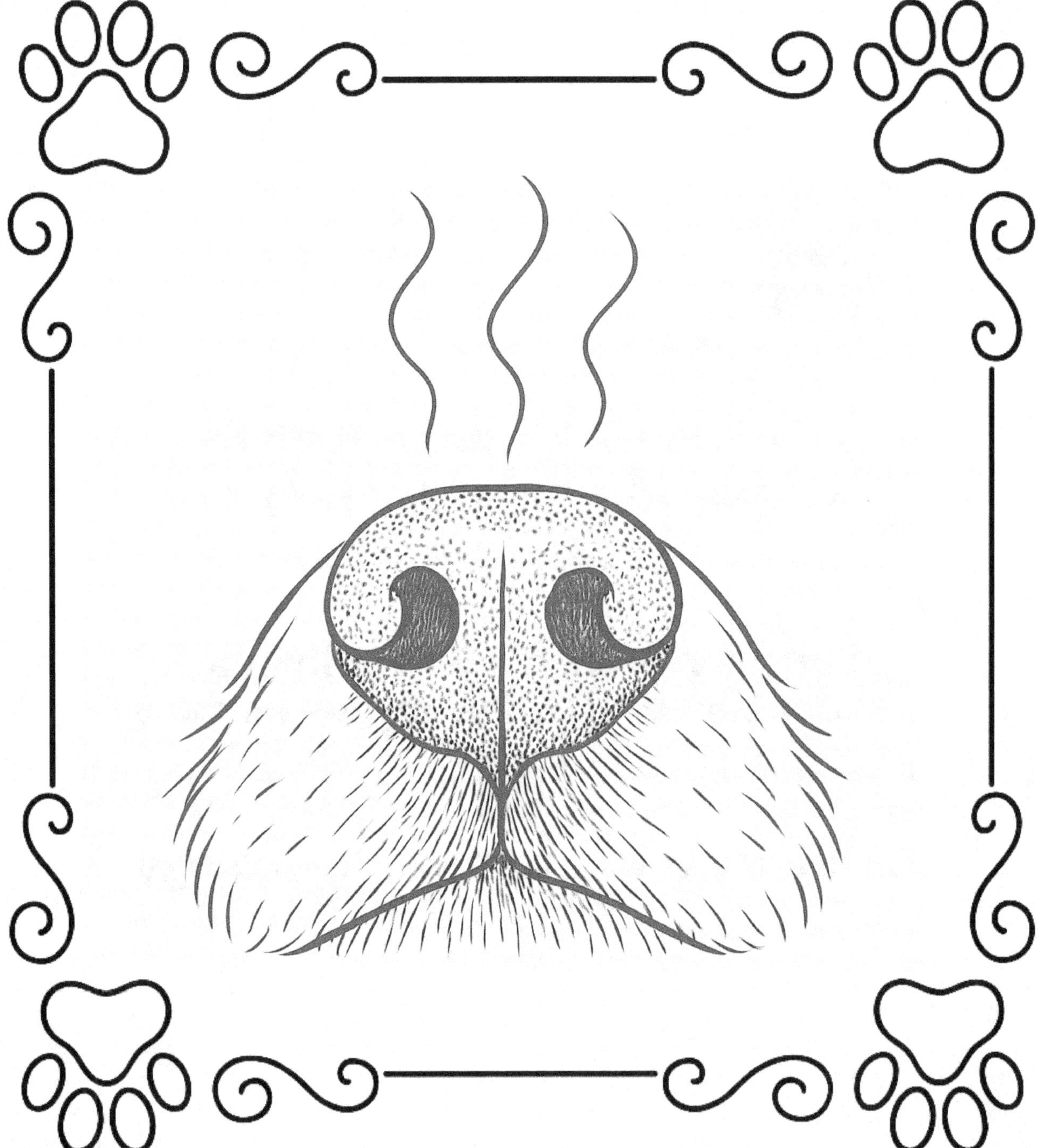

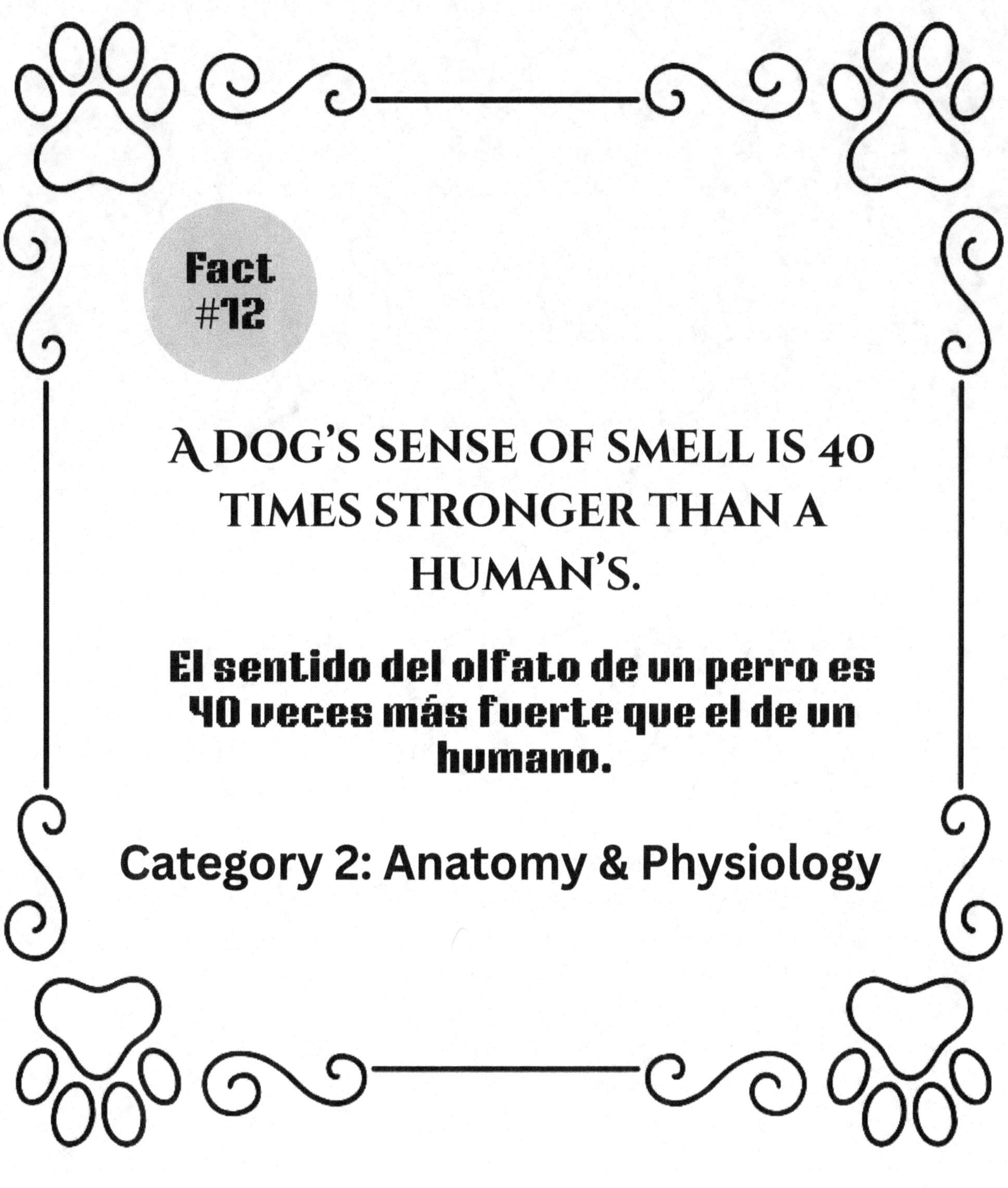
Fact #12

A DOG'S SENSE OF SMELL IS 40 TIMES STRONGER THAN A HUMAN'S.

El sentido del olfato de un perro es 40 veces más fuerte que el de un humano.

Category 2: Anatomy & Physiology

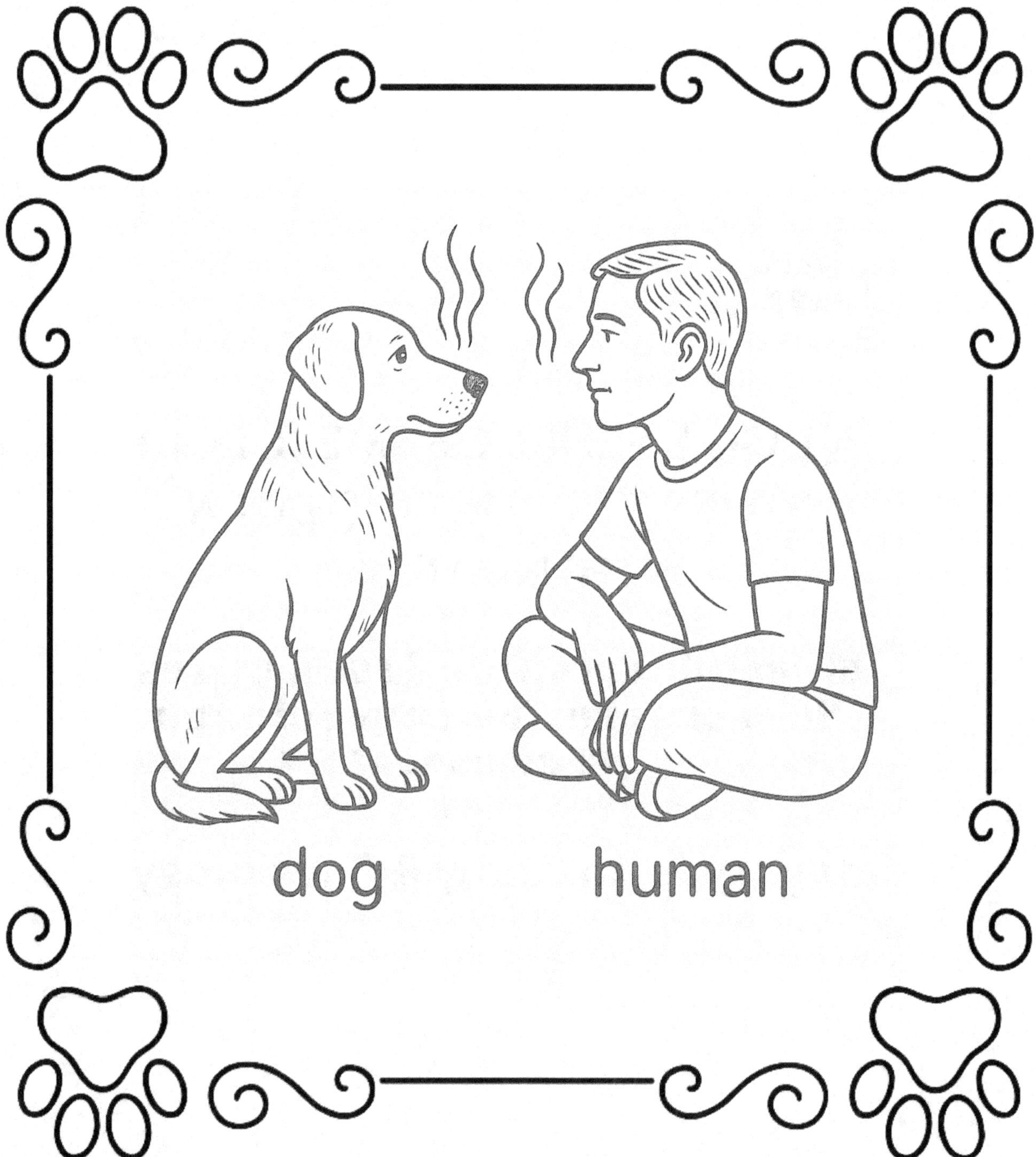

dog
human

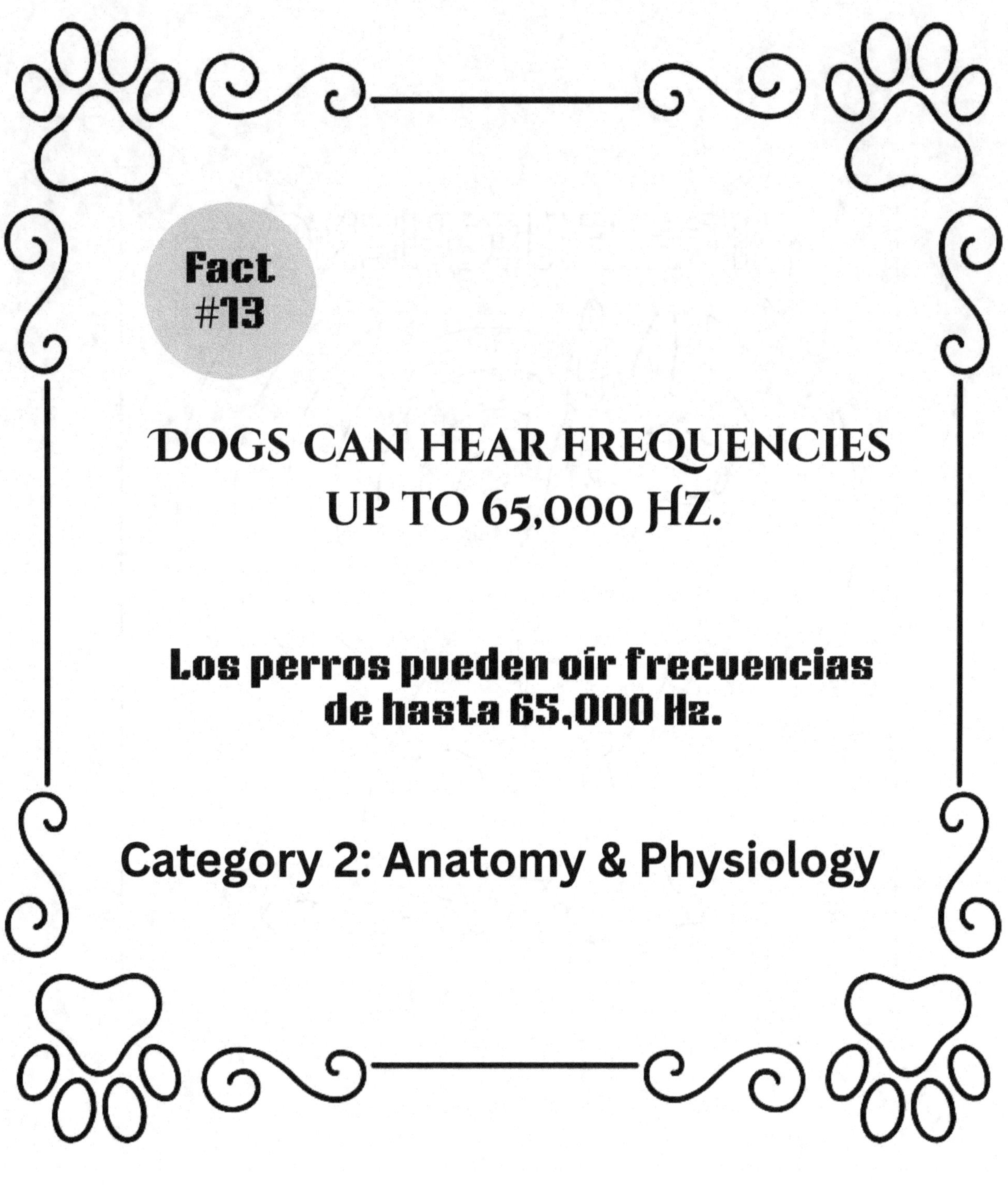

Fact #13

DOGS CAN HEAR FREQUENCIES UP TO 65,000 HZ.

Los perros pueden oír frecuencias de hasta 65,000 Hz.

Category 2: Anatomy & Physiology

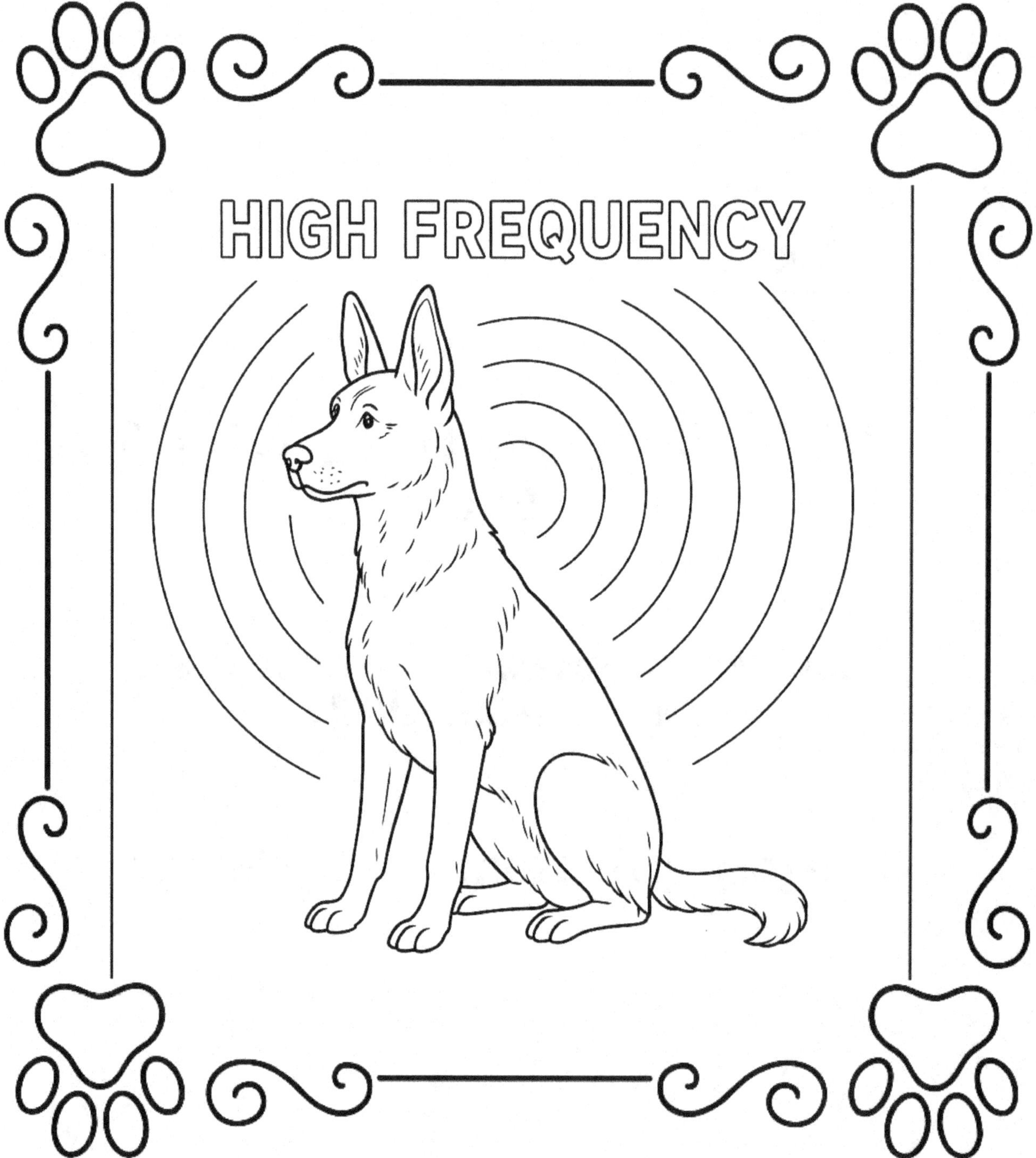
HIGH FREQUENCY

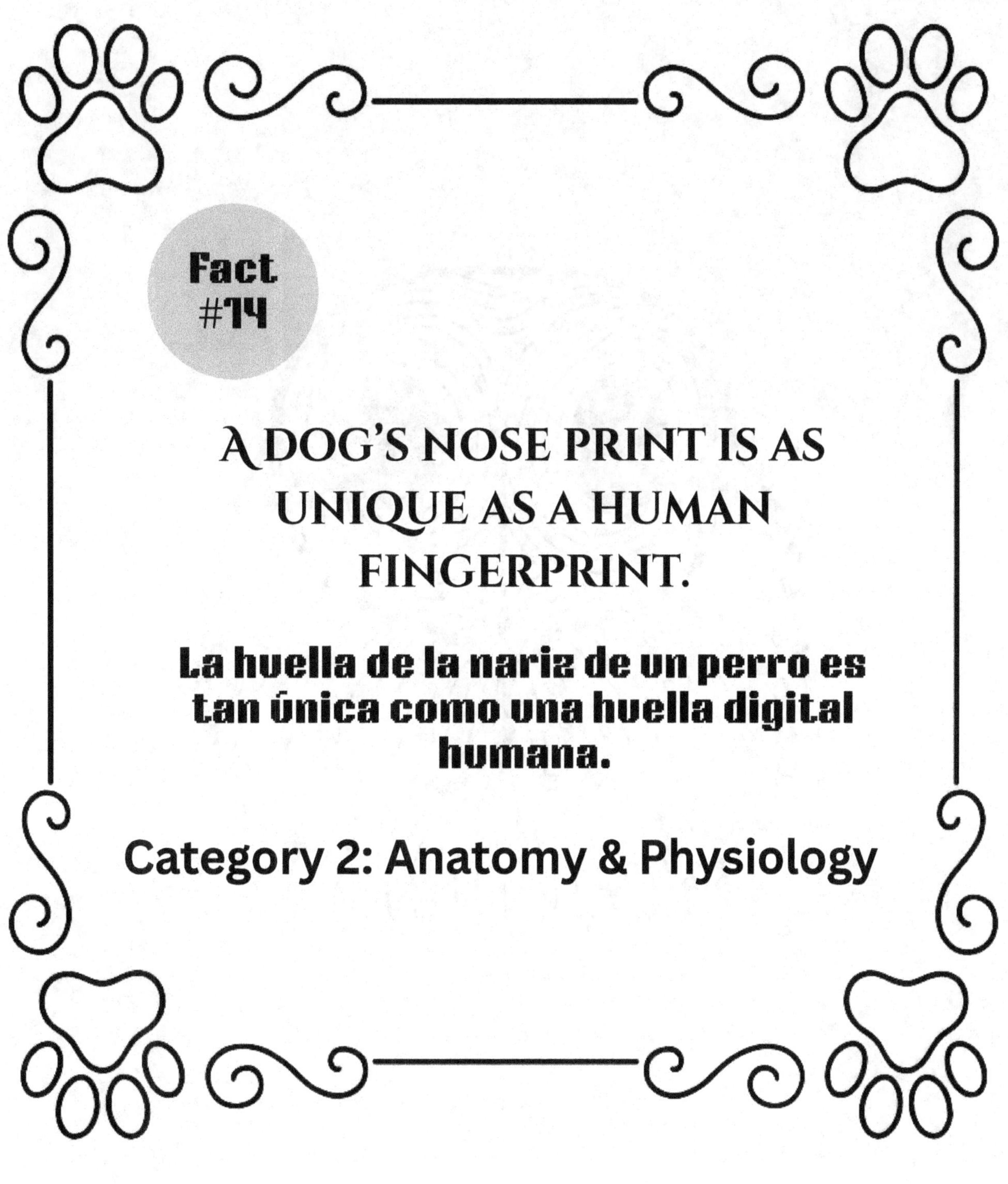

A DOG'S NOSE PRINT IS AS UNIQUE AS A HUMAN FINGERPRINT.

La huella de la nariz de un perro es tan única como una huella digital humana.

Category 2: Anatomy & Physiology

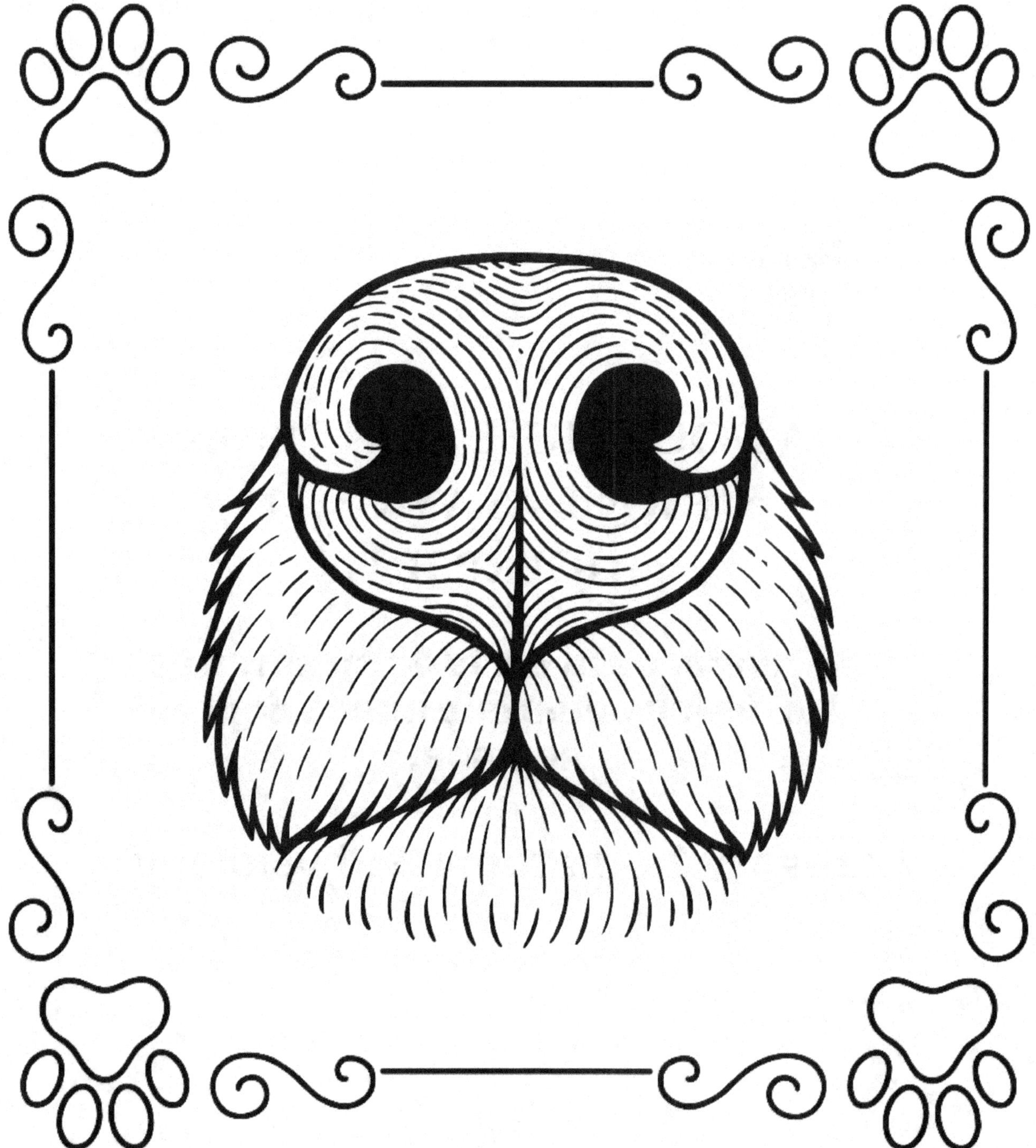

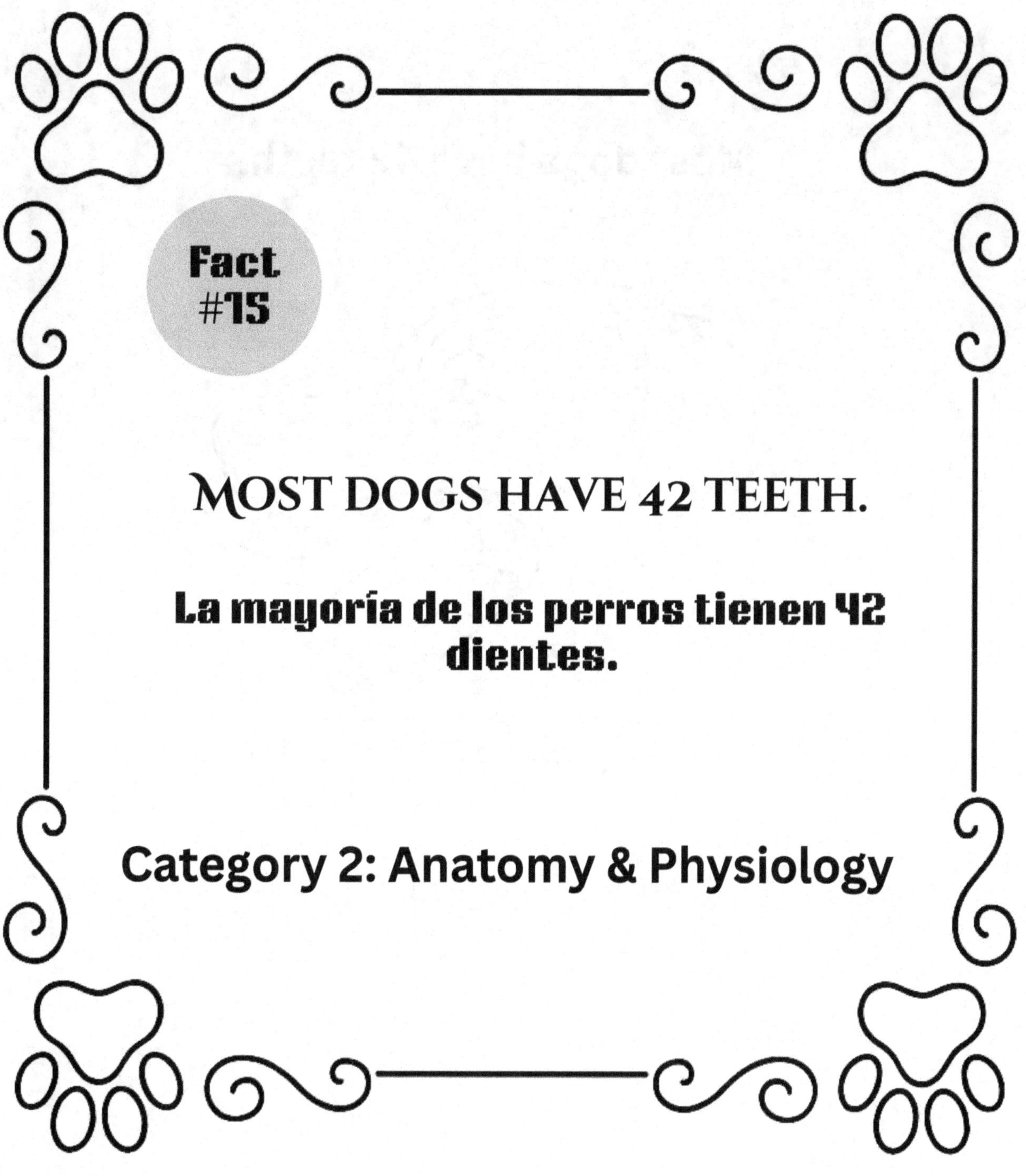

Fact #15

MOST DOGS HAVE 42 TEETH.

La mayoría de los perros tienen 42 dientes.

Category 2: Anatomy & Physiology

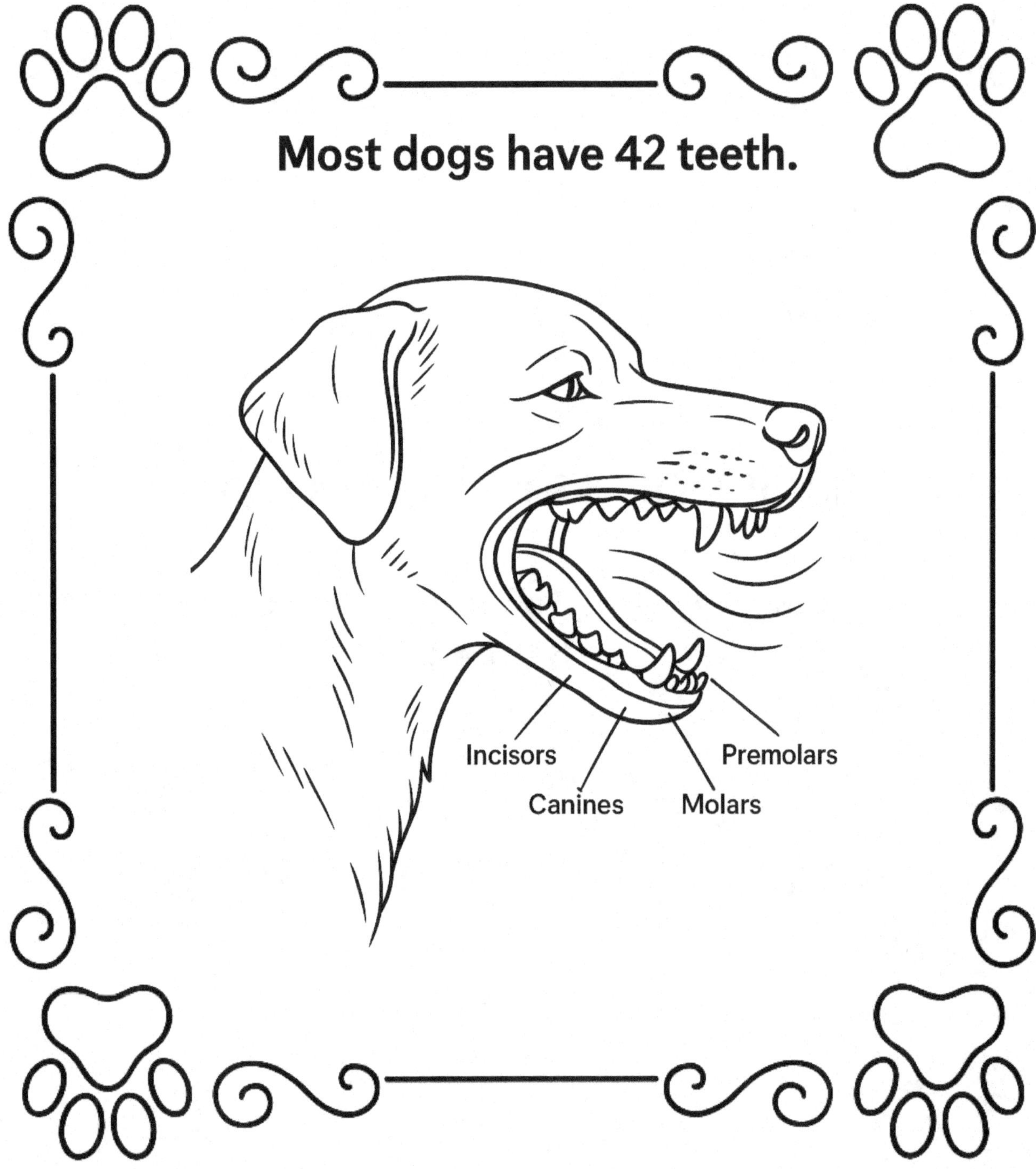

Most dogs have 42 teeth.
Incisors
Canines
Premolars
Molars

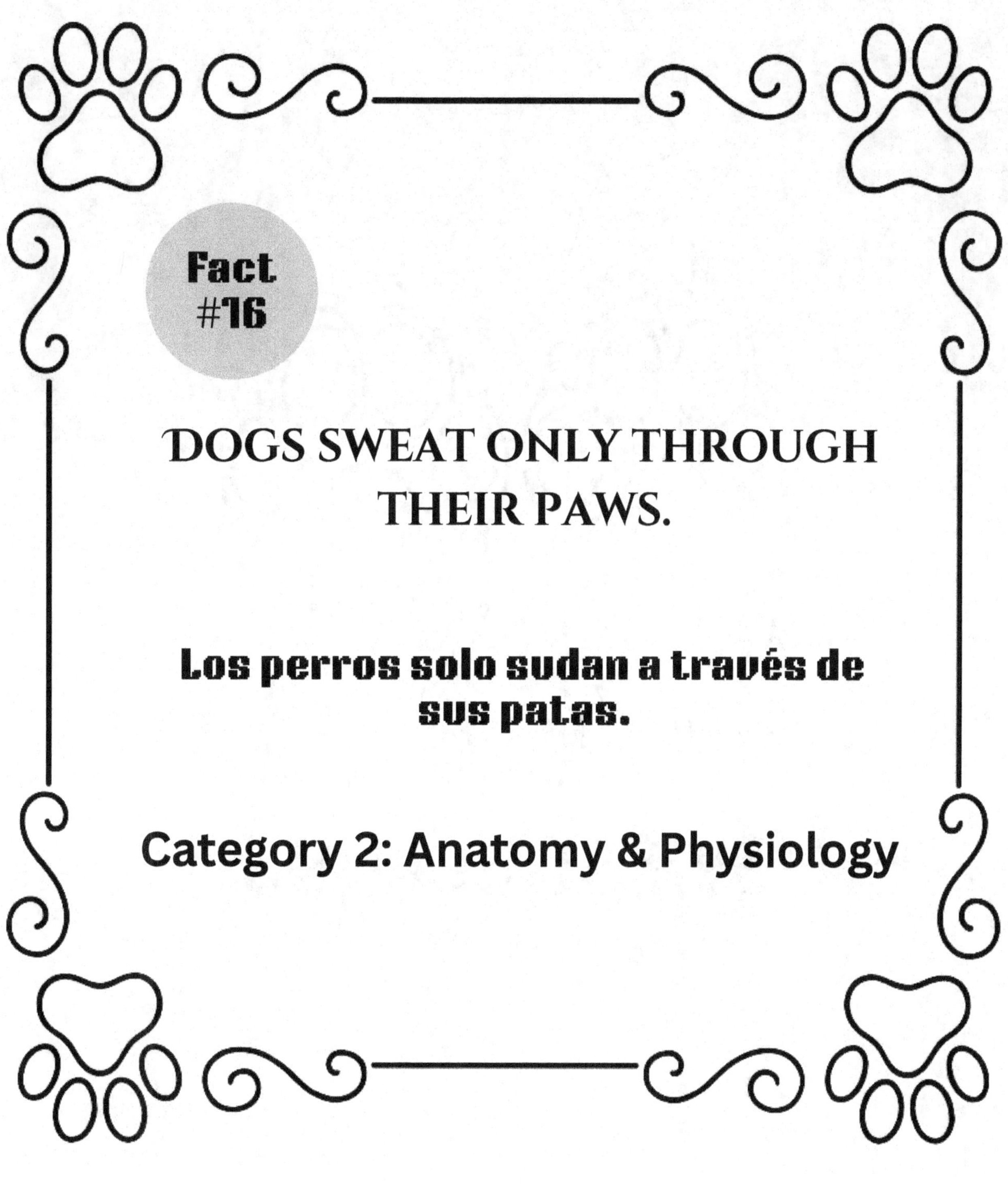

DOGS SWEAT ONLY THROUGH THEIR PAWS.

Los perros solo sudan a través de sus patas.

Category 2: Anatomy & Physiology

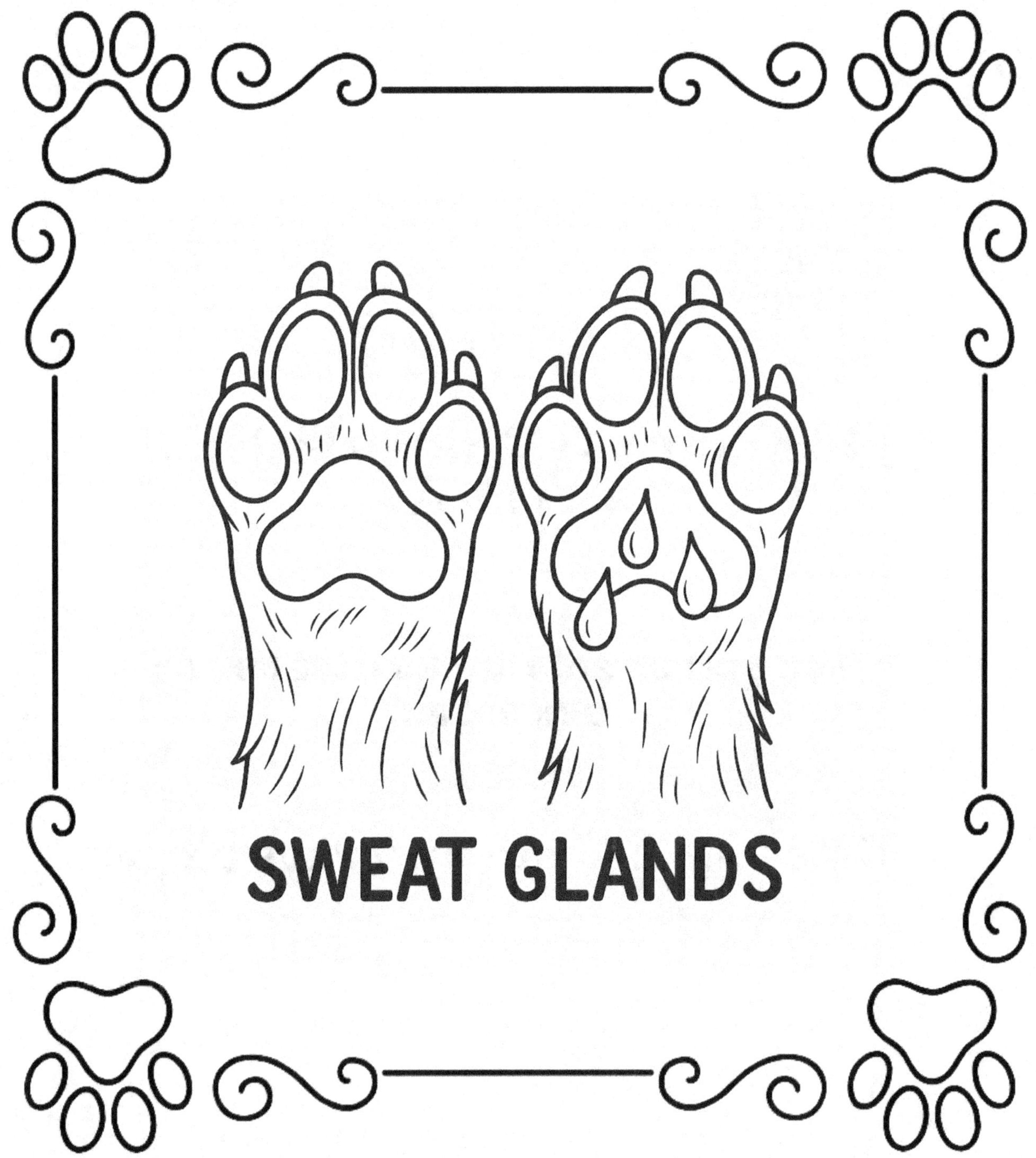

SWEAT GLANDS

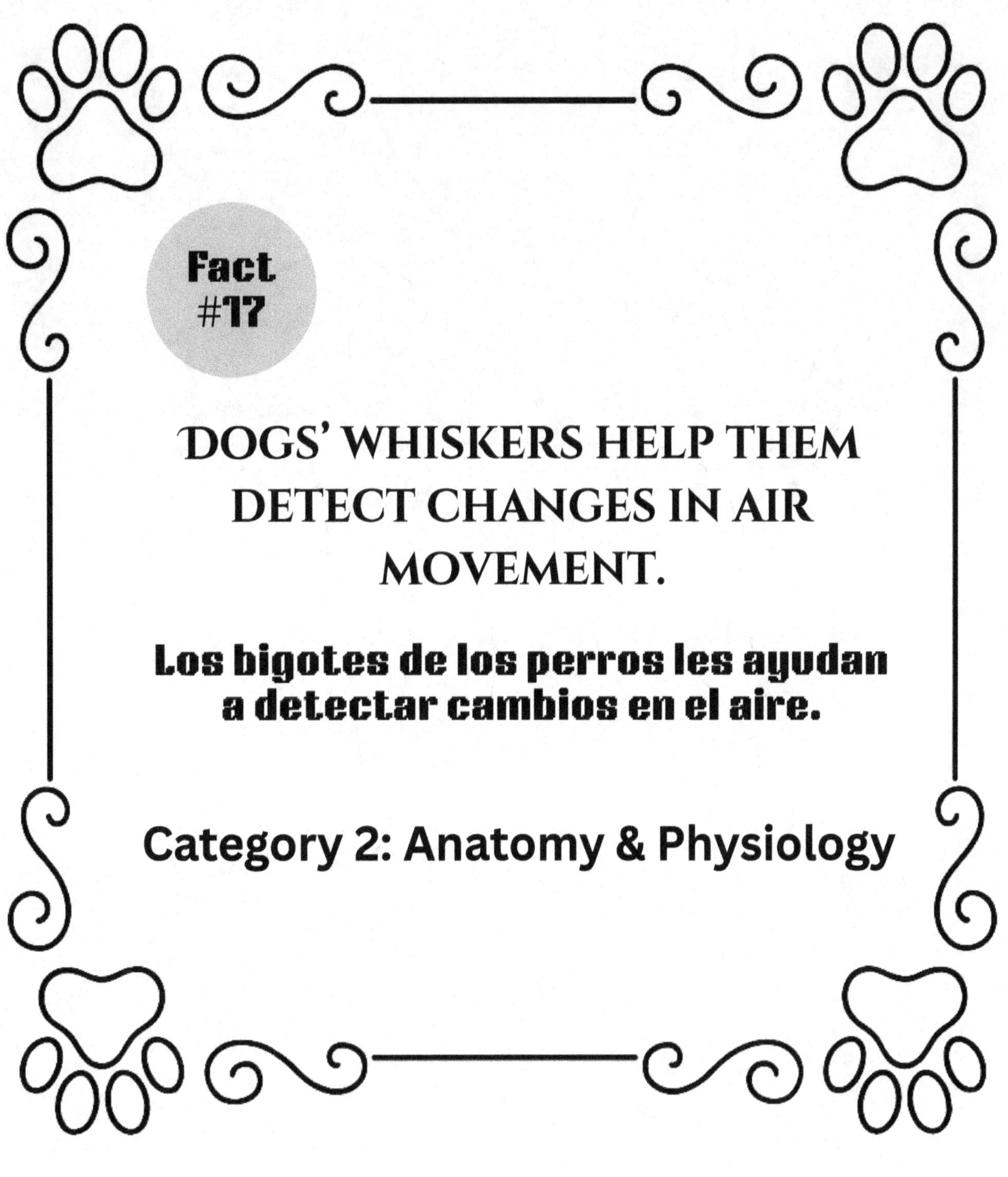

Fact #17

DOGS' WHISKERS HELP THEM DETECT CHANGES IN AIR MOVEMENT.

Los bigotes de los perros les ayudan a detectar cambios en el aire.

Category 2: Anatomy & Physiology

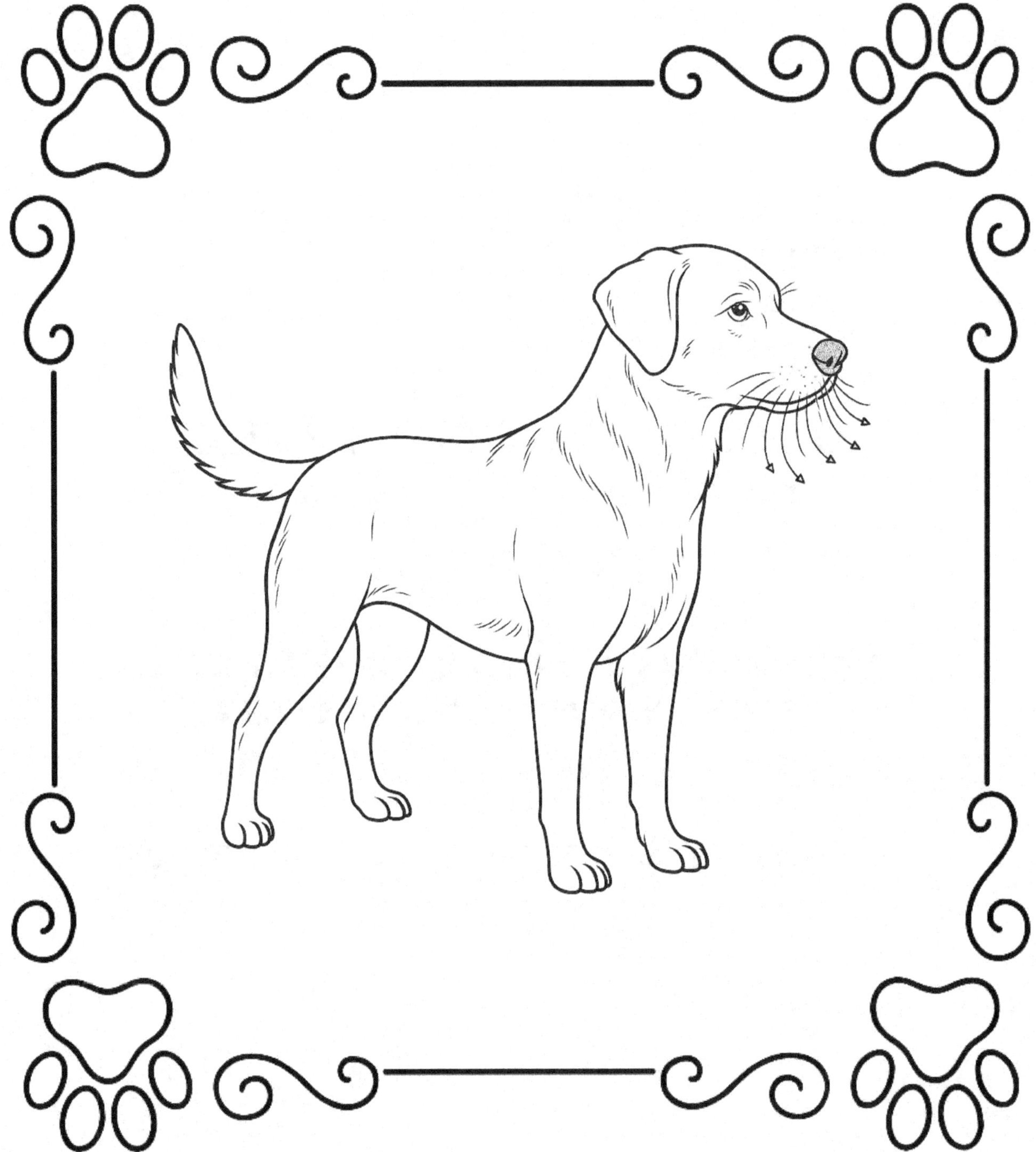

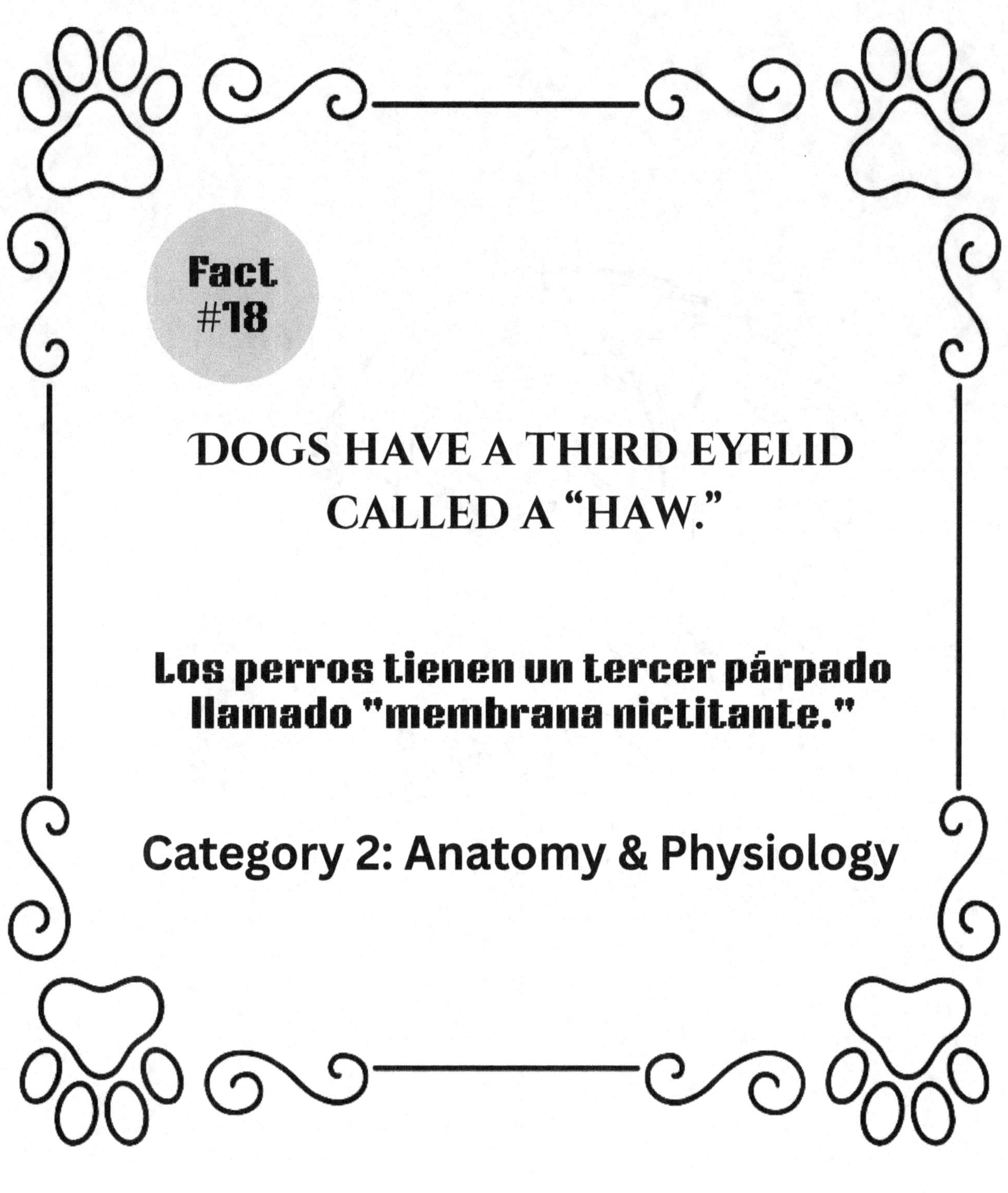

Fact
#18

DOGS HAVE A THIRD EYELID
CALLED A "HAW."

Los perros tienen un tercer párpado
llamado "membrana nictitante."

Category 2: Anatomy & Physiology

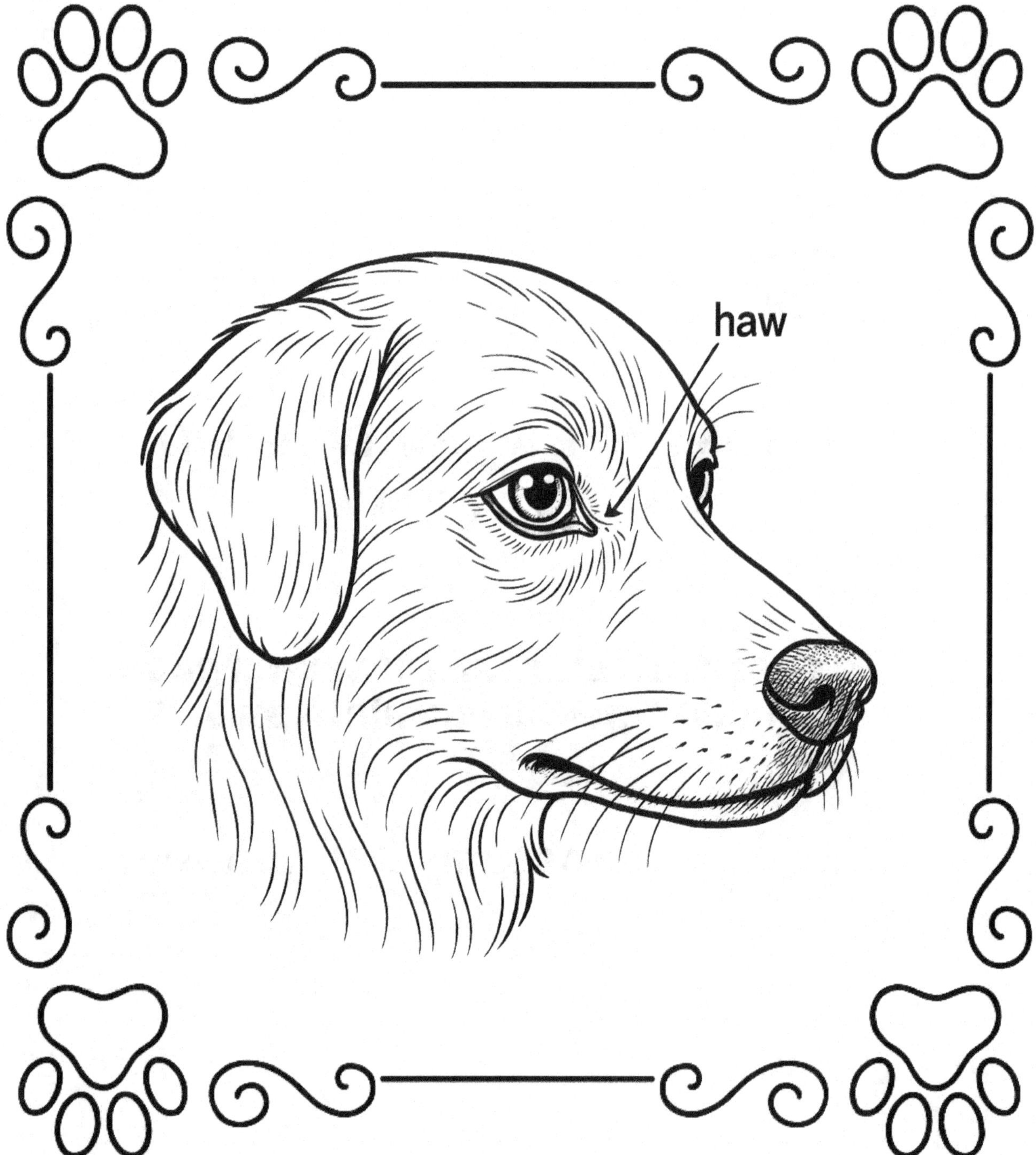
haw

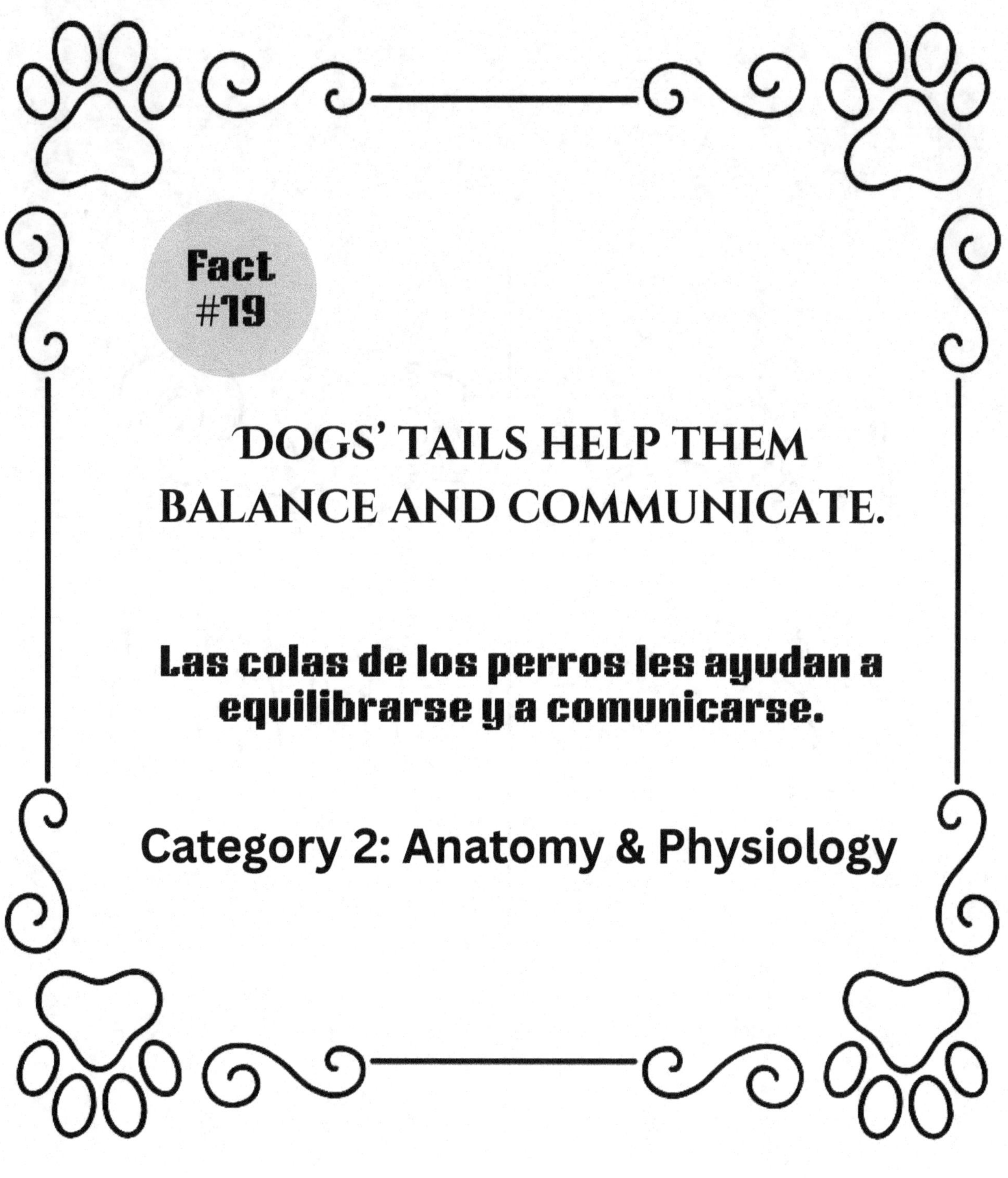

Fact #19

DOGS' TAILS HELP THEM BALANCE AND COMMUNICATE.

Las colas de los perros les ayudan a equilibrarse y a comunicarse.

Category 2: Anatomy & Physiology

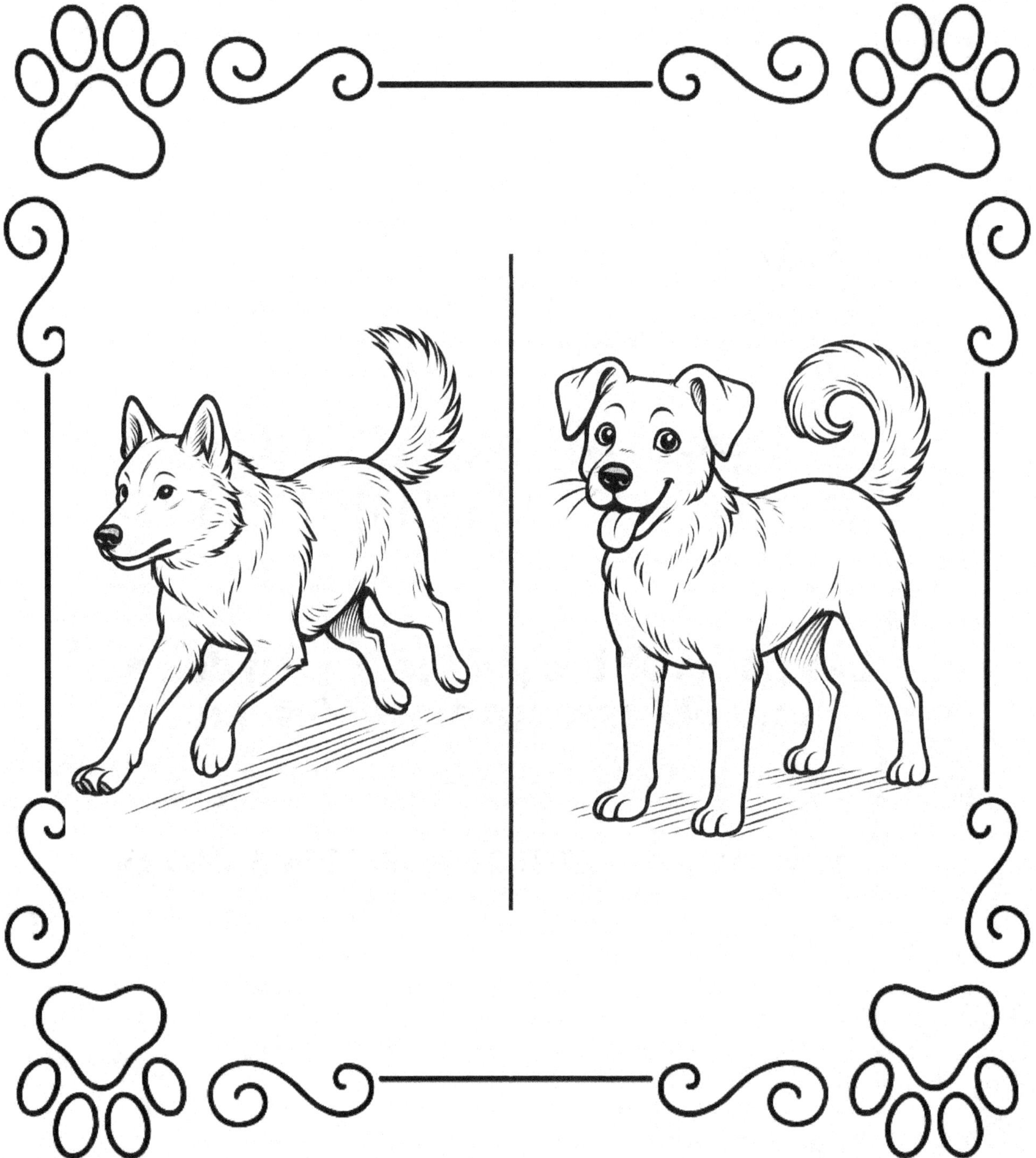

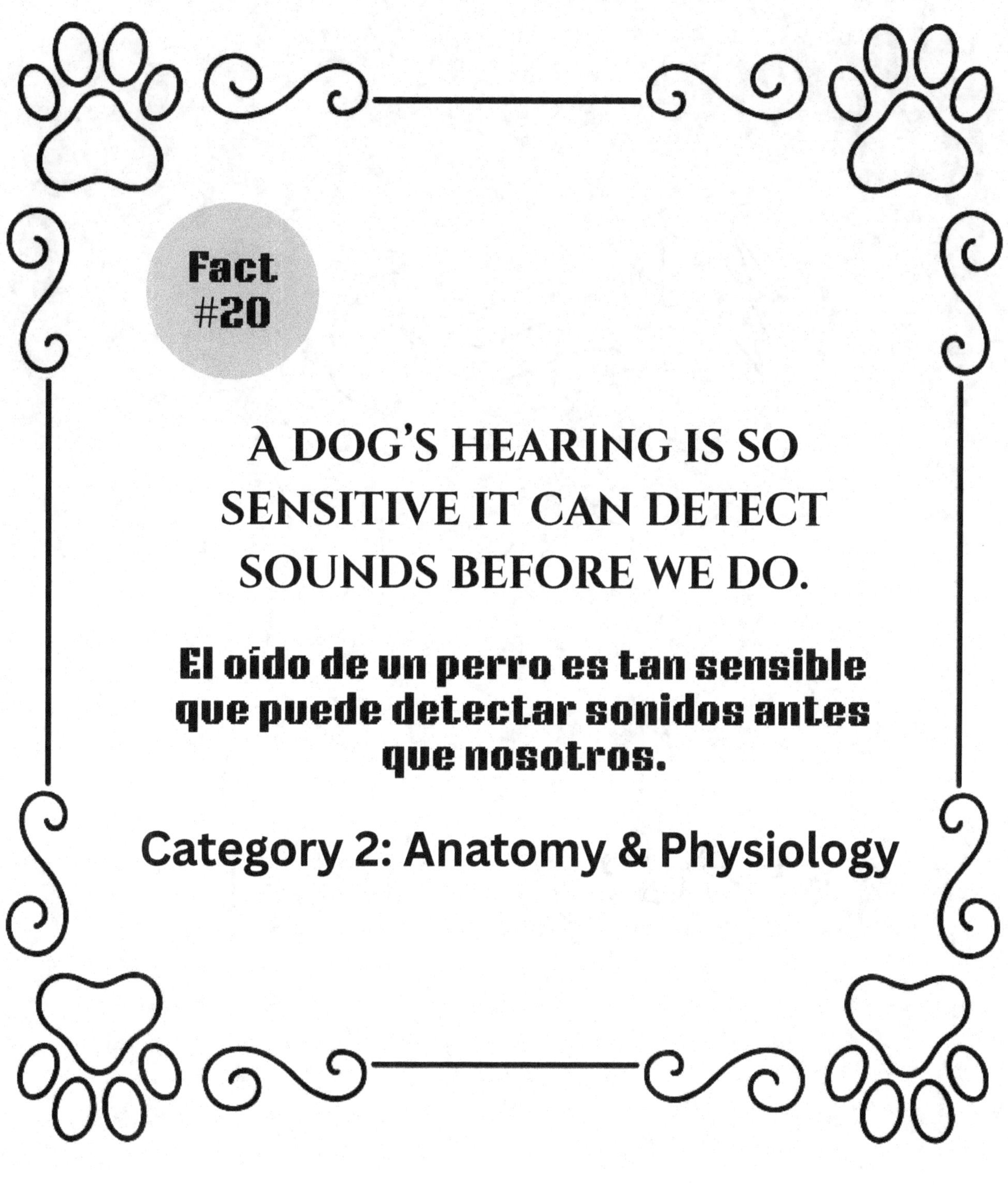

Fact
#20

A DOG'S HEARING IS SO SENSITIVE IT CAN DETECT SOUNDS BEFORE WE DO.

El oído de un perro es tan sensible que puede detectar sonidos antes que nosotros.

Category 2: Anatomy & Physiology

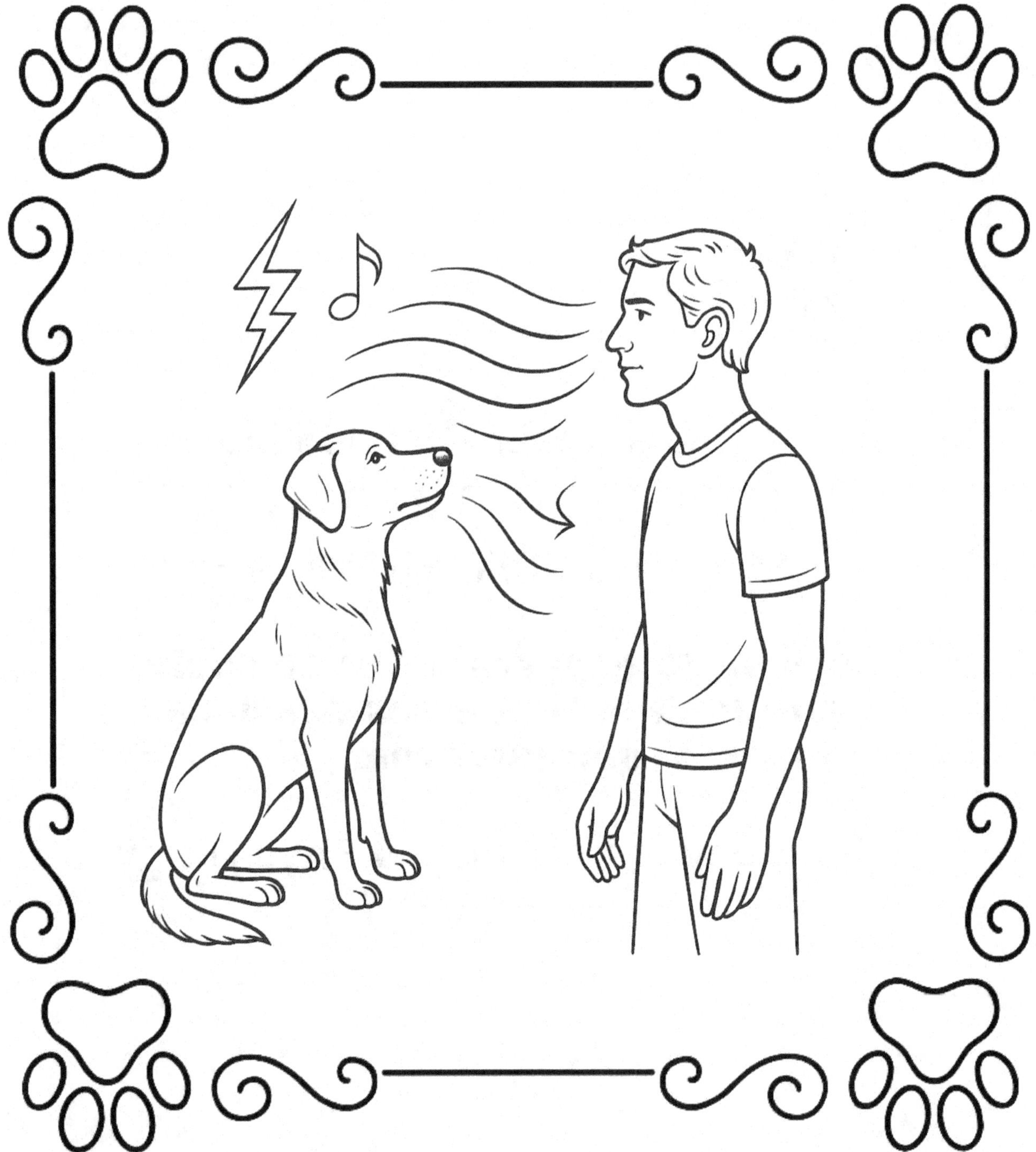

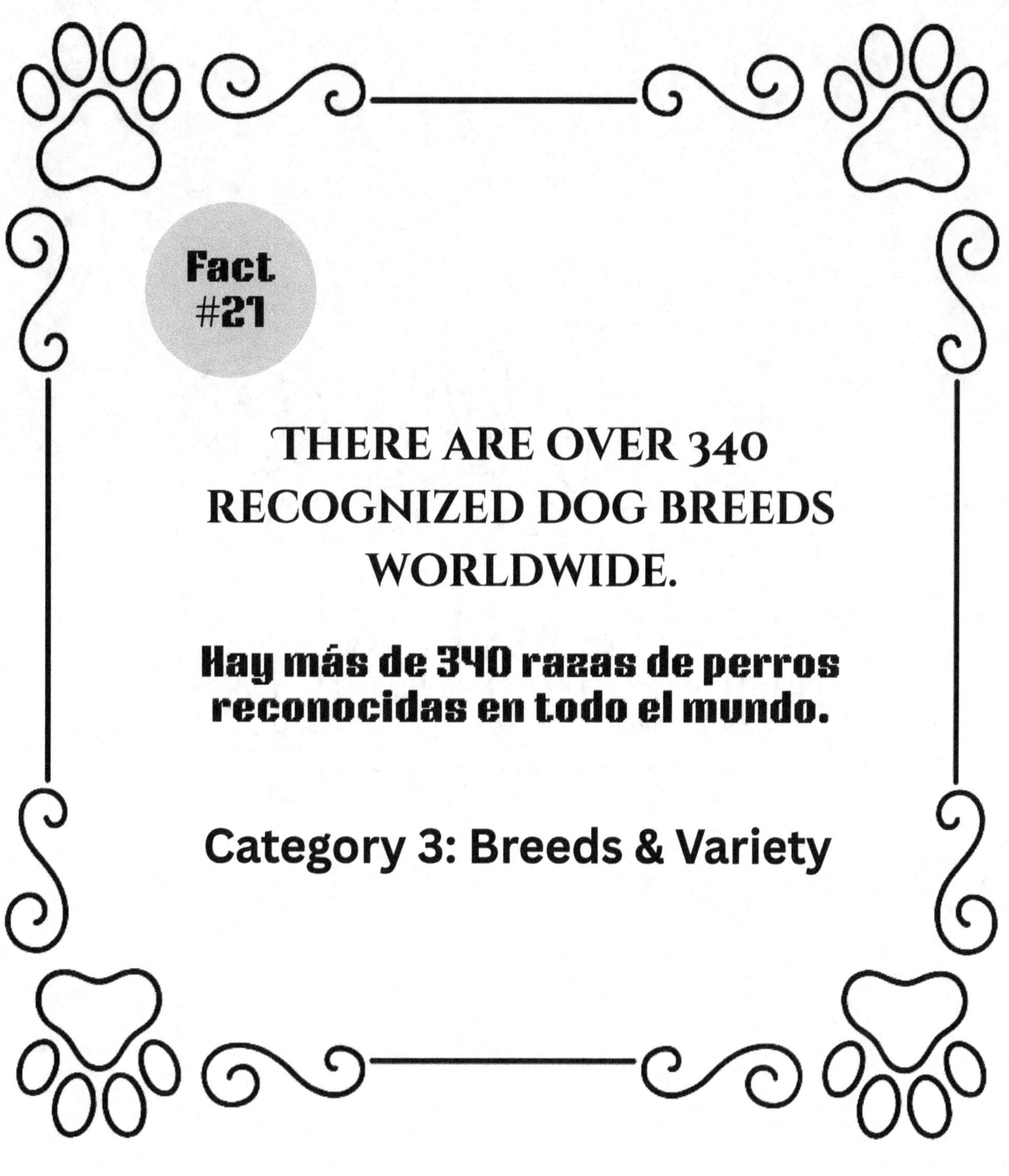

Fact #21
THERE ARE OVER 340 RECOGNIZED DOG BREEDS WORLDWIDE.
Hay más de 340 razas de perros reconocidas en todo el mundo.
Category 3: Breeds & Variety

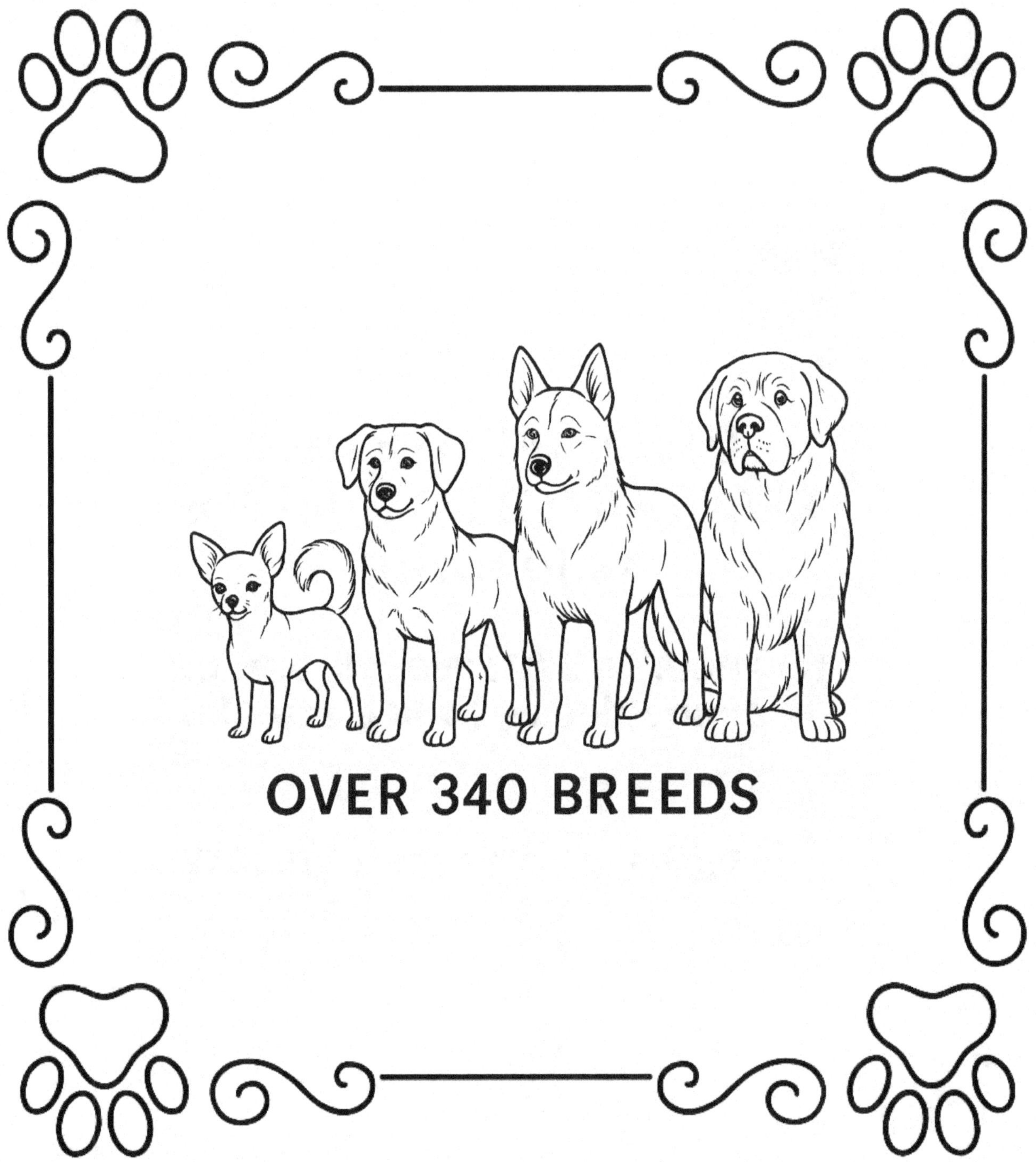

OVER 340 BREEDS

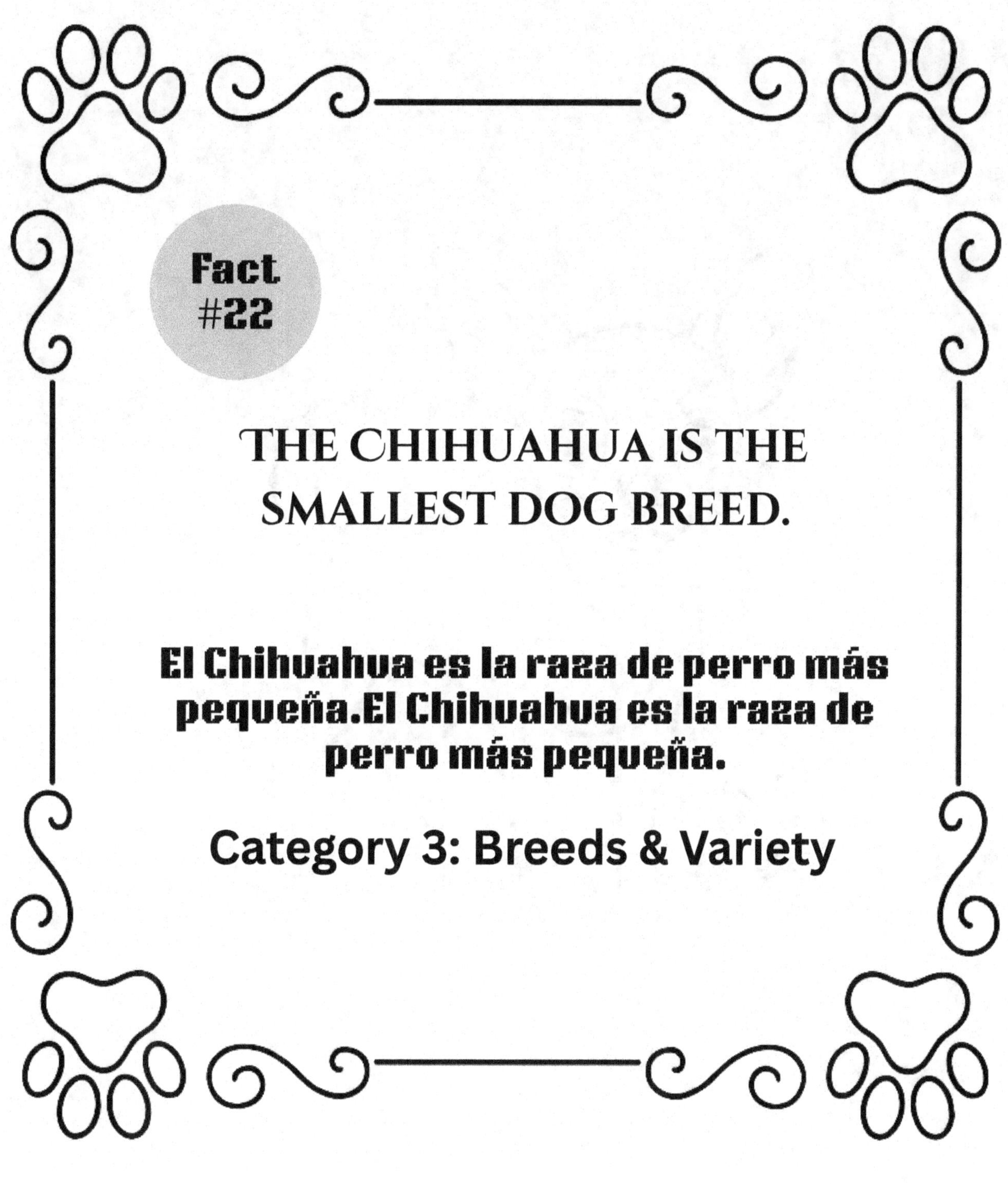
Fact #22

THE CHIHUAHUA IS THE SMALLEST DOG BREED.

El Chihuahua es la raza de perro más pequeña.El Chihuahua es la raza de perro más pequeña.

Category 3: Breeds & Variety

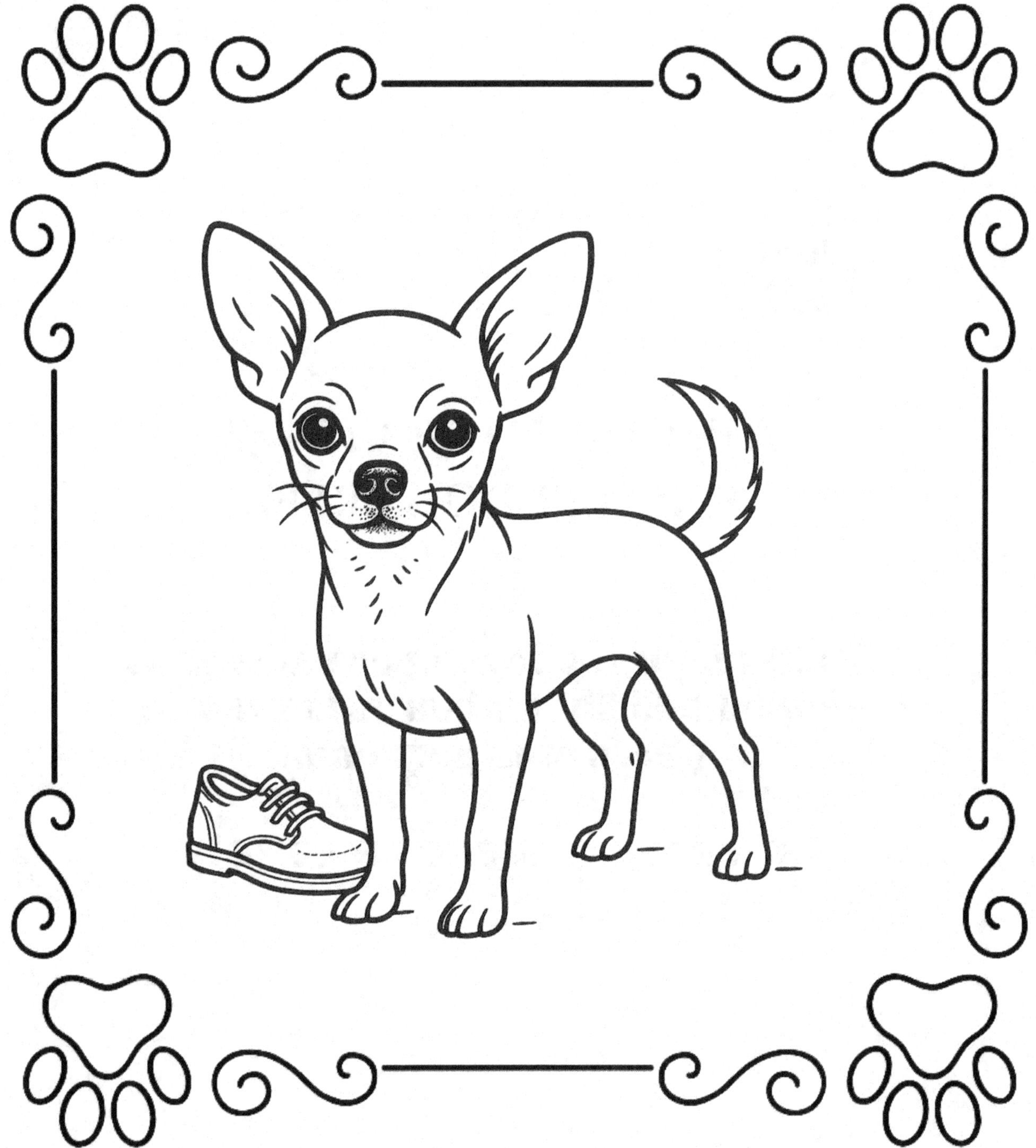

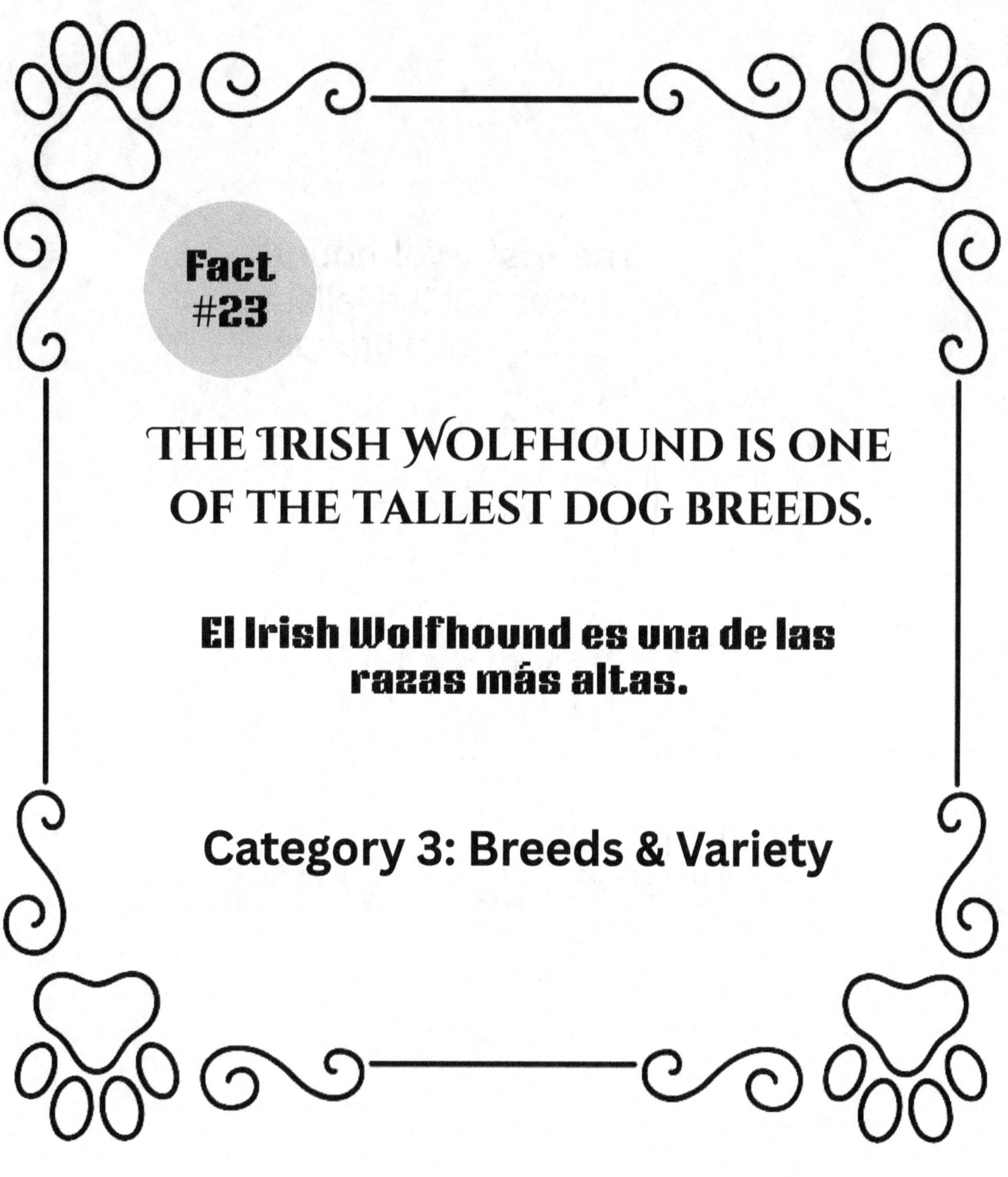

Fact #23

THE IRISH WOLFHOUND IS ONE OF THE TALLEST DOG BREEDS.

El Irish Wolfhound es una de las razas más altas.

Category 3: Breeds & Variety

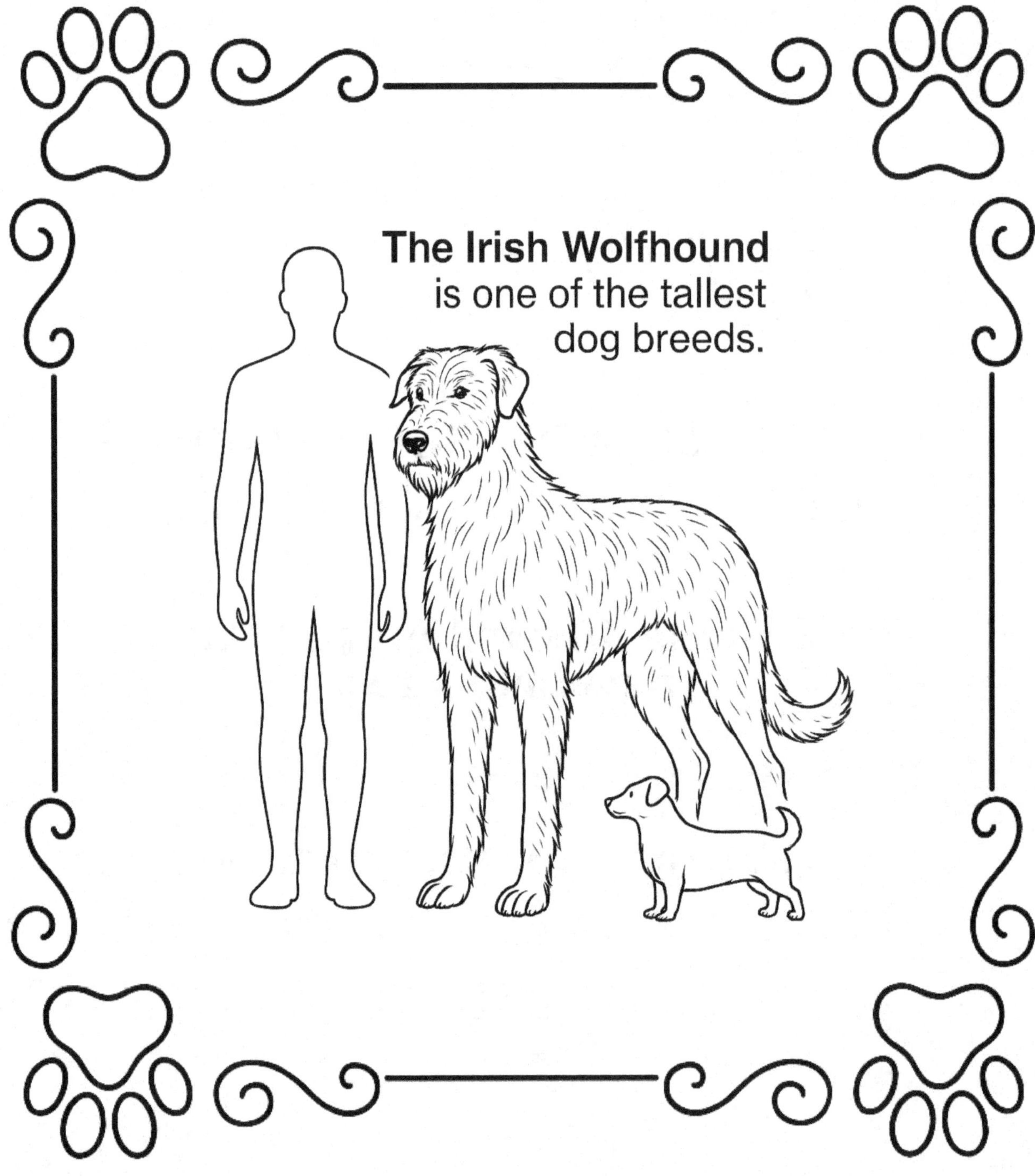
The Irish Wolfhound
is one of the tallest
dog breeds.

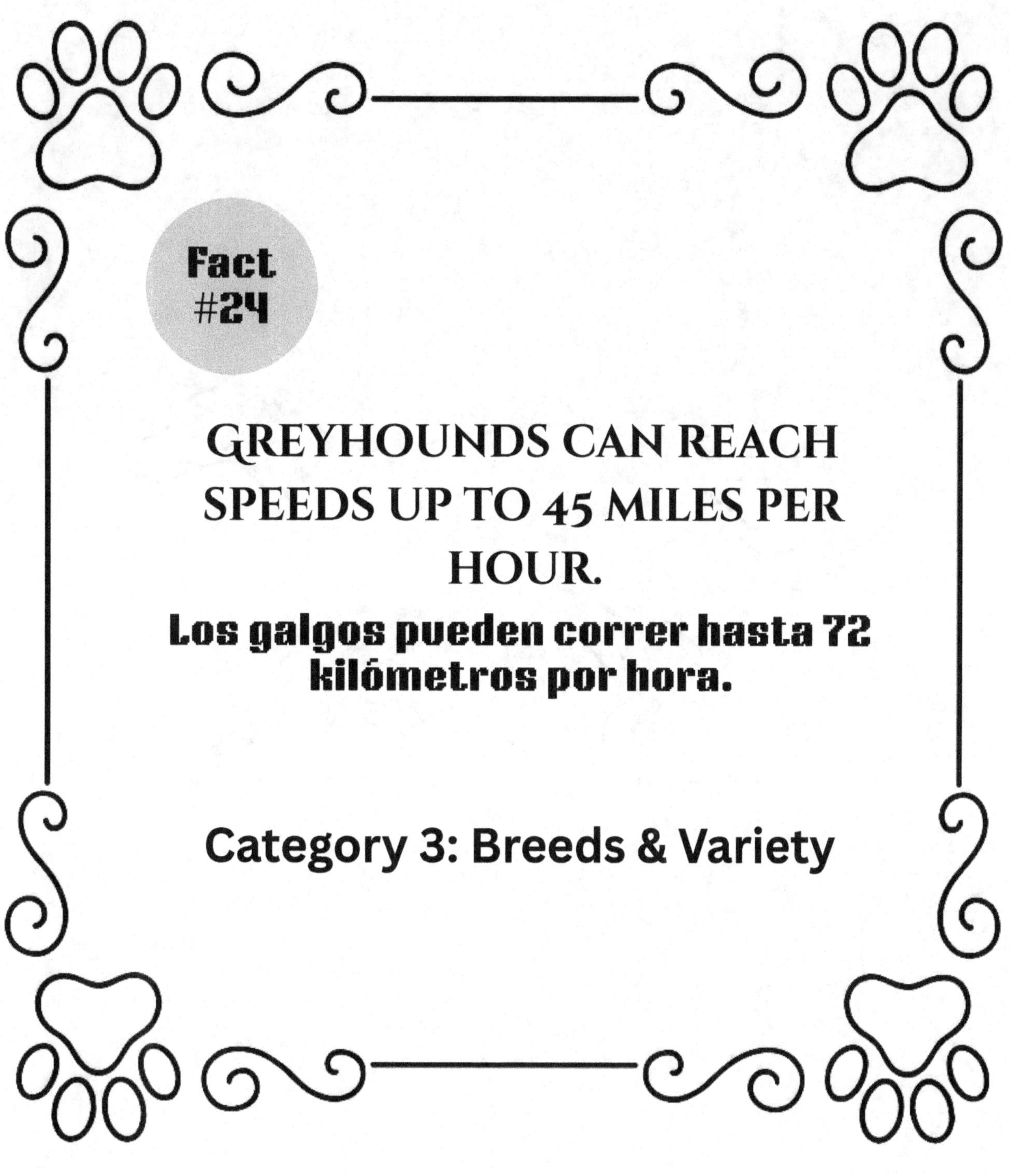

Fact #24

GREYHOUNDS CAN REACH SPEEDS UP TO 45 MILES PER HOUR.

Los galgos pueden correr hasta 72 kilómetros por hora.

Category 3: Breeds & Variety

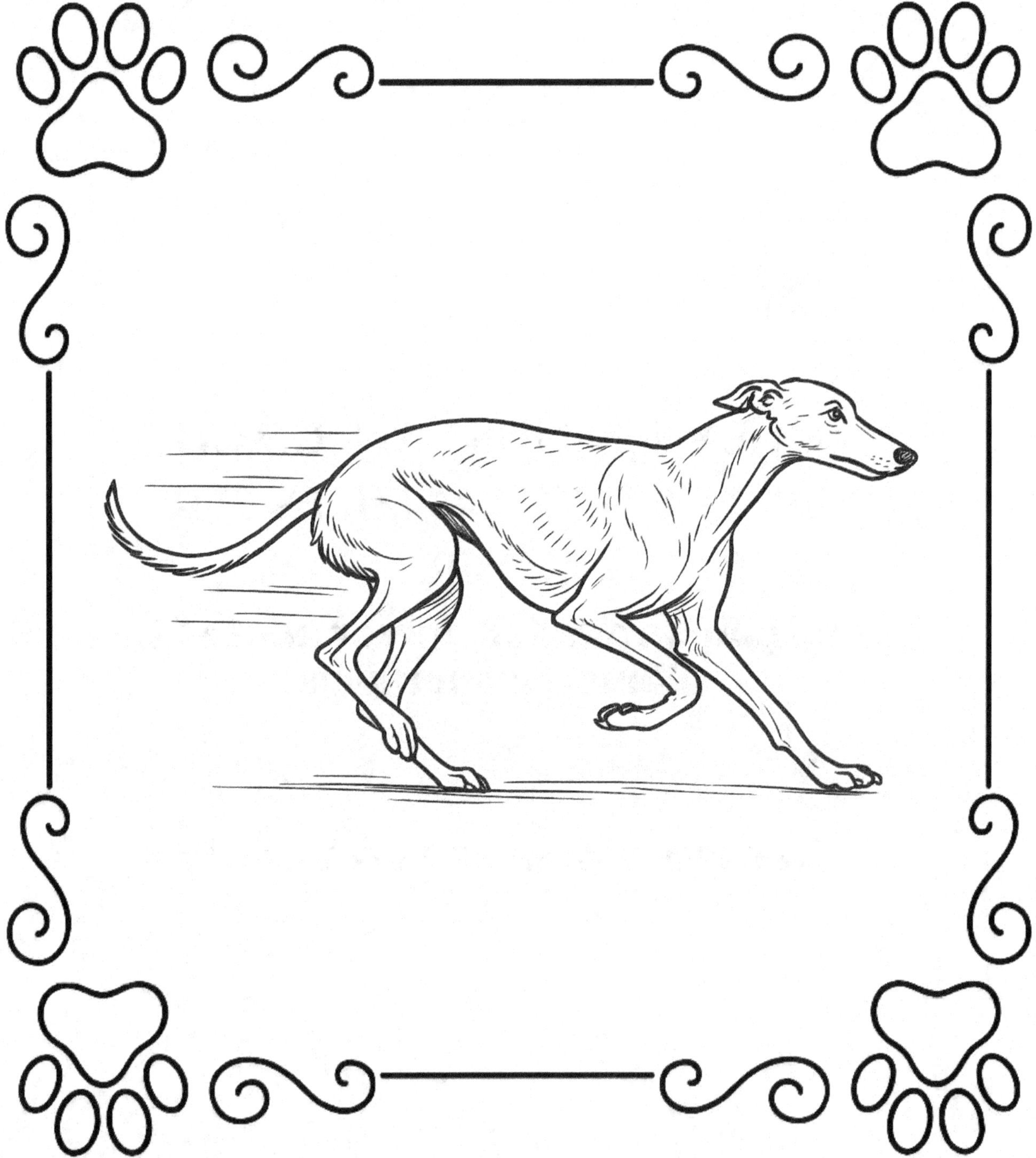

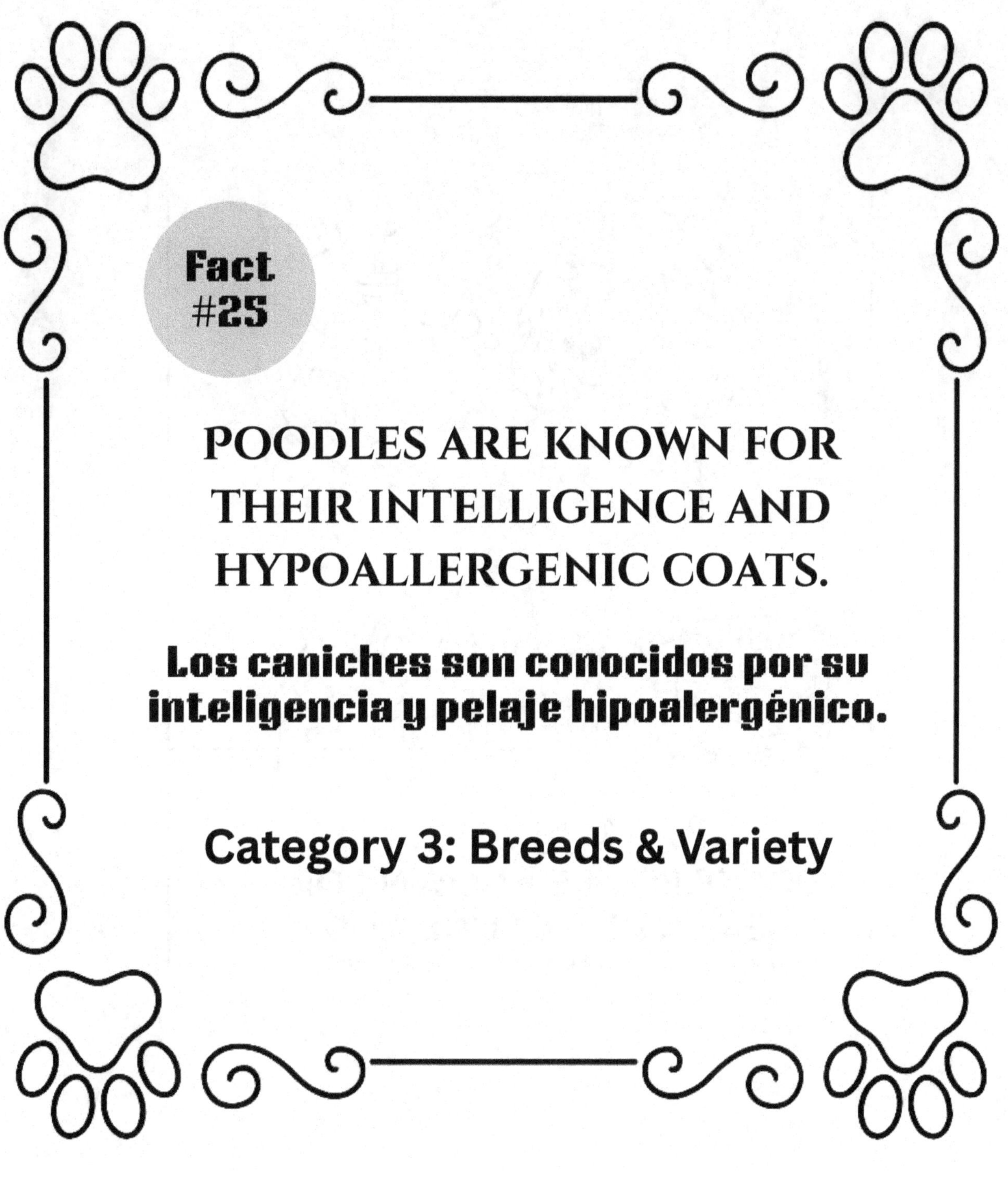

Fact #25

POODLES ARE KNOWN FOR THEIR INTELLIGENCE AND HYPOALLERGENIC COATS.

Los caniches son conocidos por su inteligencia y pelaje hipoalergénico.

Category 3: Breeds & Variety

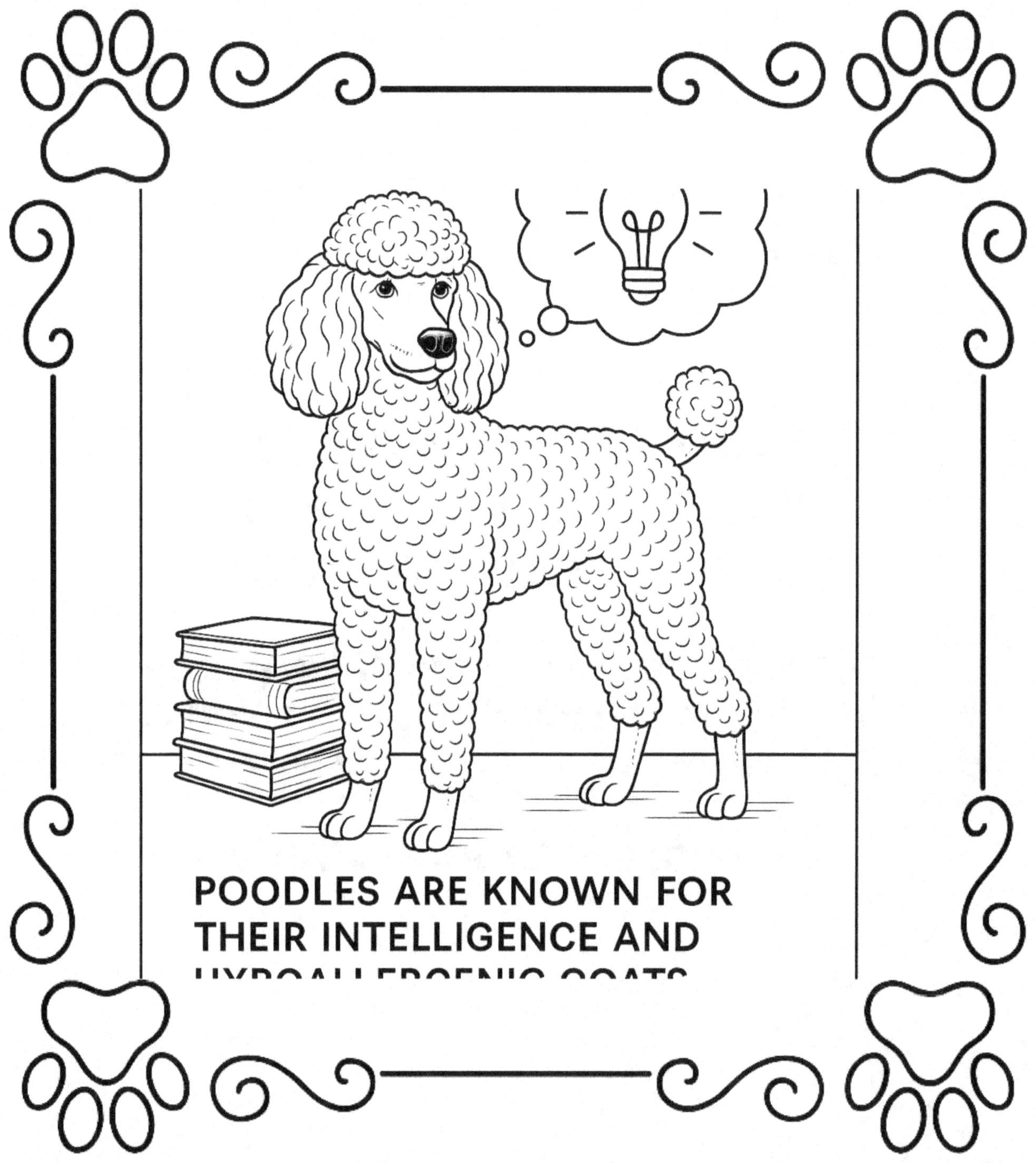

POODLES ARE KNOWN FOR
THEIR INTELLIGENCE AND
HYPOALLERGENIC COATS

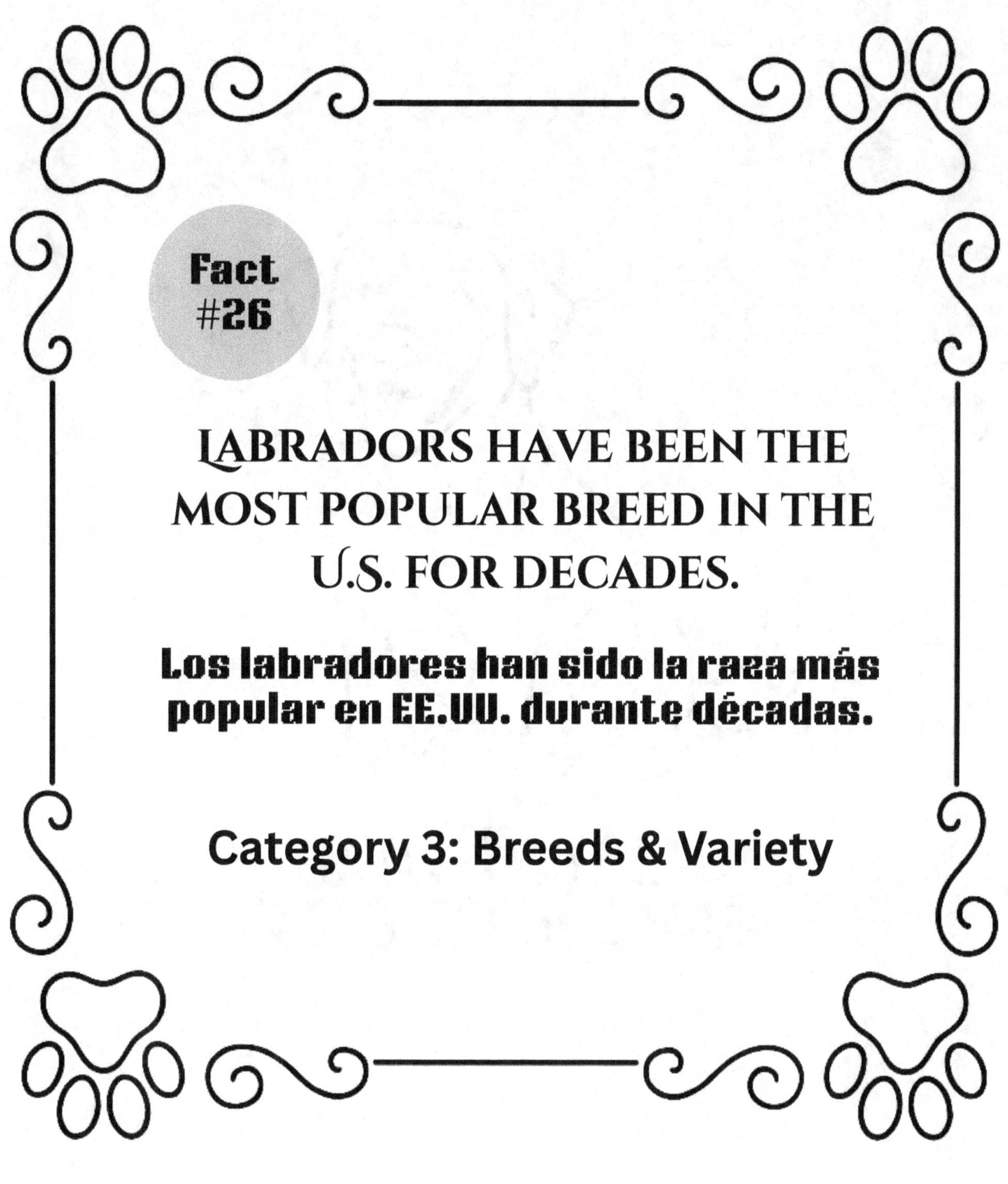

Fact #26

LABRADORS HAVE BEEN THE MOST POPULAR BREED IN THE U.S. FOR DECADES.

Los labradores han sido la raza más popular en EE.UU. durante décadas.

Category 3: Breeds & Variety

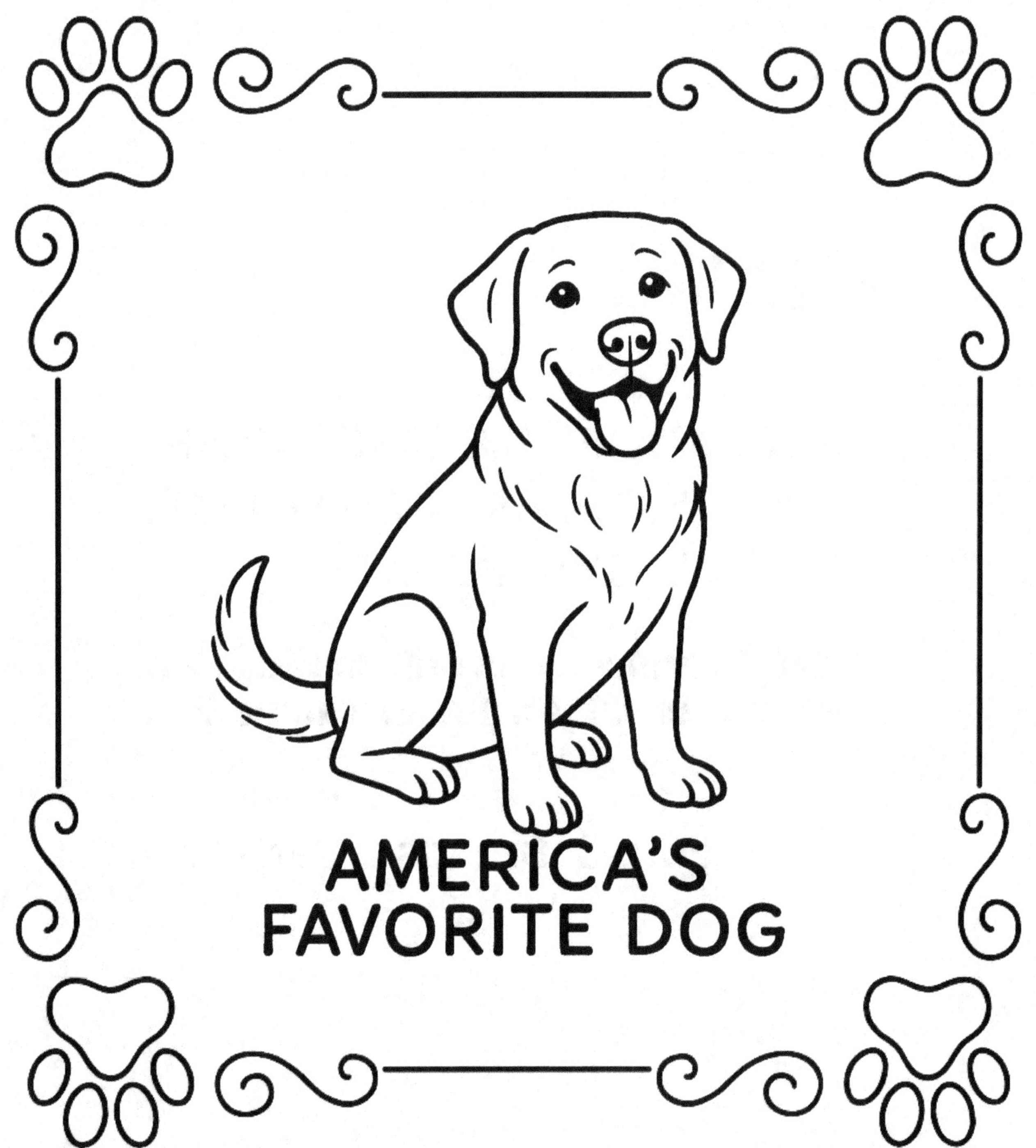

AMERICA'S
FAVORITE DOG

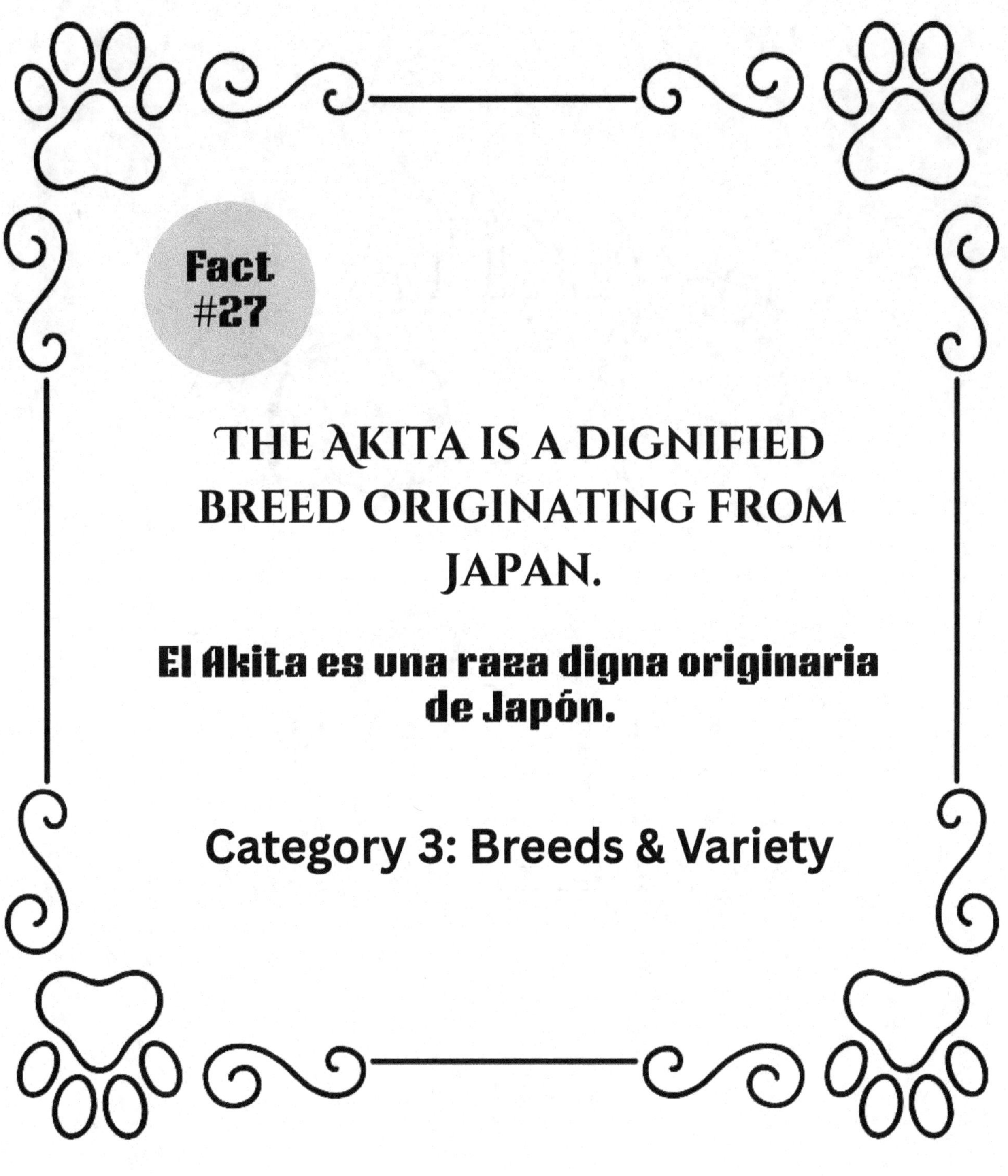

THE AKITA IS A DIGNIFIED BREED ORIGINATING FROM JAPAN.

El Akita es una raza digna originaria de Japón.

Category 3: Breeds & Variety

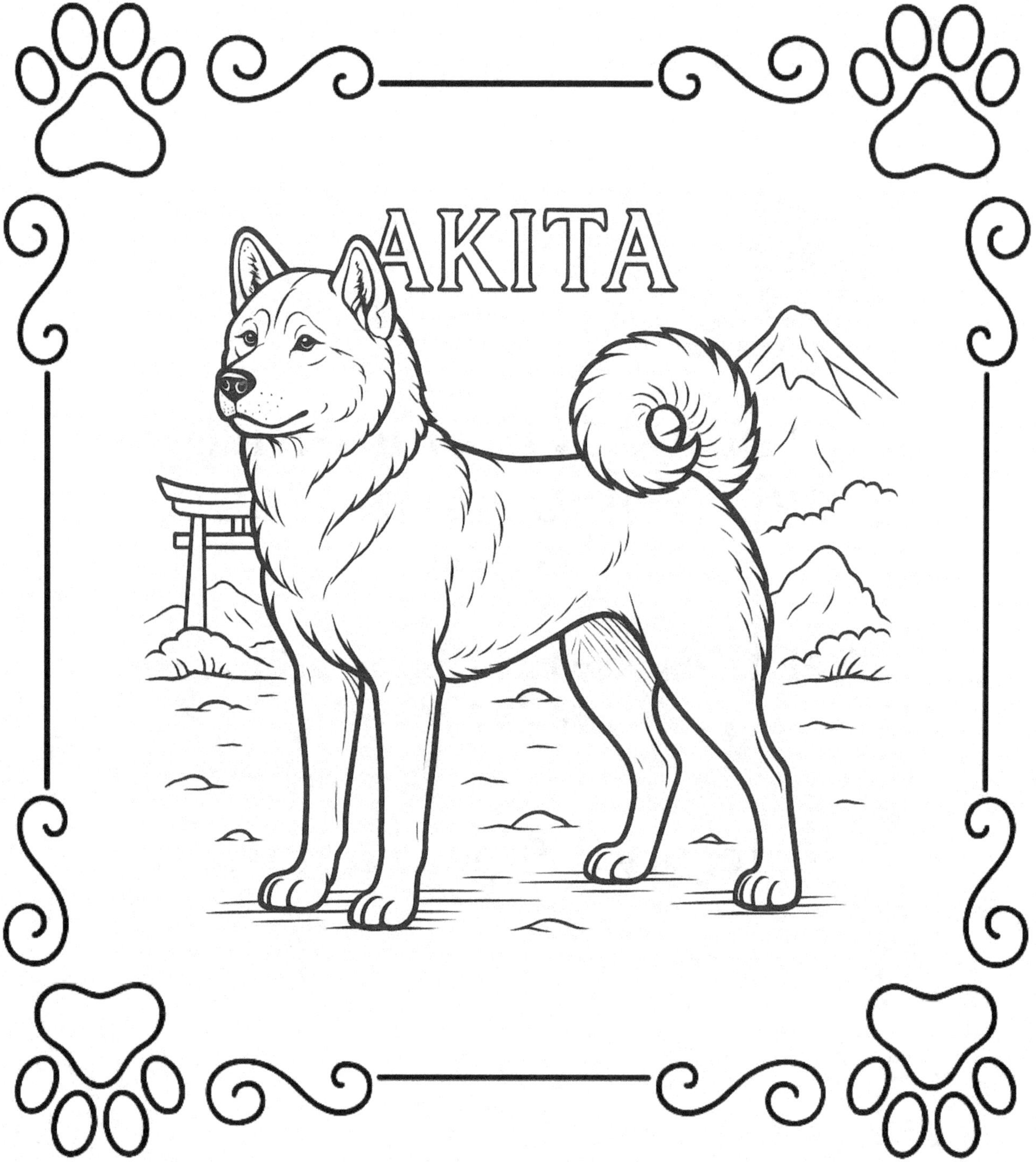
AKITA

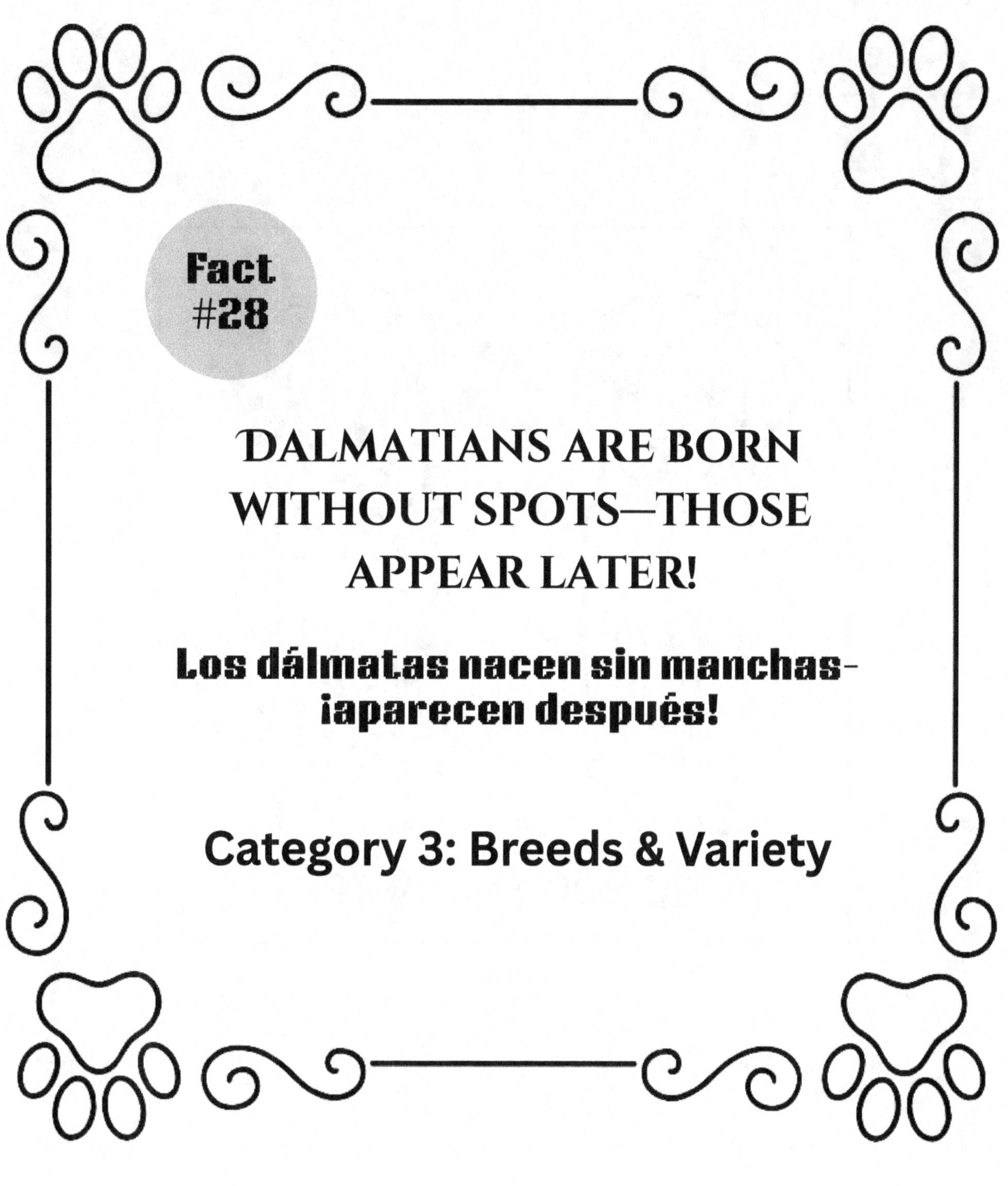

Fact #28

DALMATIANS ARE BORN WITHOUT SPOTS—THOSE APPEAR LATER!

Los dálmatas nacen sin manchas- ¡aparecen después!

Category 3: Breeds & Variety

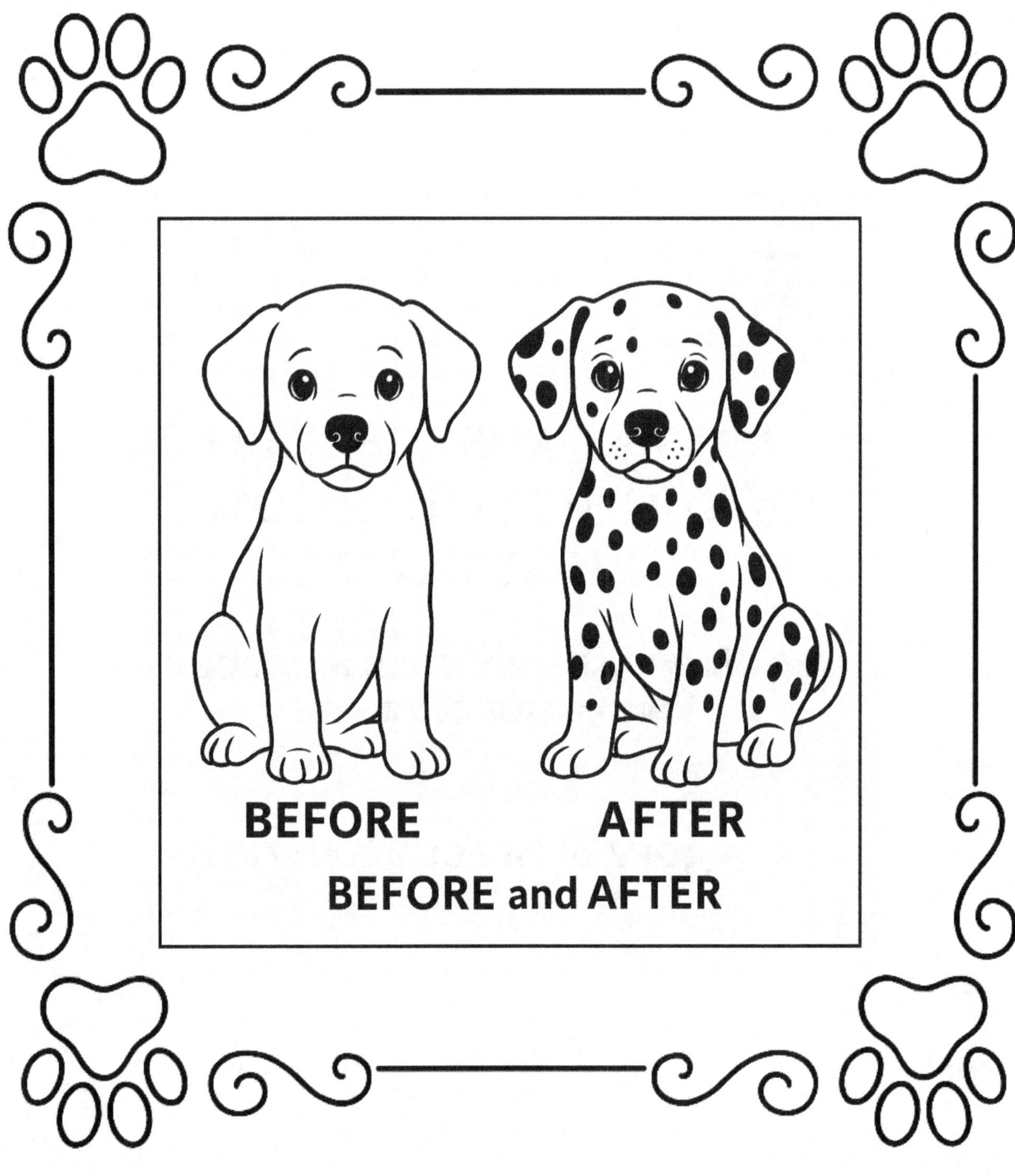
BEFORE
AFTER
BEFORE and AFTER

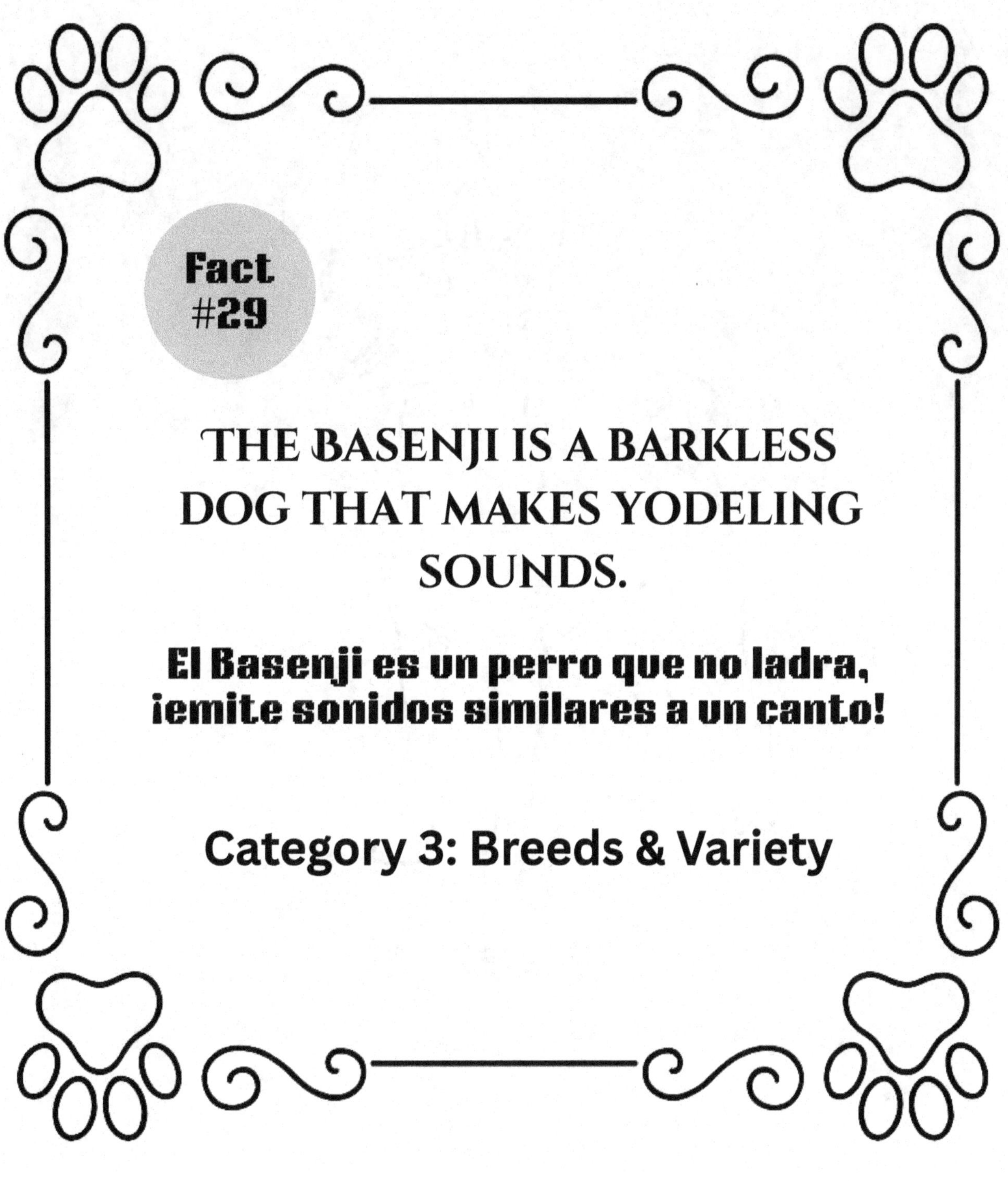

Fact #29

THE BASENJI IS A BARKLESS DOG THAT MAKES YODELING SOUNDS.

El Basenji es un perro que no ladra, ¡emite sonidos similares a un canto!

Category 3: Breeds & Variety

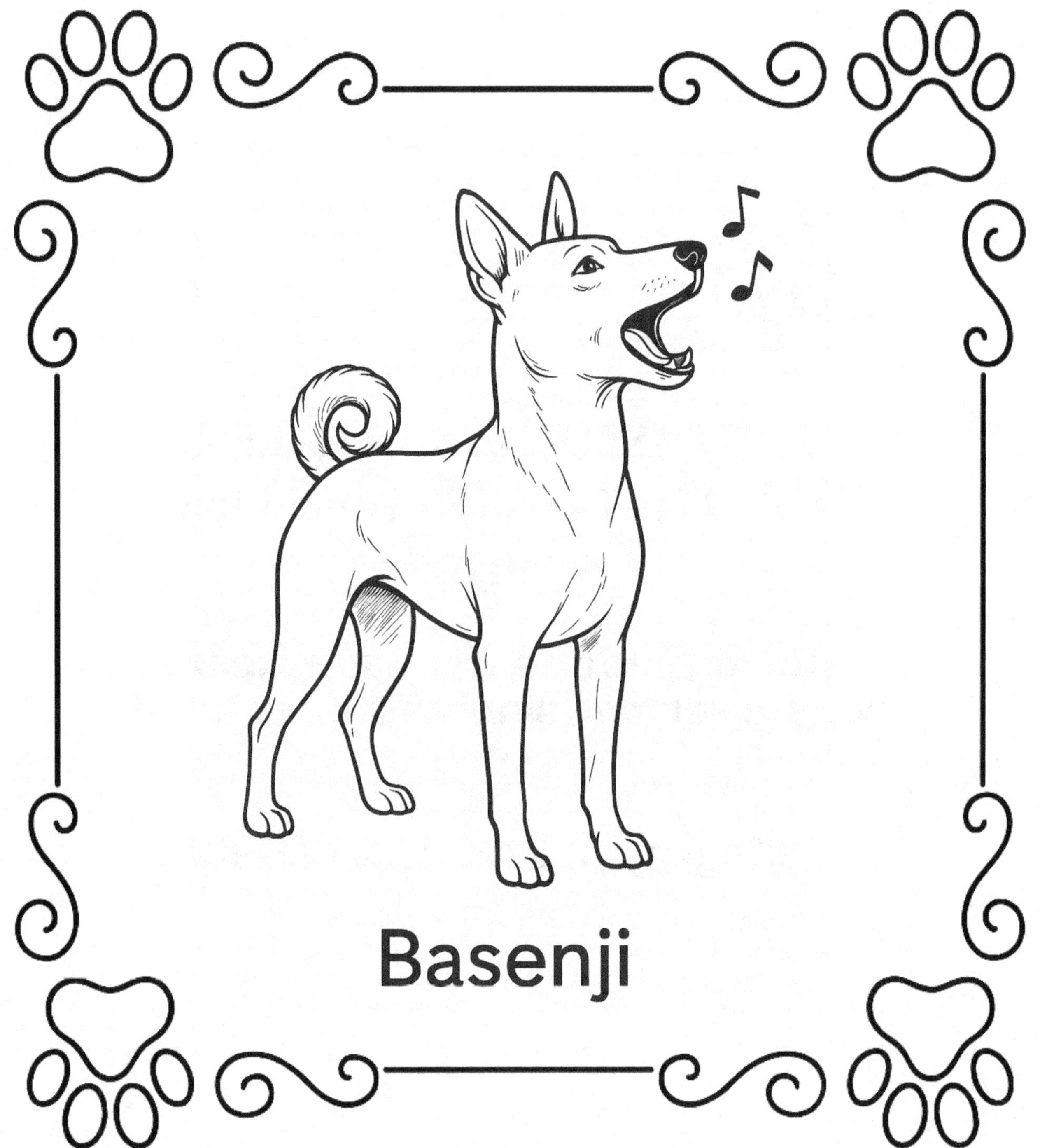

Basenji

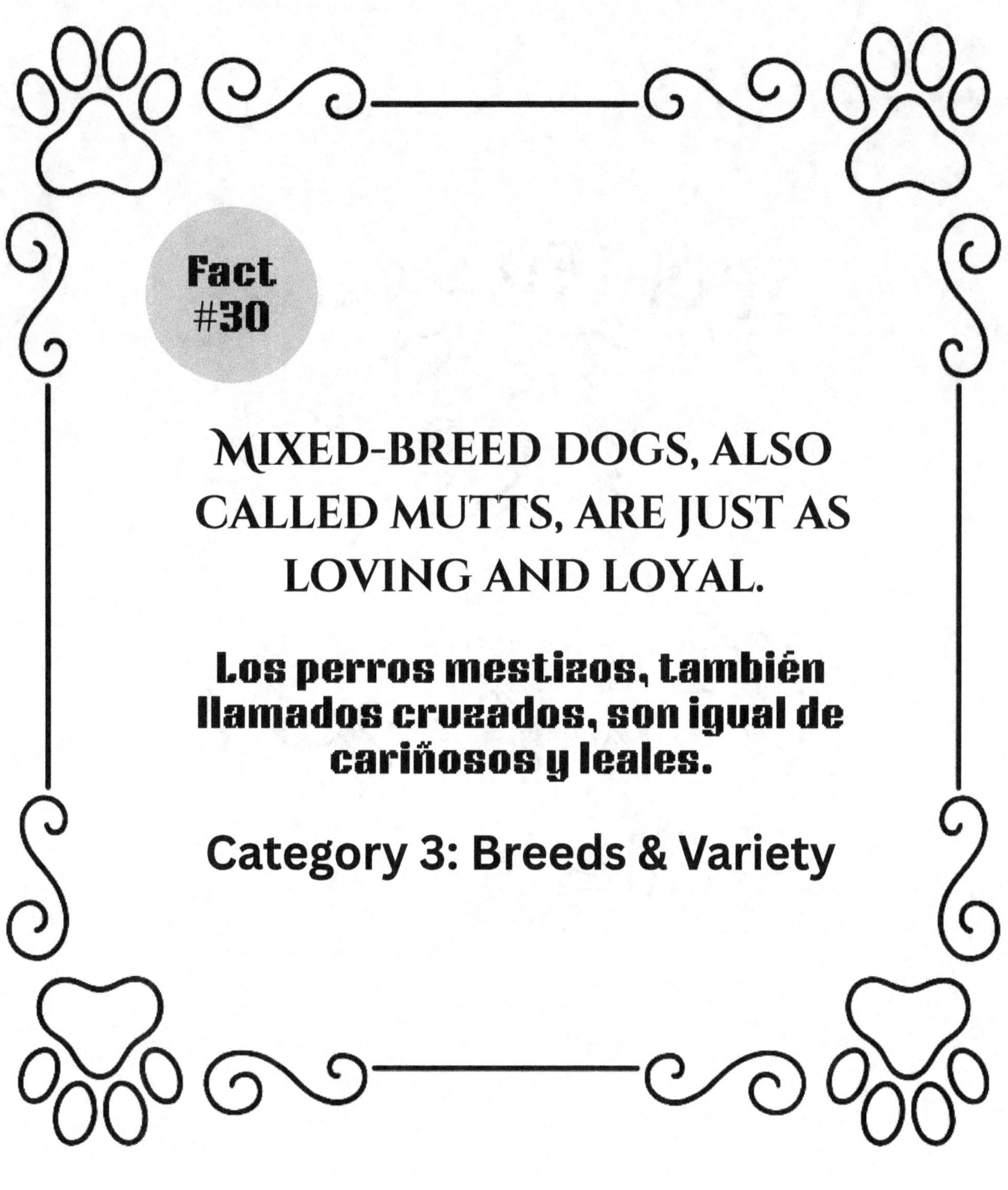

Fact #30

Mixed-breed dogs, also called mutts, are just as loving and loyal.

Los perros mestizos, también llamados cruzados, son igual de cariñosos y leales.

Category 3: Breeds & Variety

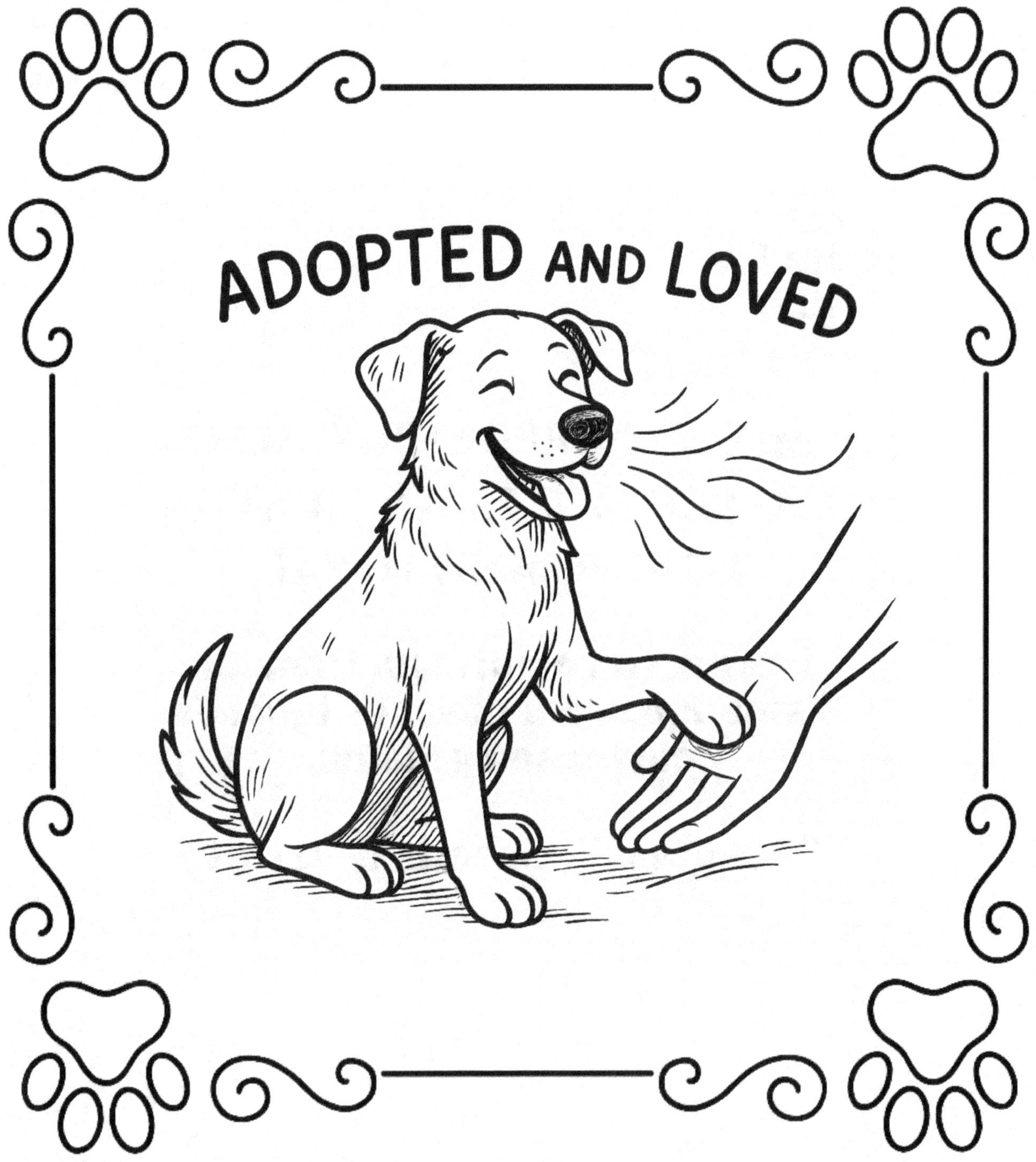
ADOPTED AND LOVED

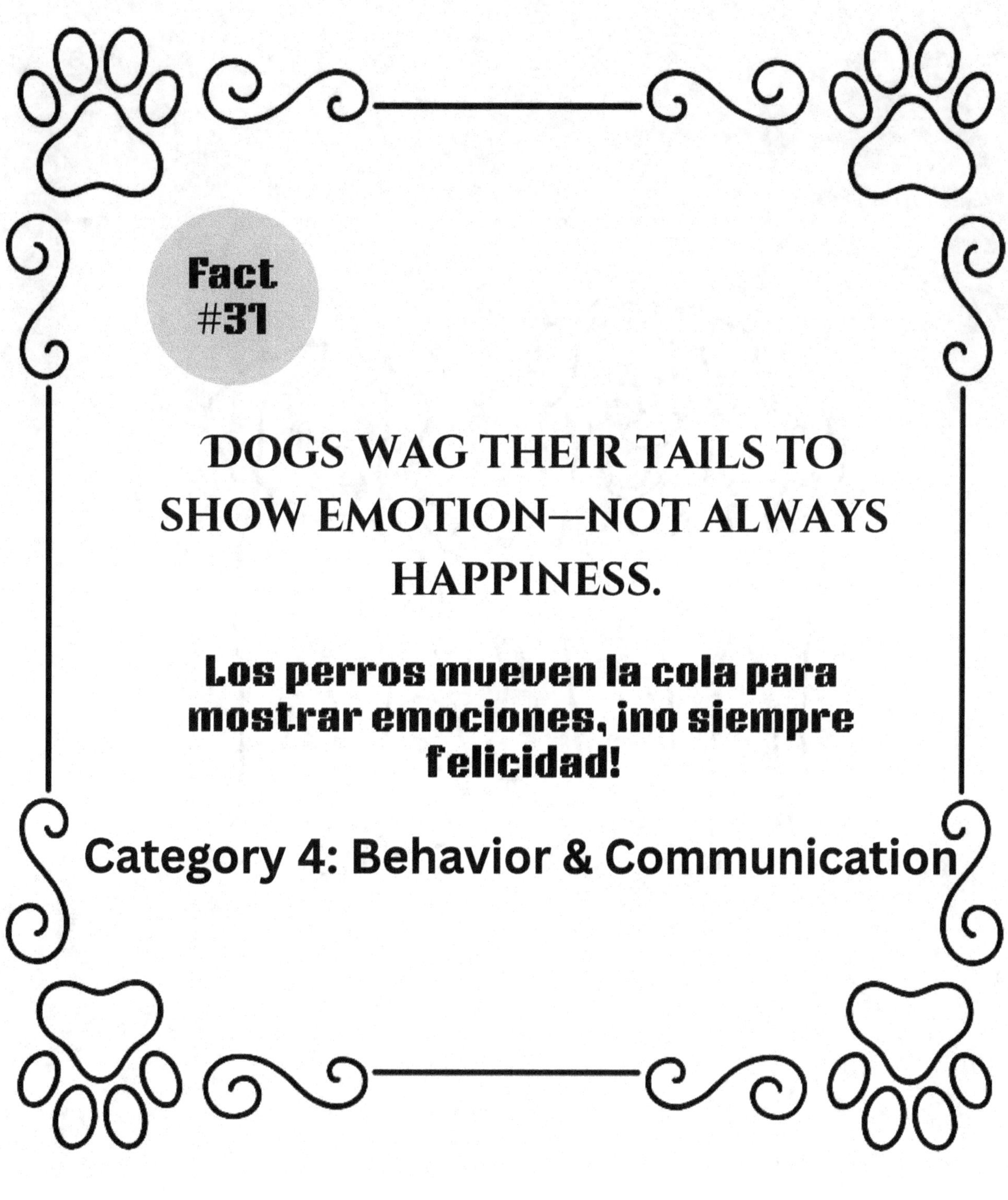

Fact #31

DOGS WAG THEIR TAILS TO SHOW EMOTION—NOT ALWAYS HAPPINESS.

Los perros mueven la cola para mostrar emociones, ¡no siempre felicidad!

Category 4: Behavior & Communication

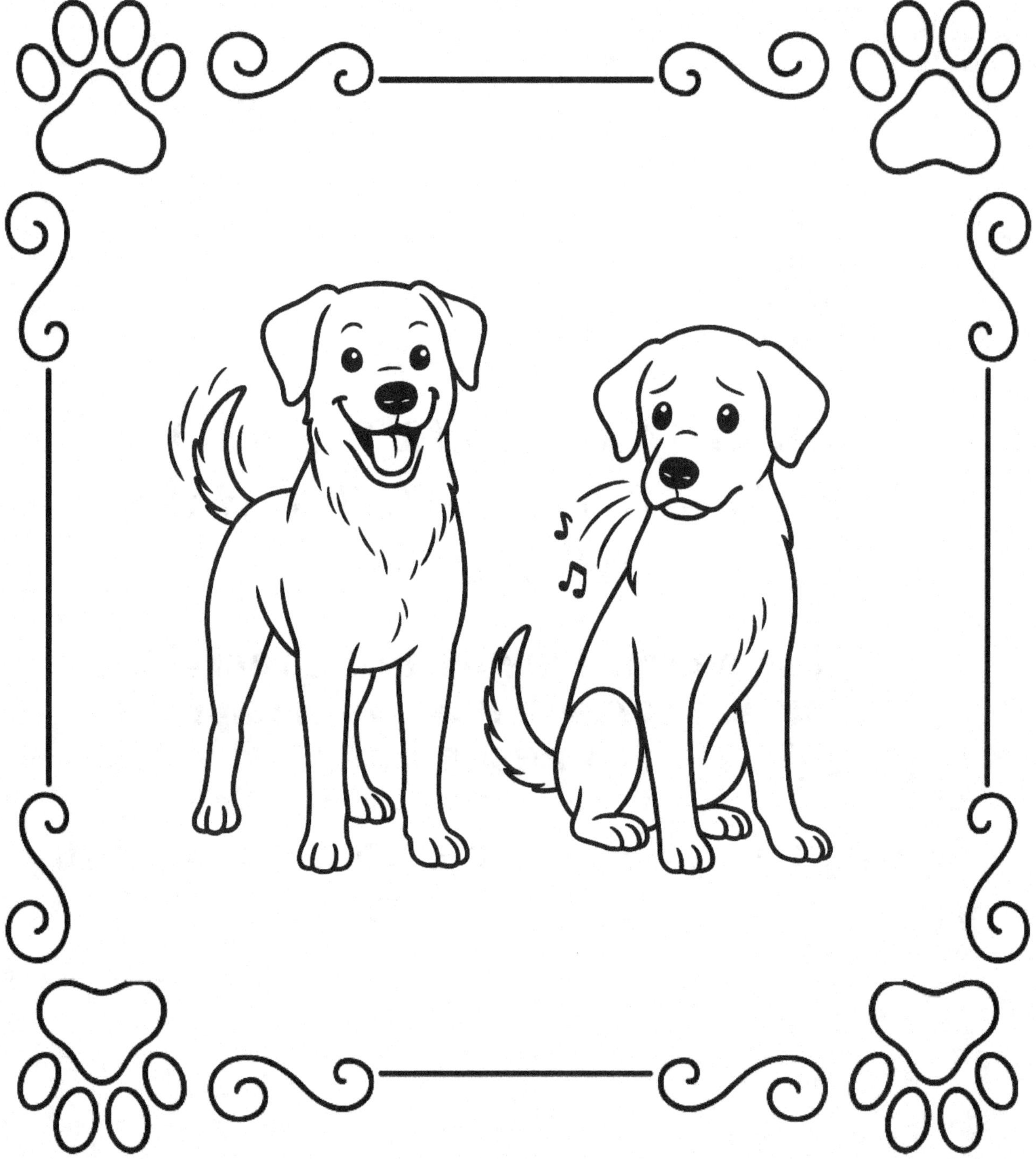

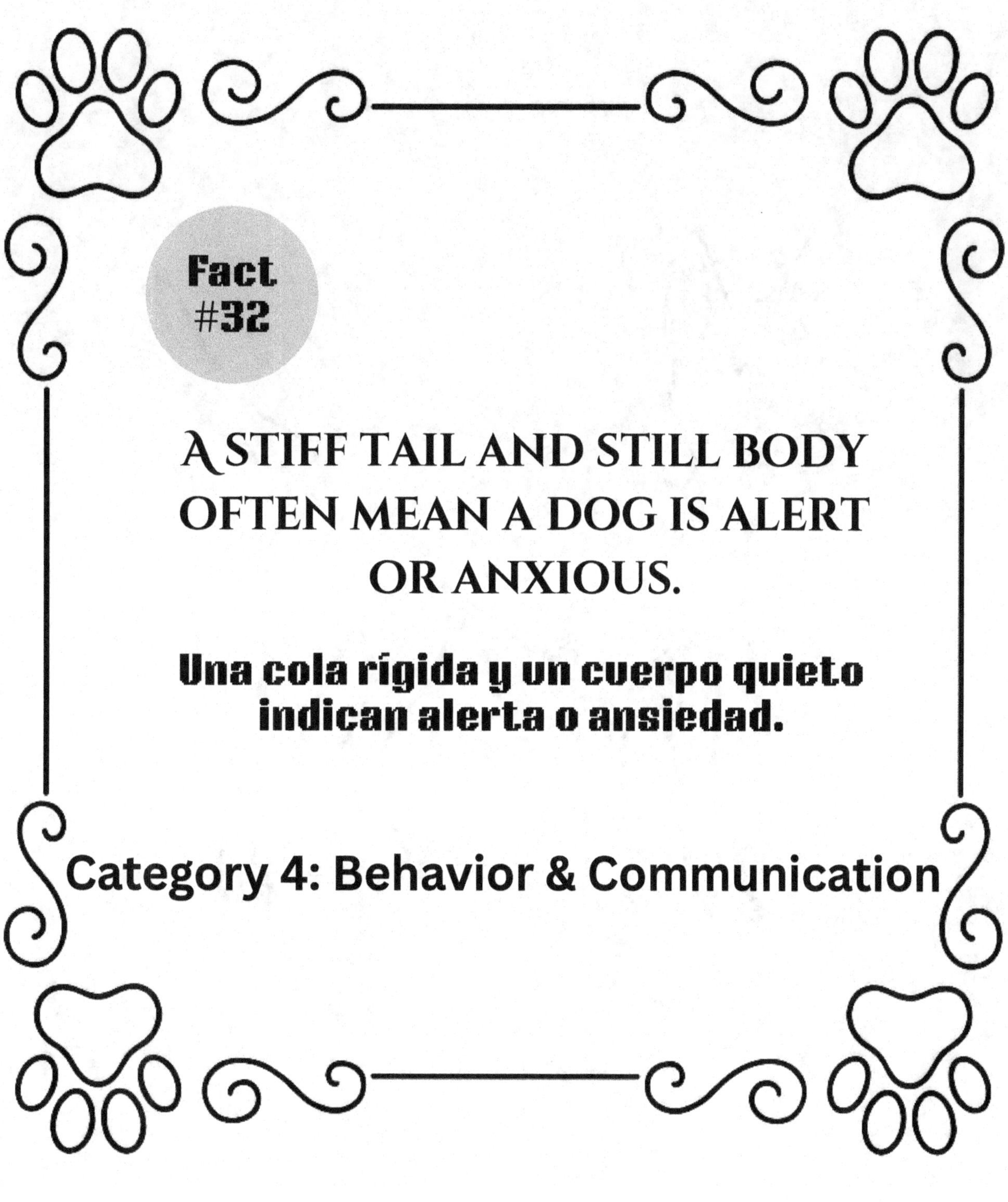

A STIFF TAIL AND STILL BODY OFTEN MEAN A DOG IS ALERT OR ANXIOUS.

Una cola rígida y un cuerpo quieto indican alerta o ansiedad.

Category 4: Behavior & Communication

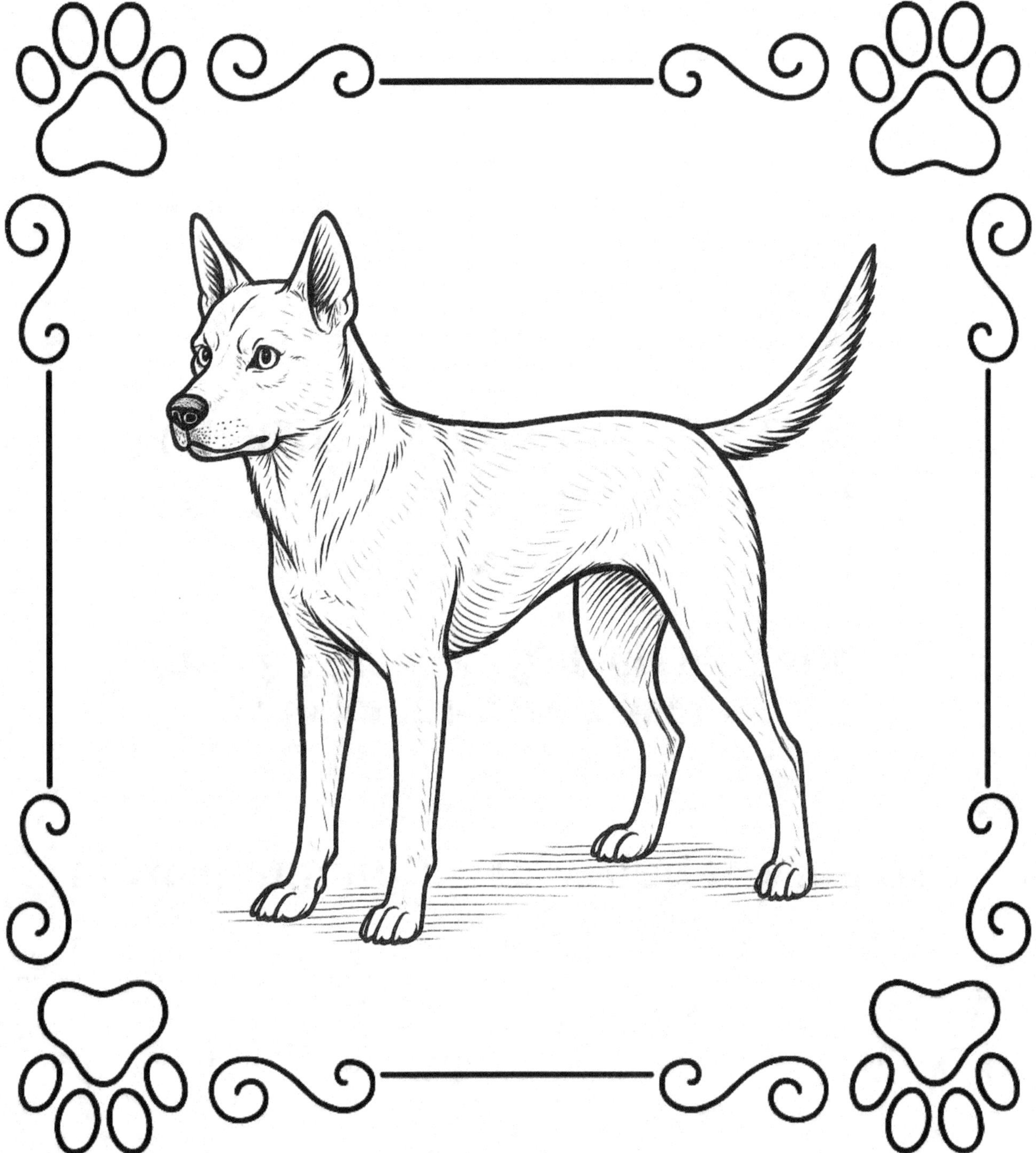

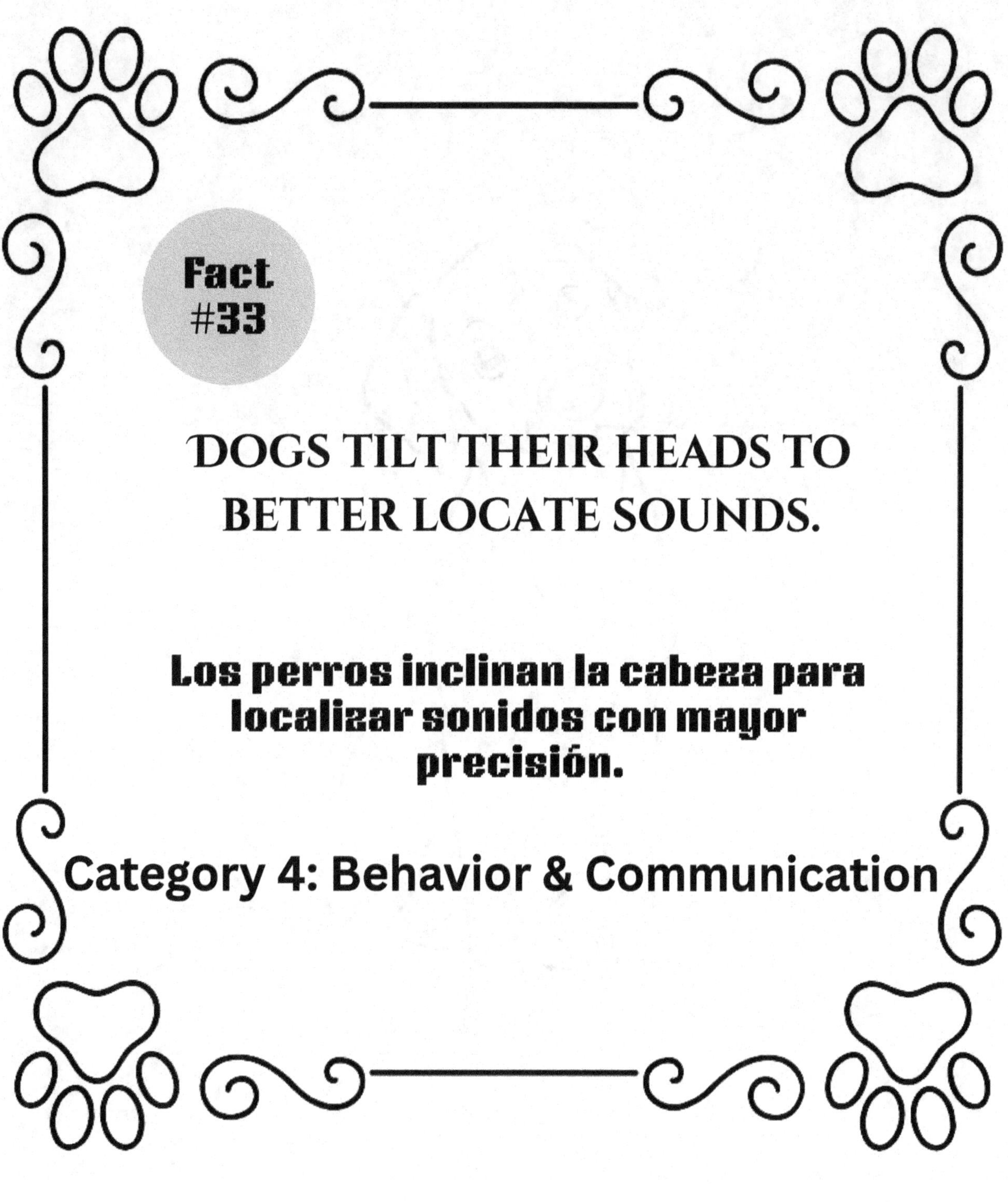

Fact #33

DOGS TILT THEIR HEADS TO BETTER LOCATE SOUNDS.

Los perros inclinan la cabeza para localizar sonidos con mayor precisión.

Category 4: Behavior & Communication

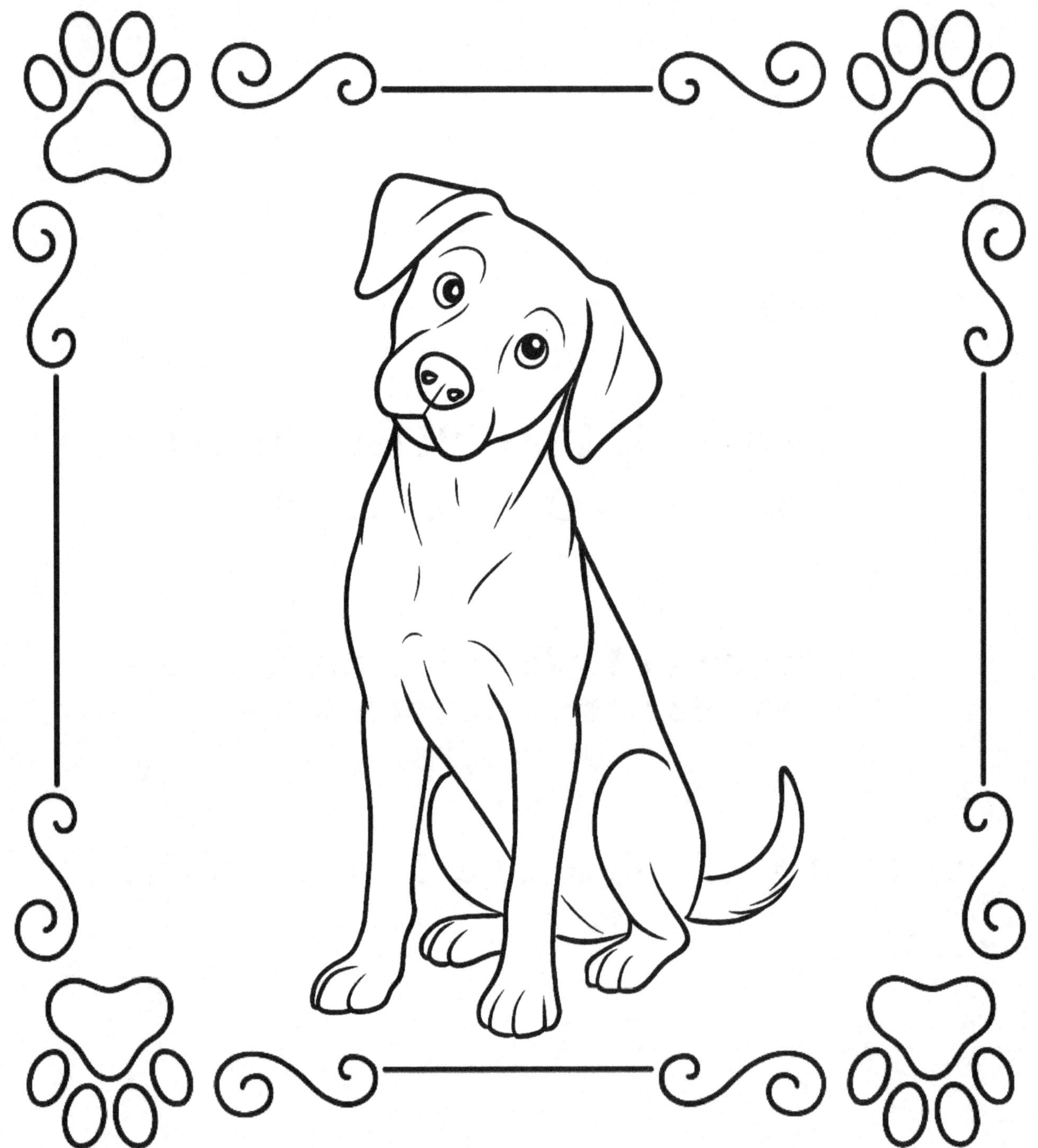

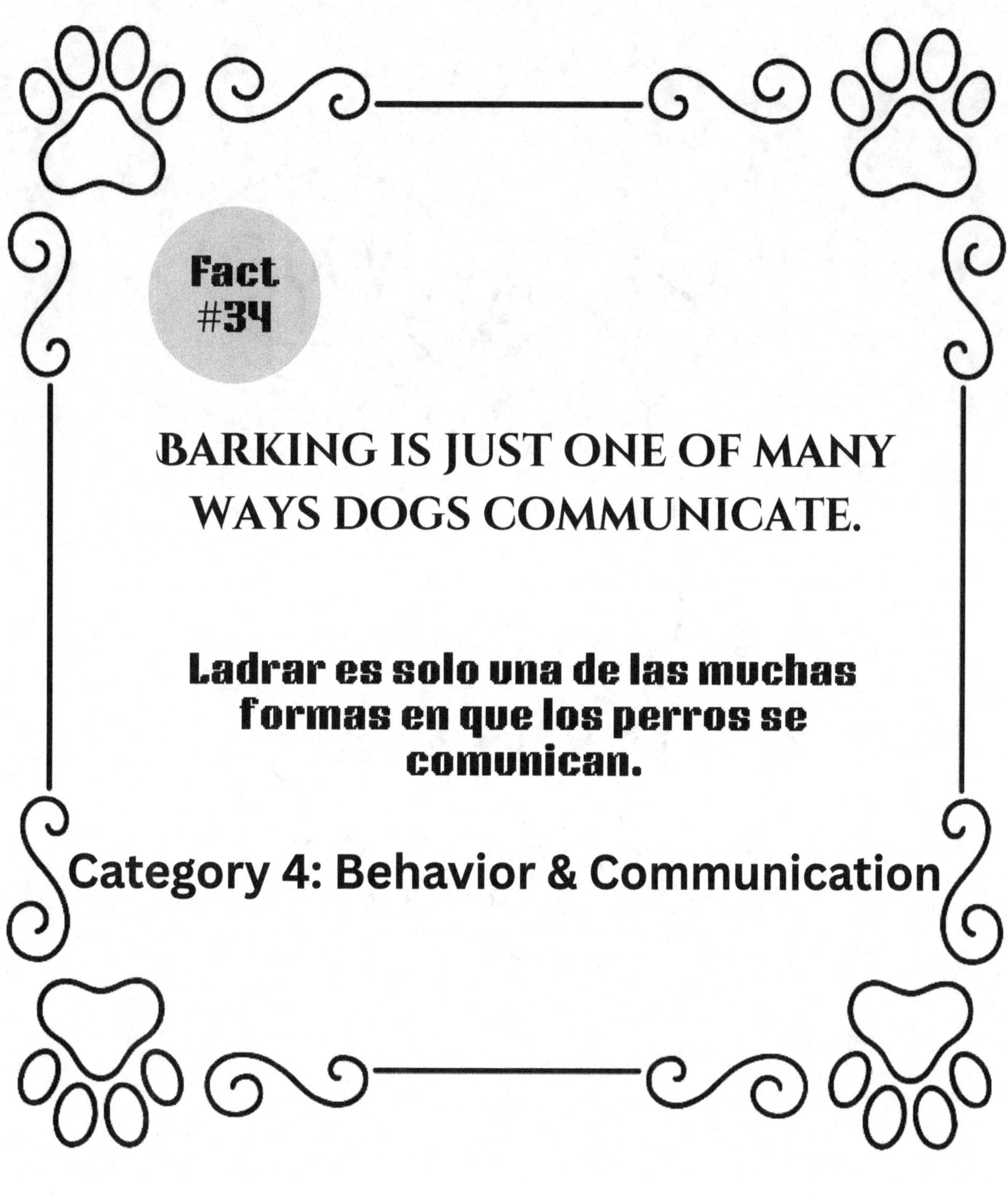

Fact #34

BARKING IS JUST ONE OF MANY WAYS DOGS COMMUNICATE.

Ladrar es solo una de las muchas formas en que los perros se comunican.

Category 4: Behavior & Communication

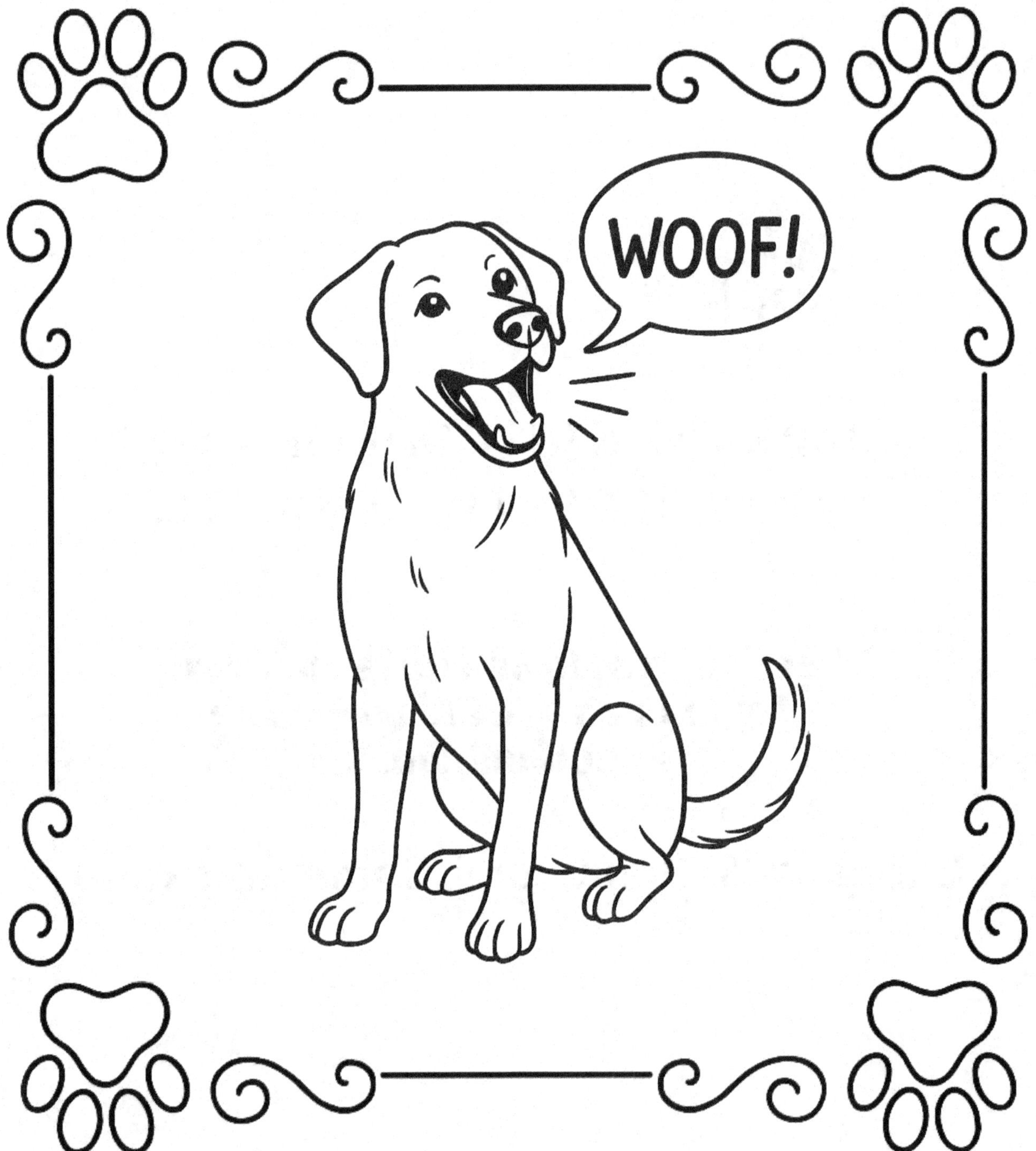
WOOF!

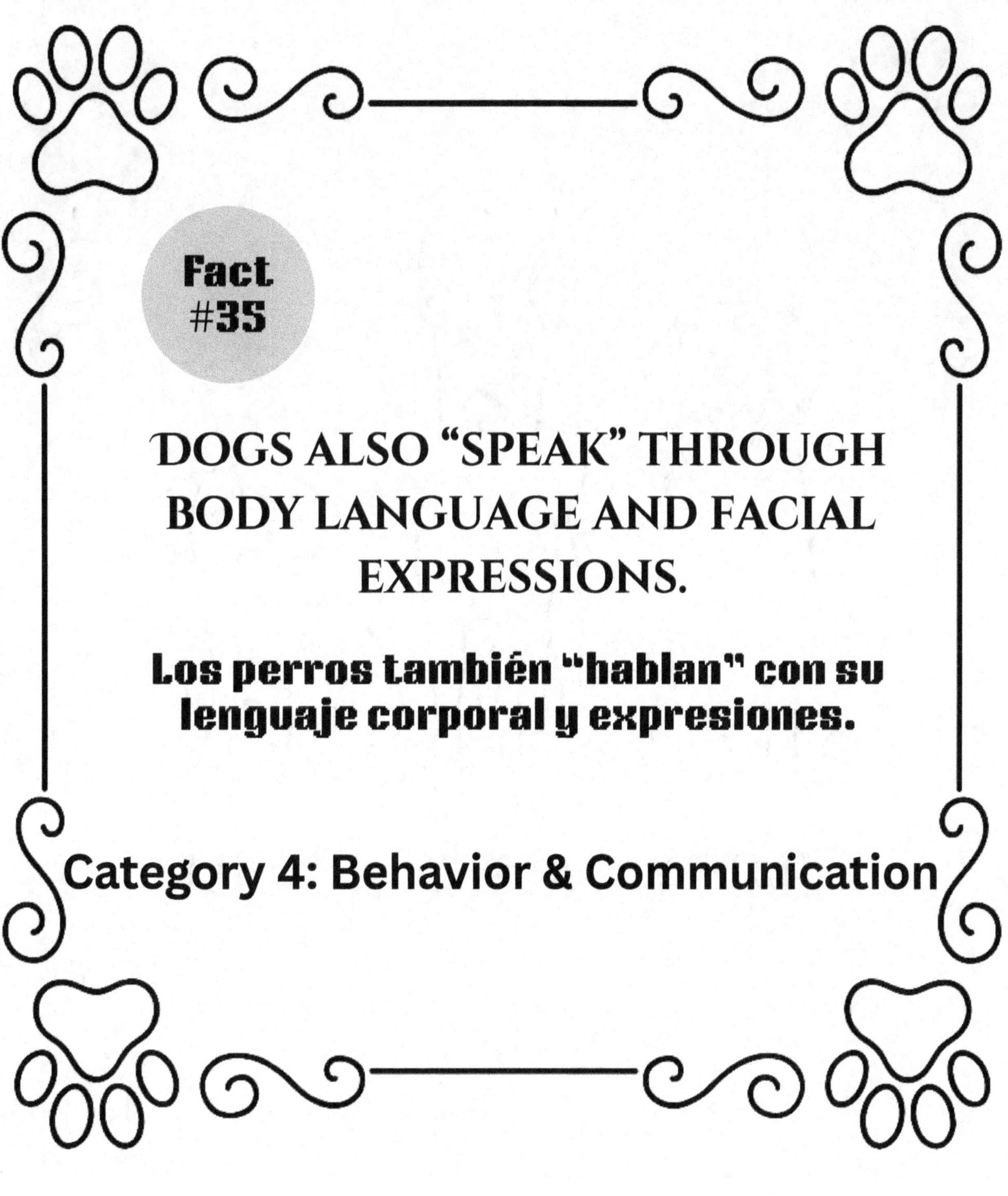

Fact #35

DOGS ALSO "SPEAK" THROUGH BODY LANGUAGE AND FACIAL EXPRESSIONS.

Los perros también "hablan" con su lenguaje corporal y expresiones.

Category 4: Behavior & Communication

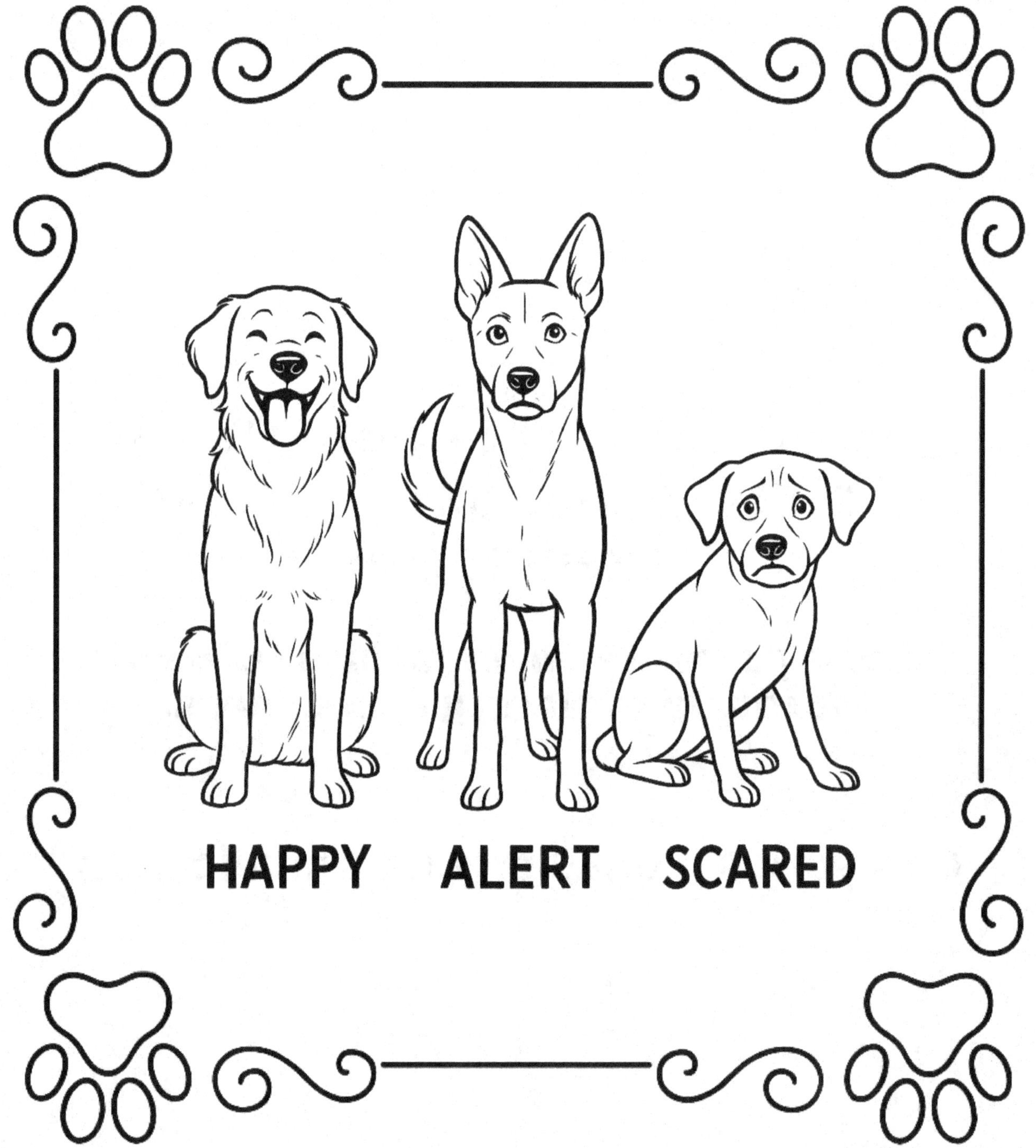

HAPPY
ALERT
SCARED

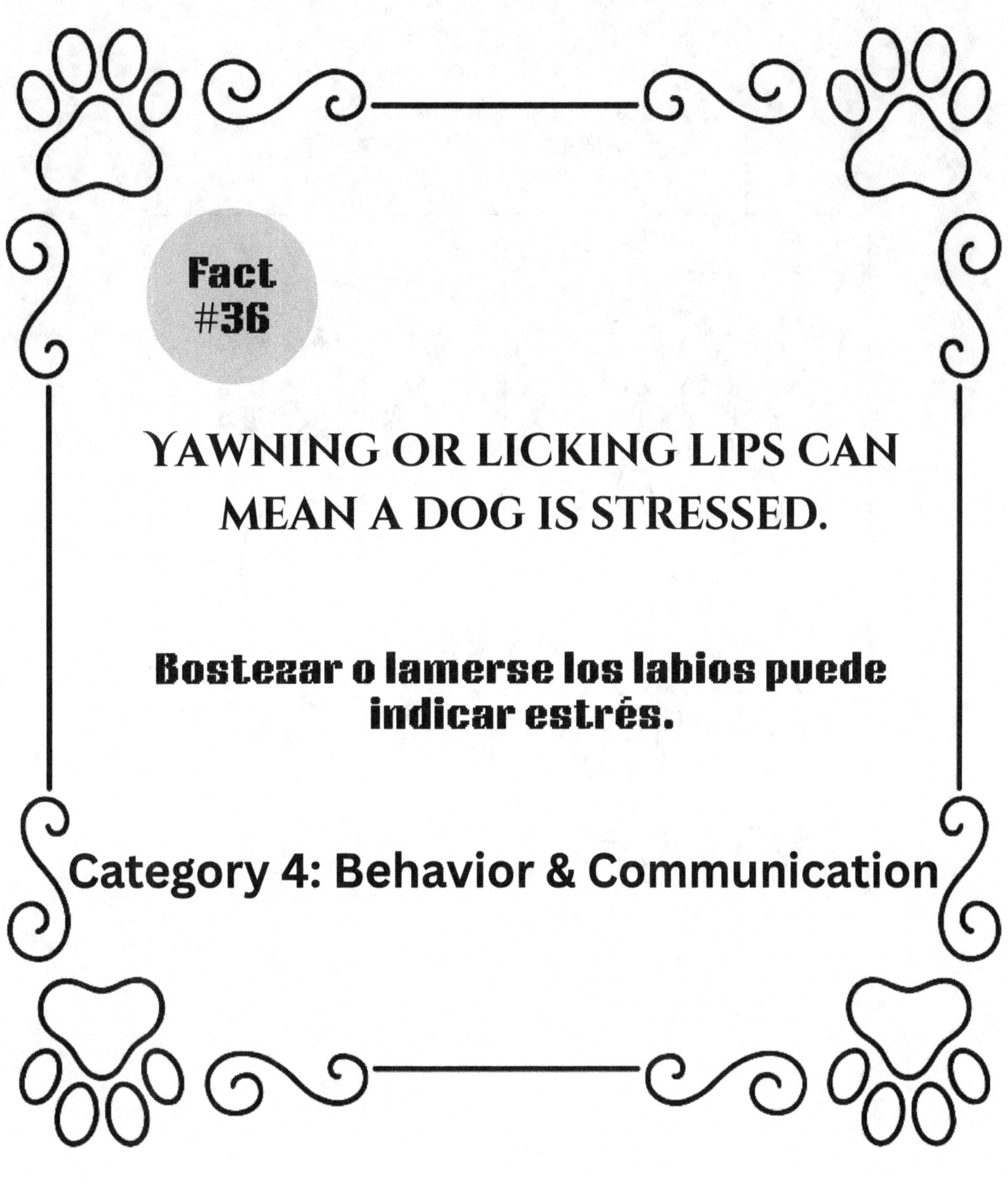

Fact #36

YAWNING OR LICKING LIPS CAN MEAN A DOG IS STRESSED.

Bostezar o lamerse los labios puede indicar estrés.

Category 4: Behavior & Communication

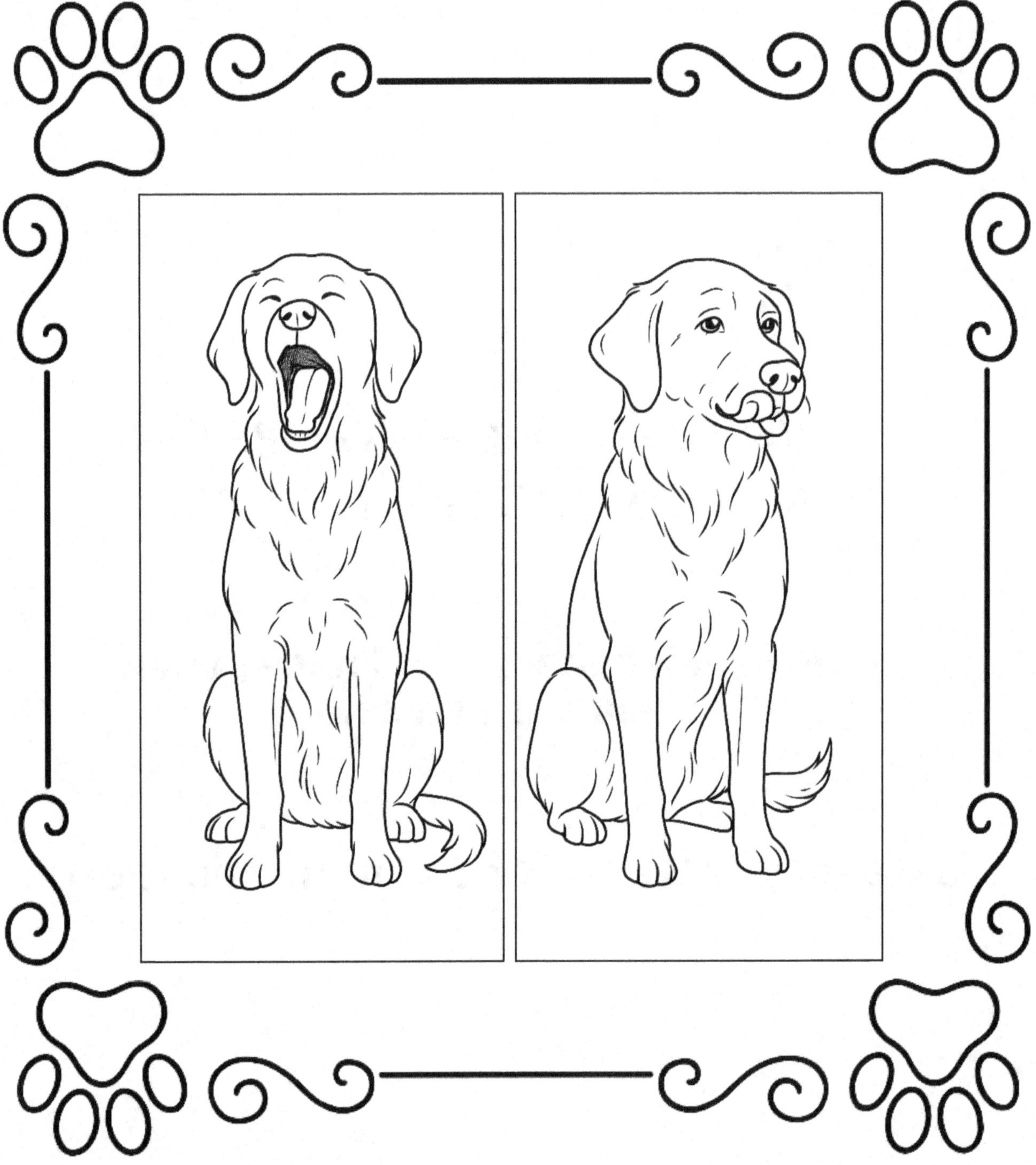

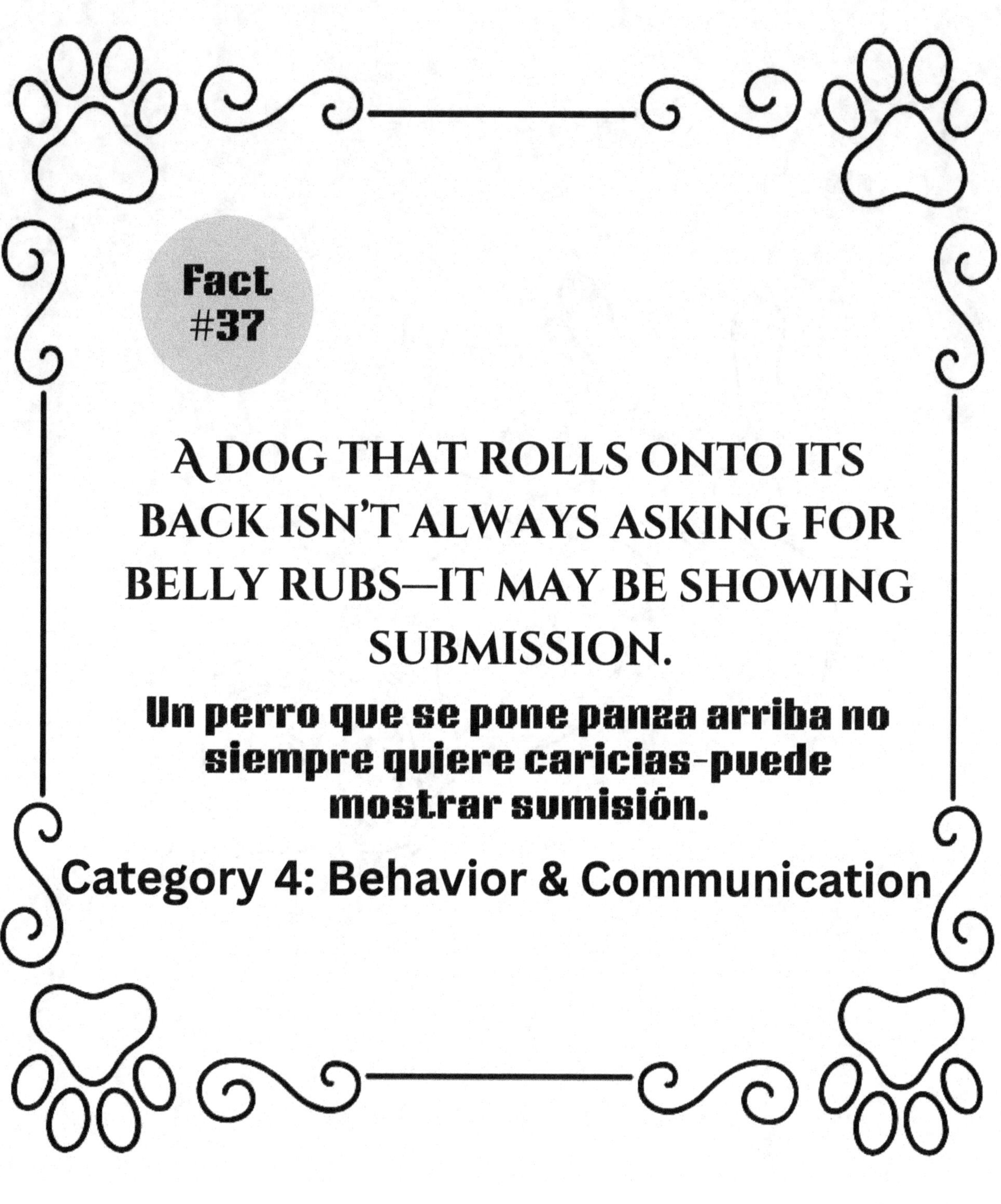

Fact #37

A DOG THAT ROLLS ONTO ITS BACK ISN'T ALWAYS ASKING FOR BELLY RUBS—IT MAY BE SHOWING SUBMISSION.

Un perro que se pone panza arriba no siempre quiere caricias-puede mostrar sumisión.

Category 4: Behavior & Communication

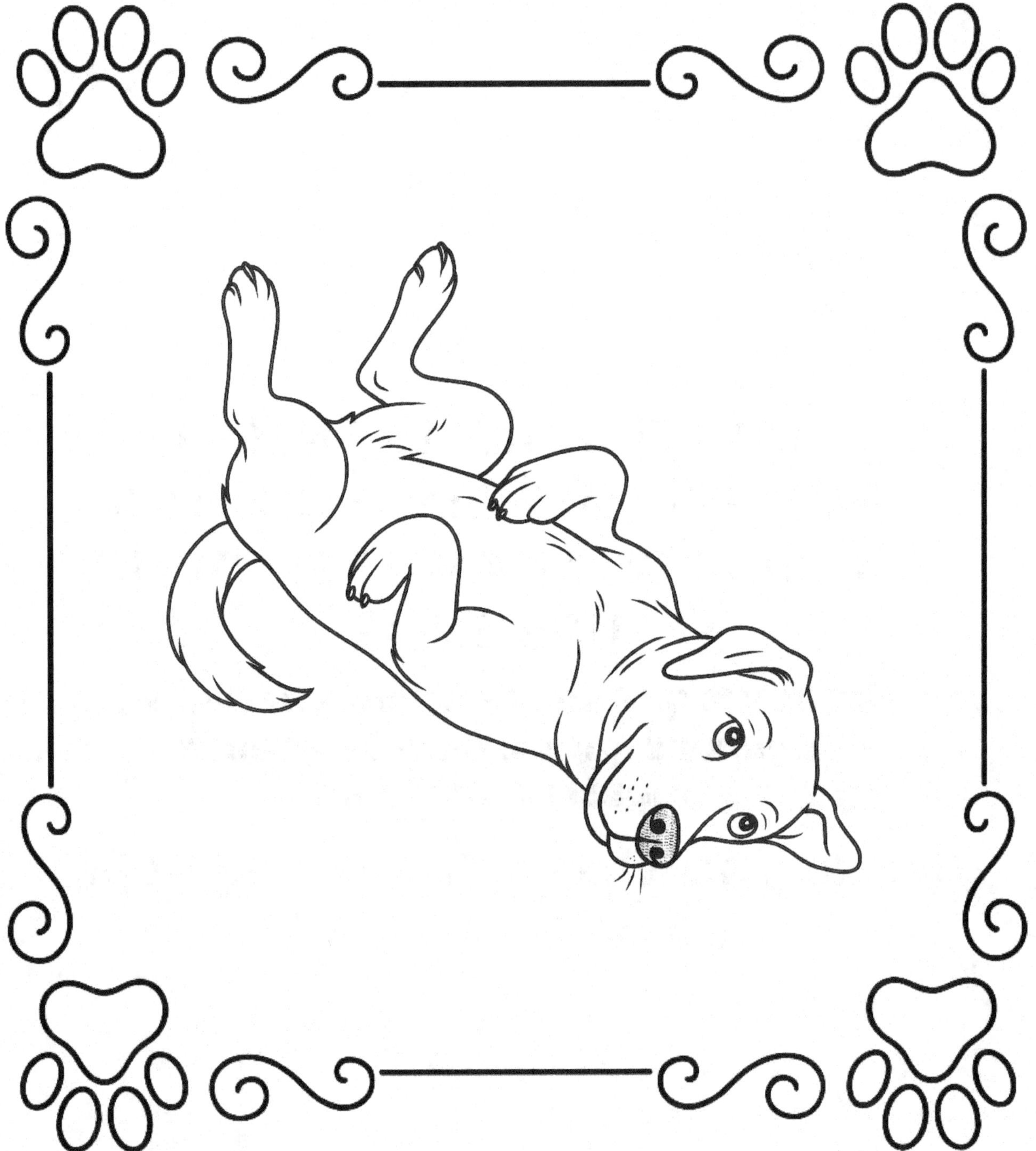

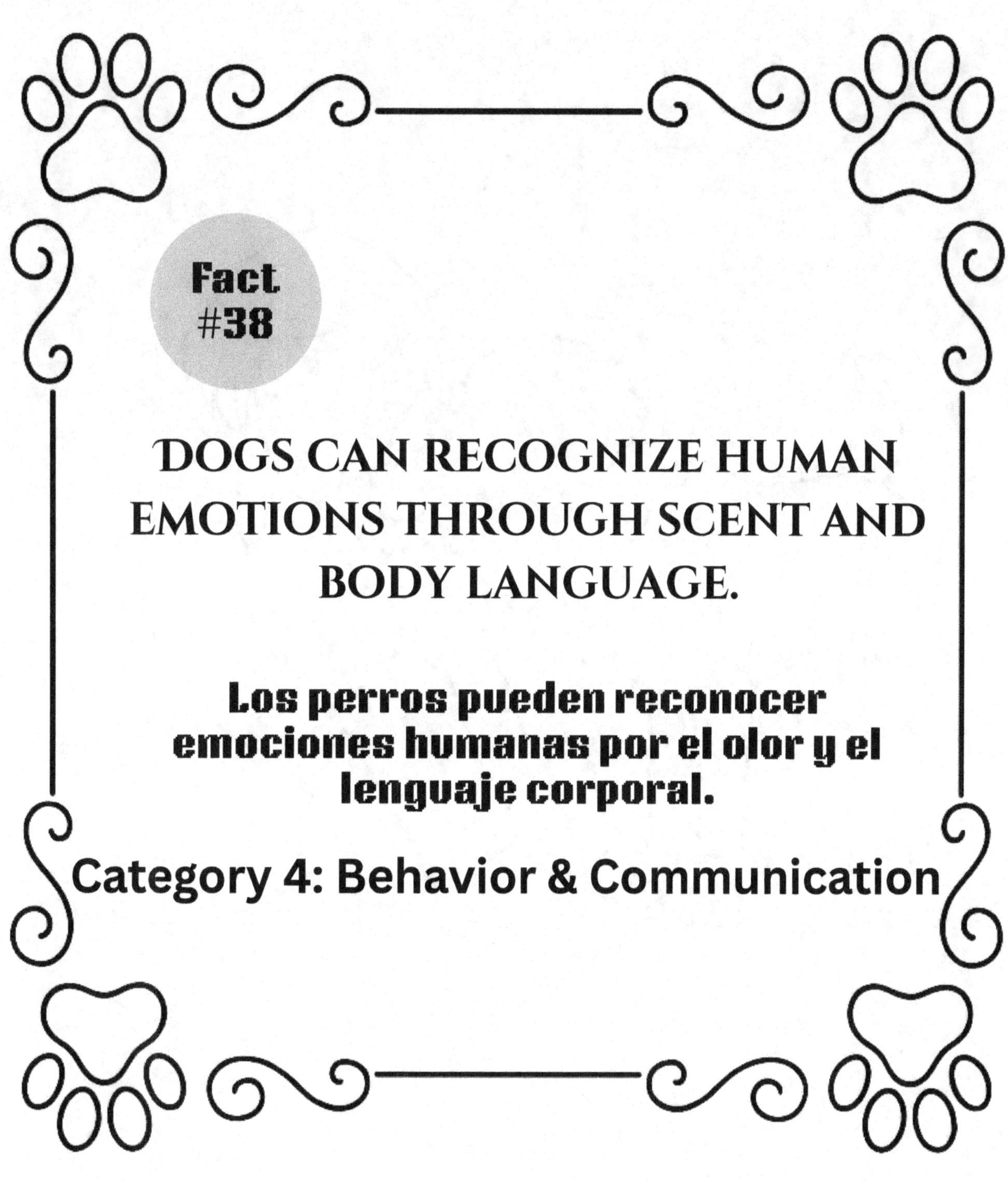

Fact #38

DOGS CAN RECOGNIZE HUMAN EMOTIONS THROUGH SCENT AND BODY LANGUAGE.

Los perros pueden reconocer emociones humanas por el olor y el lenguaje corporal.

Category 4: Behavior & Communication

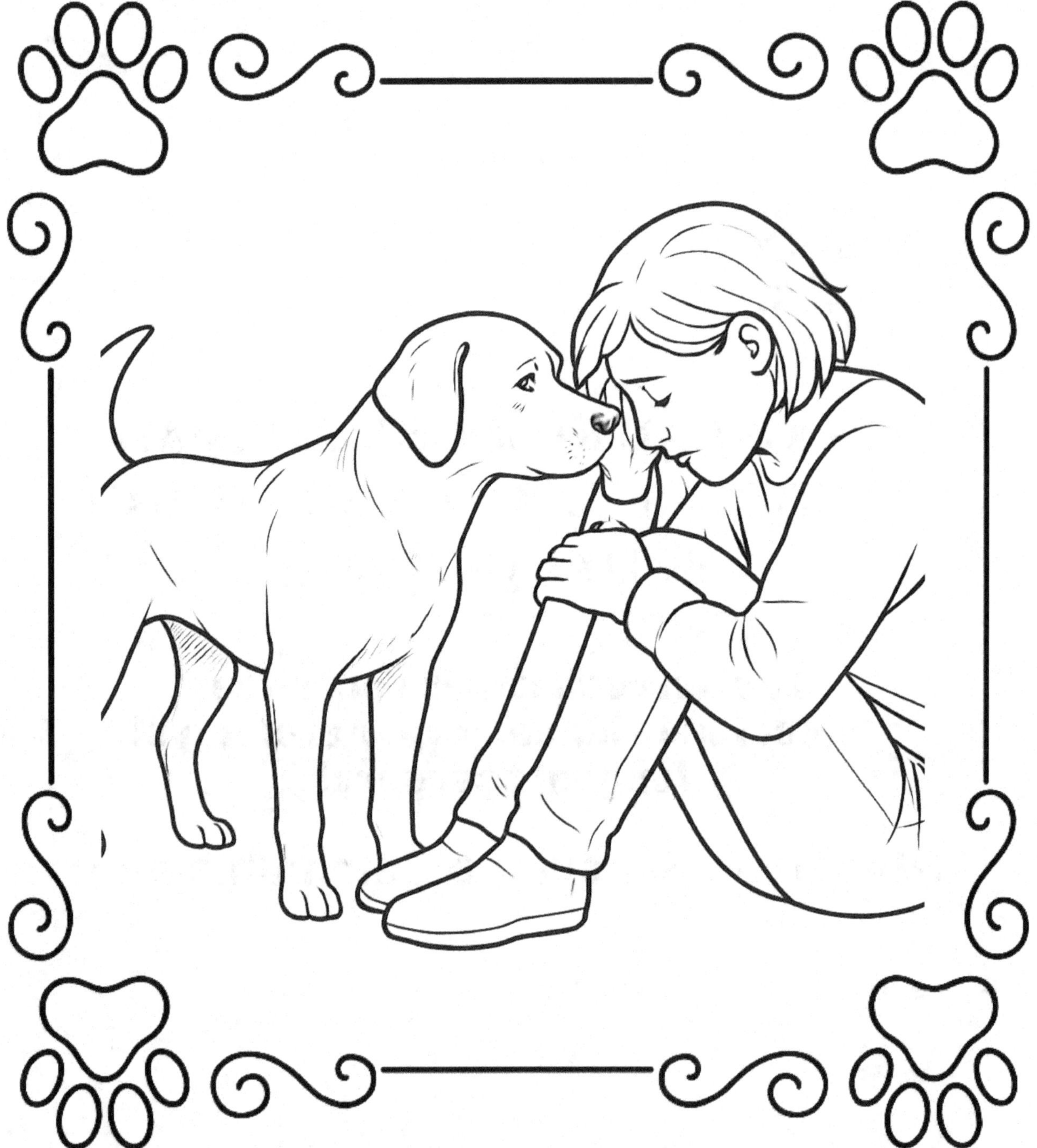

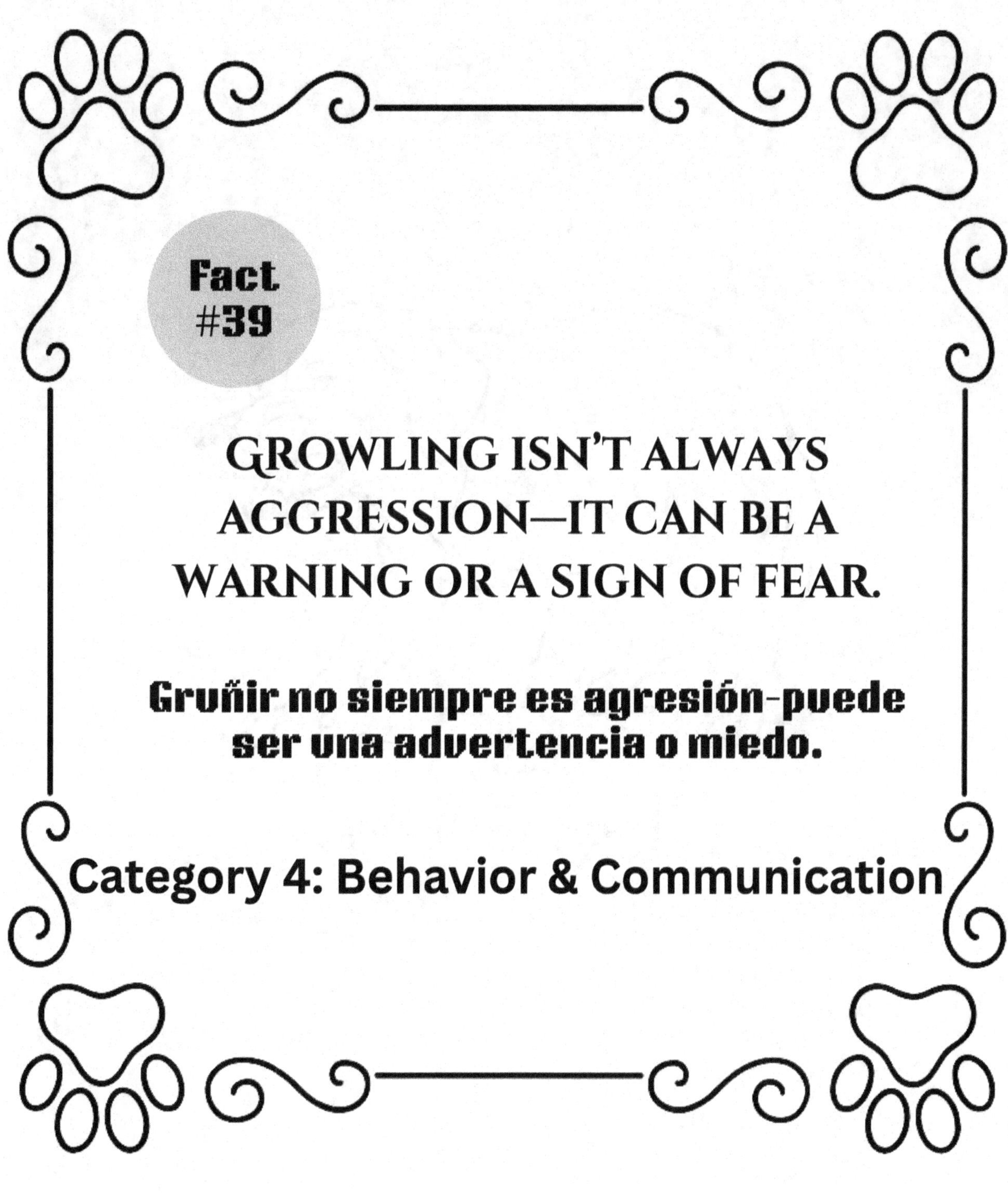

GROWLING ISN'T ALWAYS AGGRESSION—IT CAN BE A WARNING OR A SIGN OF FEAR.

Gruñir no siempre es agresión-puede ser una advertencia o miedo.

Category 4: Behavior & Communication

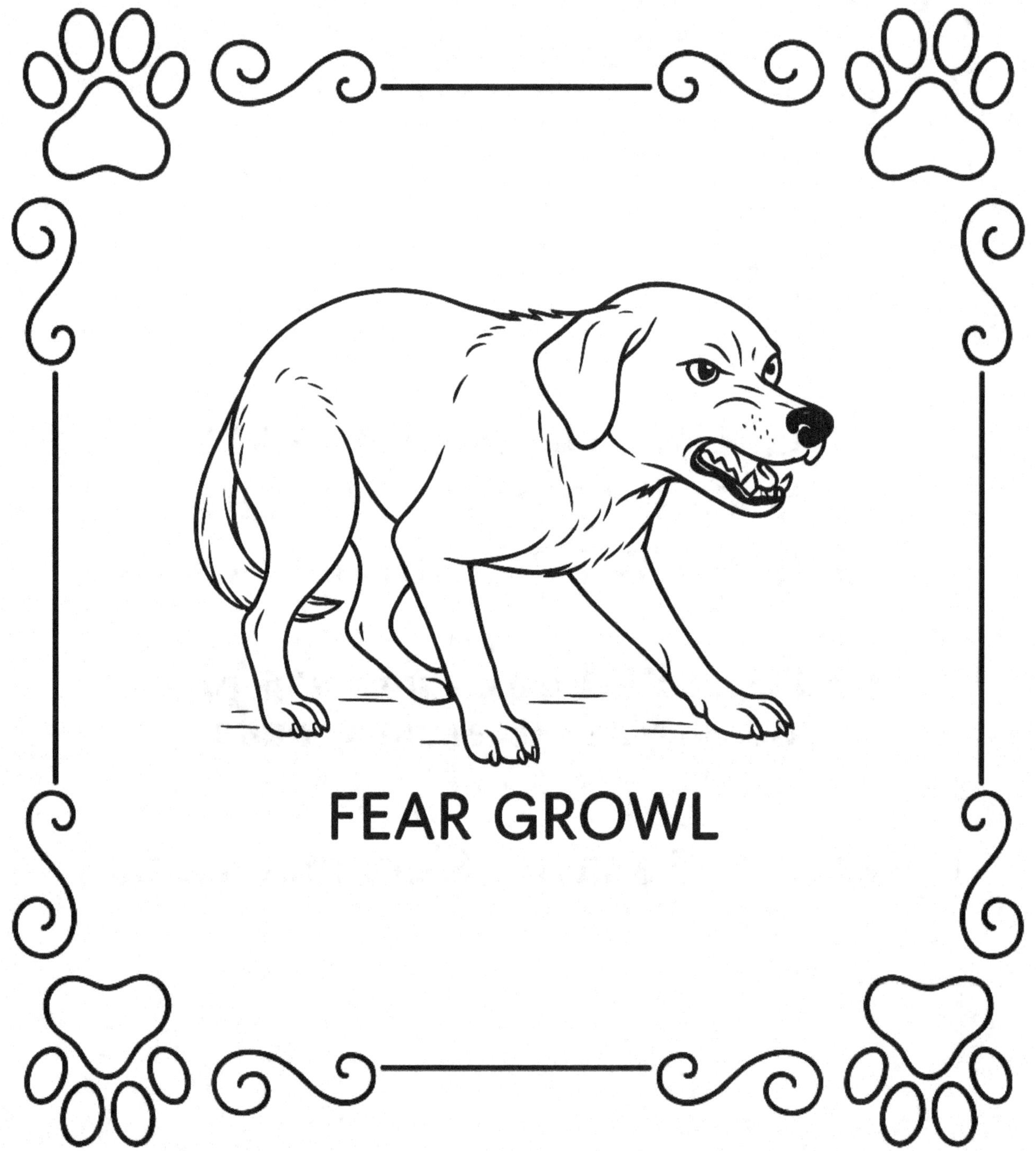

FEAR GROWL

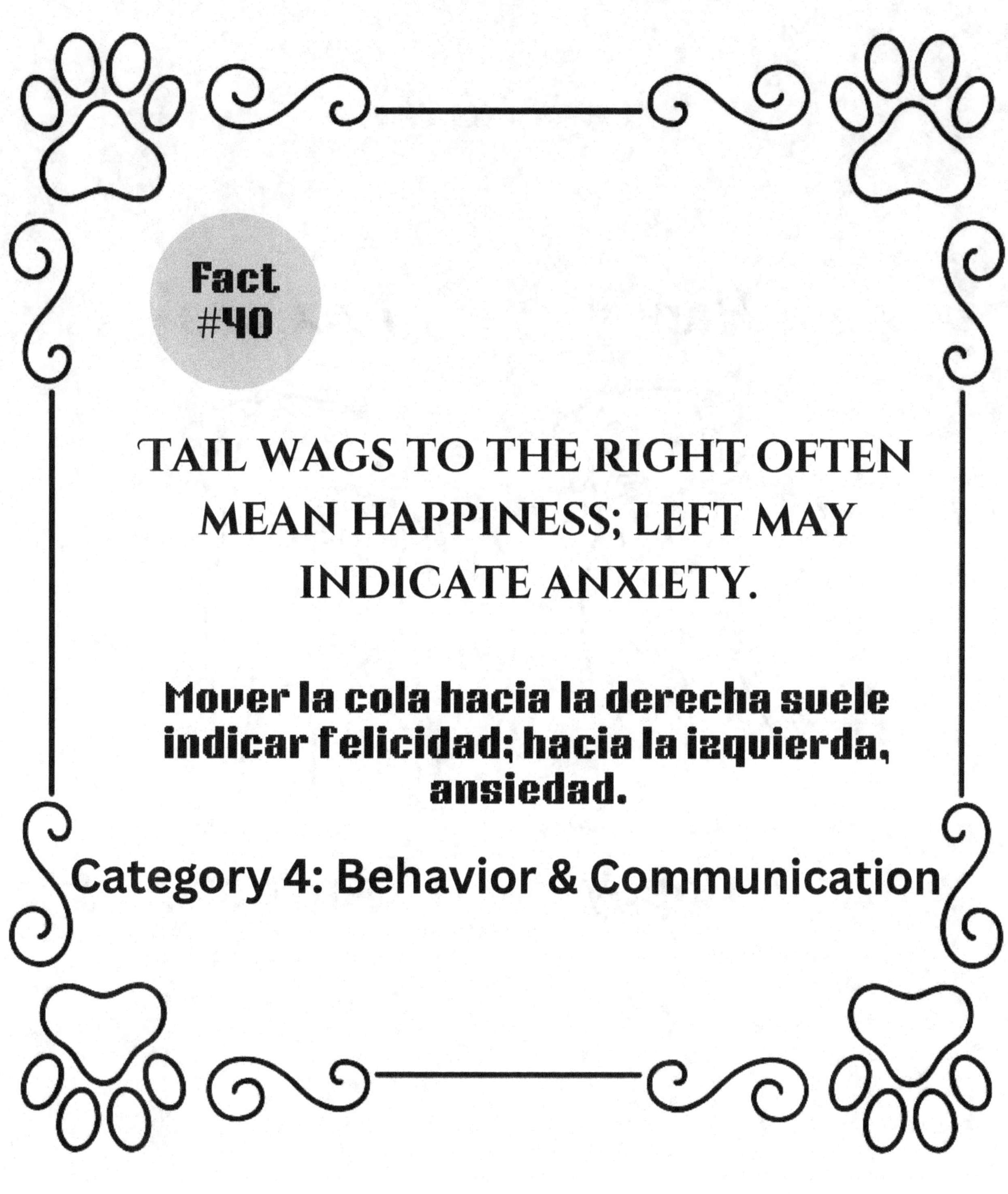
Fact #40

TAIL WAGS TO THE RIGHT OFTEN MEAN HAPPINESS; LEFT MAY INDICATE ANXIETY.

Mover la cola hacia la derecha suele indicar felicidad; hacia la izquierda, ansiedad.

Category 4: Behavior & Communication

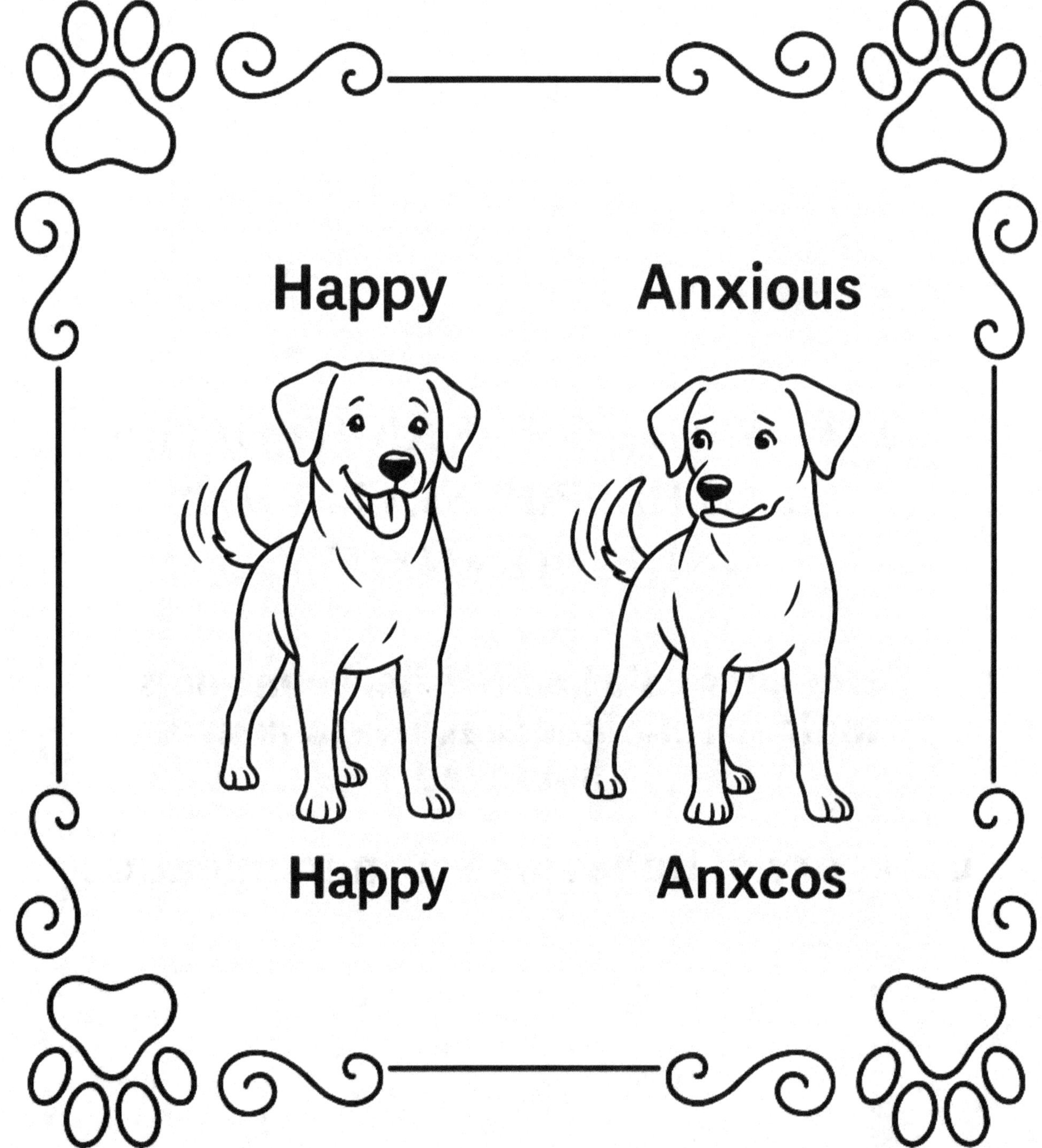
Happy
Anxious
Happy
Anxcos

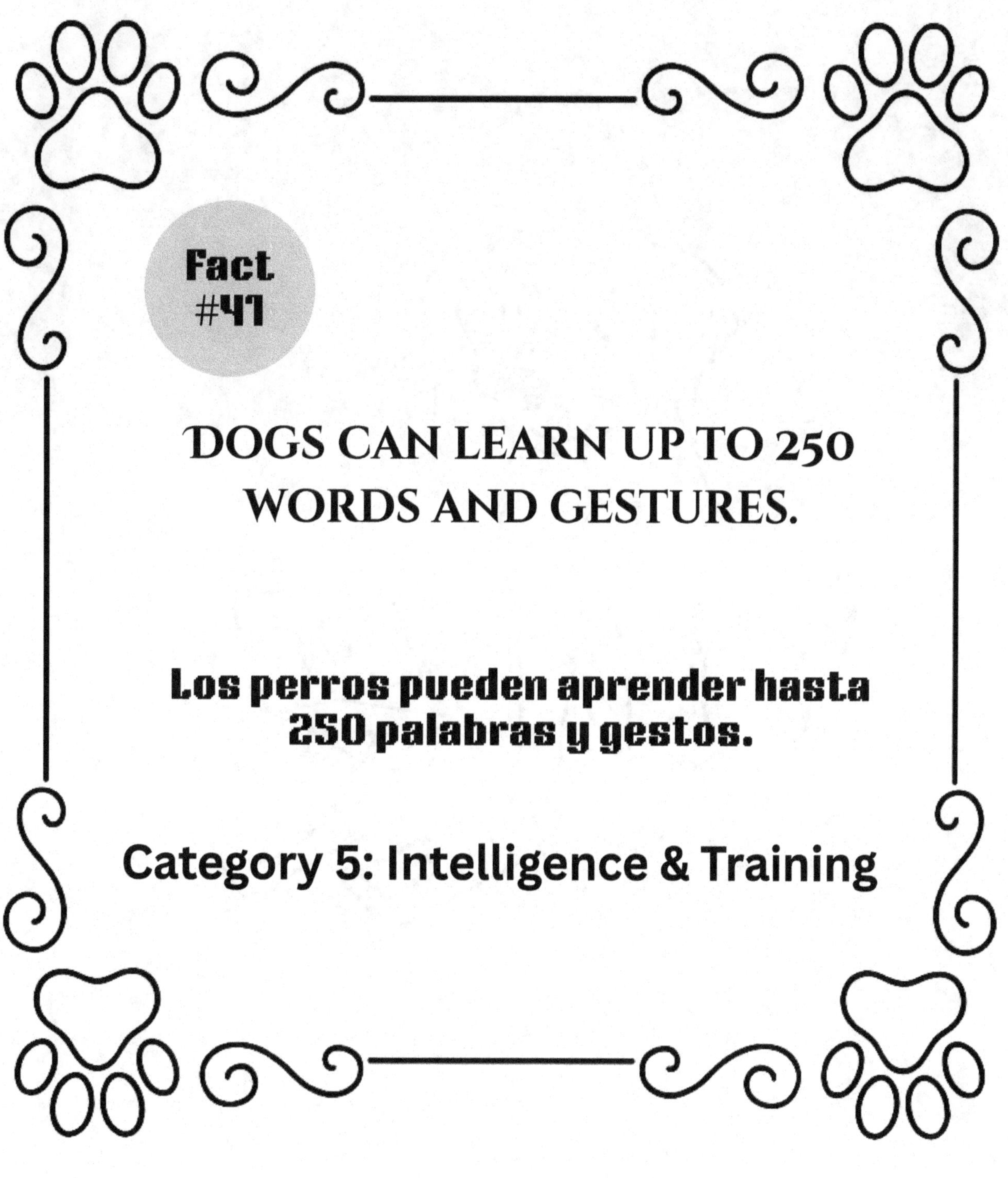

Fact #47

DOGS CAN LEARN UP TO 250 WORDS AND GESTURES.

Los perros pueden aprender hasta 250 palabras y gestos.

Category 5: Intelligence & Training

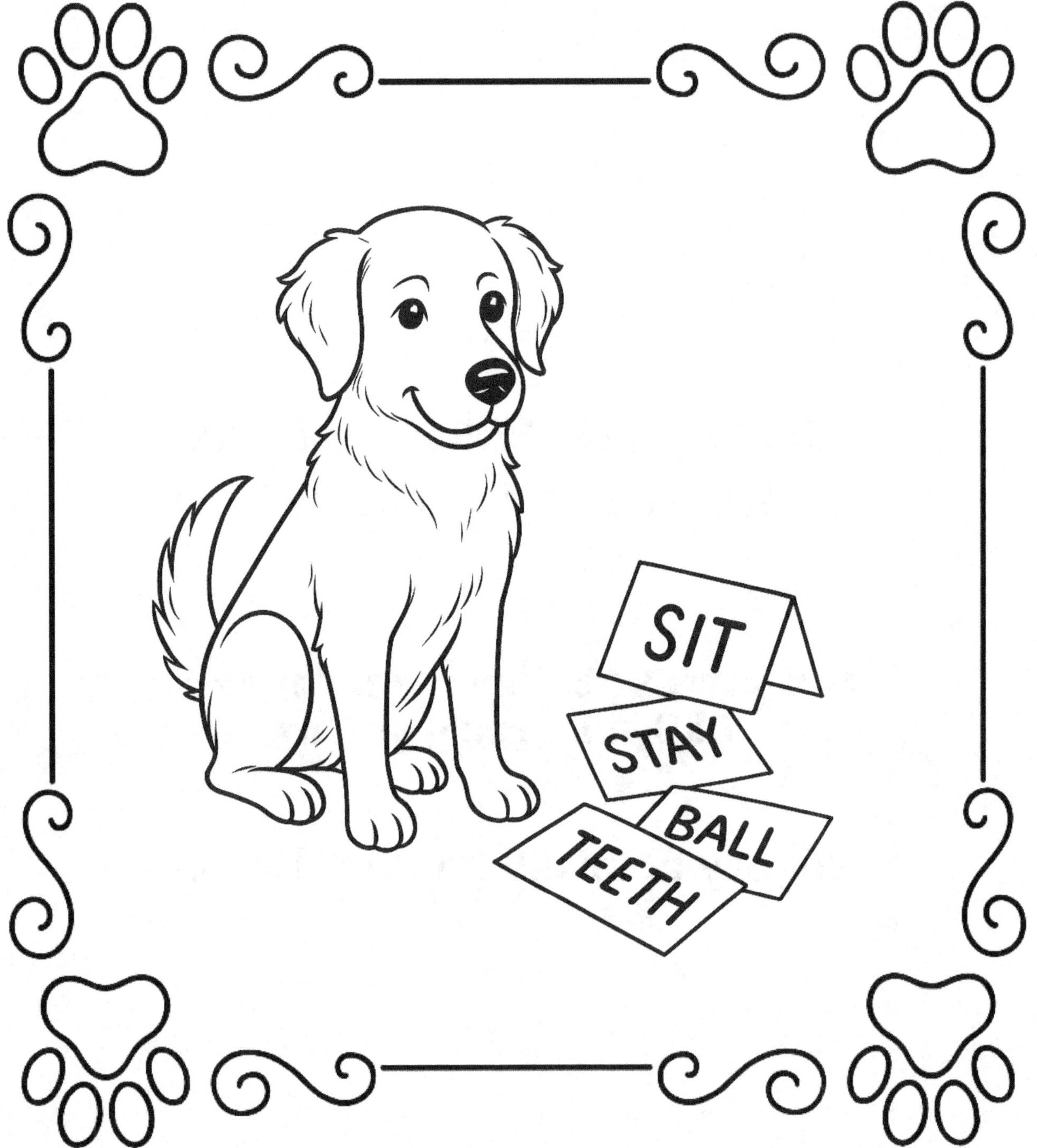

SIT
STAY
BALL
TEETH

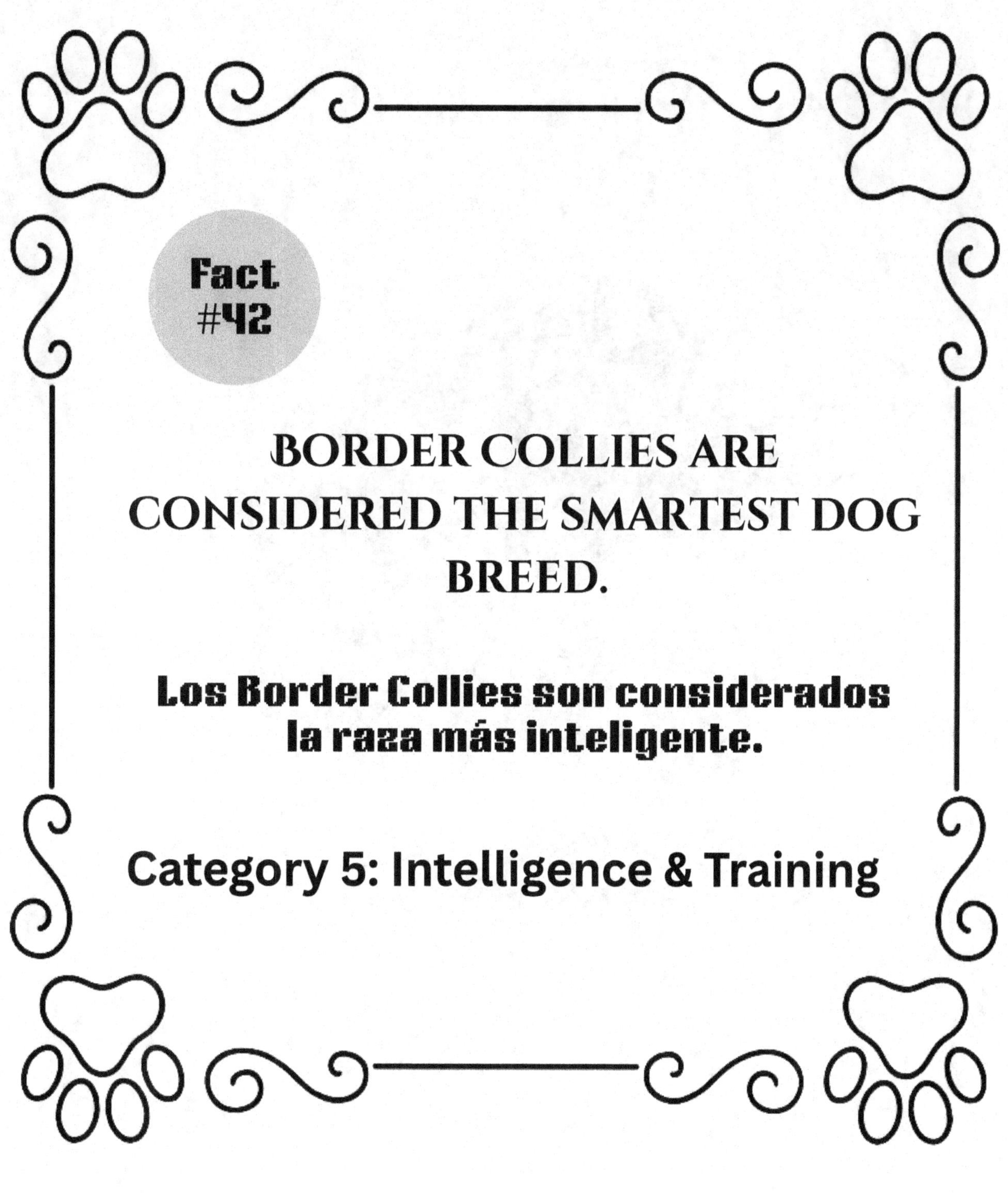

Fact #42

BORDER COLLIES ARE CONSIDERED THE SMARTEST DOG BREED.

Los Border Collies son considerados la raza más inteligente.

Category 5: Intelligence & Training

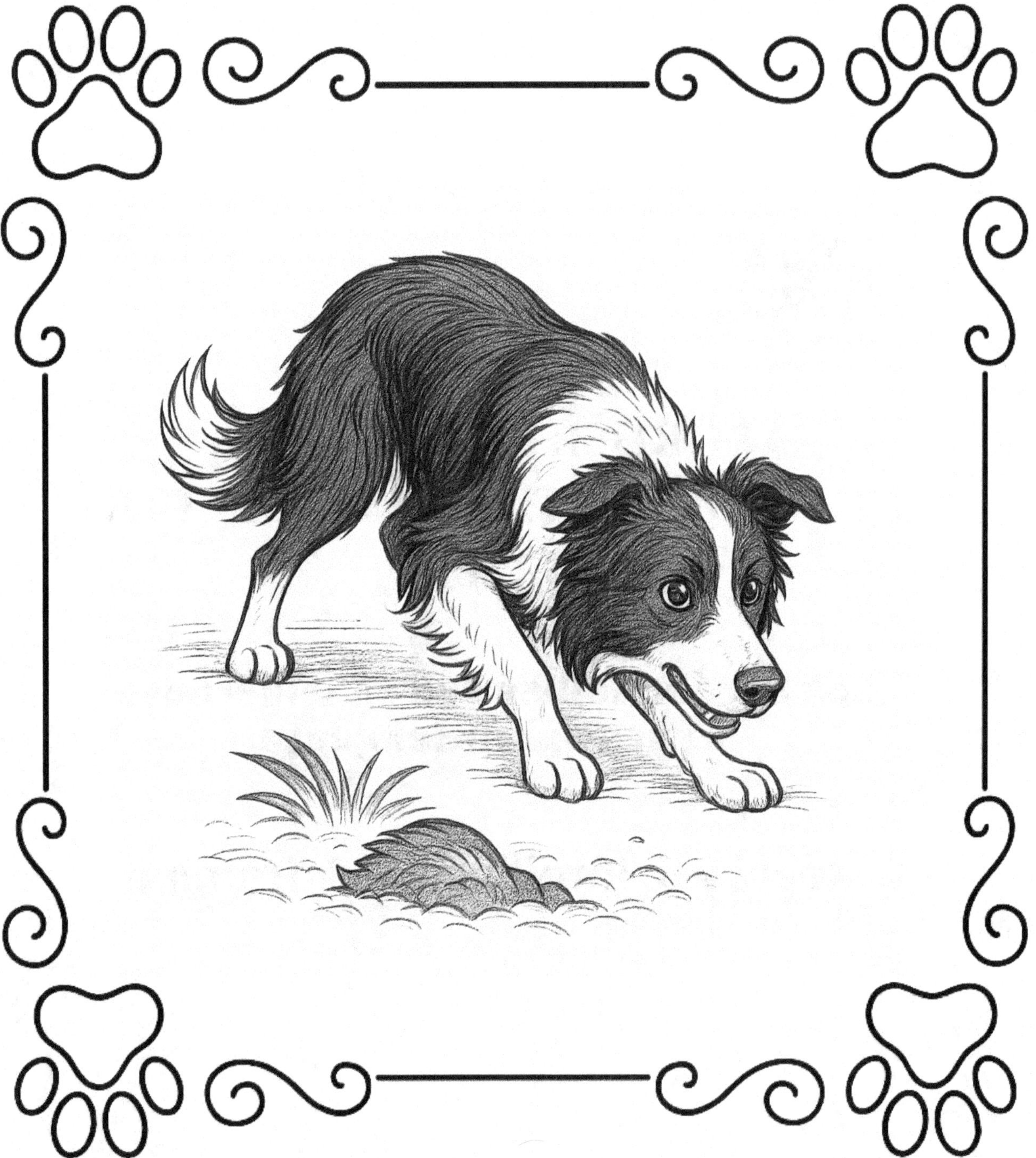

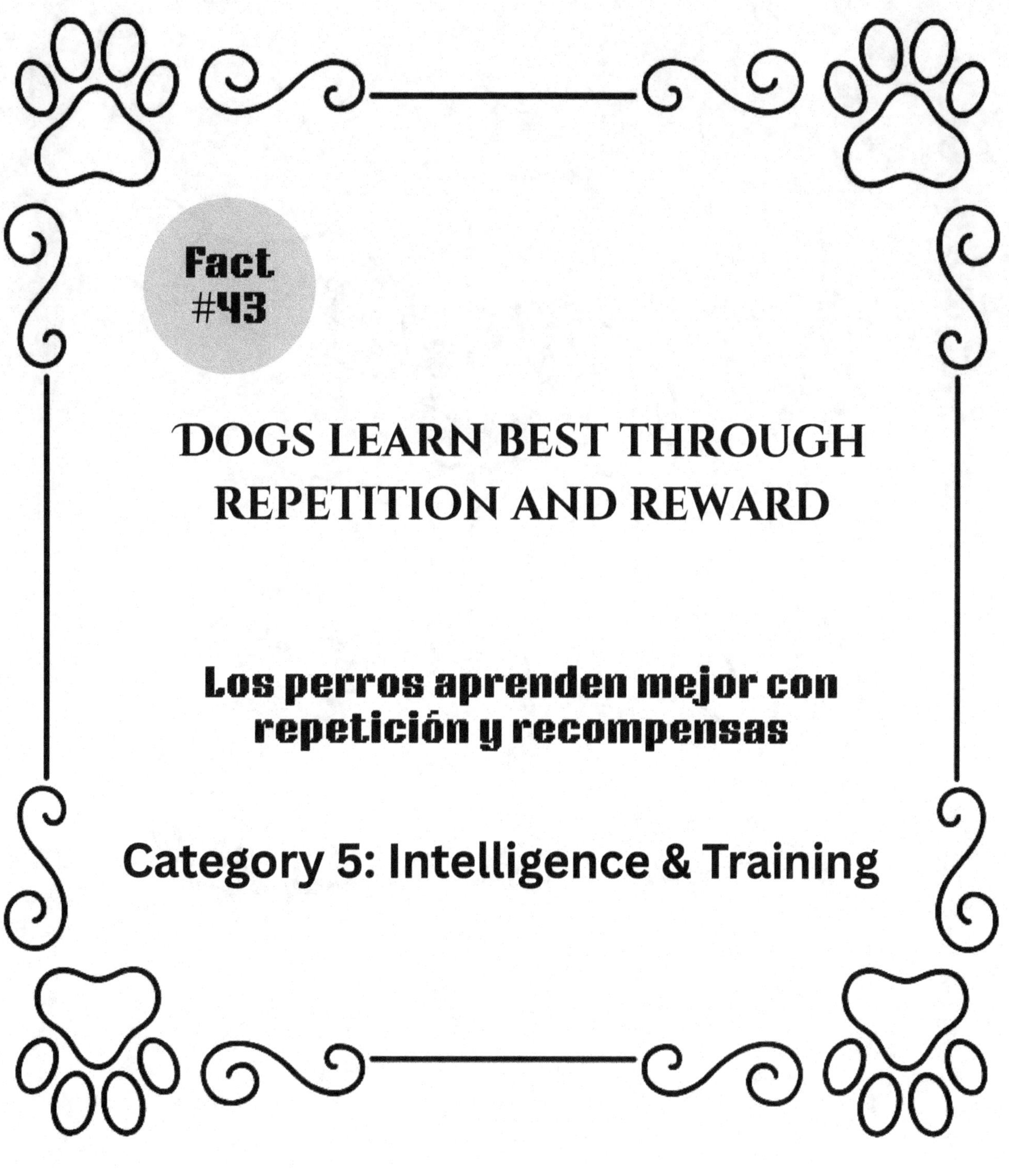

Fact #43

DOGS LEARN BEST THROUGH REPETITION AND REWARD

Los perros aprenden mejor con repetición y recompensas

Category 5: Intelligence & Training

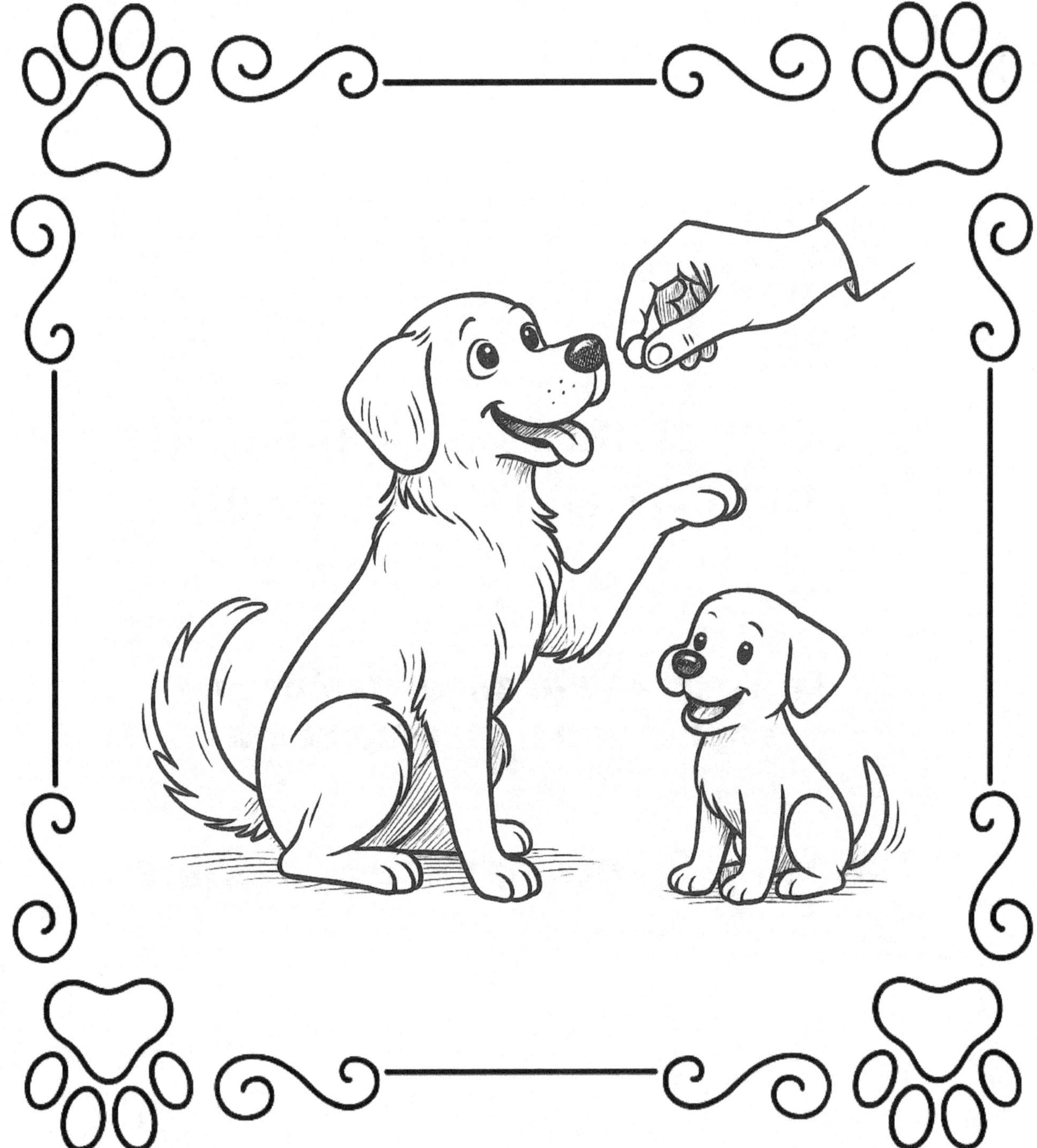

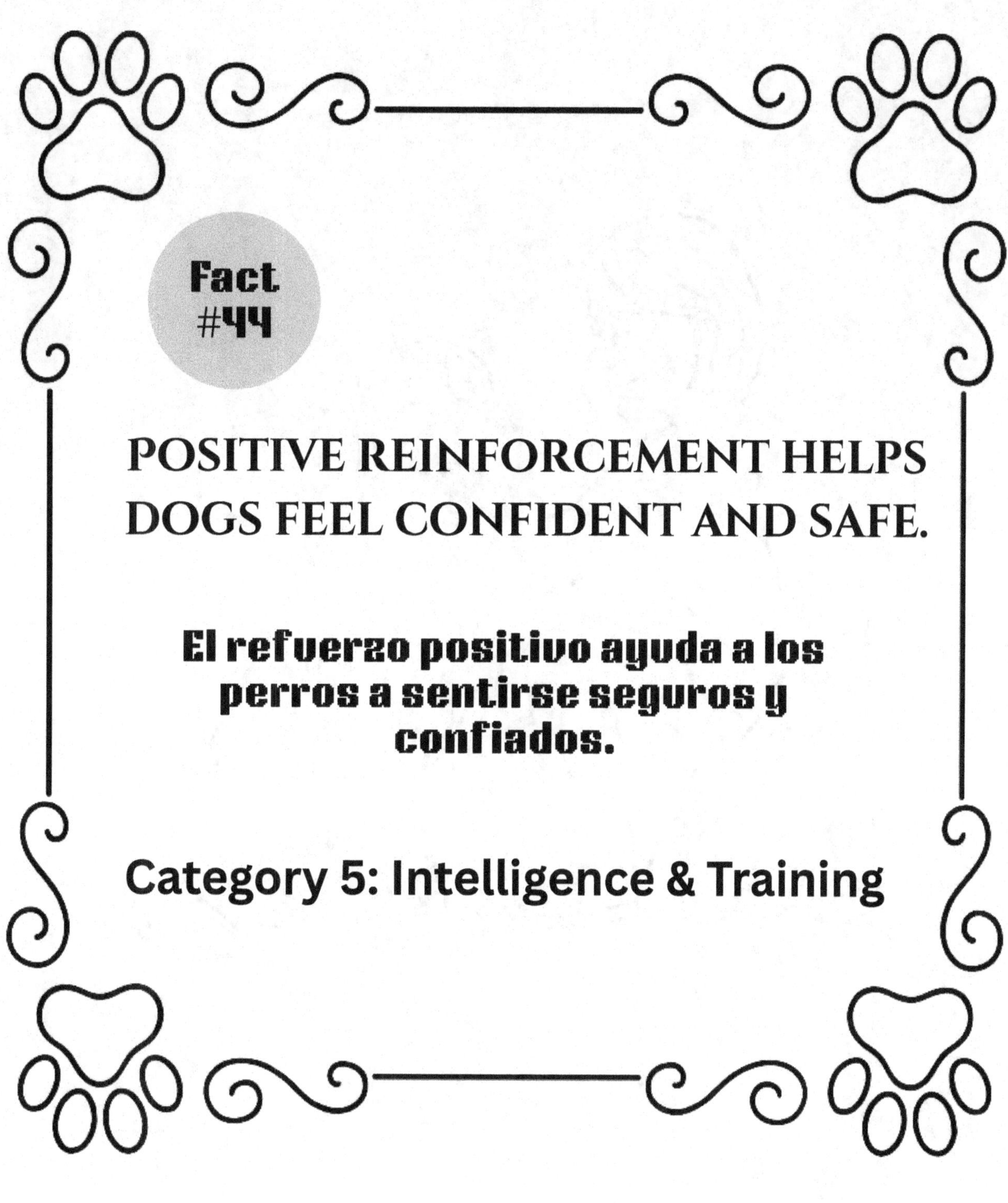

Fact
#44

POSITIVE REINFORCEMENT HELPS DOGS FEEL CONFIDENT AND SAFE.

El refuerzo positivo ayuda a los perros a sentirse seguros y confiados.

Category 5: Intelligence & Training

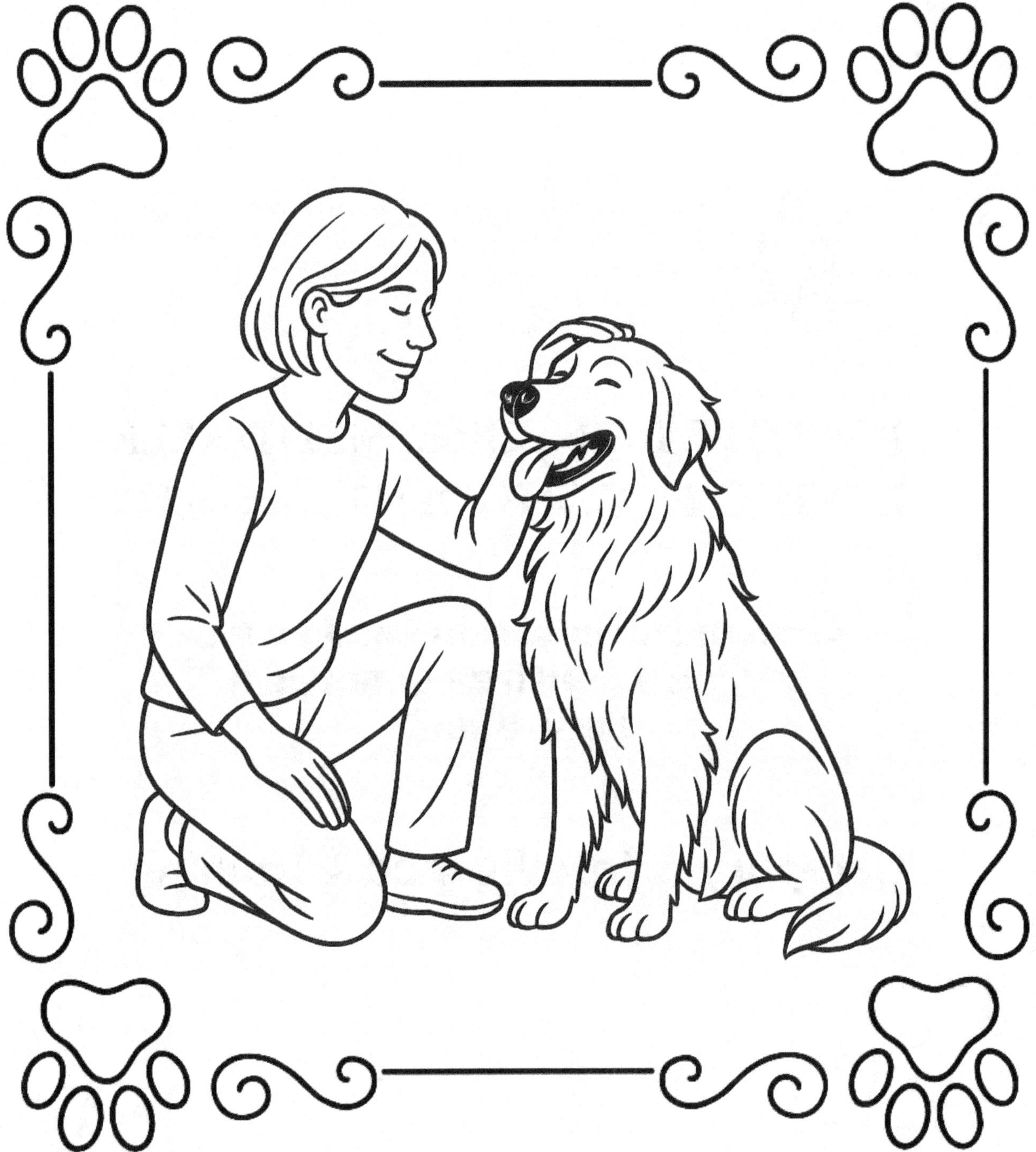

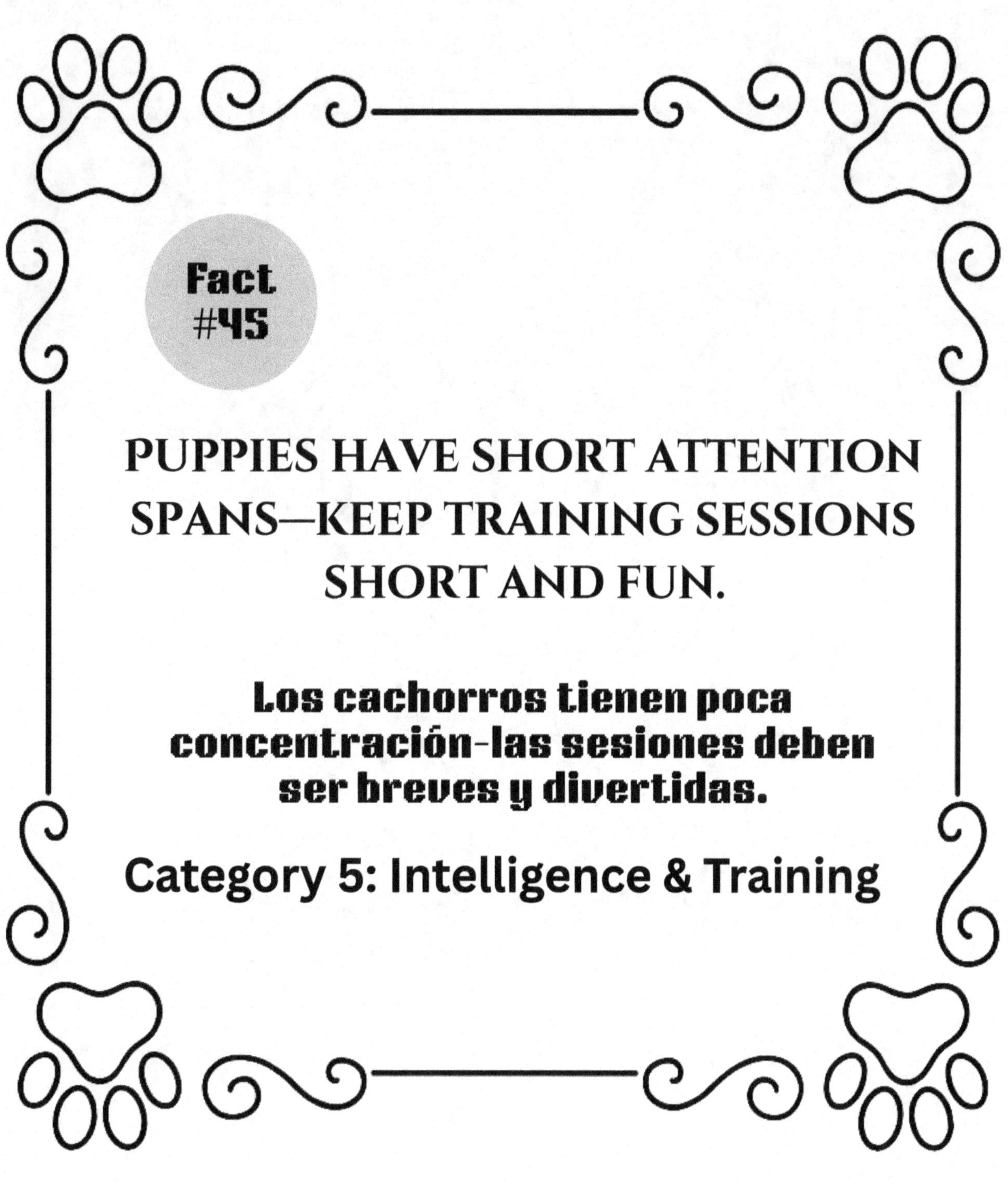

Fact #45

PUPPIES HAVE SHORT ATTENTION SPANS—KEEP TRAINING SESSIONS SHORT AND FUN.

Los cachorros tienen poca concentración-las sesiones deben ser breves y divertidas.

Category 5: Intelligence & Training

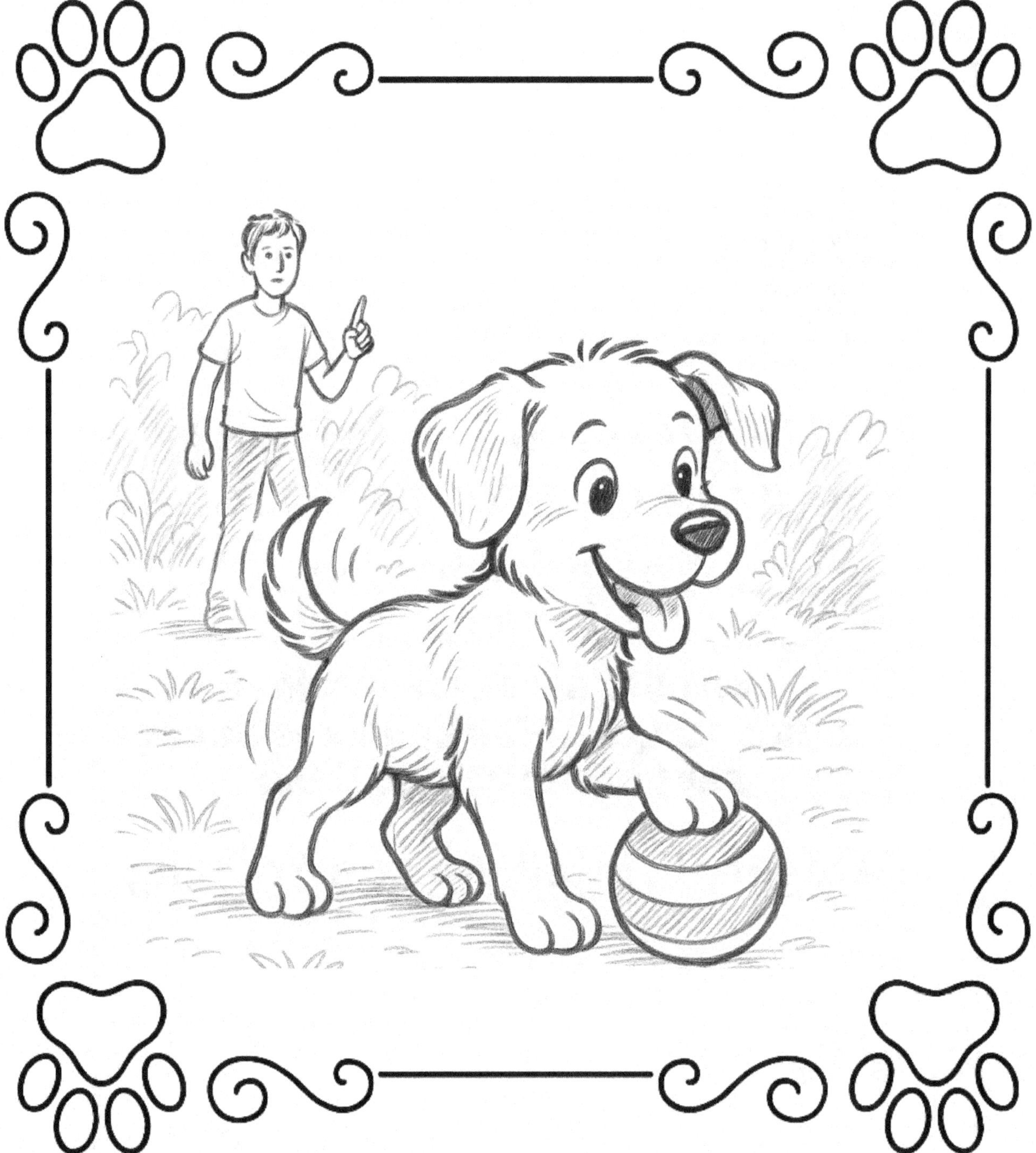

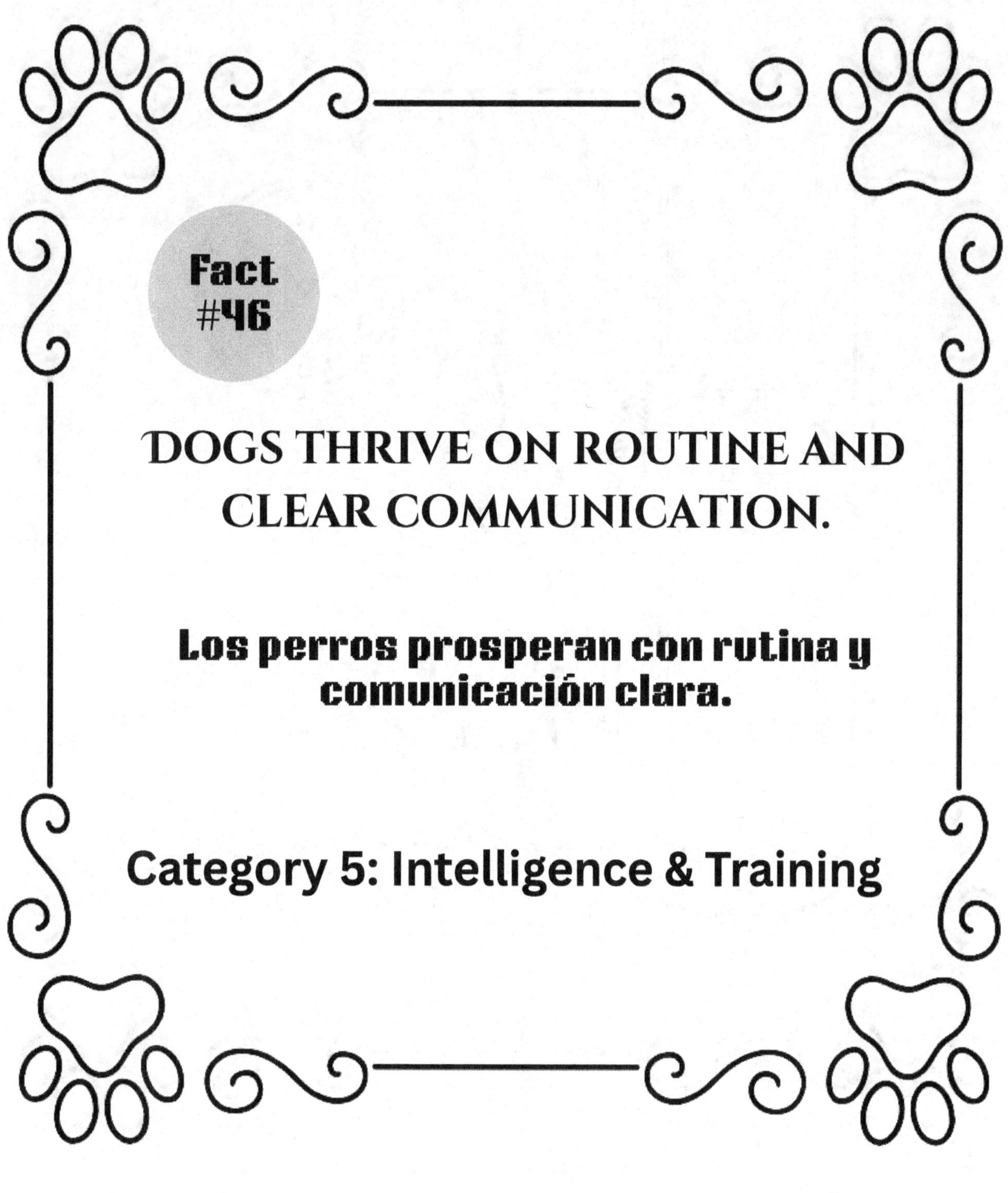

Fact
#46

DOGS THRIVE ON ROUTINE AND
CLEAR COMMUNICATION.

Los perros prosperan con rutina y
comunicación clara.

Category 5: Intelligence & Training

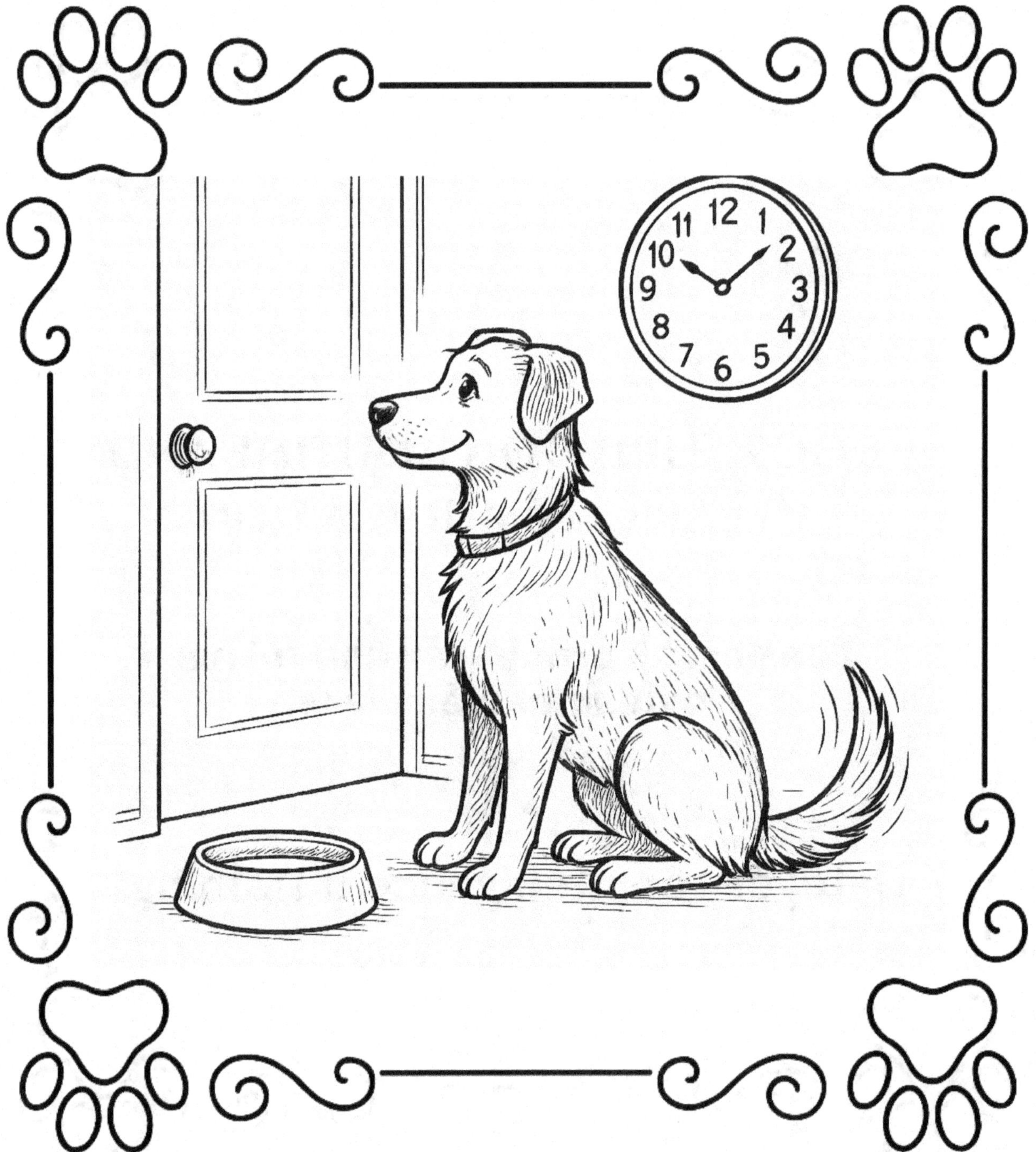

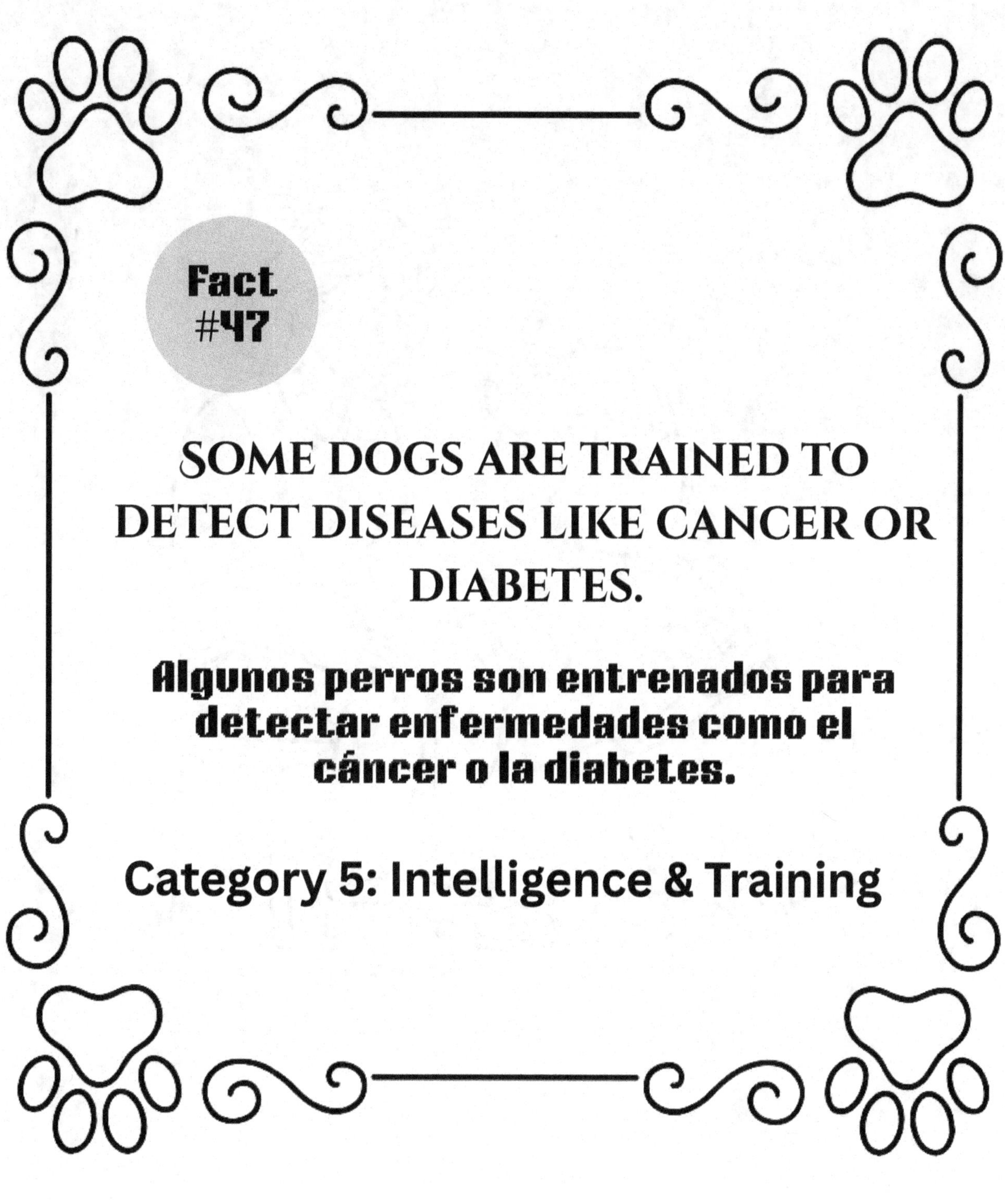

SOME DOGS ARE TRAINED TO DETECT DISEASES LIKE CANCER OR DIABETES.

Algunos perros son entrenados para detectar enfermedades como el cáncer o la diabetes.

Category 5: Intelligence & Training

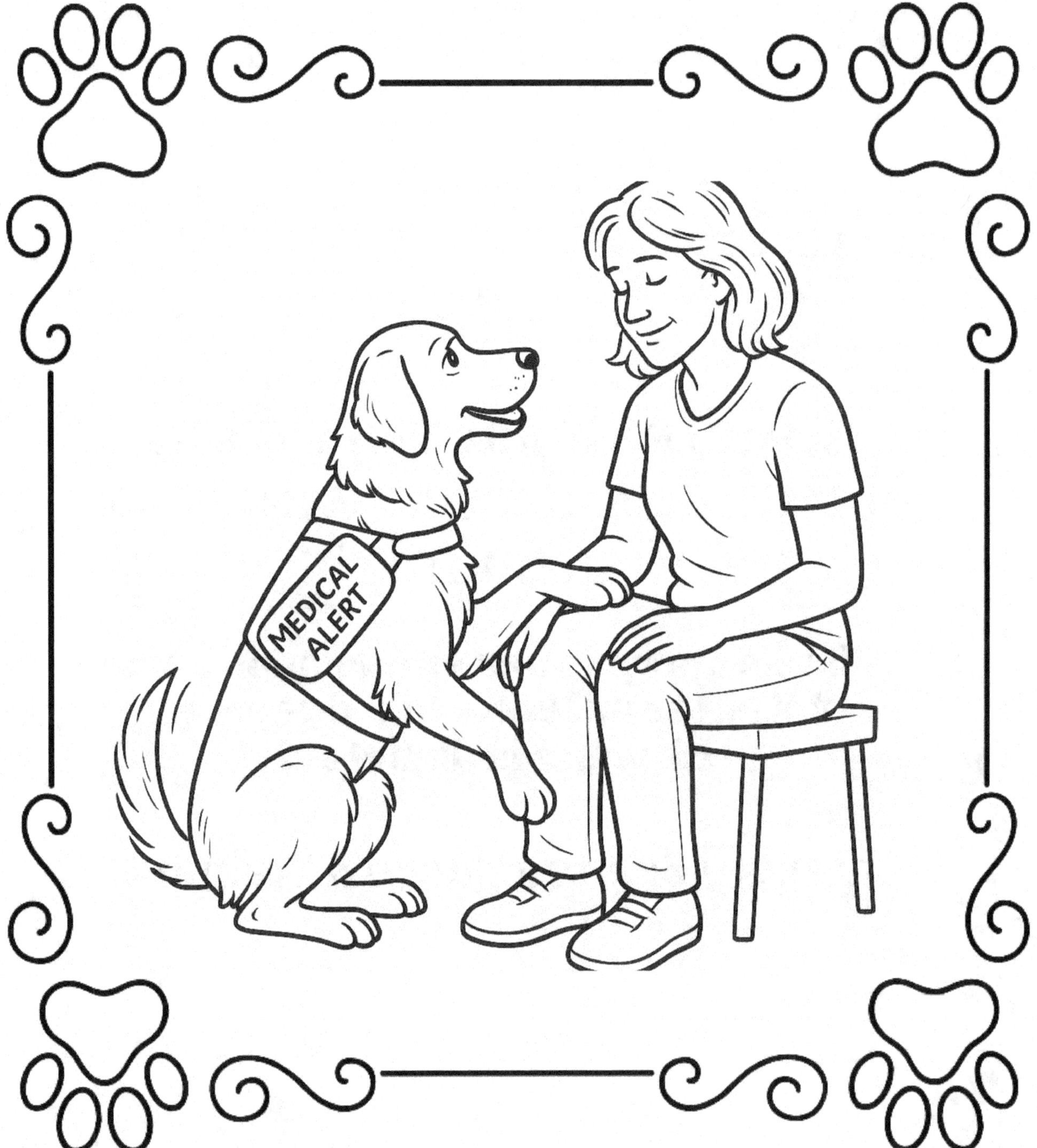

MEDICAL ALERT

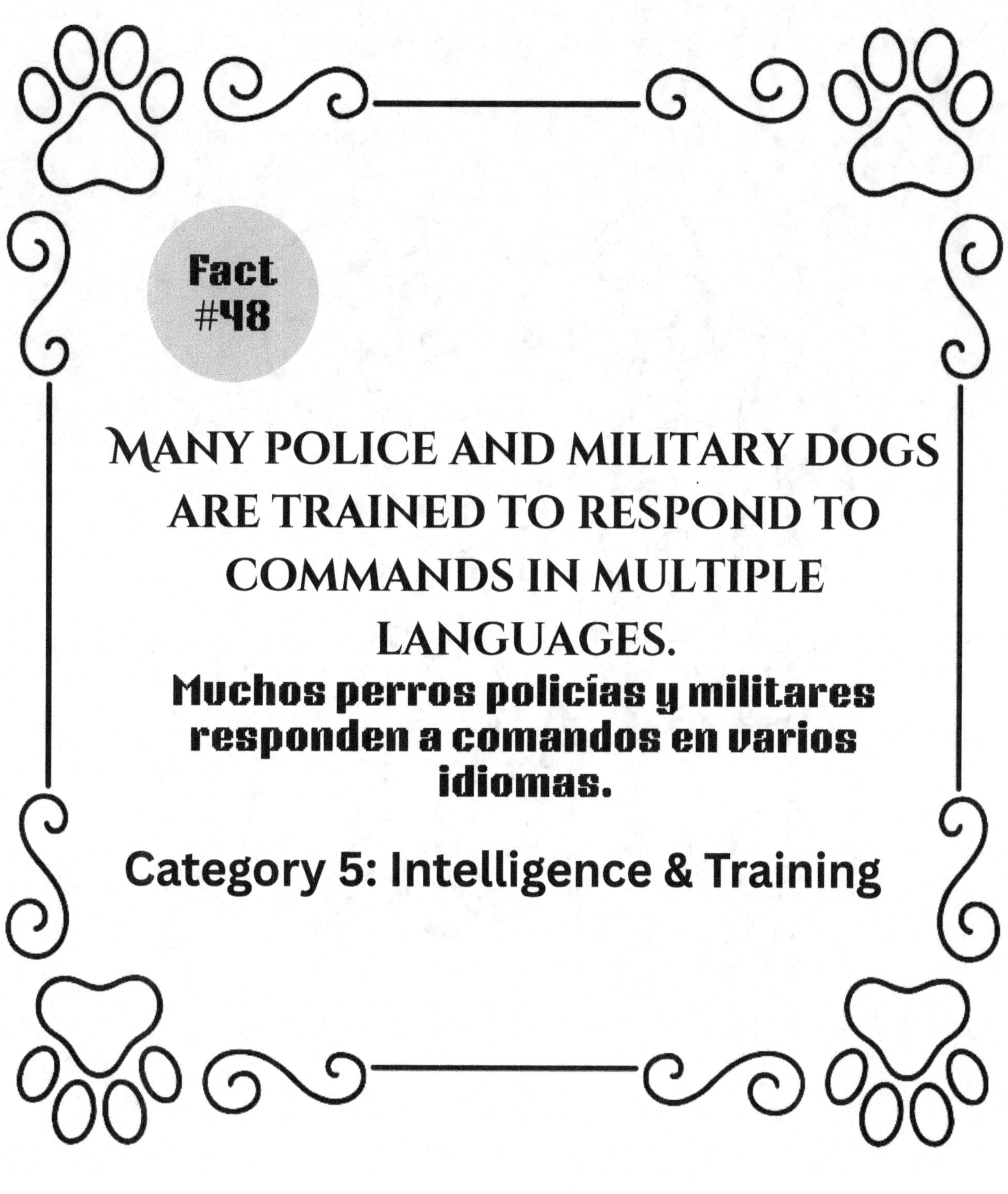
Fact
#48

MANY POLICE AND MILITARY DOGS ARE TRAINED TO RESPOND TO COMMANDS IN MULTIPLE LANGUAGES.

Muchos perros policías y militares responden a comandos en varios idiomas.

Category 5: Intelligence & Training

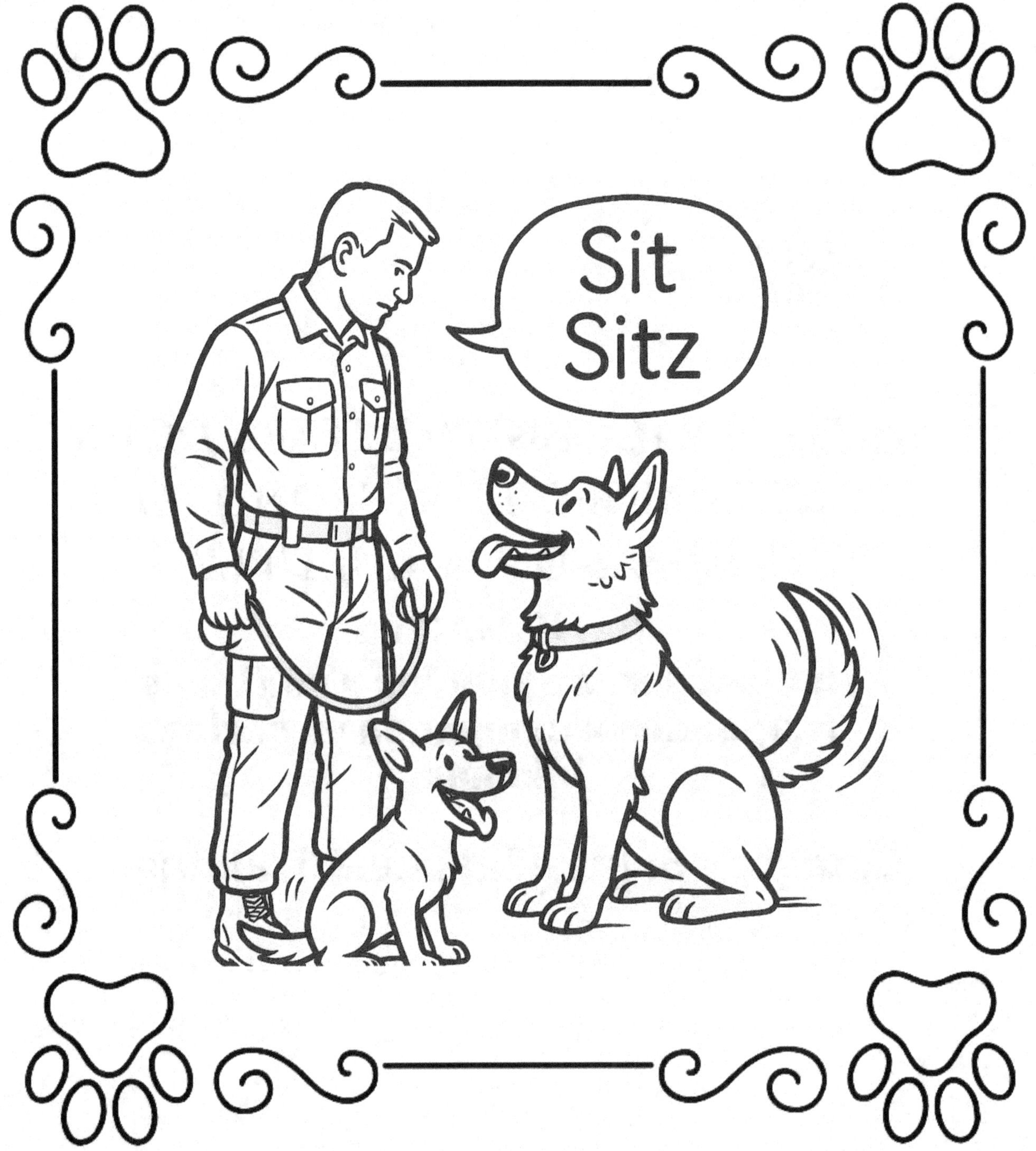

Sit
Sitz

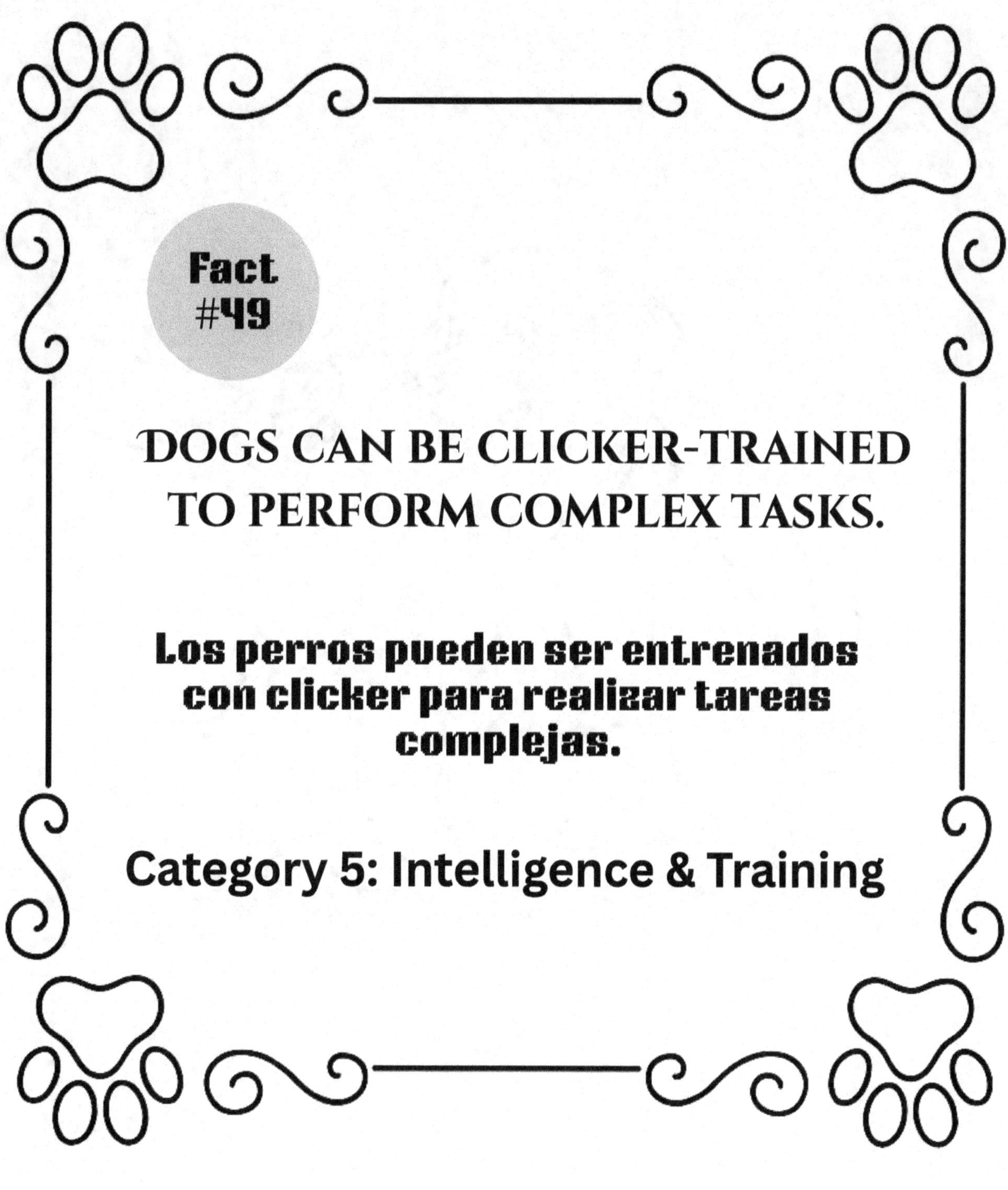

Fact #49

DOGS CAN BE CLICKER-TRAINED TO PERFORM COMPLEX TASKS.

Los perros pueden ser entrenados con clicker para realizar tareas complejas.

Category 5: Intelligence & Training

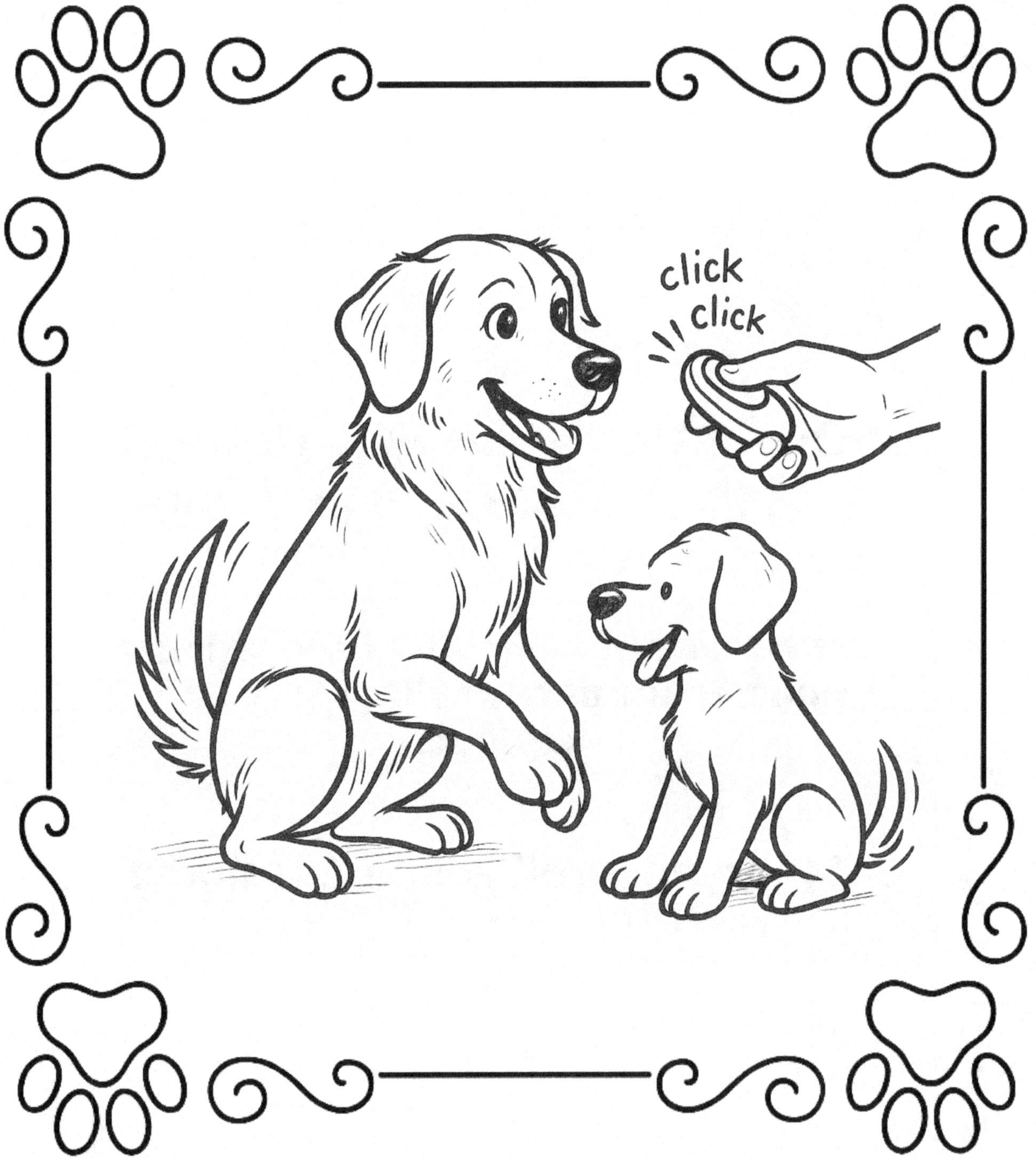

click
click

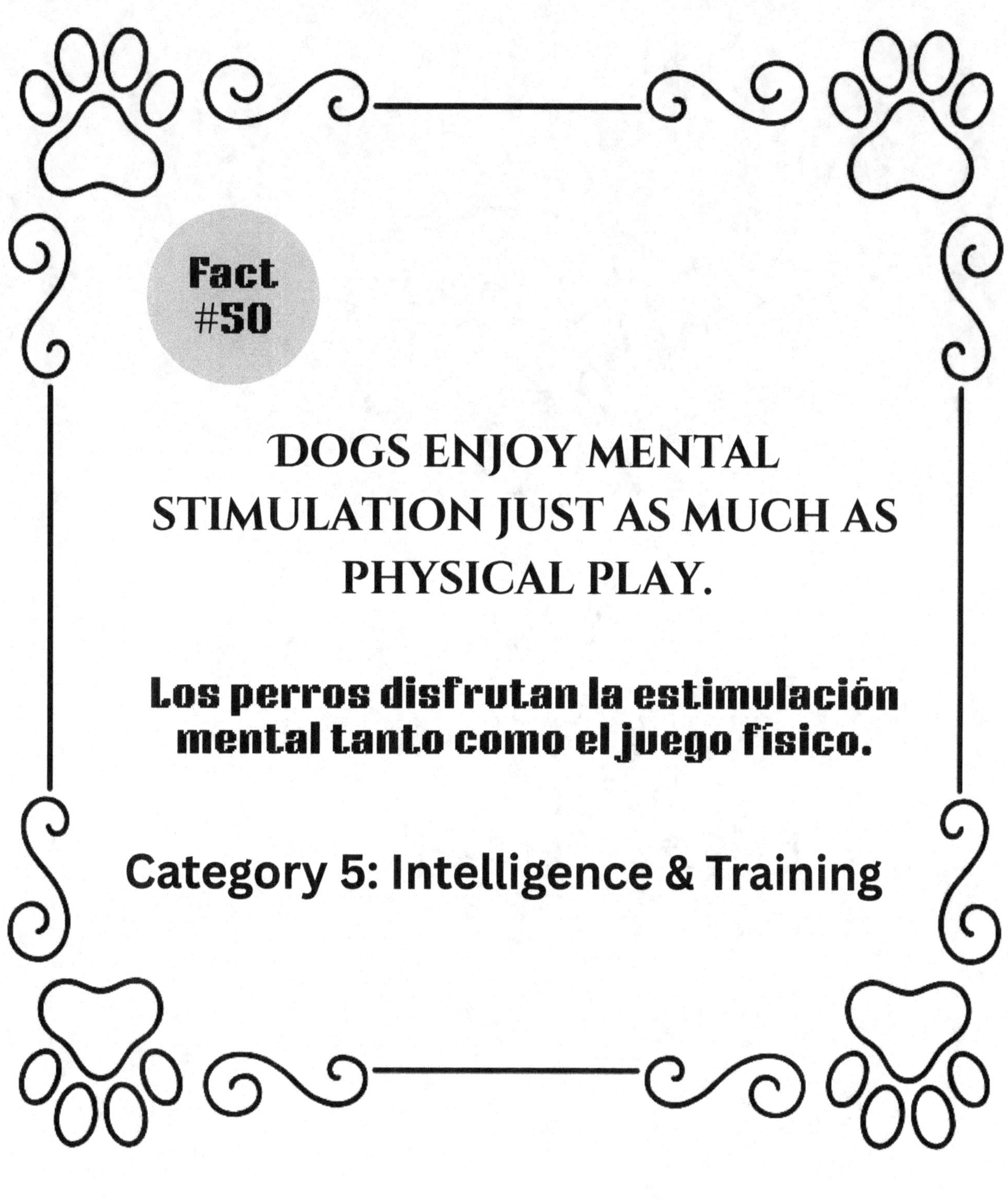

Fact #50

DOGS ENJOY MENTAL STIMULATION JUST AS MUCH AS PHYSICAL PLAY.

Los perros disfrutan la estimulación mental tanto como el juego físico.

Category 5: Intelligence & Training

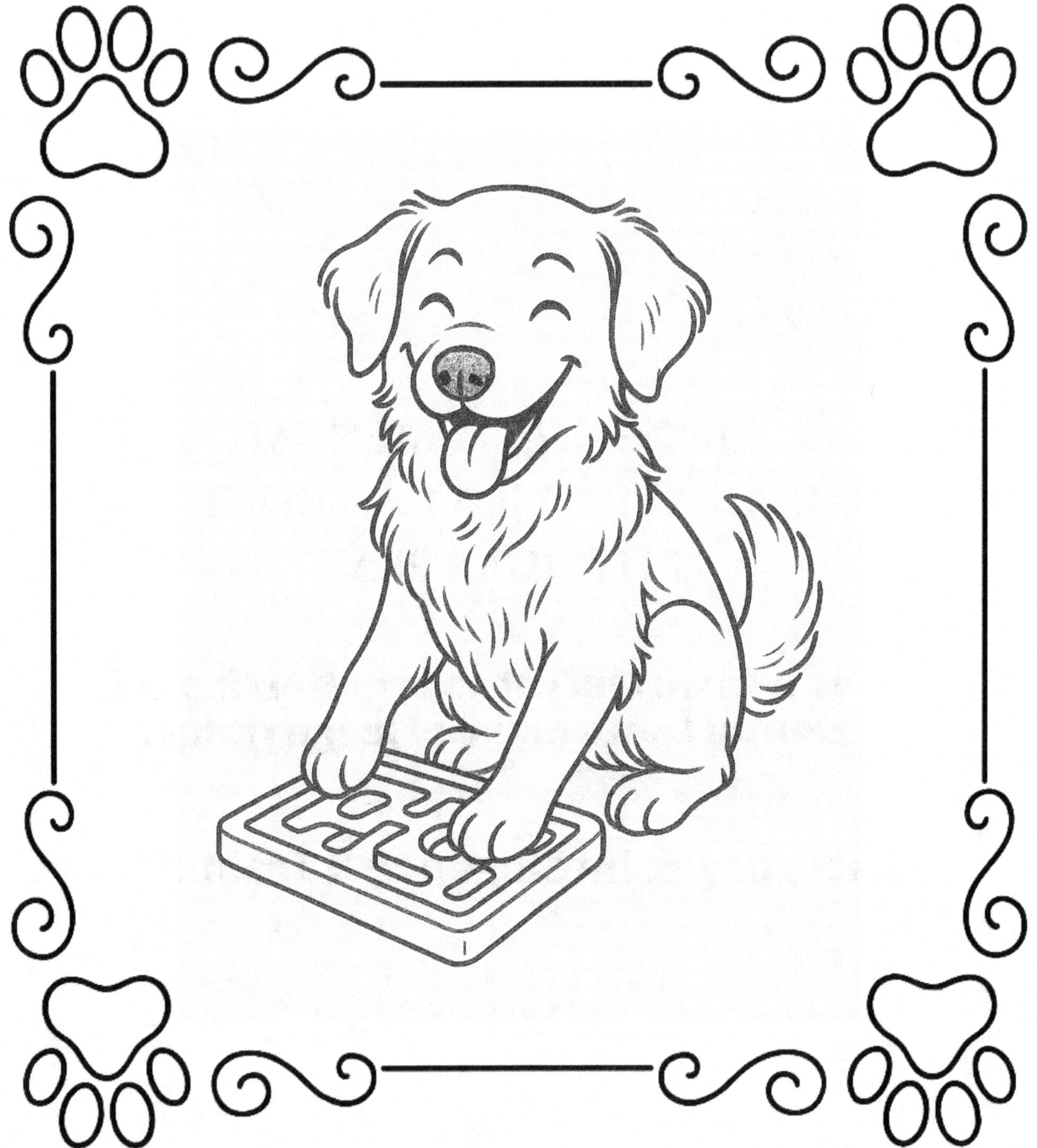

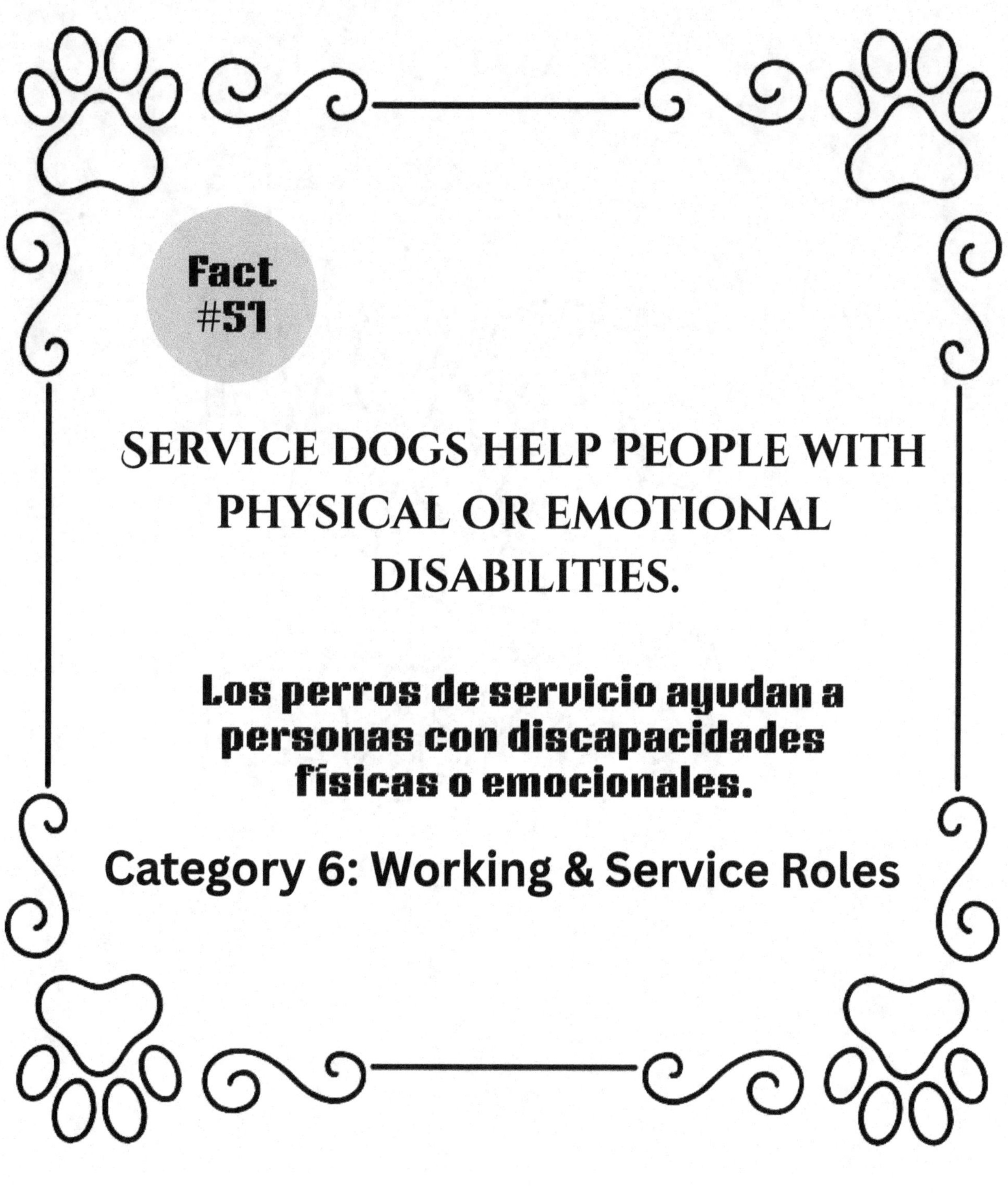

Fact #51

SERVICE DOGS HELP PEOPLE WITH PHYSICAL OR EMOTIONAL DISABILITIES.

Los perros de servicio ayudan a personas con discapacidades físicas o emocionales.

Category 6: Working & Service Roles

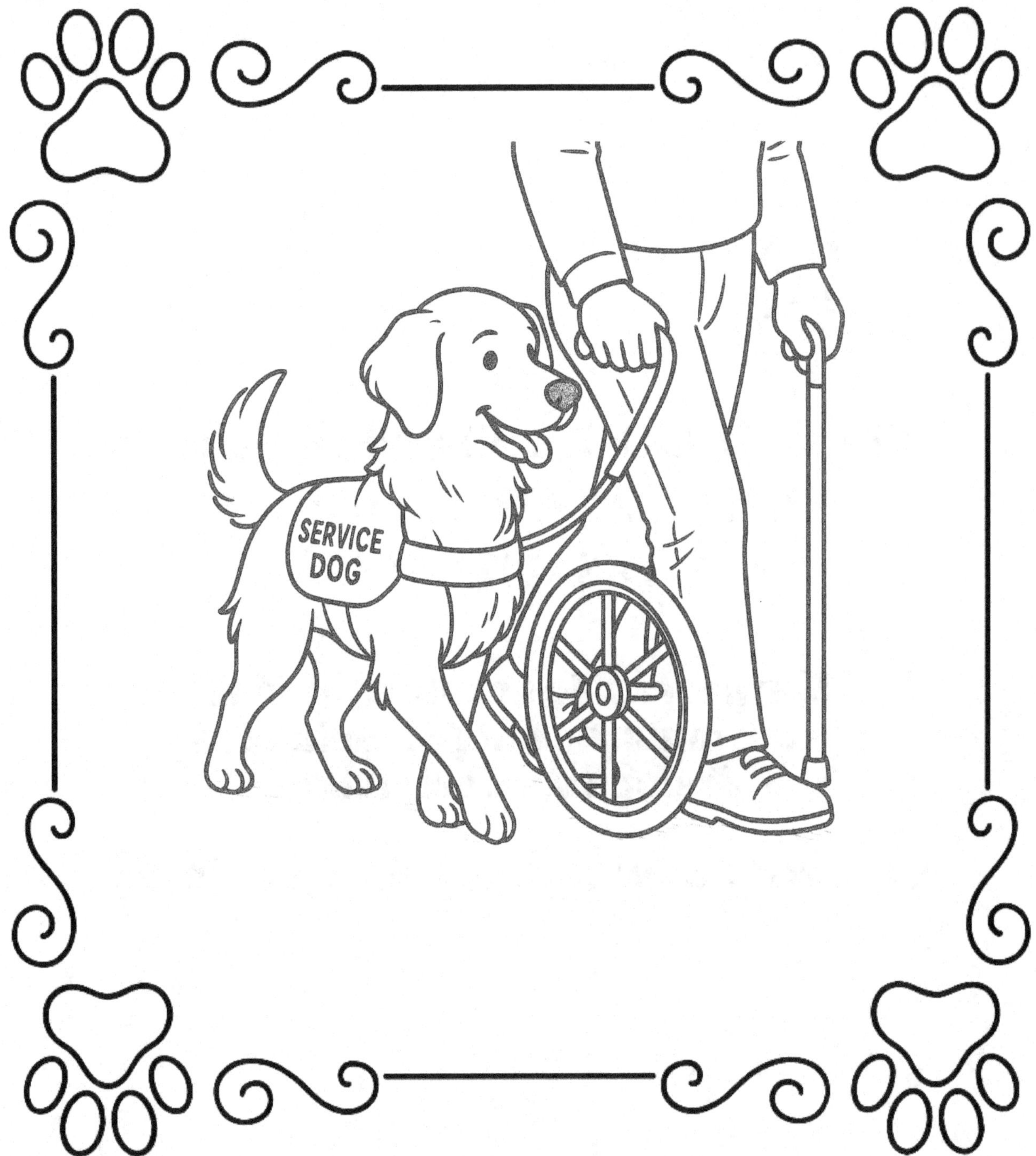

SERVICE
DOG

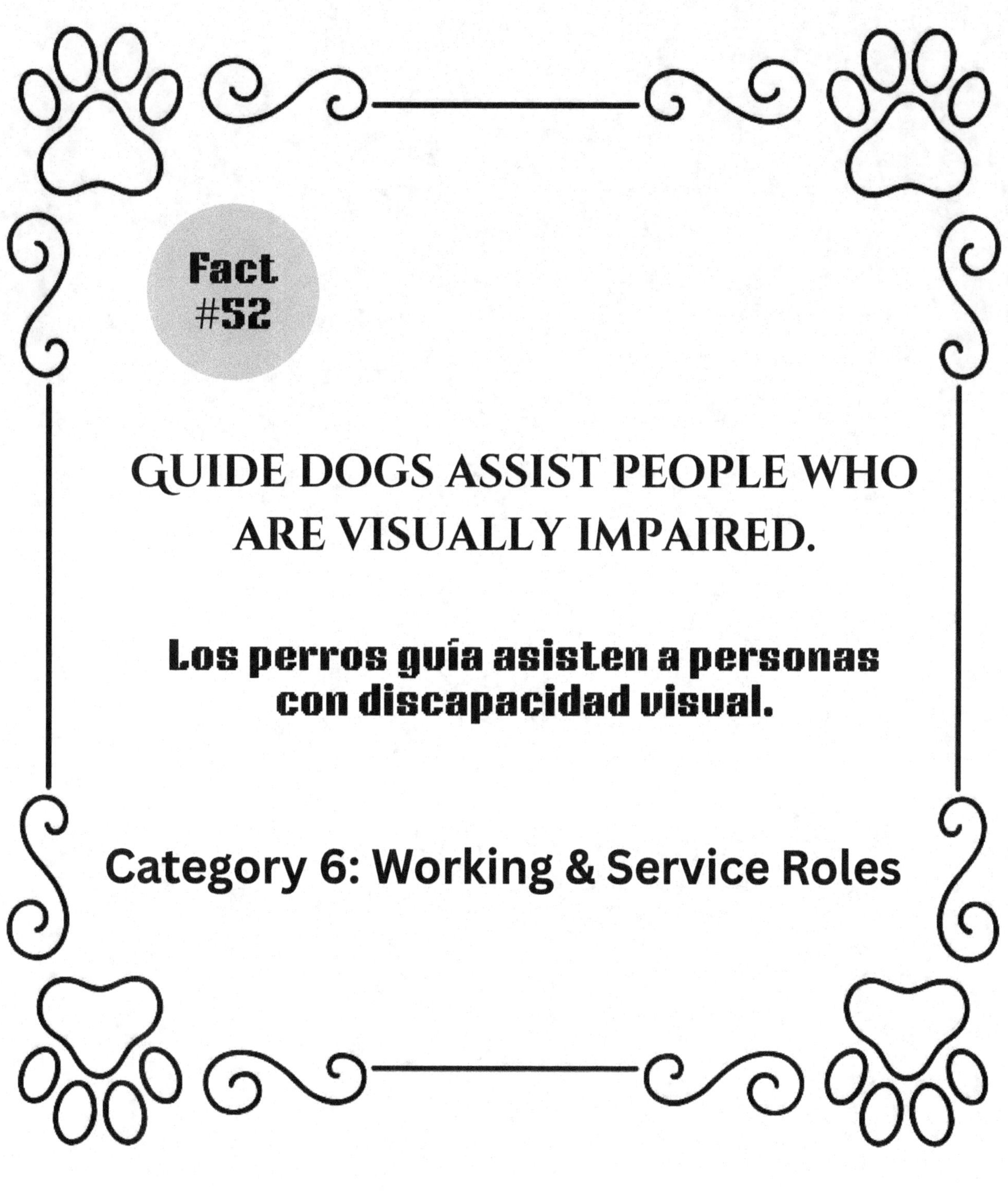

Fact #52

GUIDE DOGS ASSIST PEOPLE WHO ARE VISUALLY IMPAIRED.

Los perros guía asisten a personas con discapacidad visual.

Category 6: Working & Service Roles

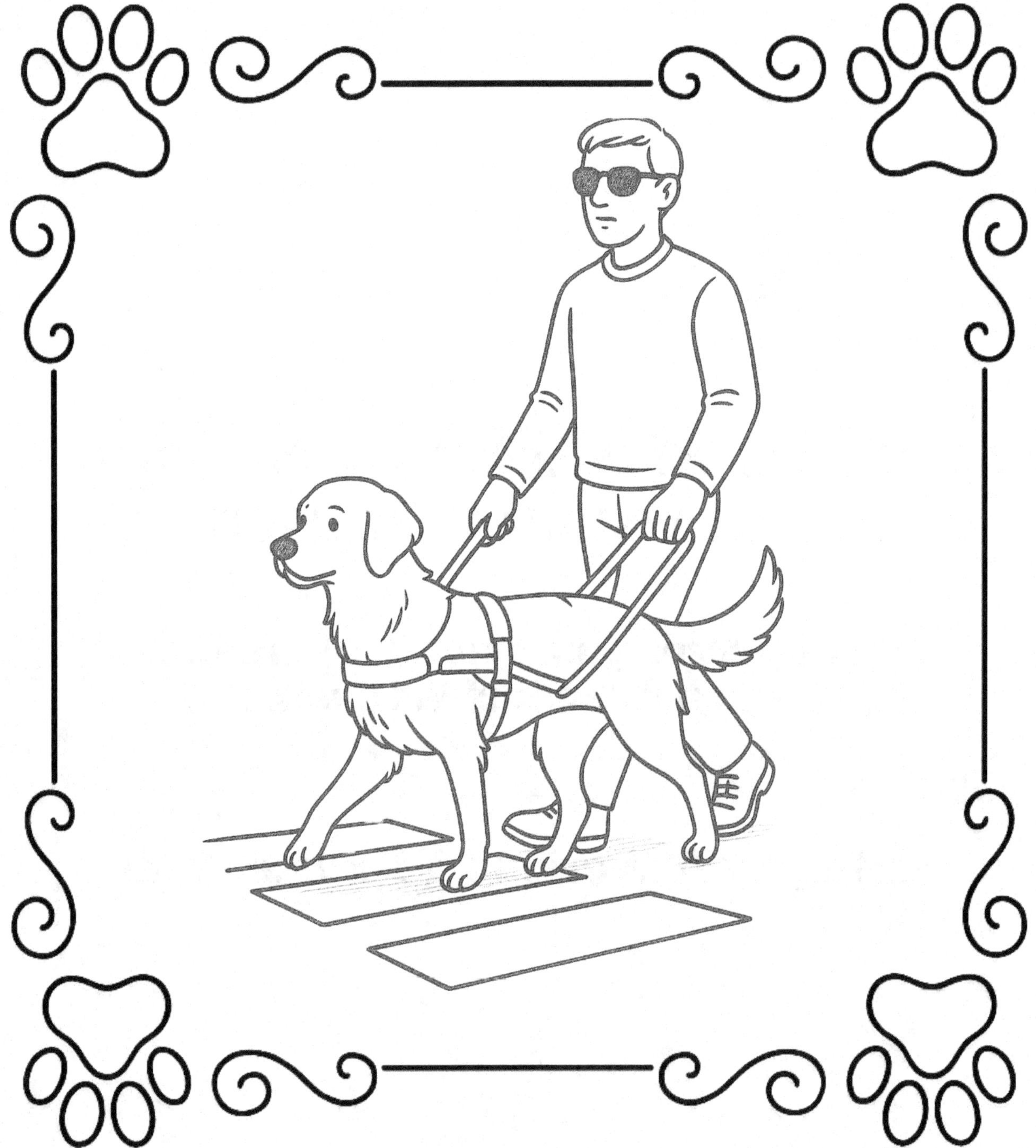

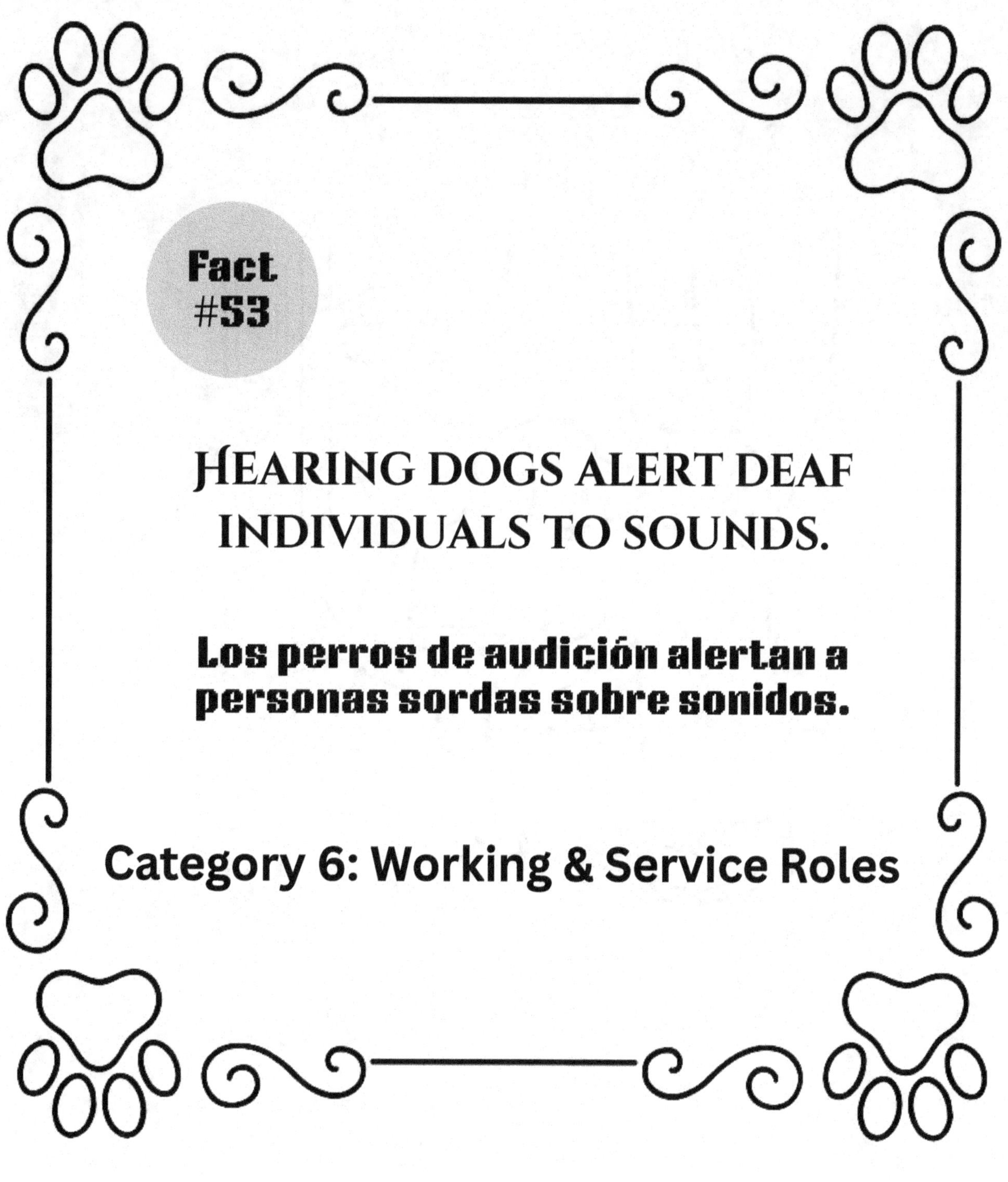

HEARING DOGS ALERT DEAF INDIVIDUALS TO SOUNDS.

Los perros de audición alertan a personas sordas sobre sonidos.

Category 6: Working & Service Roles

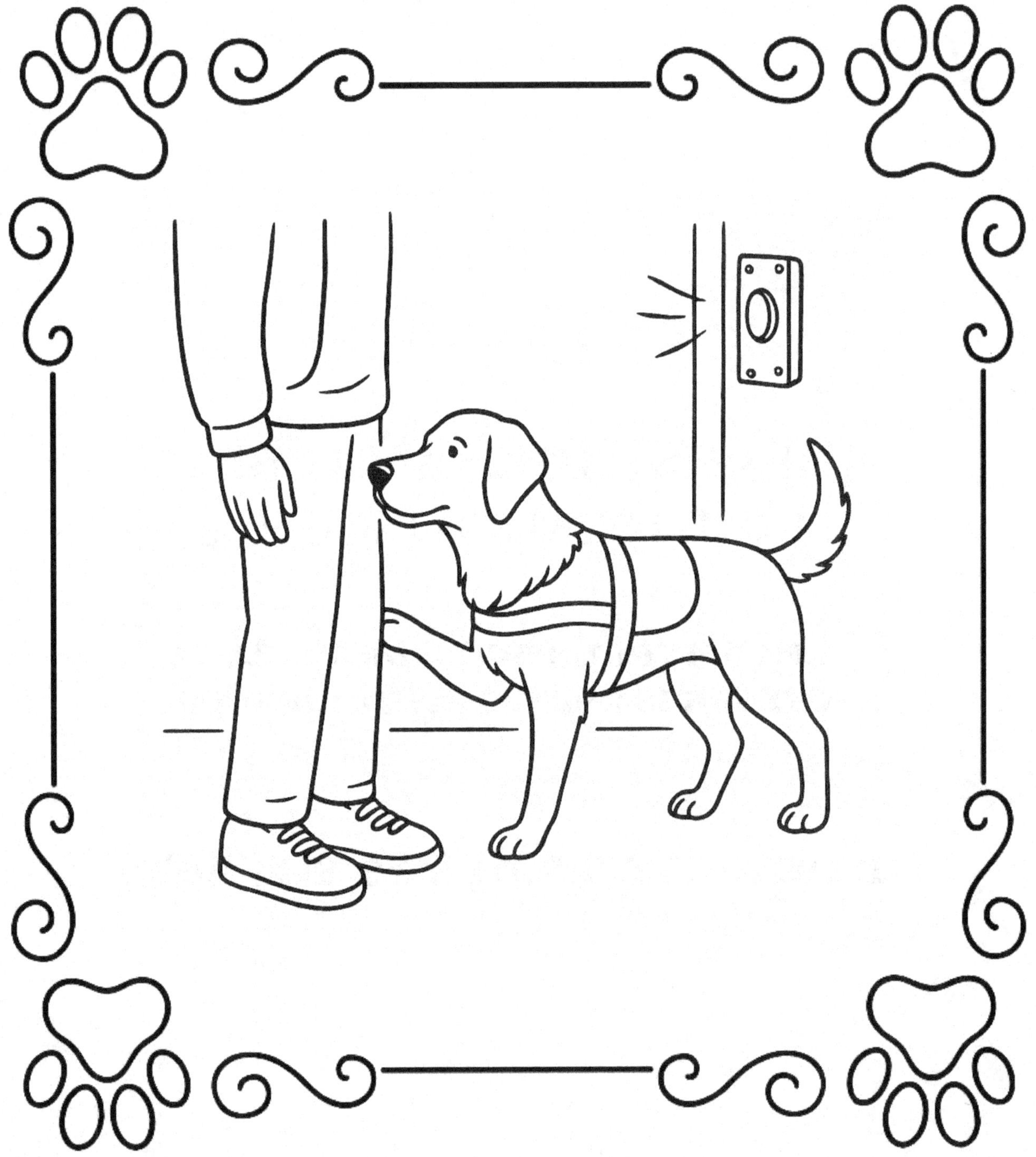

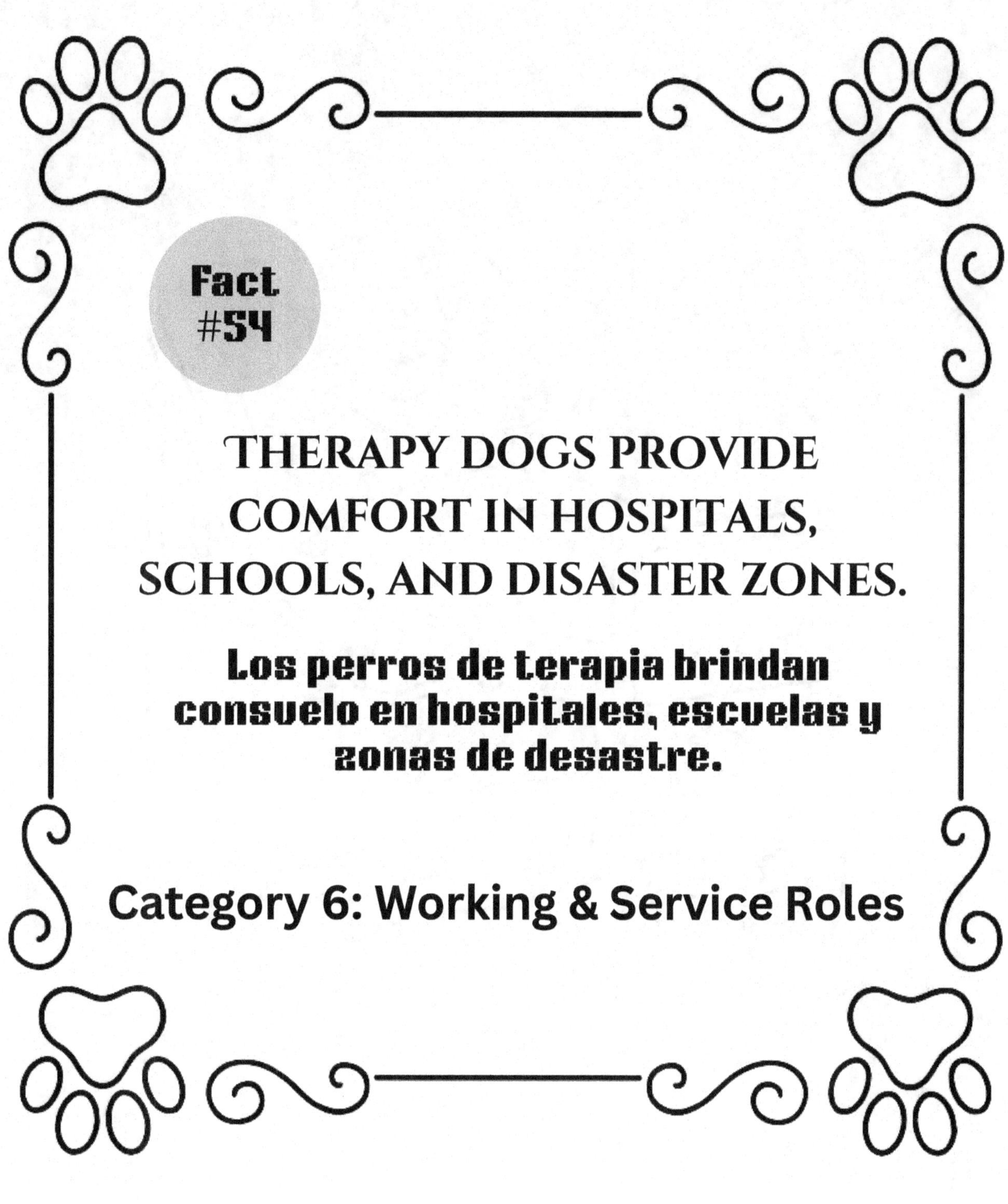

Fact #54

THERAPY DOGS PROVIDE COMFORT IN HOSPITALS, SCHOOLS, AND DISASTER ZONES.

Los perros de terapia brindan consuelo en hospitales, escuelas y zonas de desastre.

Category 6: Working & Service Roles

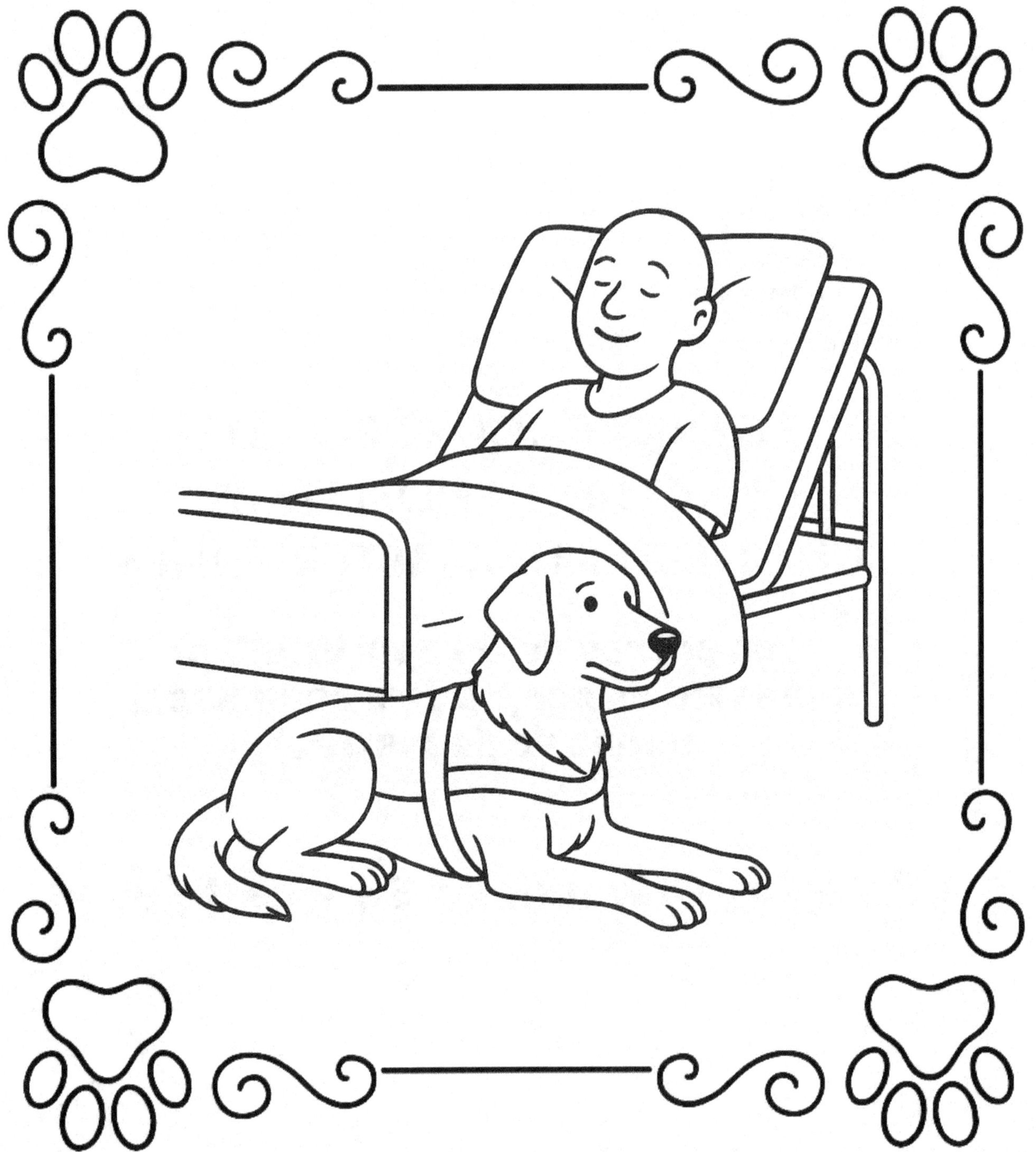

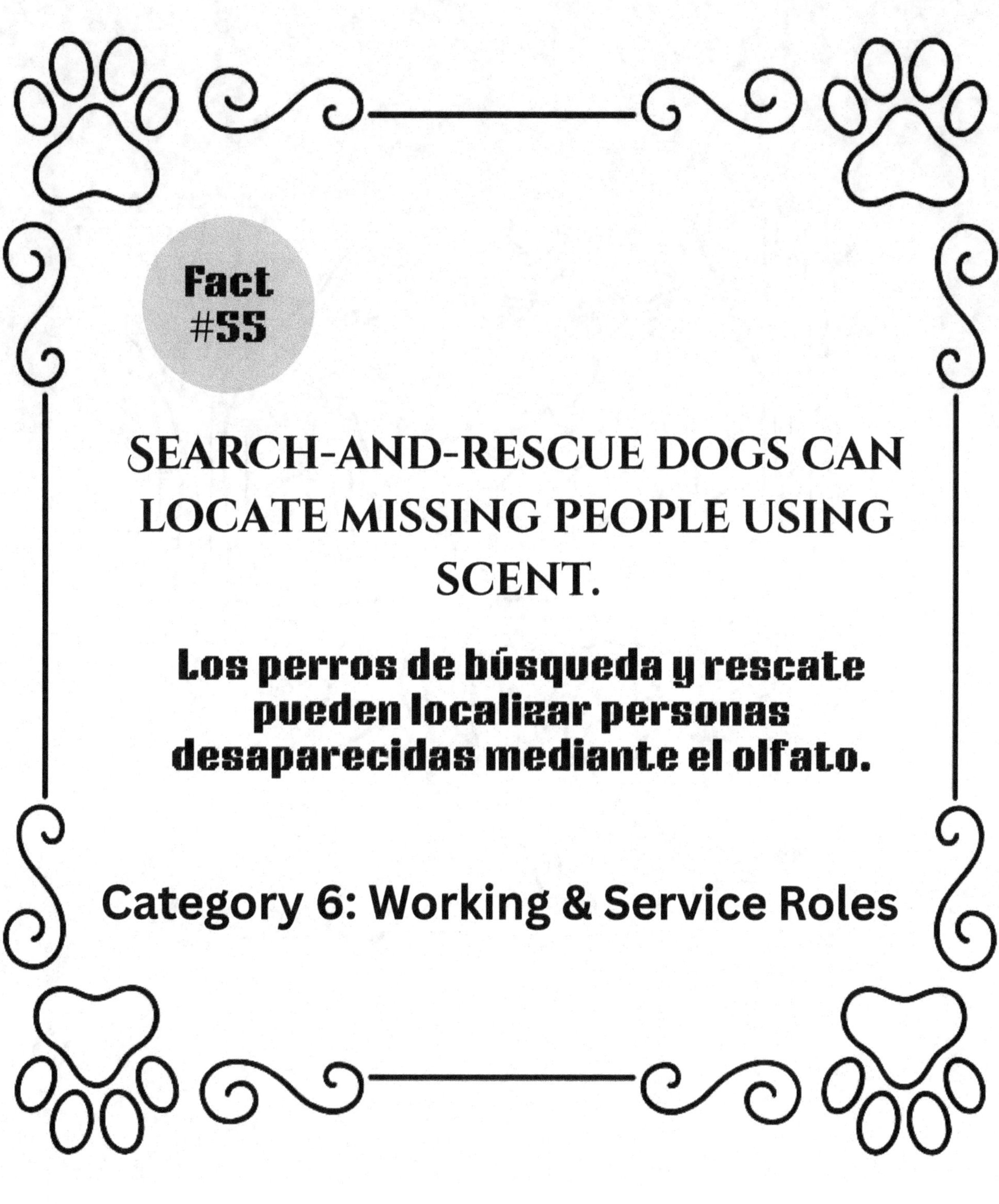

Fact #55

SEARCH-AND-RESCUE DOGS CAN LOCATE MISSING PEOPLE USING SCENT.

Los perros de búsqueda y rescate pueden localizar personas desaparecidas mediante el olfato.

Category 6: Working & Service Roles

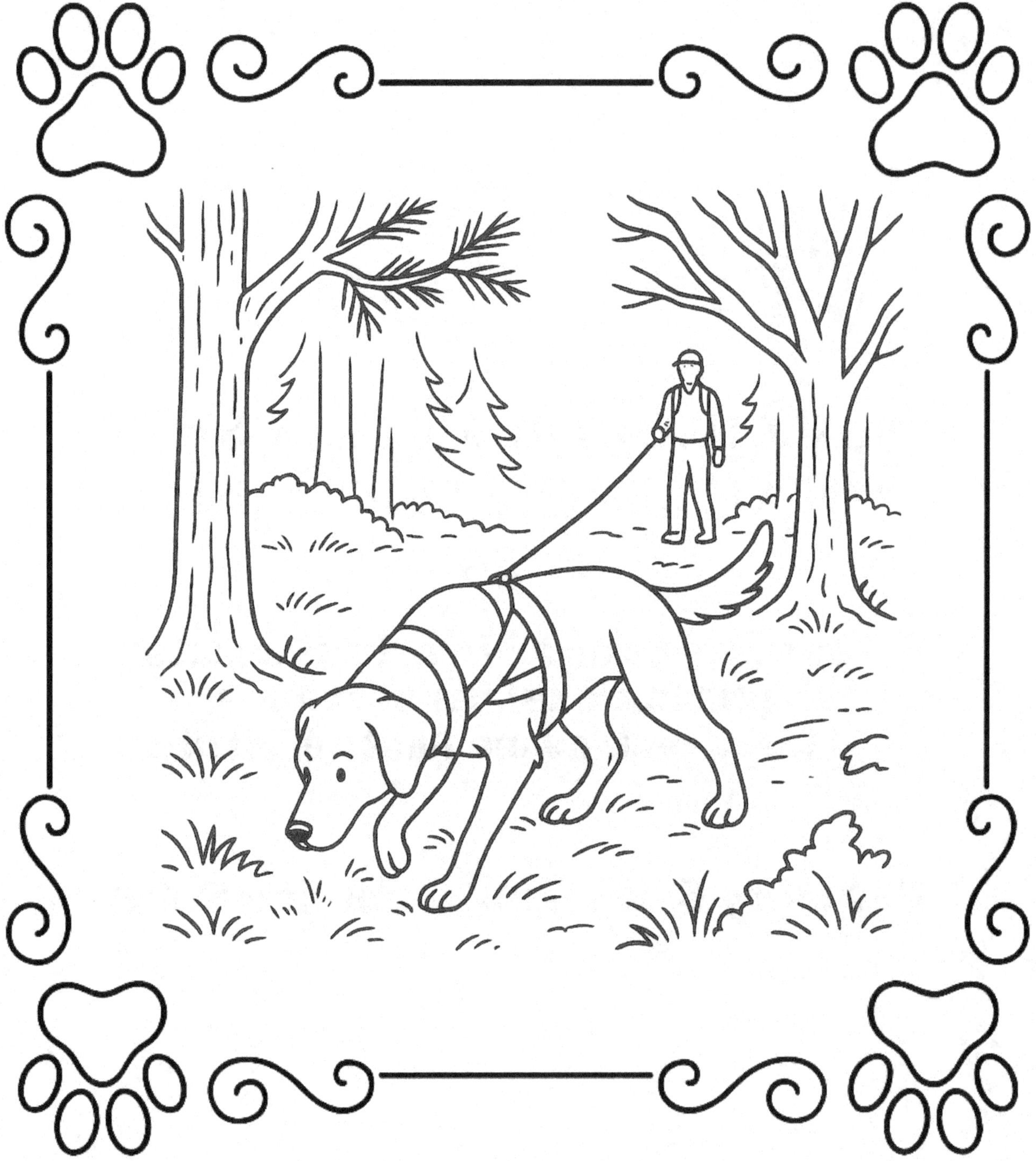

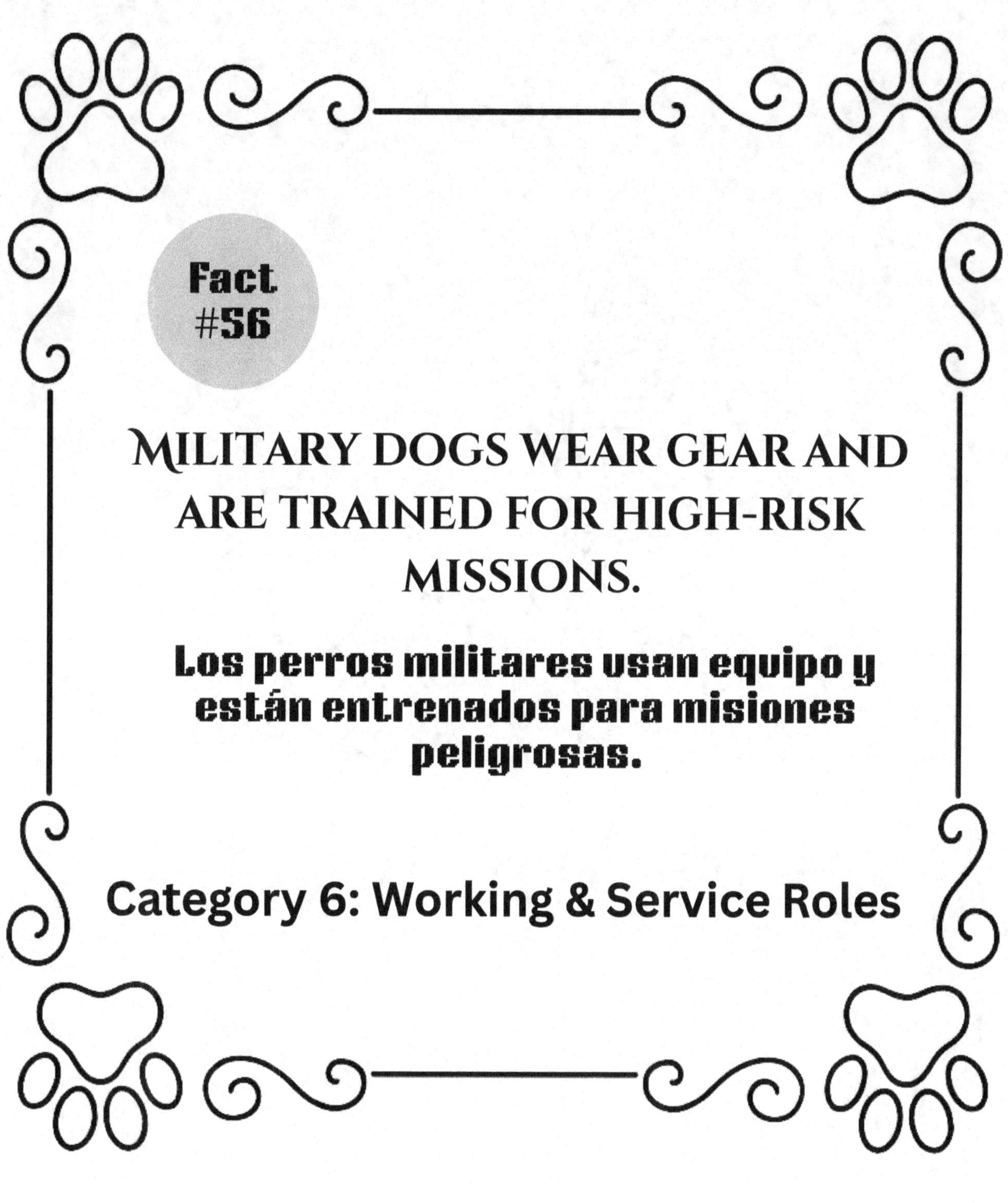

Fact
#56

MILITARY DOGS WEAR GEAR AND ARE TRAINED FOR HIGH-RISK MISSIONS.

Los perros militares usan equipo y están entrenados para misiones peligrosas.

Category 6: Working & Service Roles

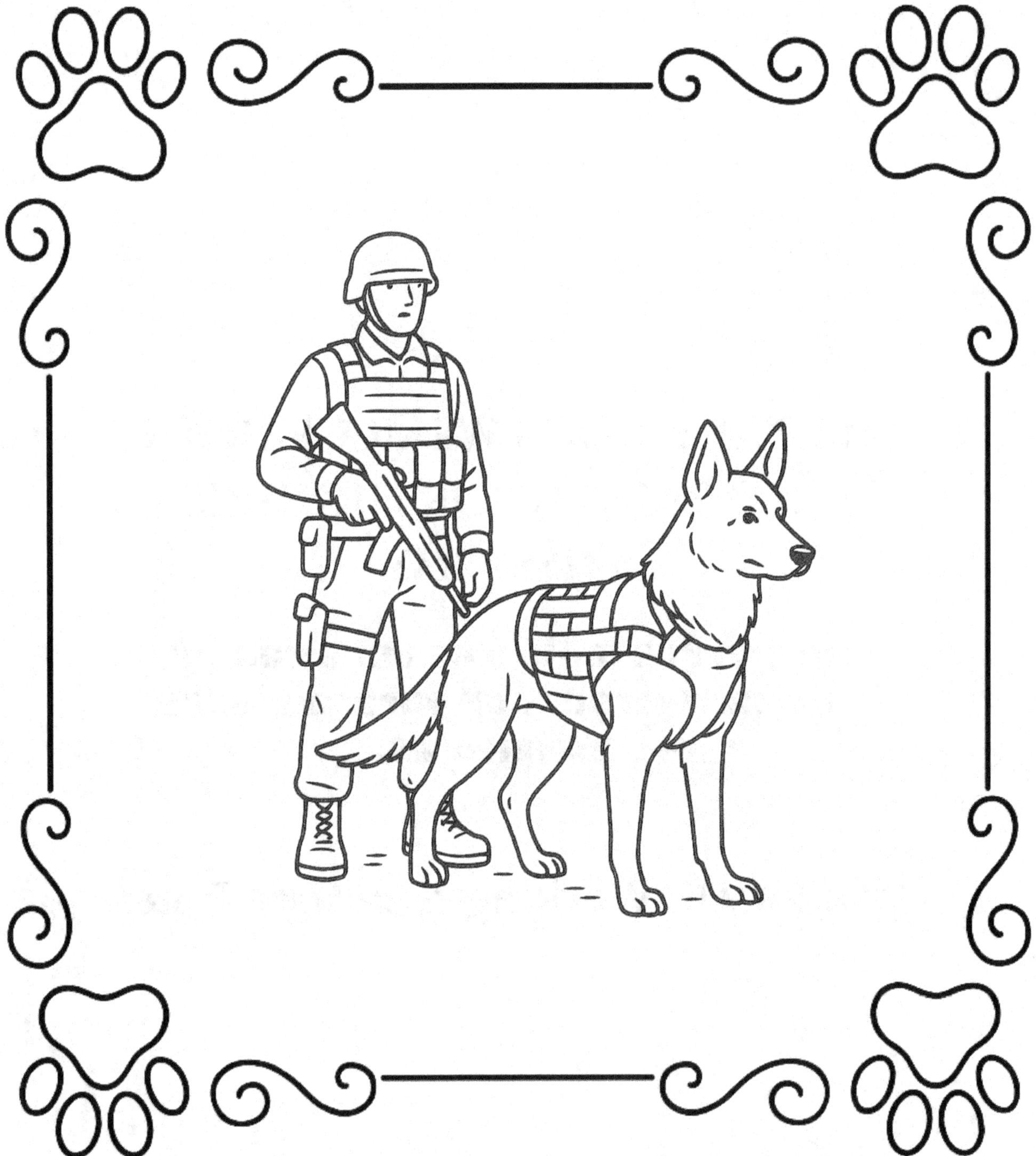

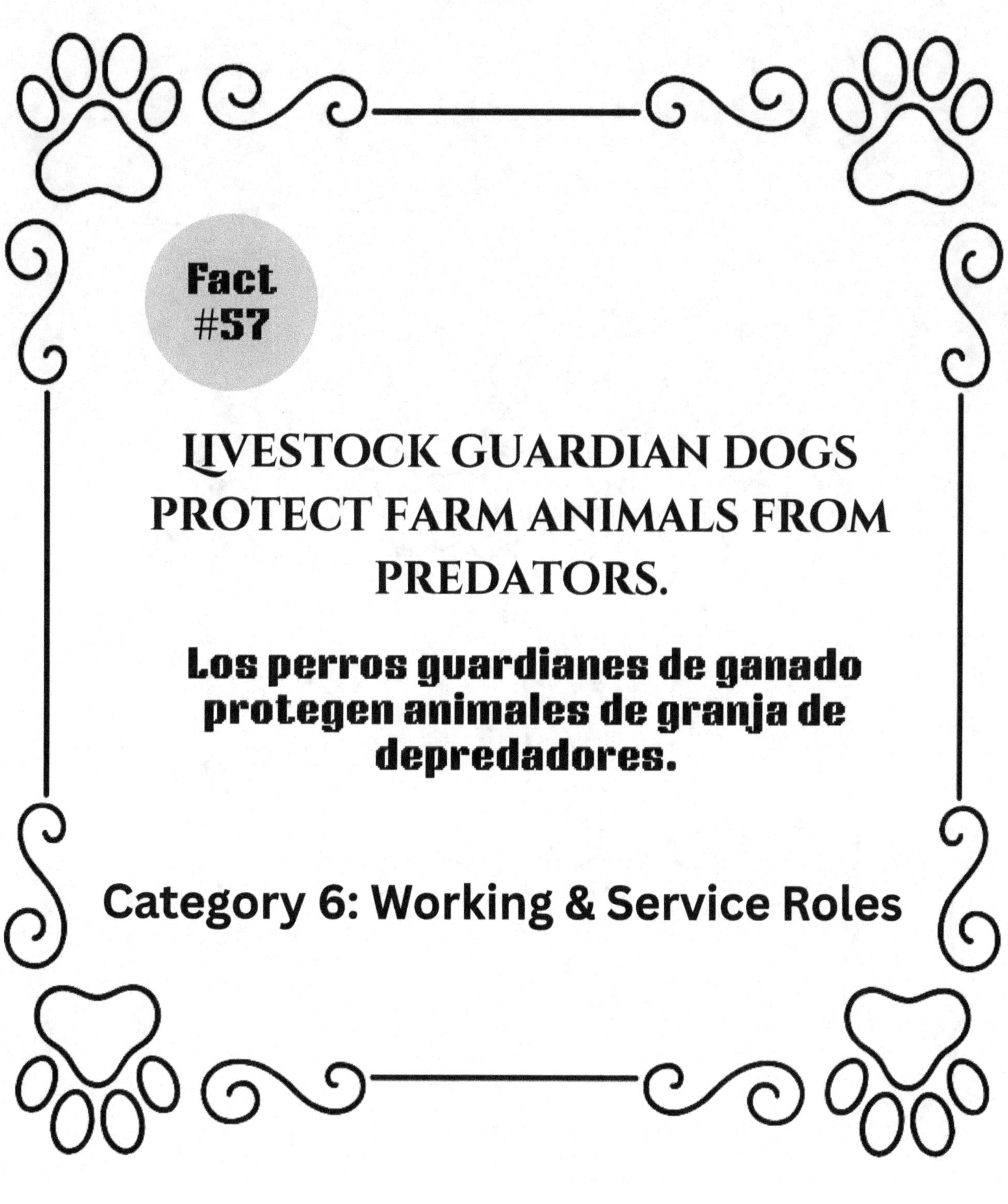

LIVESTOCK GUARDIAN DOGS PROTECT FARM ANIMALS FROM PREDATORS.

Los perros guardianes de ganado protegen animales de granja de depredadores.

Category 6: Working & Service Roles

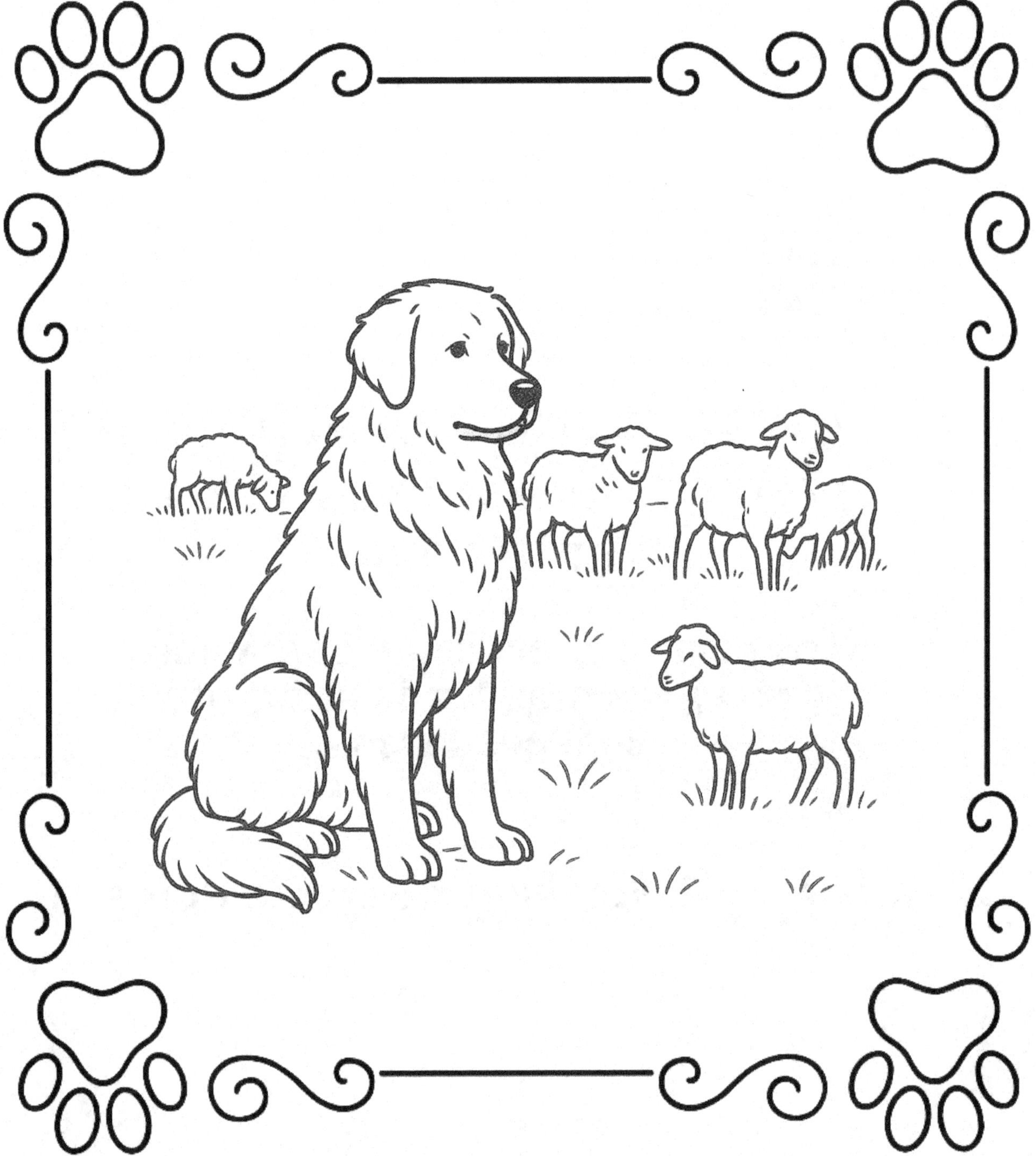

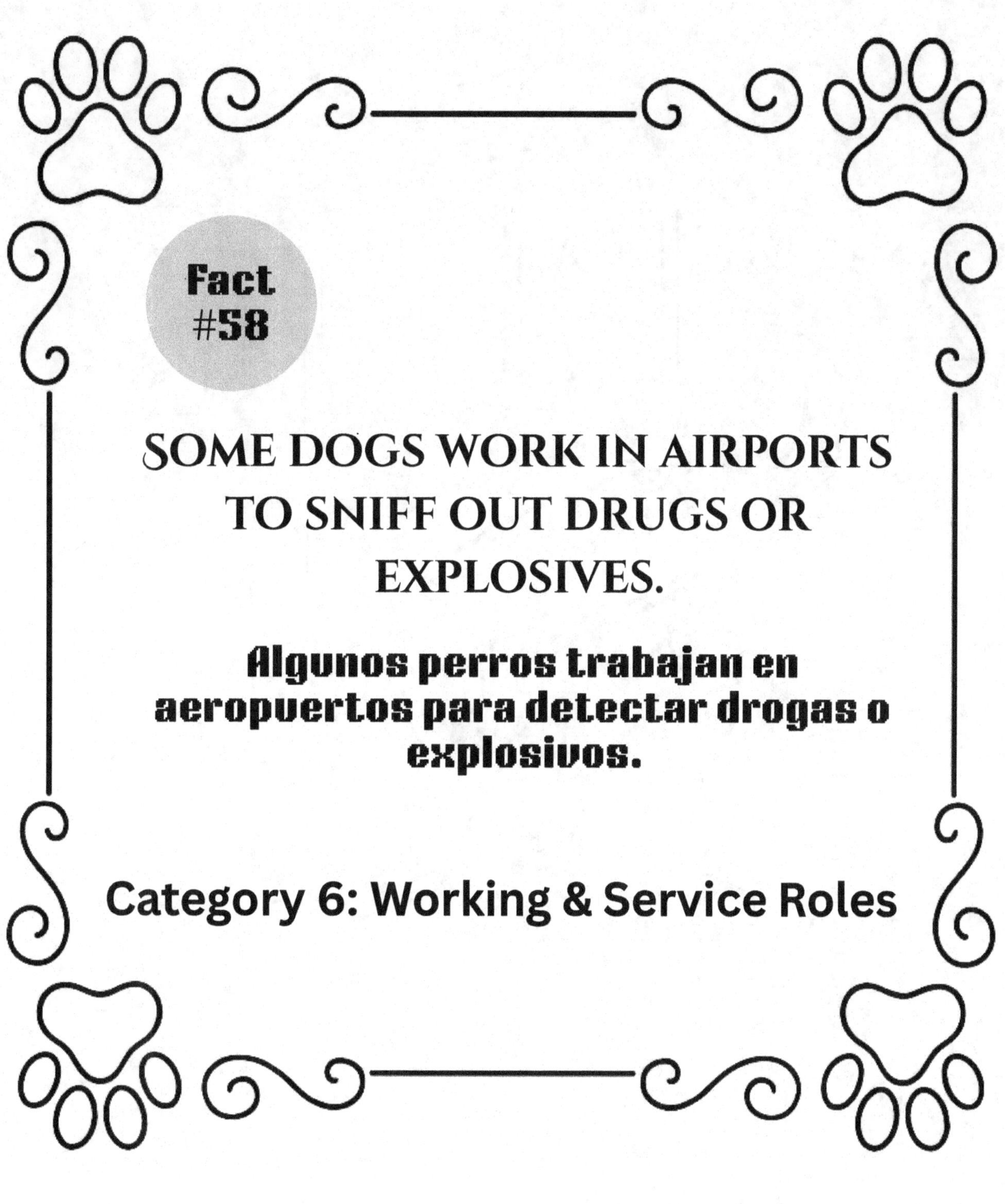

Fact #58

SOME DOGS WORK IN AIRPORTS TO SNIFF OUT DRUGS OR EXPLOSIVES.

Algunos perros trabajan en aeropuertos para detectar drogas o explosivos.

Category 6: Working & Service Roles

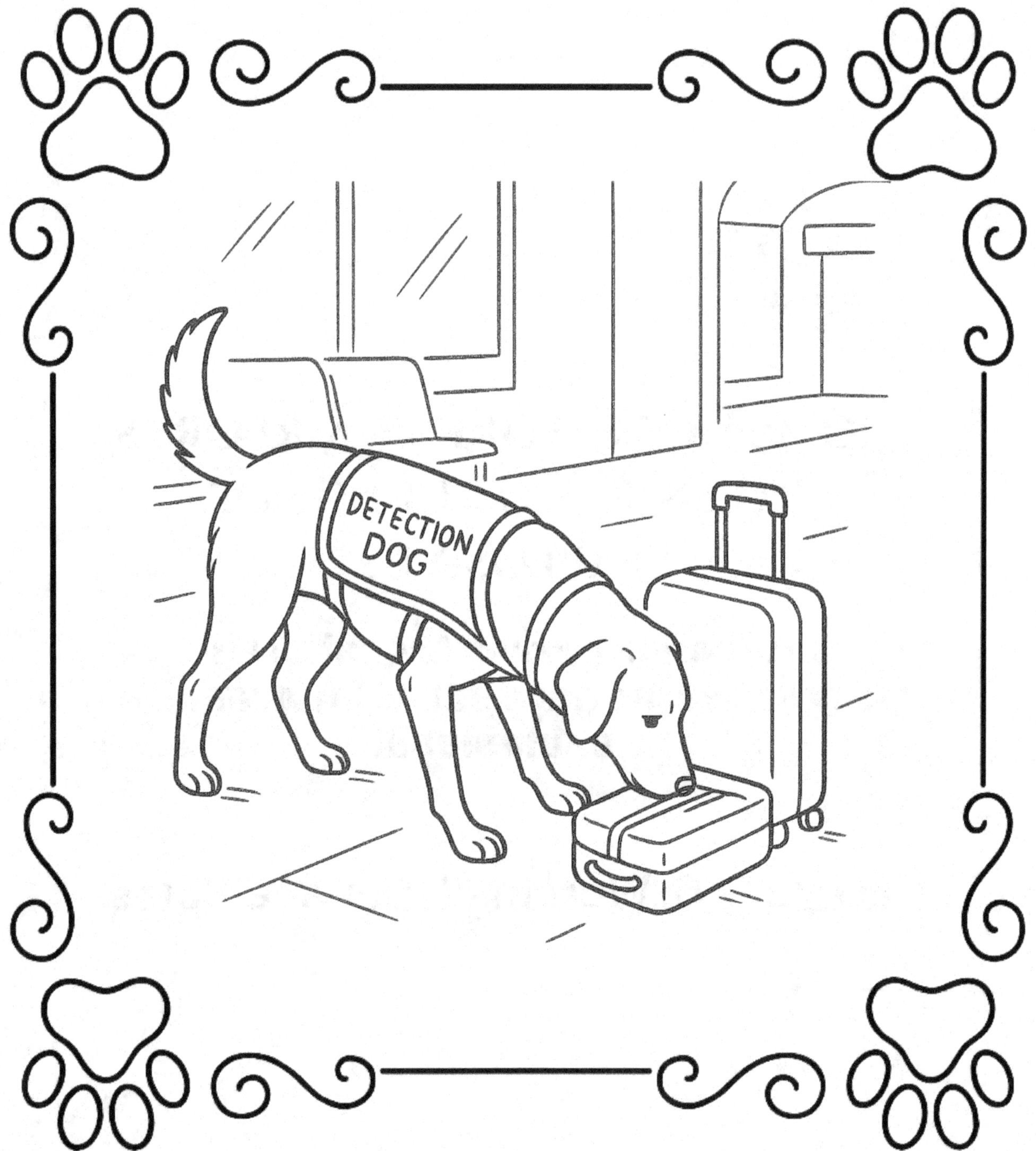

DETECTION
DOG

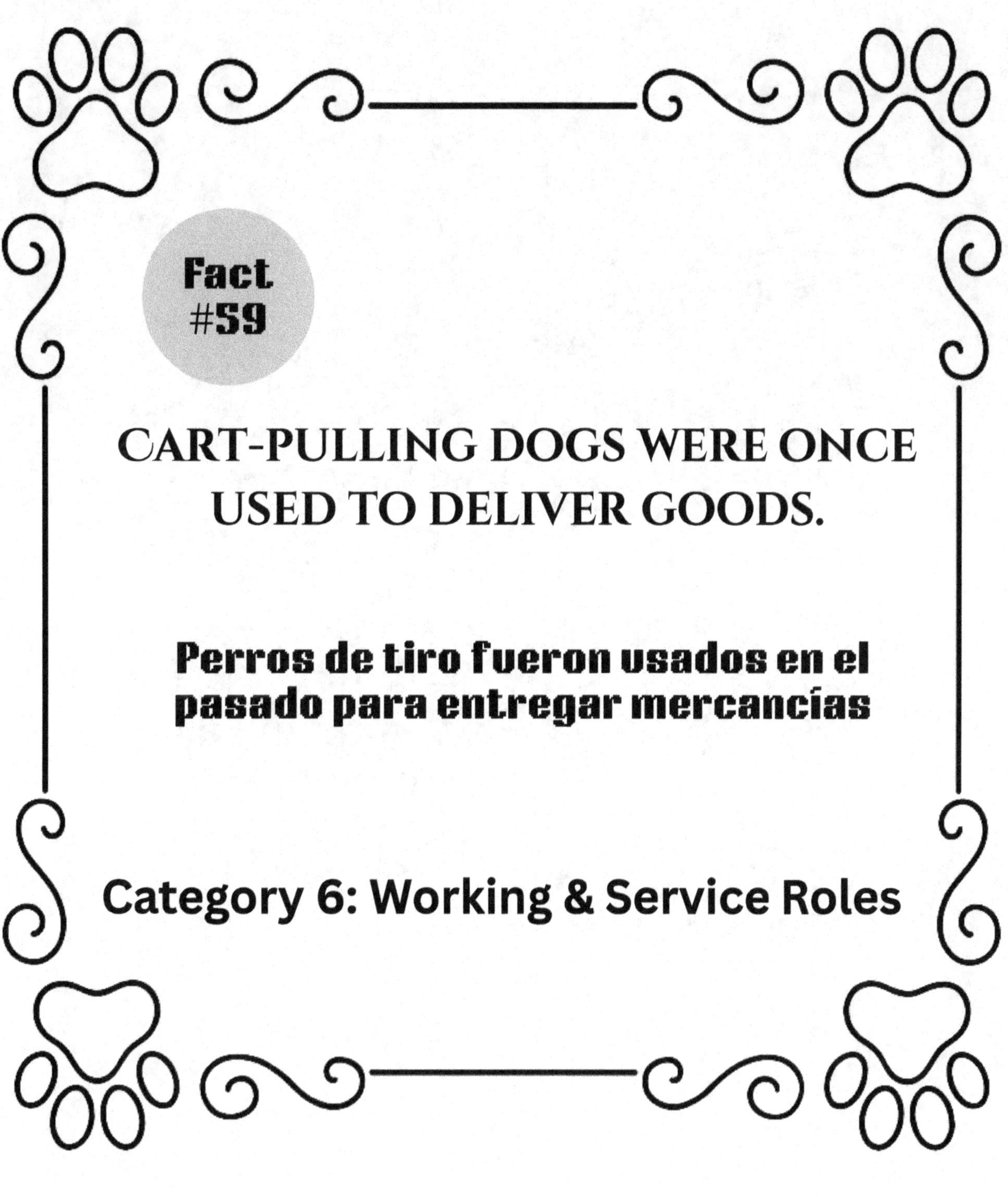

CART-PULLING DOGS WERE ONCE USED TO DELIVER GOODS.

Perros de tiro fueron usados en el pasado para entregar mercancías

Category 6: Working & Service Roles

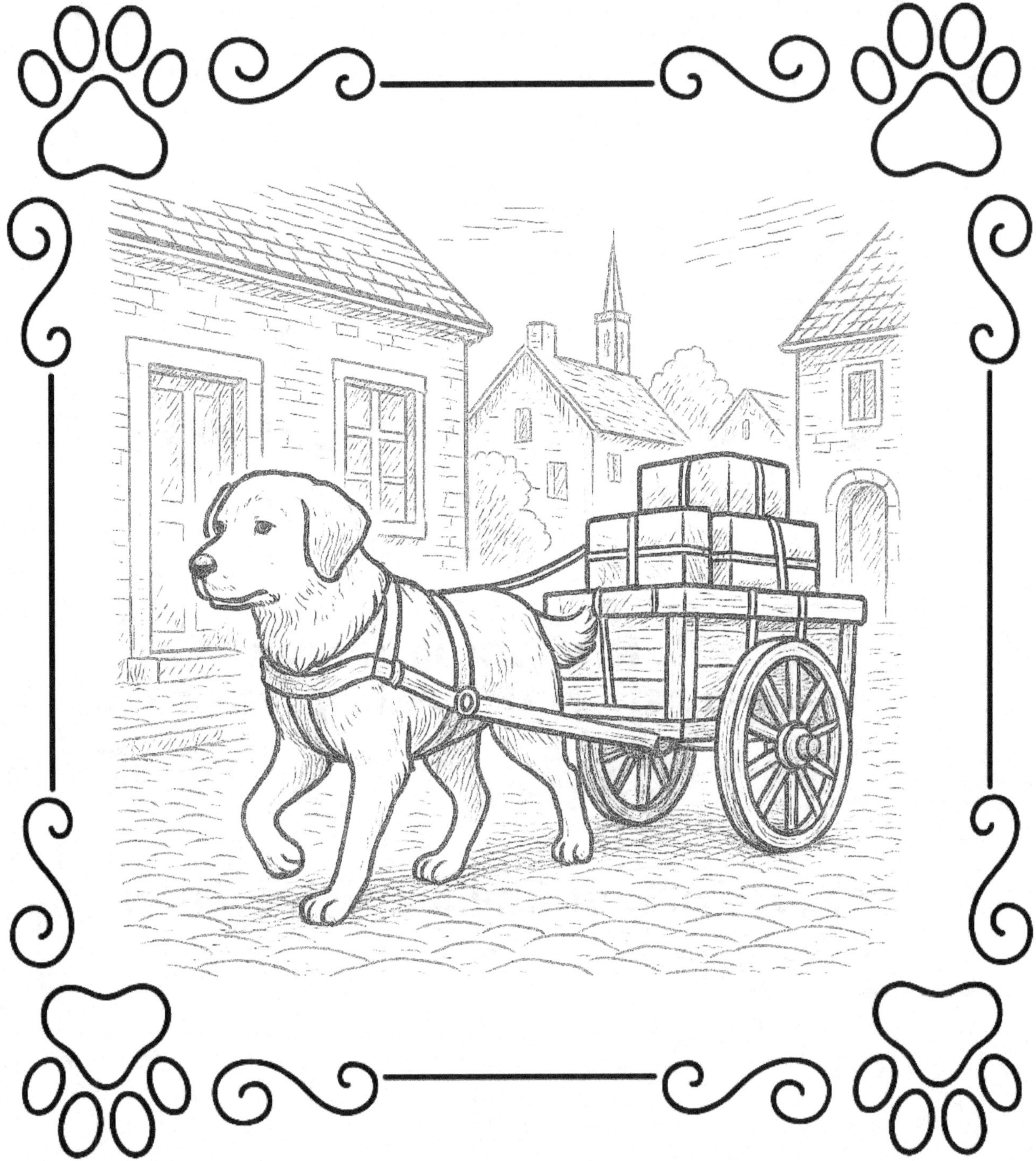

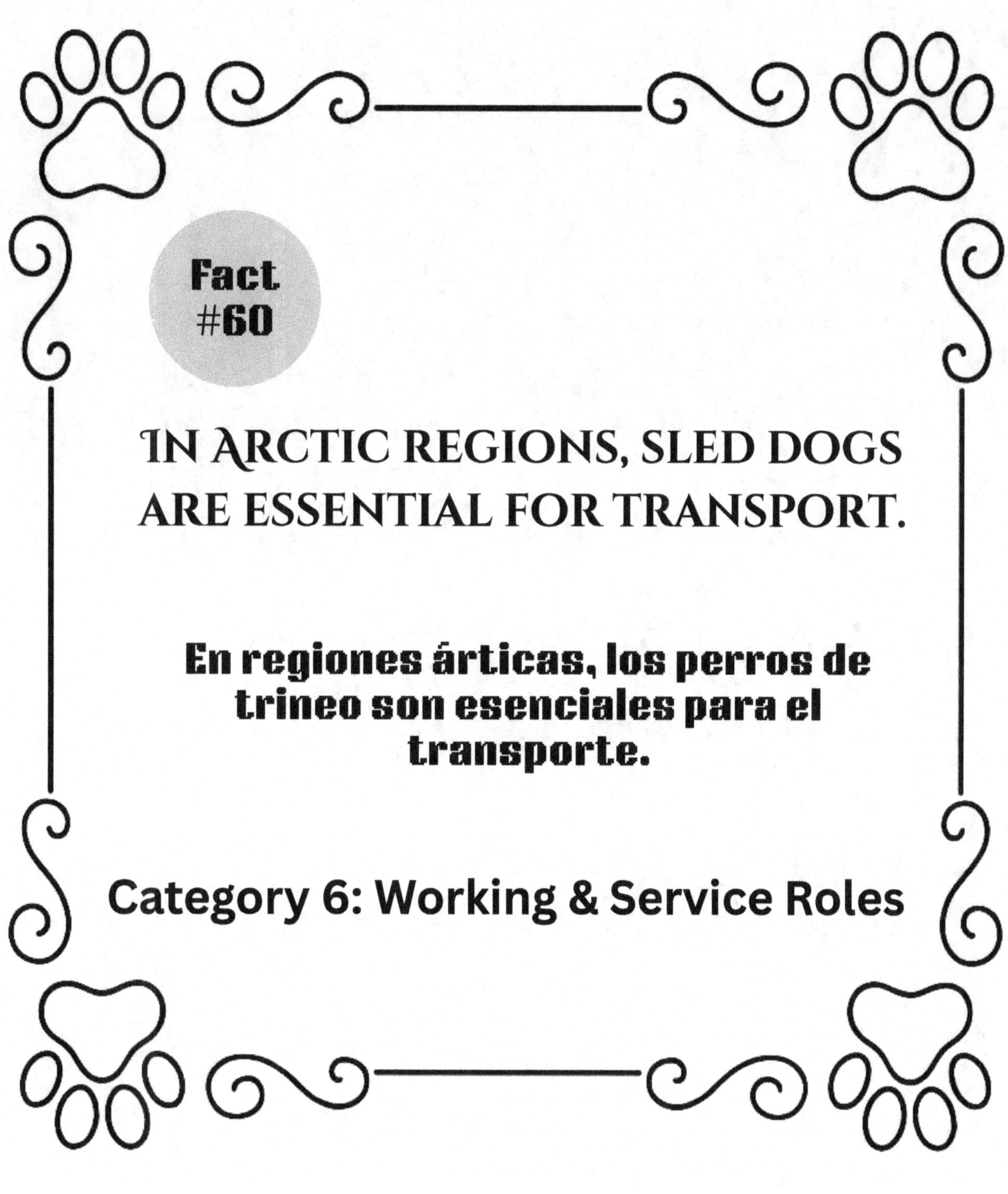

IN ARCTIC REGIONS, SLED DOGS ARE ESSENTIAL FOR TRANSPORT.

En regiones árticas, los perros de trineo son esenciales para el transporte.

Category 6: Working & Service Roles

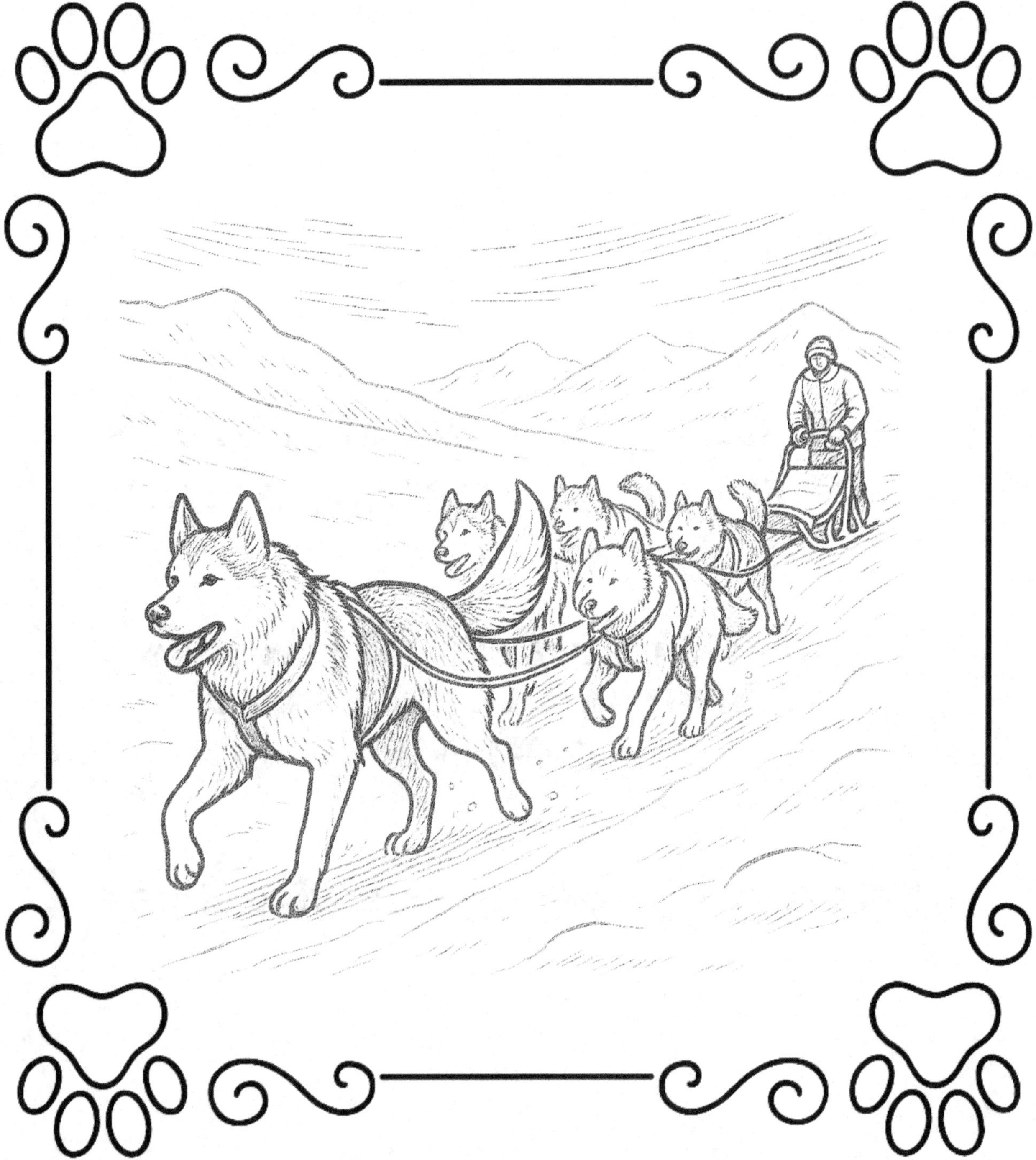

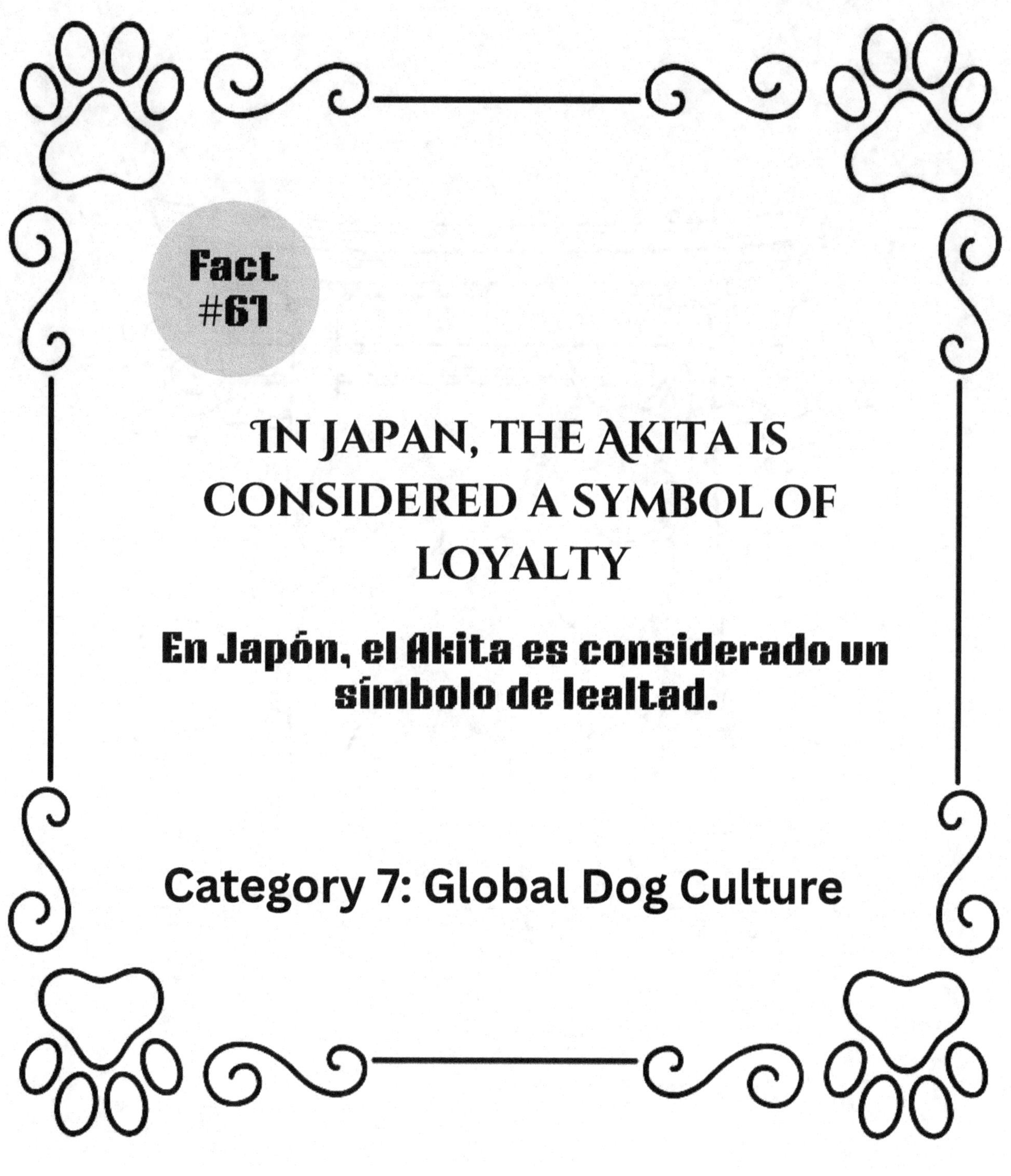

Fact #61

IN JAPAN, THE AKITA IS CONSIDERED A SYMBOL OF LOYALTY

En Japón, el Akita es considerado un símbolo de lealtad.

Category 7: Global Dog Culture

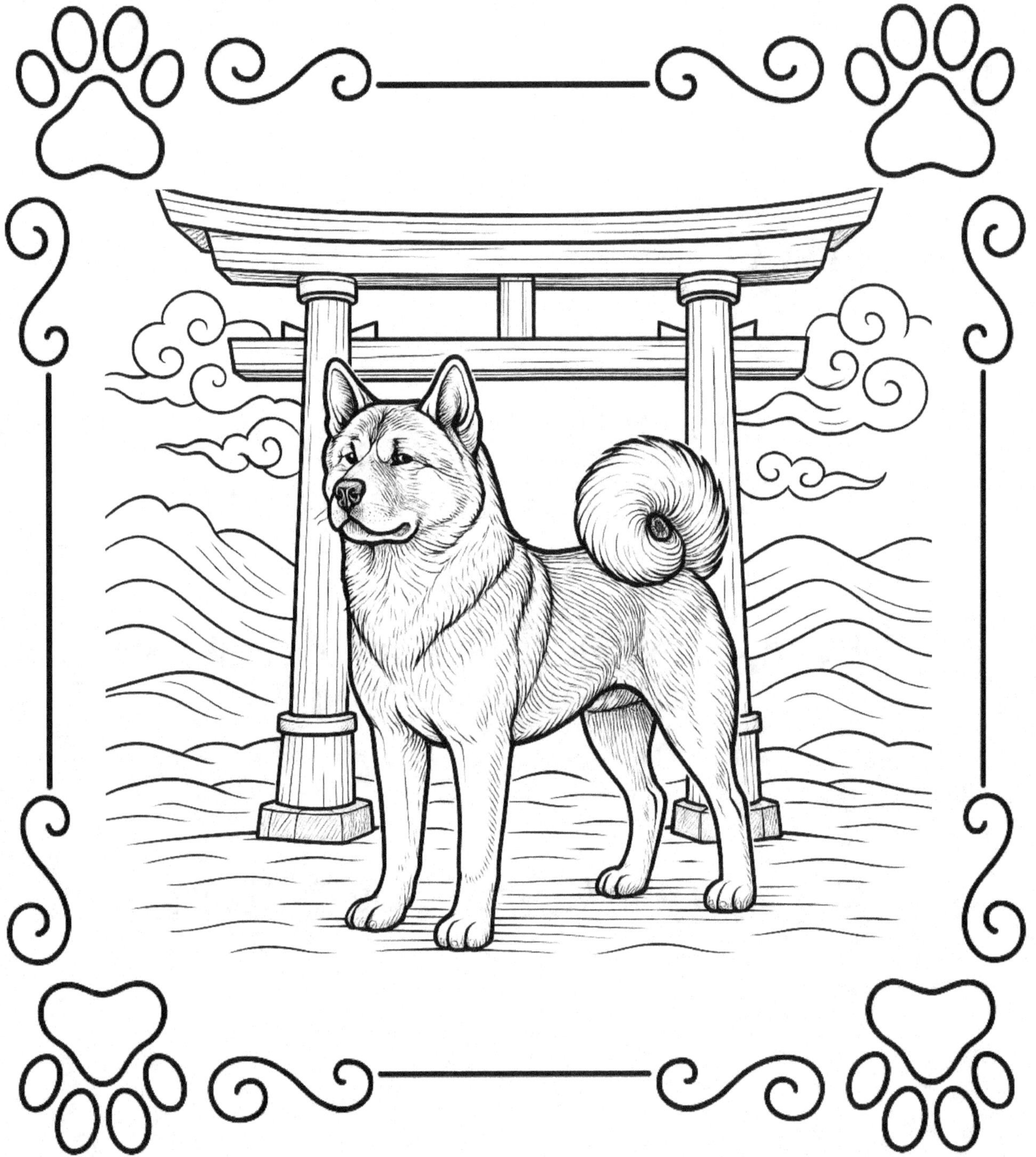

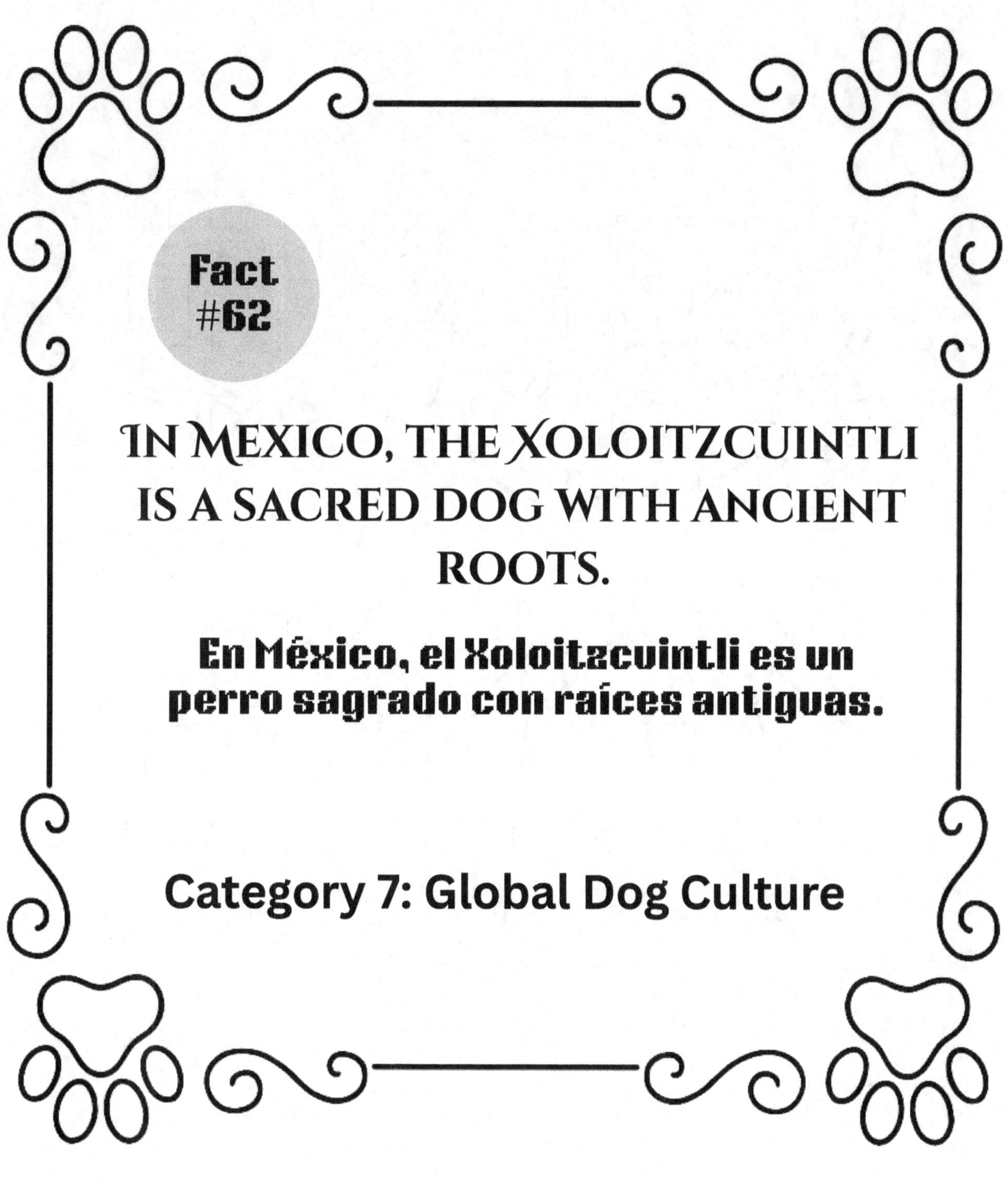

Fact #62

IN MEXICO, THE XOLOITZCUINTLI IS A SACRED DOG WITH ANCIENT ROOTS.

En México, el Xoloitzcuintli es un perro sagrado con raíces antiguas.

Category 7: Global Dog Culture

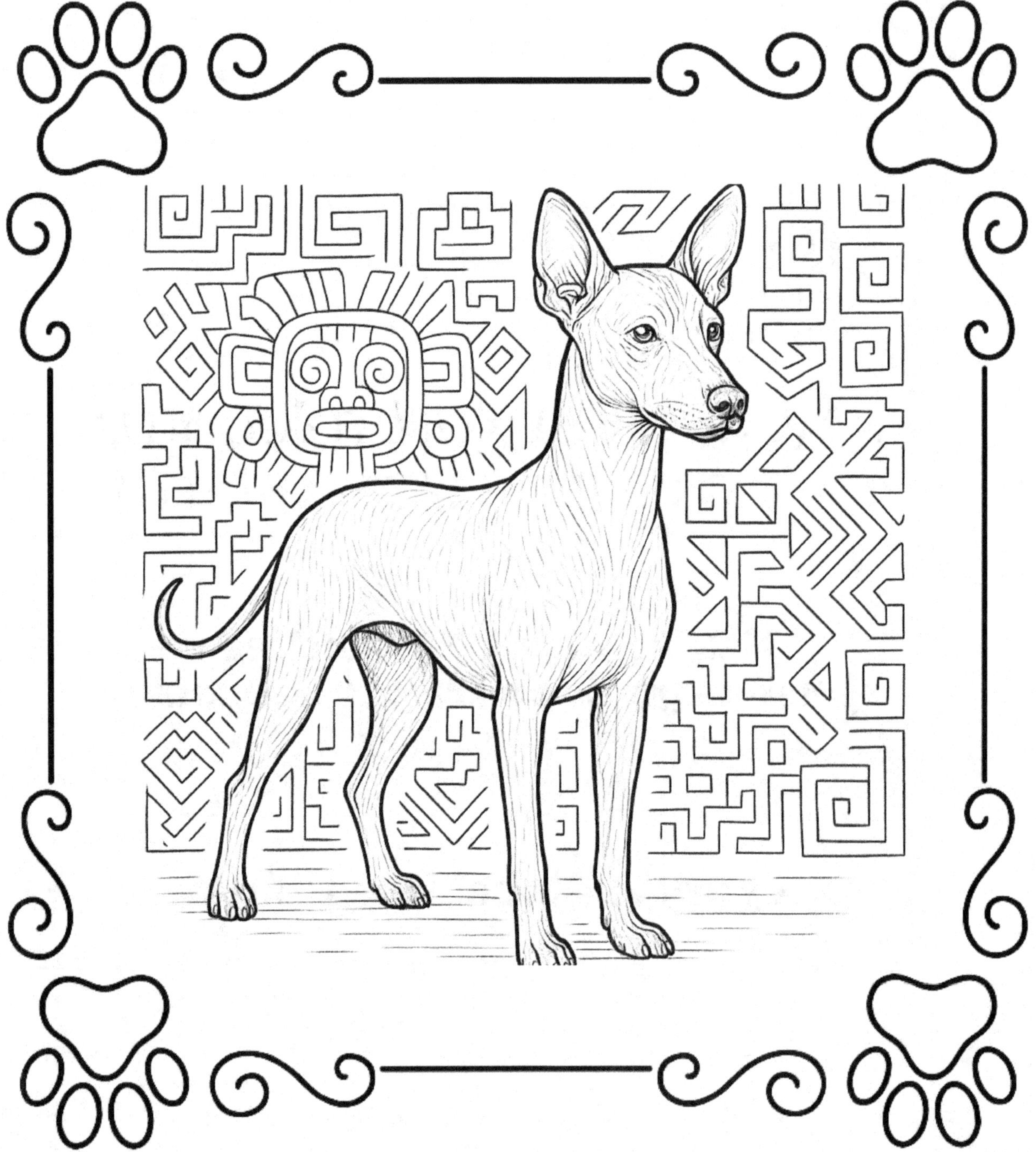

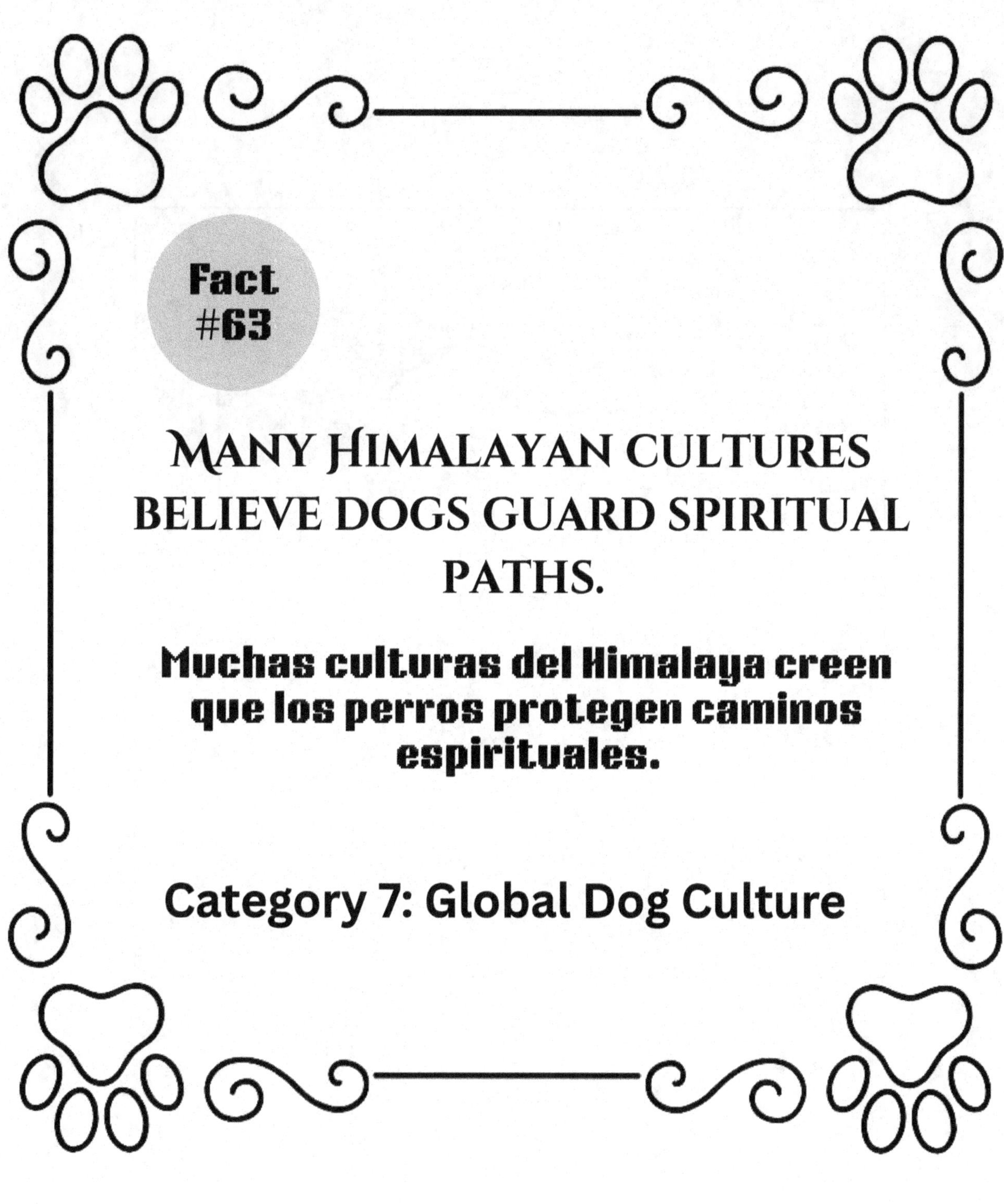

Fact #63

MANY HIMALAYAN CULTURES BELIEVE DOGS GUARD SPIRITUAL PATHS.

Muchas culturas del Himalaya creen que los perros protegen caminos espirituales.

Category 7: Global Dog Culture

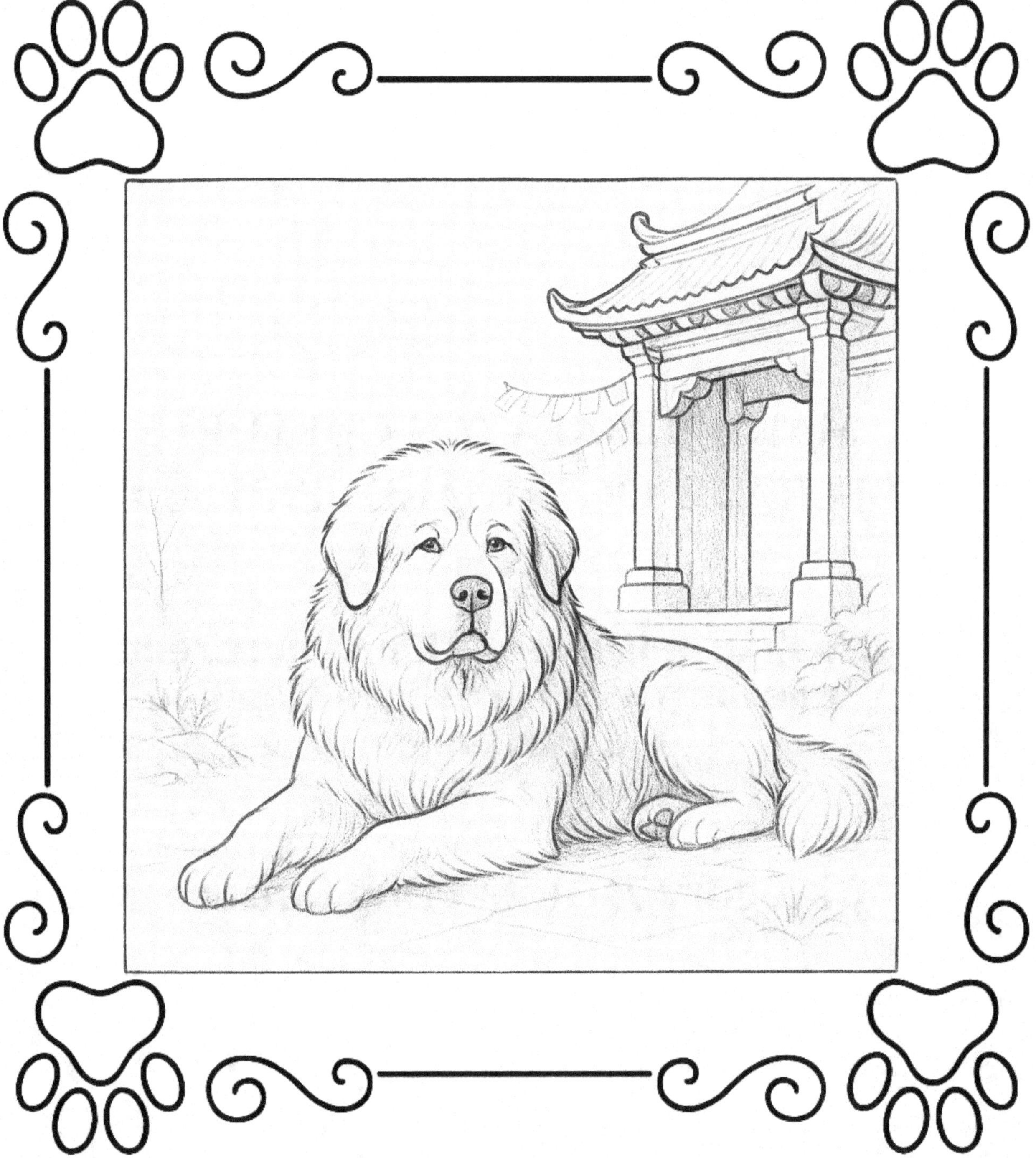

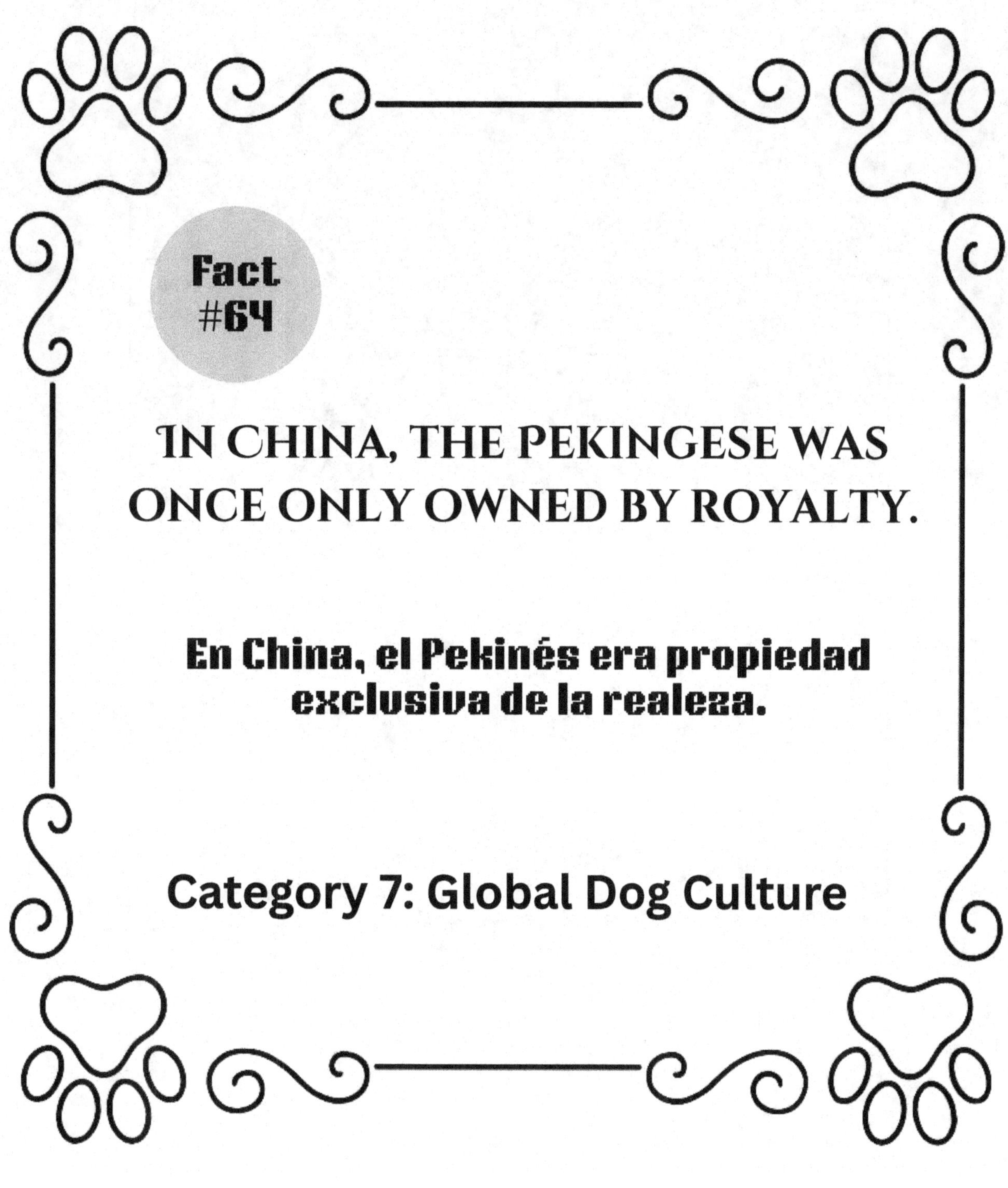

Fact #64

IN CHINA, THE PEKINGESE WAS ONCE ONLY OWNED BY ROYALTY.

En China, el Pekinés era propiedad exclusiva de la realeza.

Category 7: Global Dog Culture

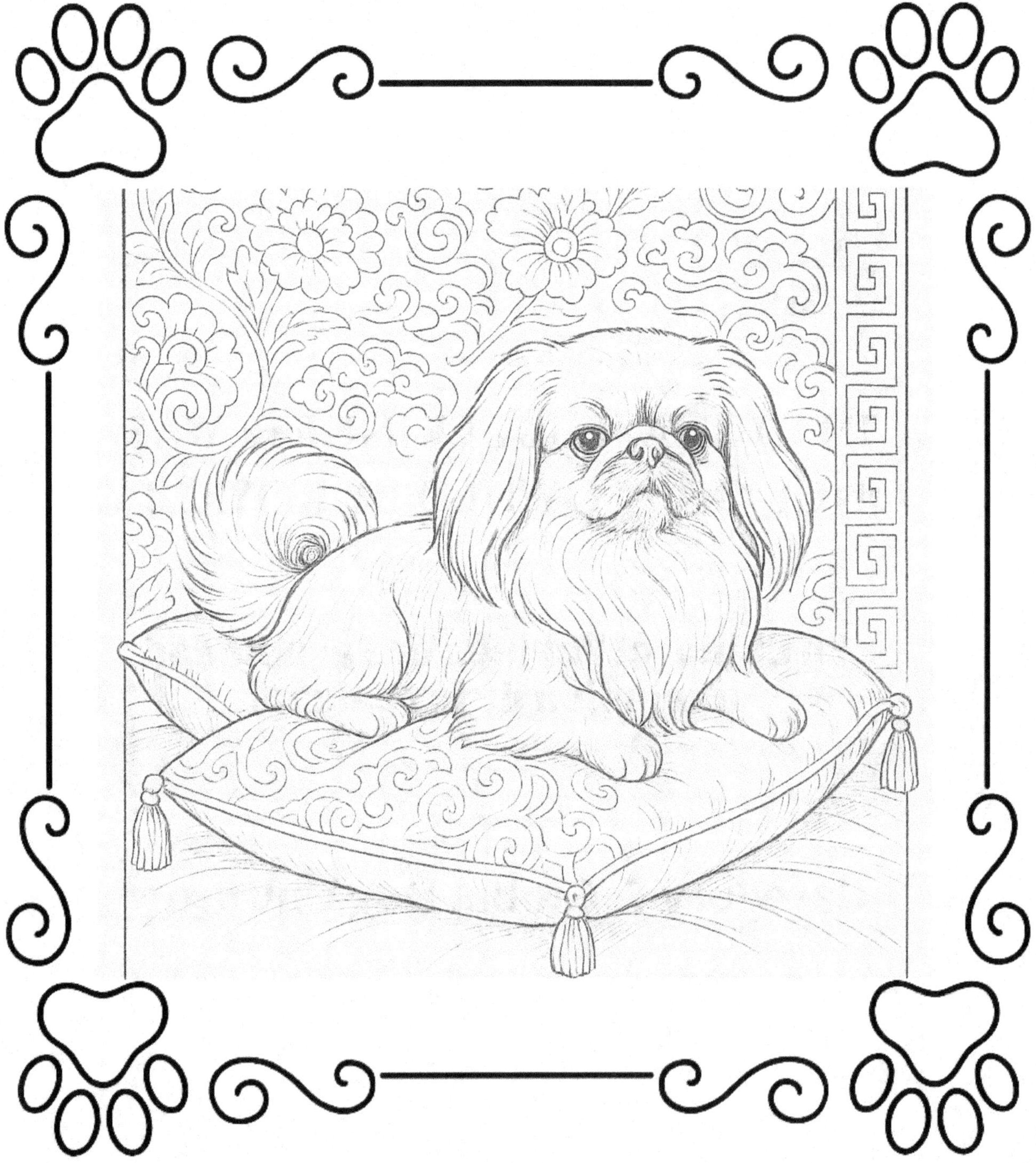

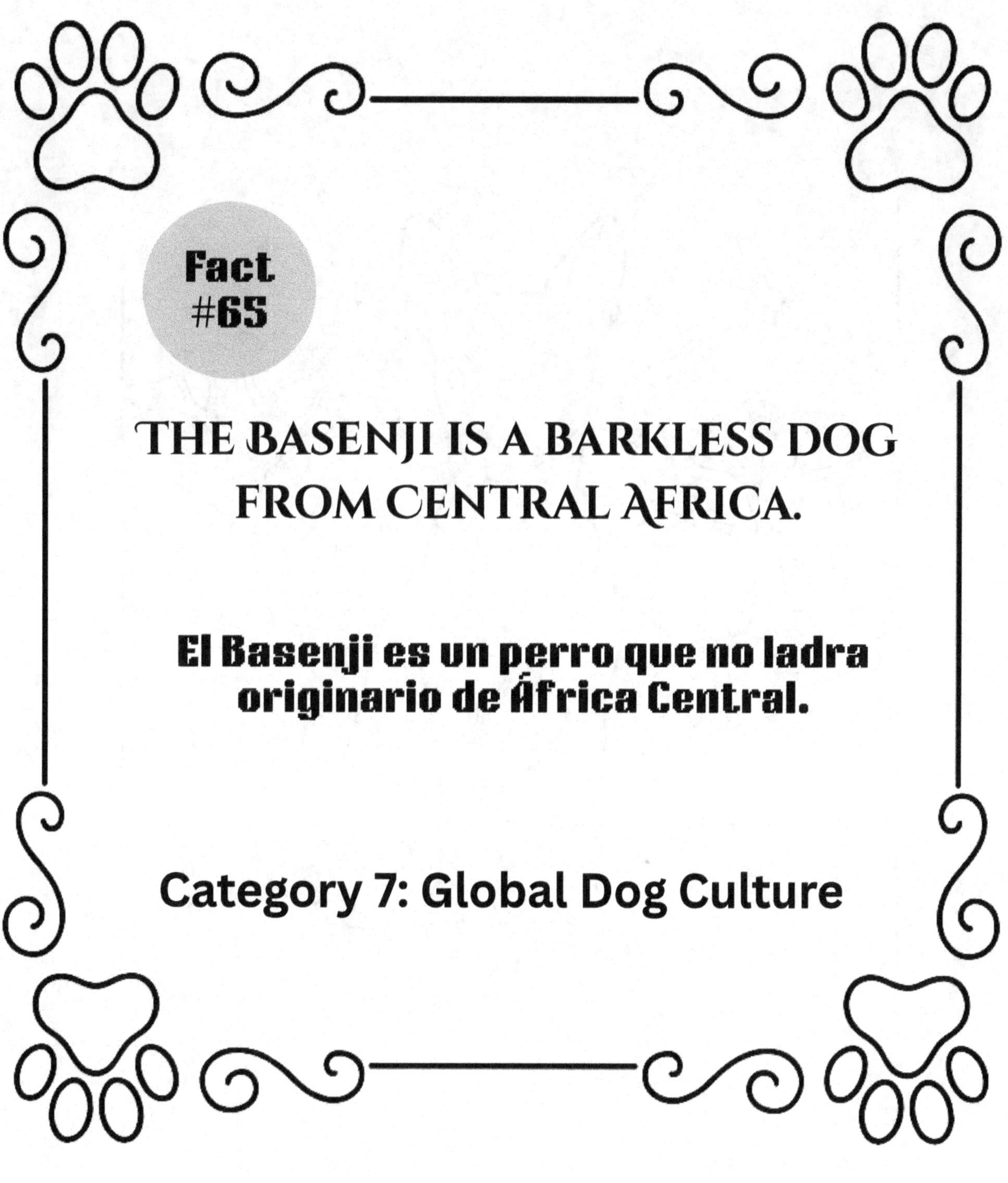

Fact #65

THE BASENJI IS A BARKLESS DOG FROM CENTRAL AFRICA.

El Basenji es un perro que no ladra originario de África Central.

Category 7: Global Dog Culture

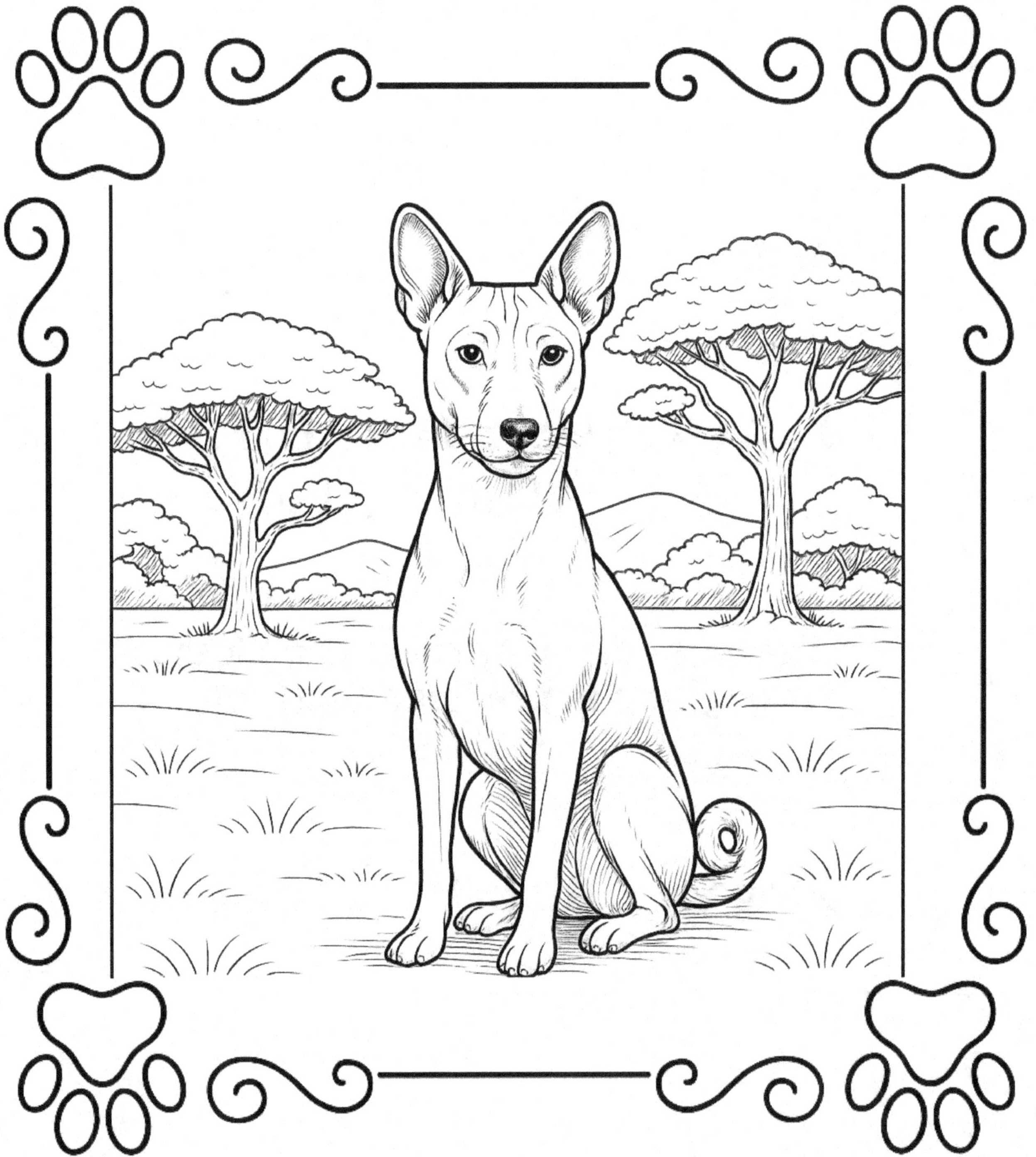

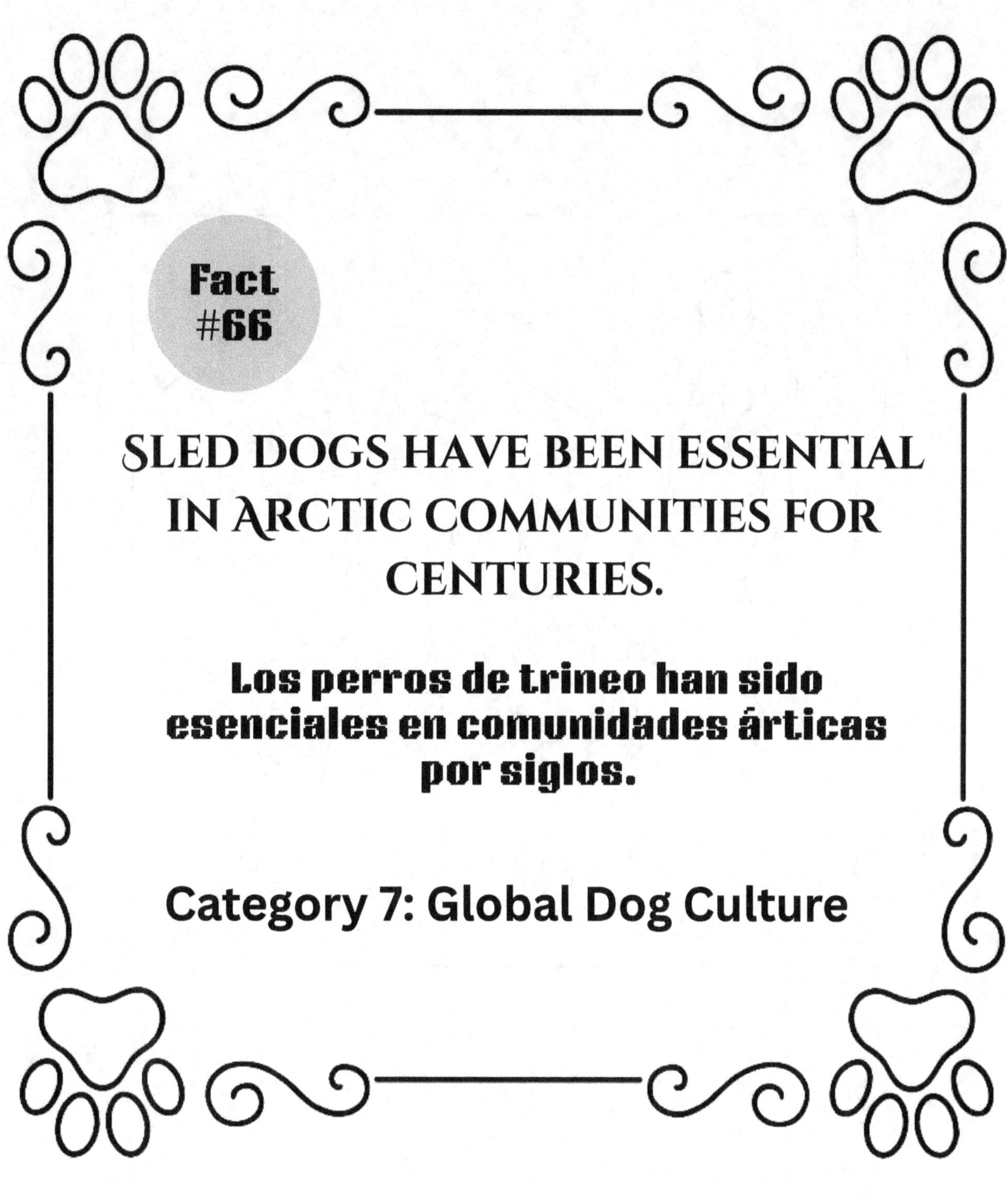

Fact #66

SLED DOGS HAVE BEEN ESSENTIAL IN ARCTIC COMMUNITIES FOR CENTURIES.

Los perros de trineo han sido esenciales en comunidades árticas por siglos.

Category 7: Global Dog Culture

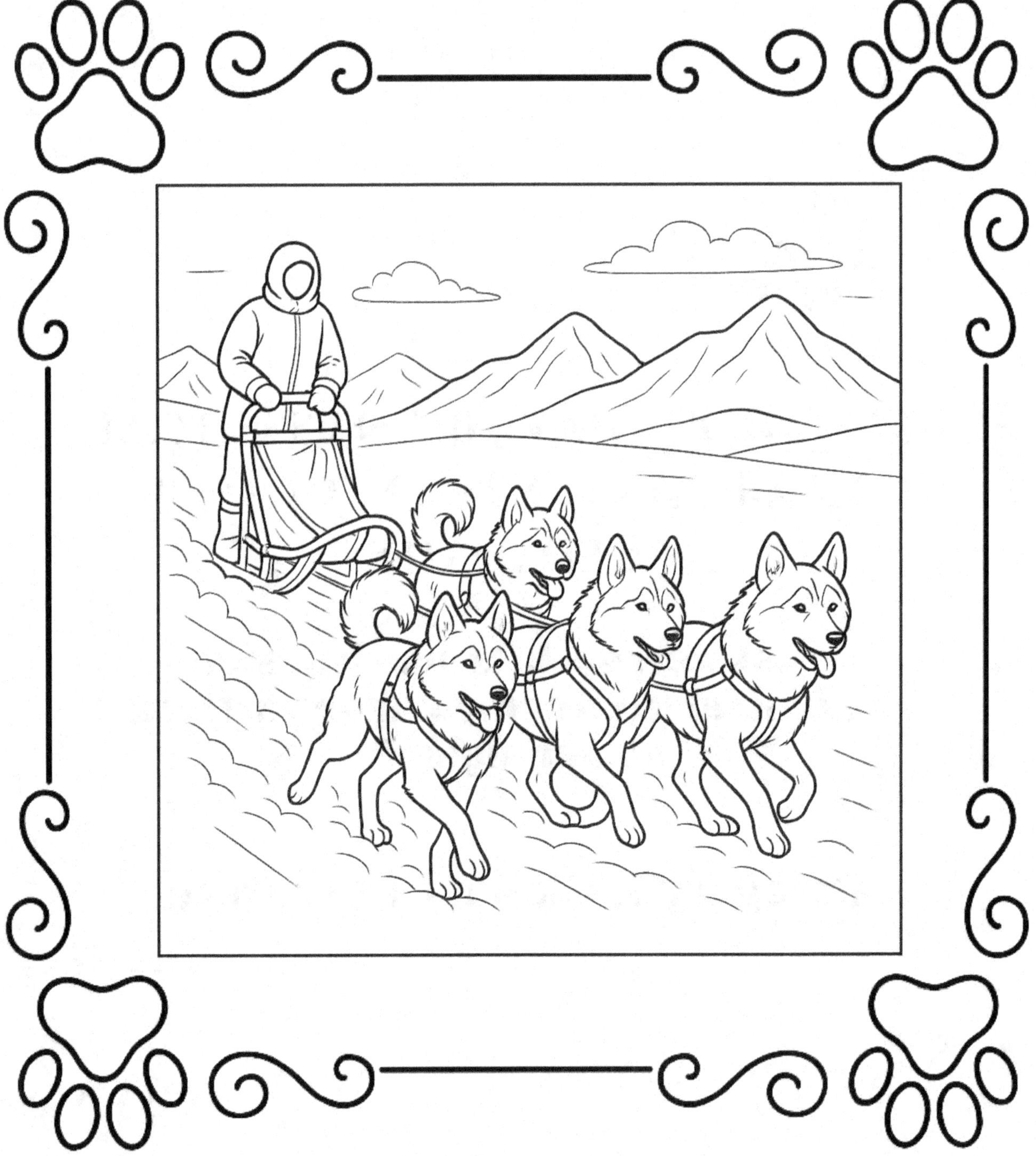

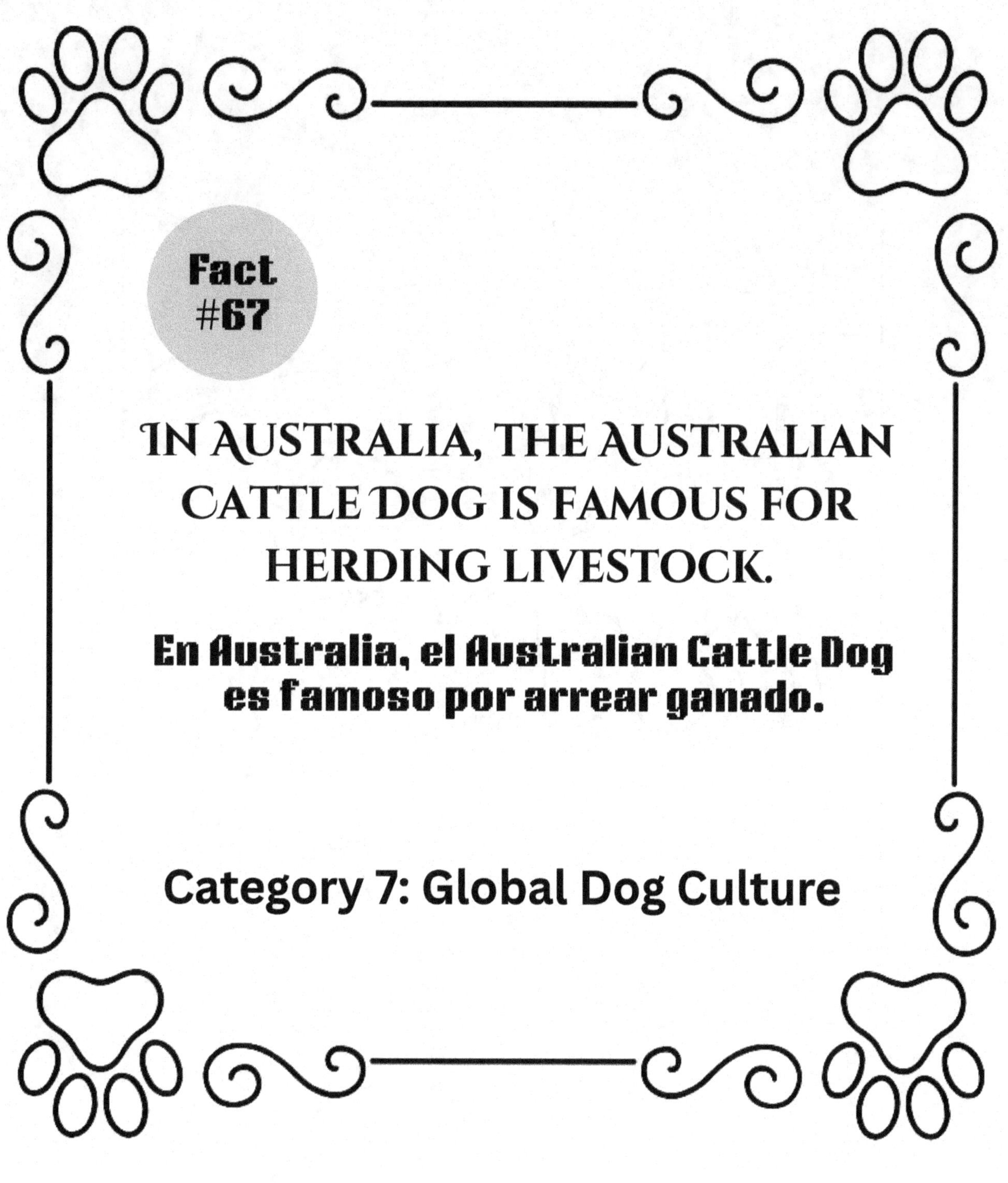
Fact #67

IN AUSTRALIA, THE AUSTRALIAN CATTLE DOG IS FAMOUS FOR HERDING LIVESTOCK.

En Australia, el Australian Cattle Dog es famoso por arrear ganado.

Category 7: Global Dog Culture

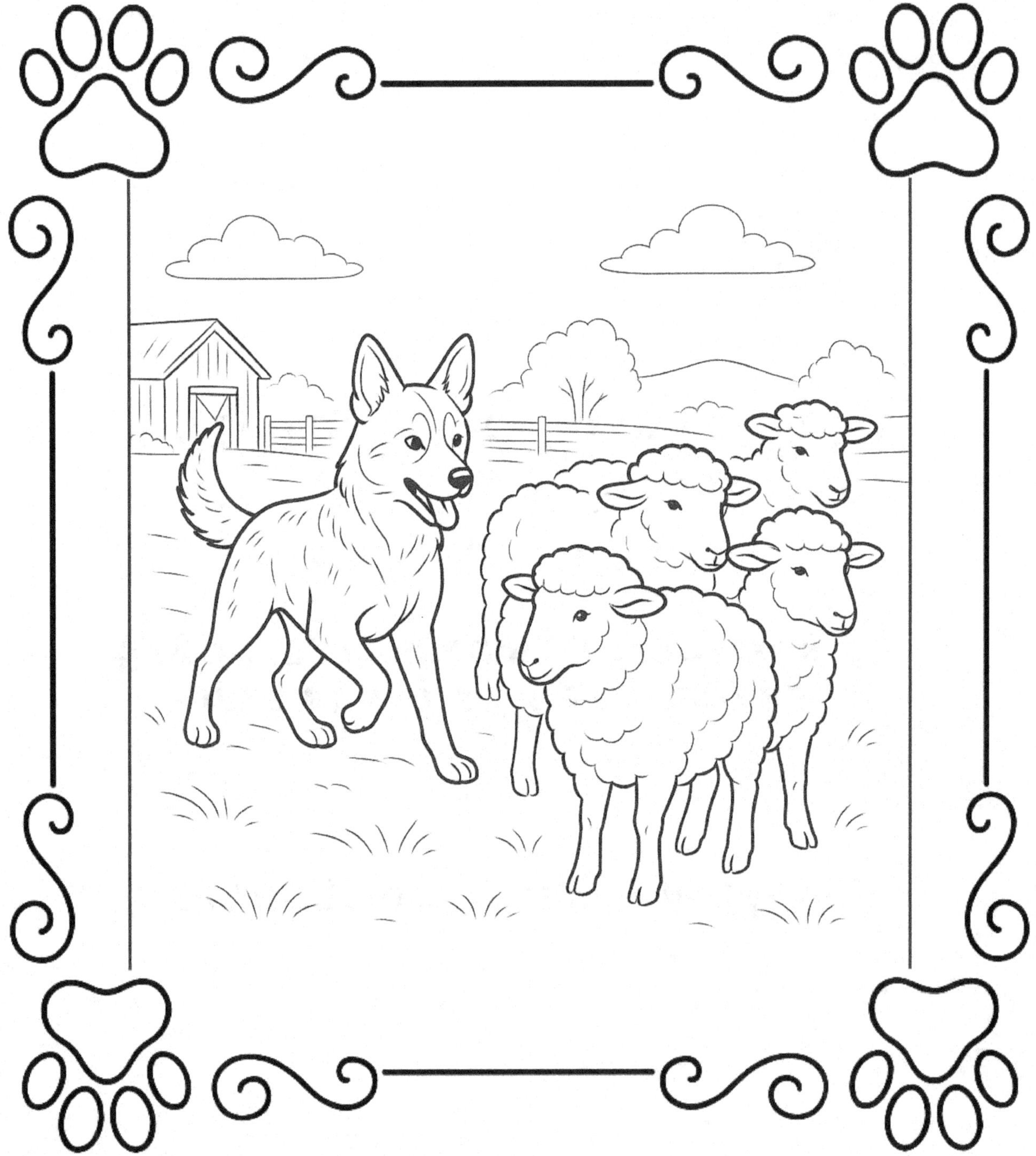

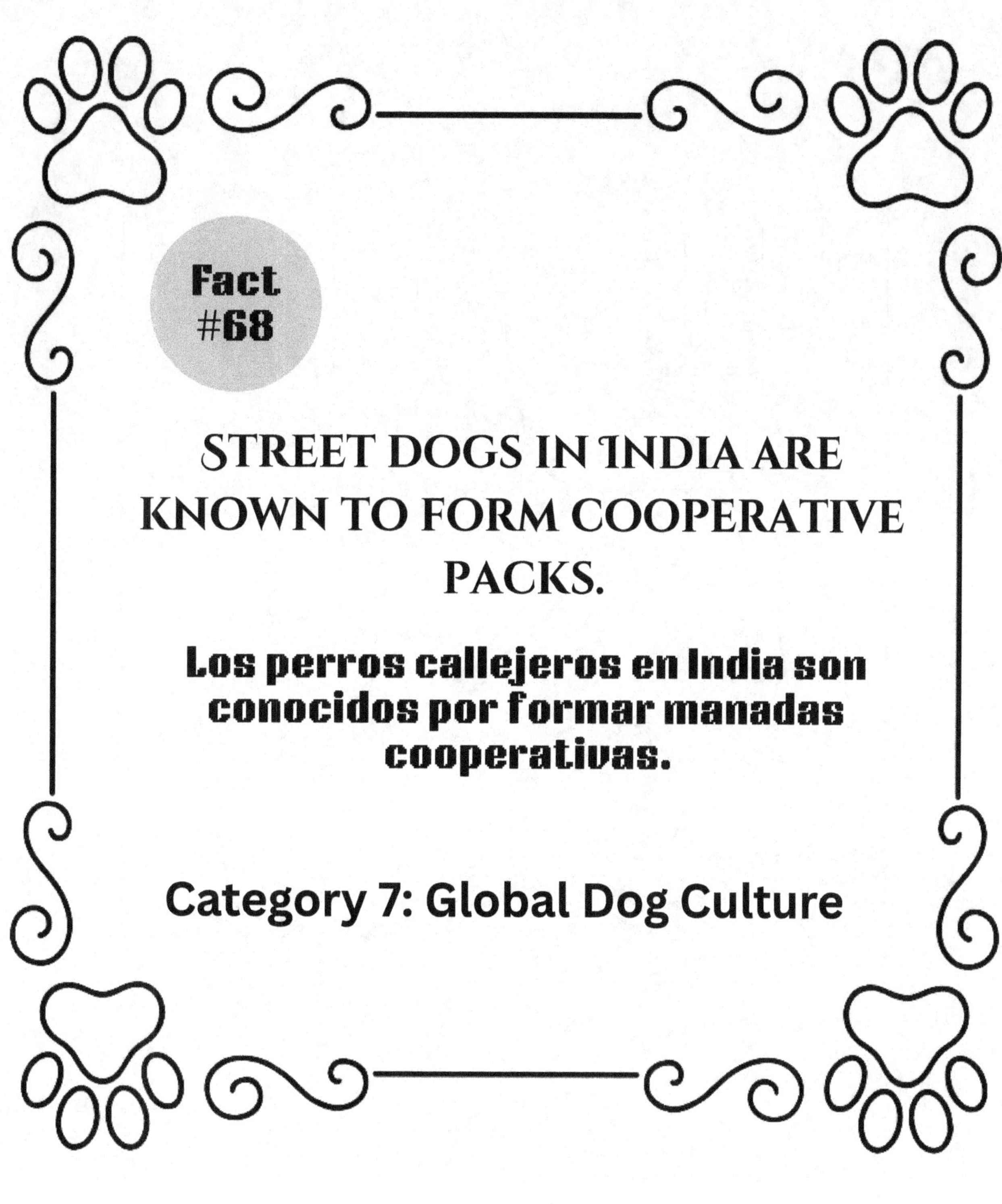

Fact #68

STREET DOGS IN INDIA ARE KNOWN TO FORM COOPERATIVE PACKS.

Los perros callejeros en India son conocidos por formar manadas cooperativas.

Category 7: Global Dog Culture

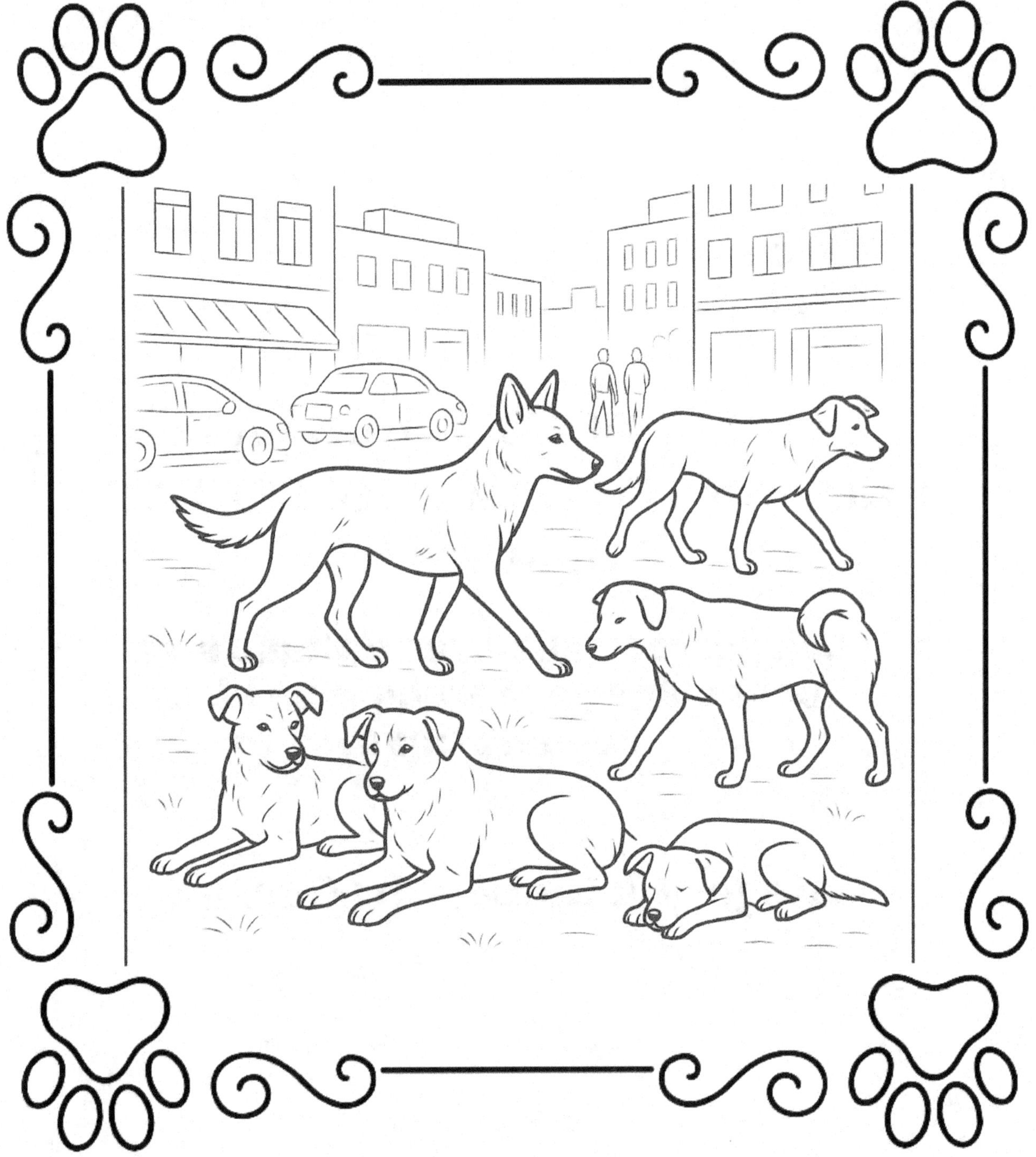

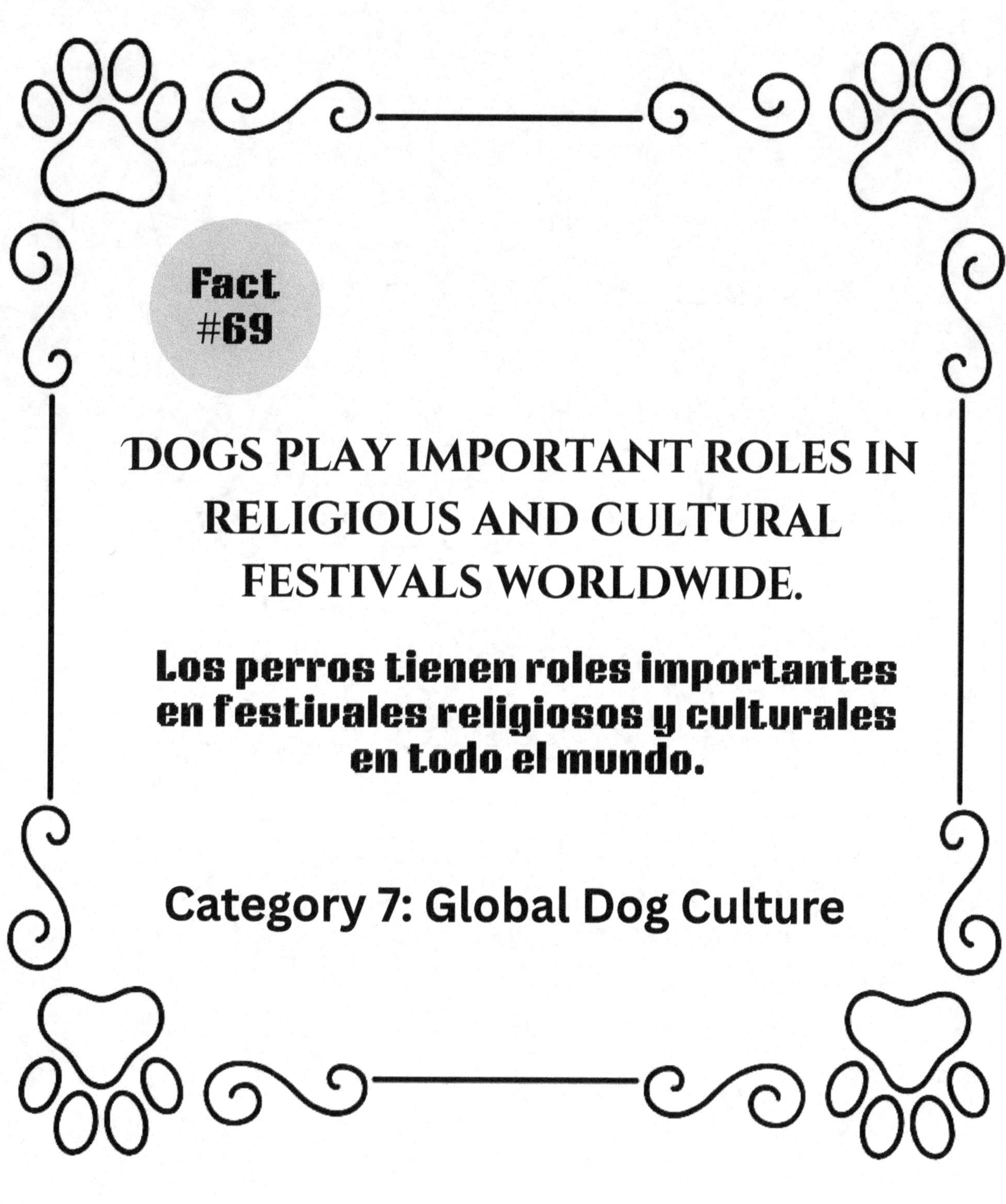

Fact
#69

DOGS PLAY IMPORTANT ROLES IN
RELIGIOUS AND CULTURAL
FESTIVALS WORLDWIDE.

Los perros tienen roles importantes
en festivales religiosos y culturales
en todo el mundo.

Category 7: Global Dog Culture

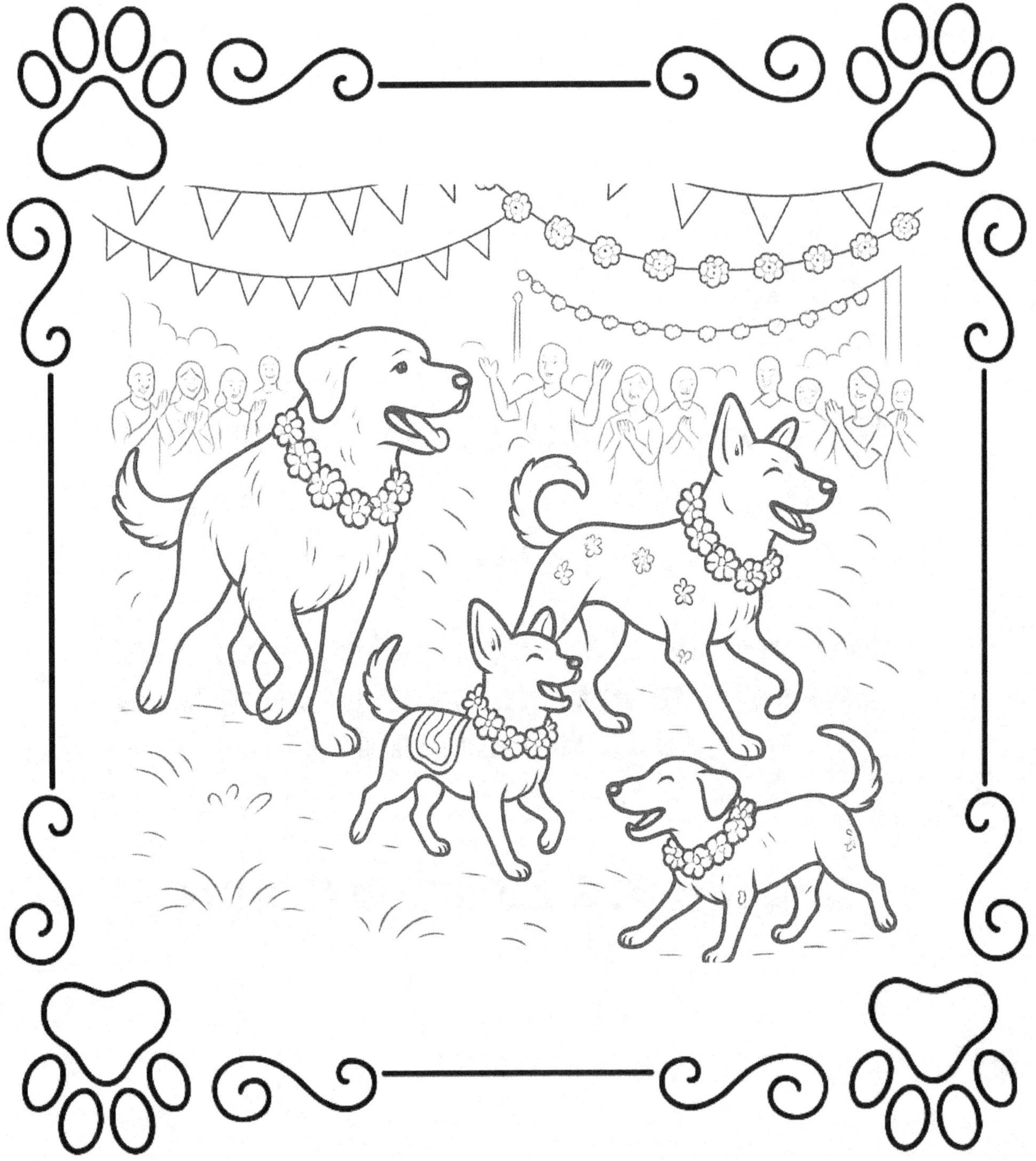

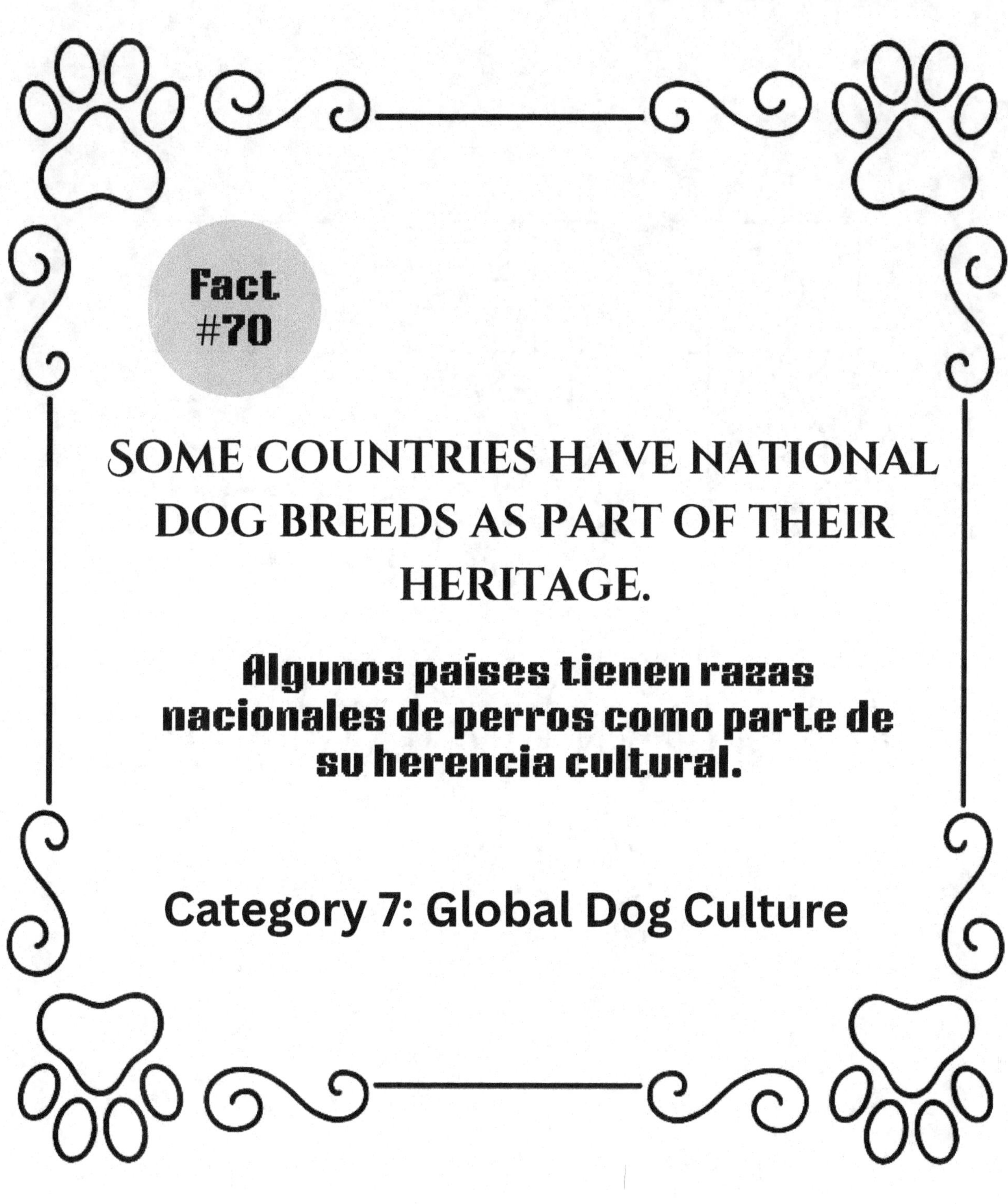
Fact #70

SOME COUNTRIES HAVE NATIONAL DOG BREEDS AS PART OF THEIR HERITAGE.

Algunos países tienen razas nacionales de perros como parte de su herencia cultural.

Category 7: Global Dog Culture

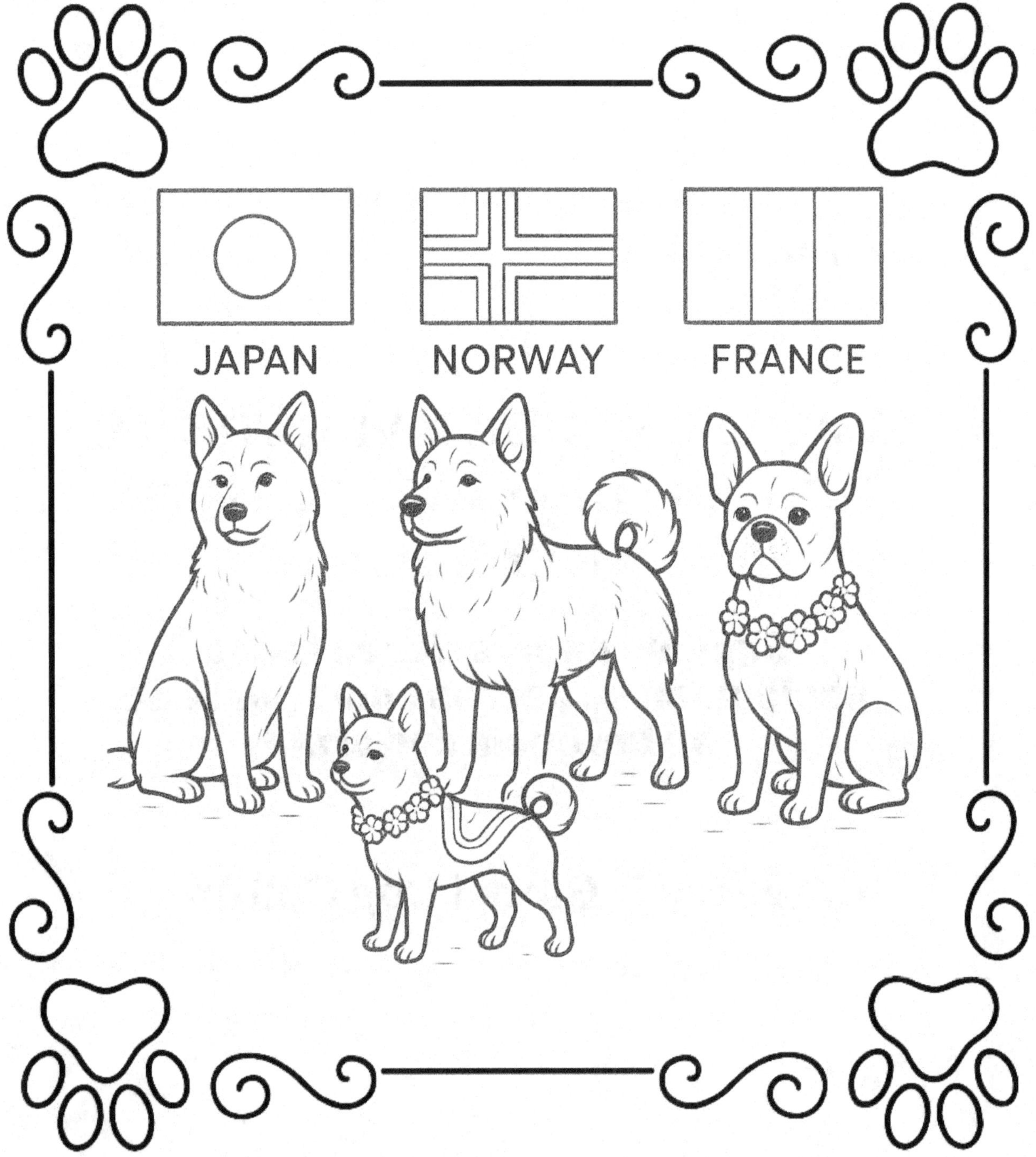

JAPAN
NORWAY
FRANCE

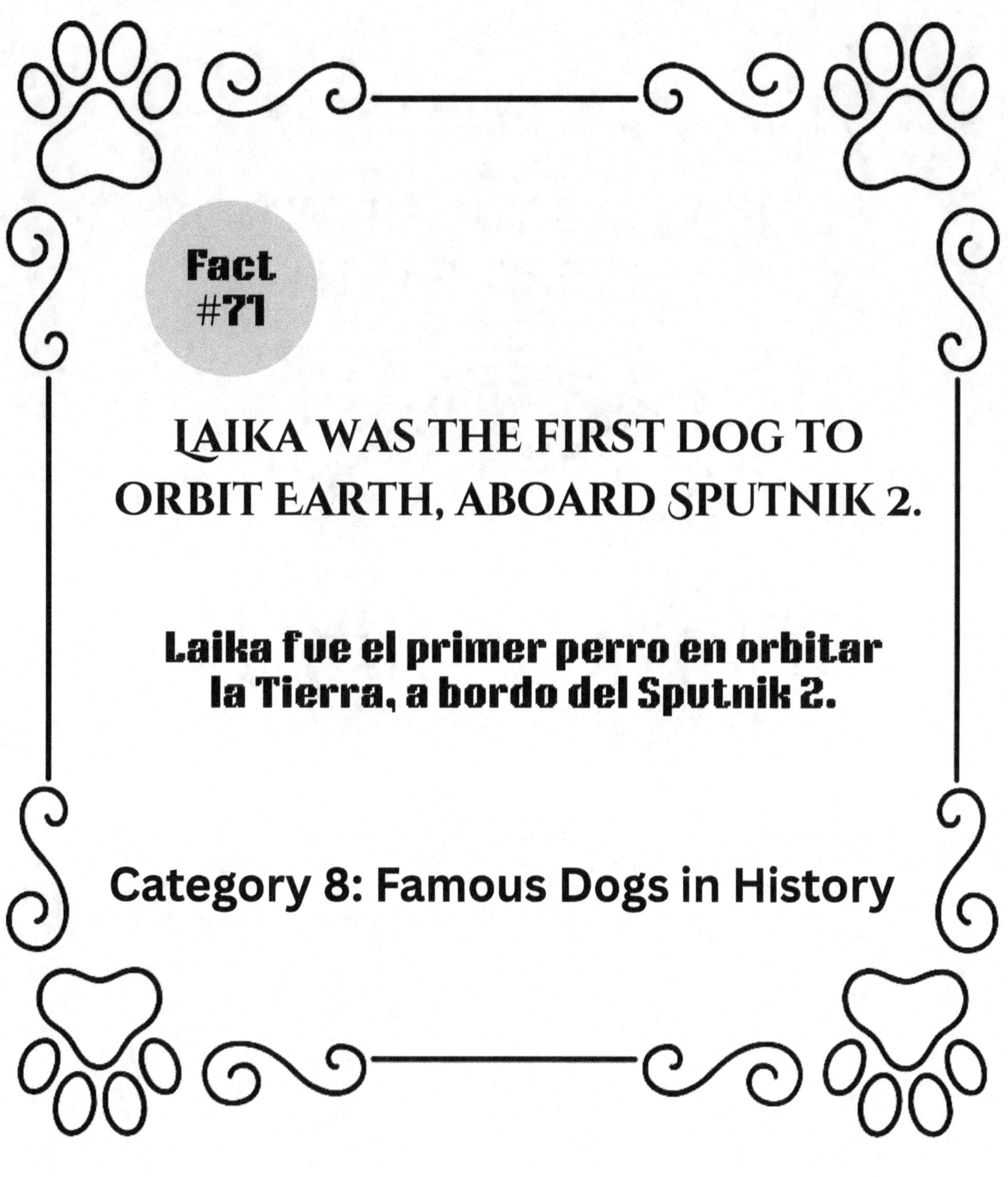

Fact #71

LAIKA WAS THE FIRST DOG TO ORBIT EARTH, ABOARD SPUTNIK 2.

Laika fue el primer perro en orbitar la Tierra, a bordo del Sputnik 2.

Category 8: Famous Dogs in History

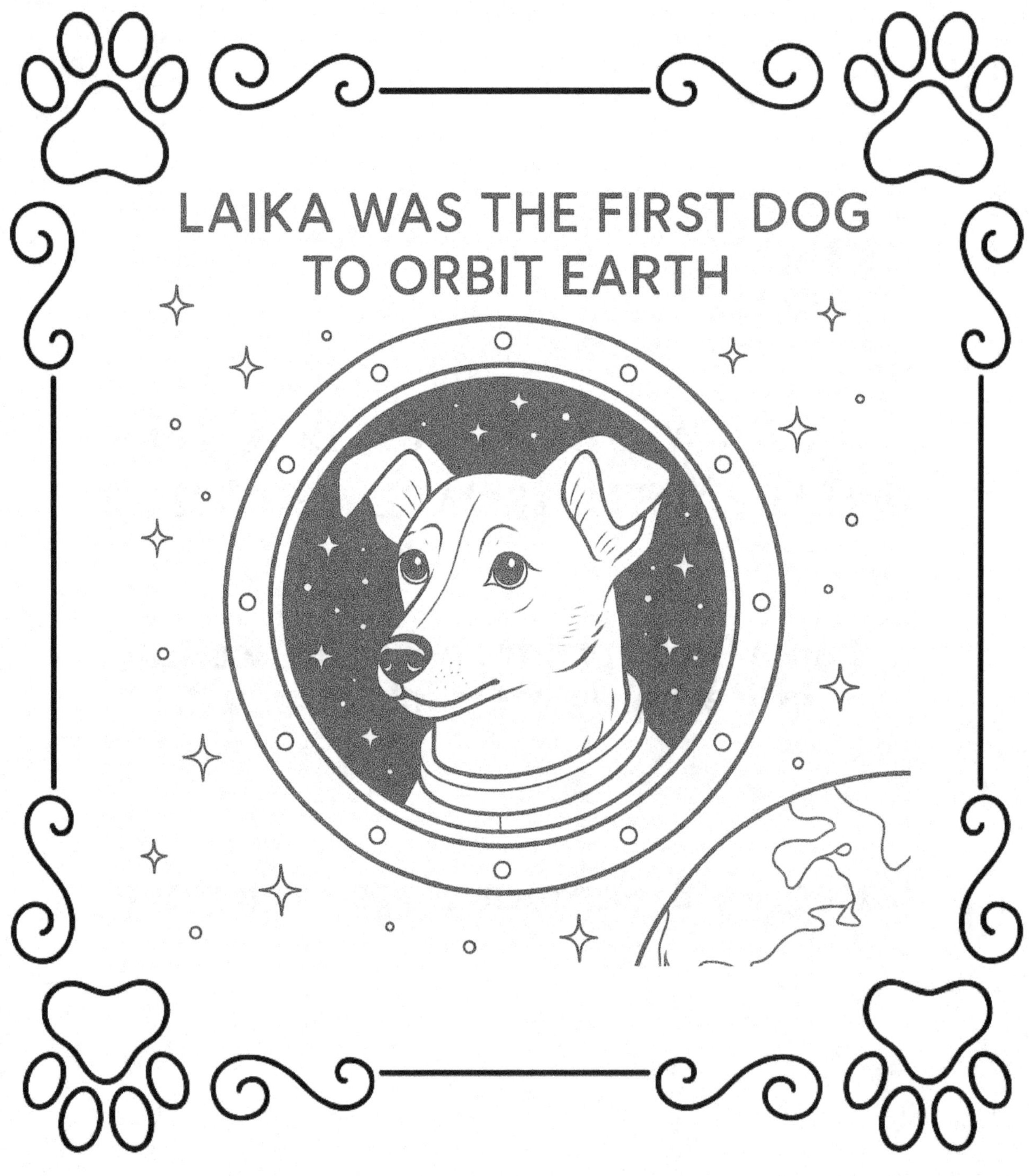

LAIKA WAS THE FIRST DOG
TO ORBIT EARTH

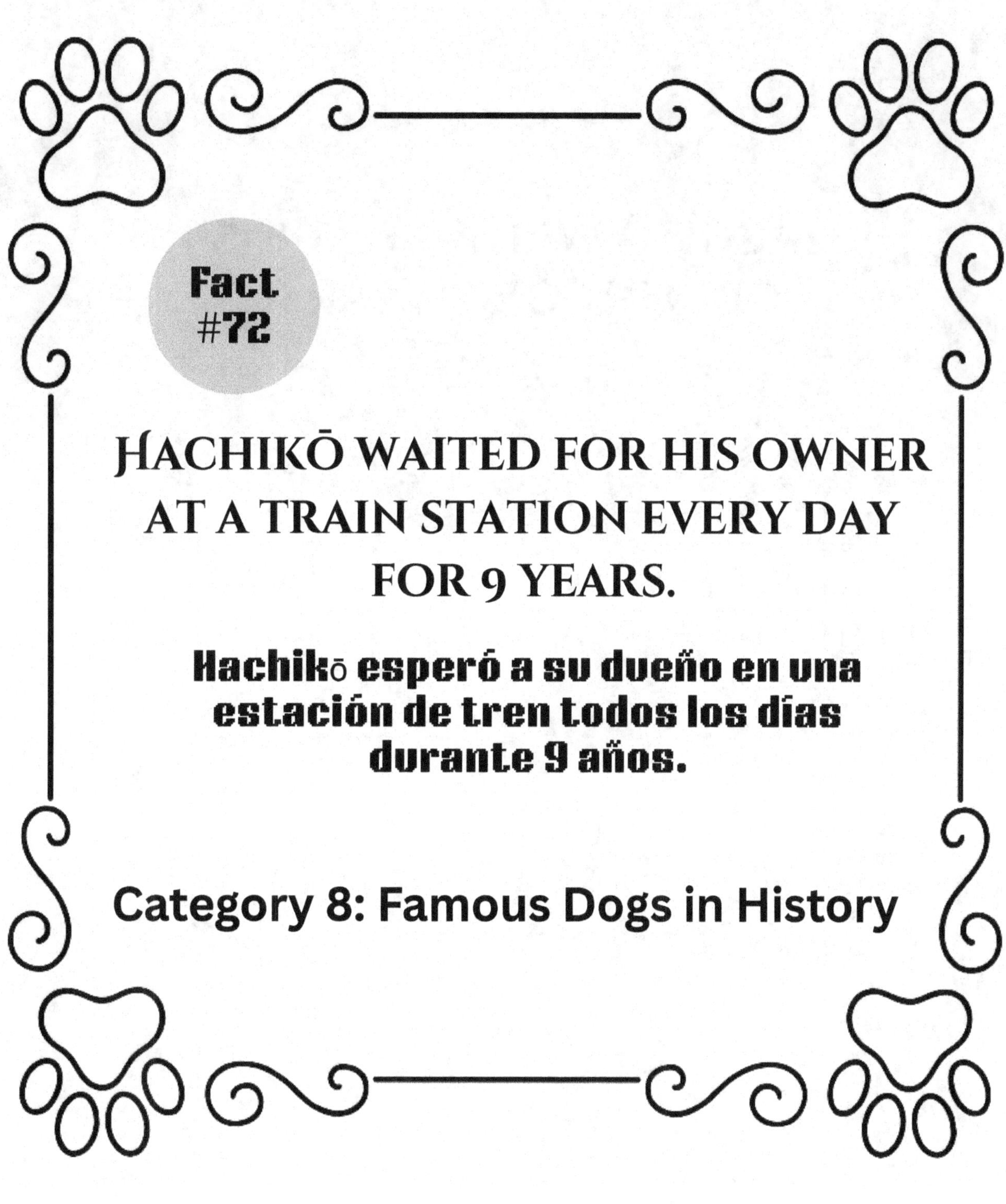
Fact #72

HACHIKŌ WAITED FOR HIS OWNER AT A TRAIN STATION EVERY DAY FOR 9 YEARS.

Hachikō esperó a su dueño en una estación de tren todos los días durante 9 años.

Category 8: Famous Dogs in History

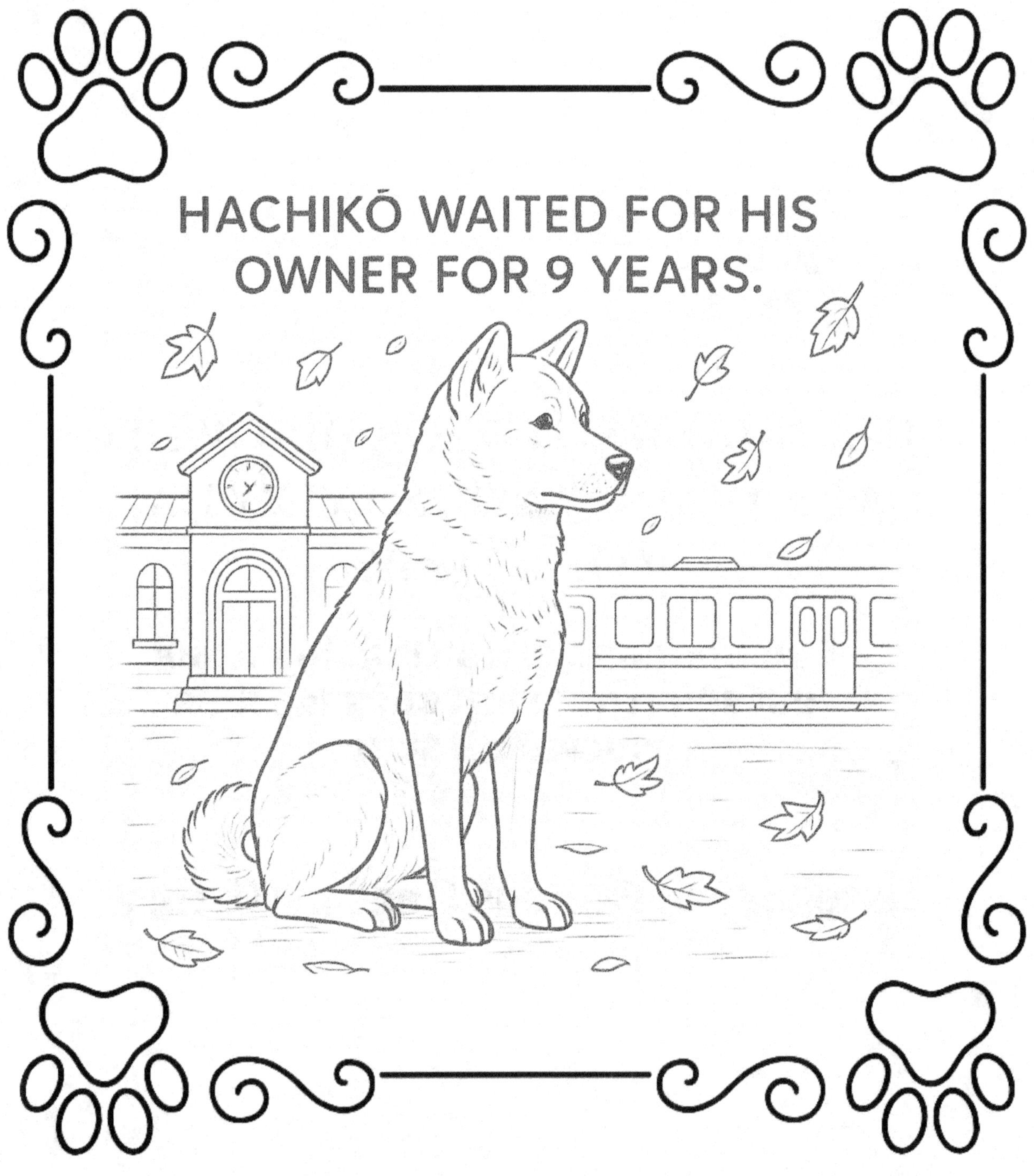

HACHIKŌ WAITED FOR HIS OWNER FOR 9 YEARS.

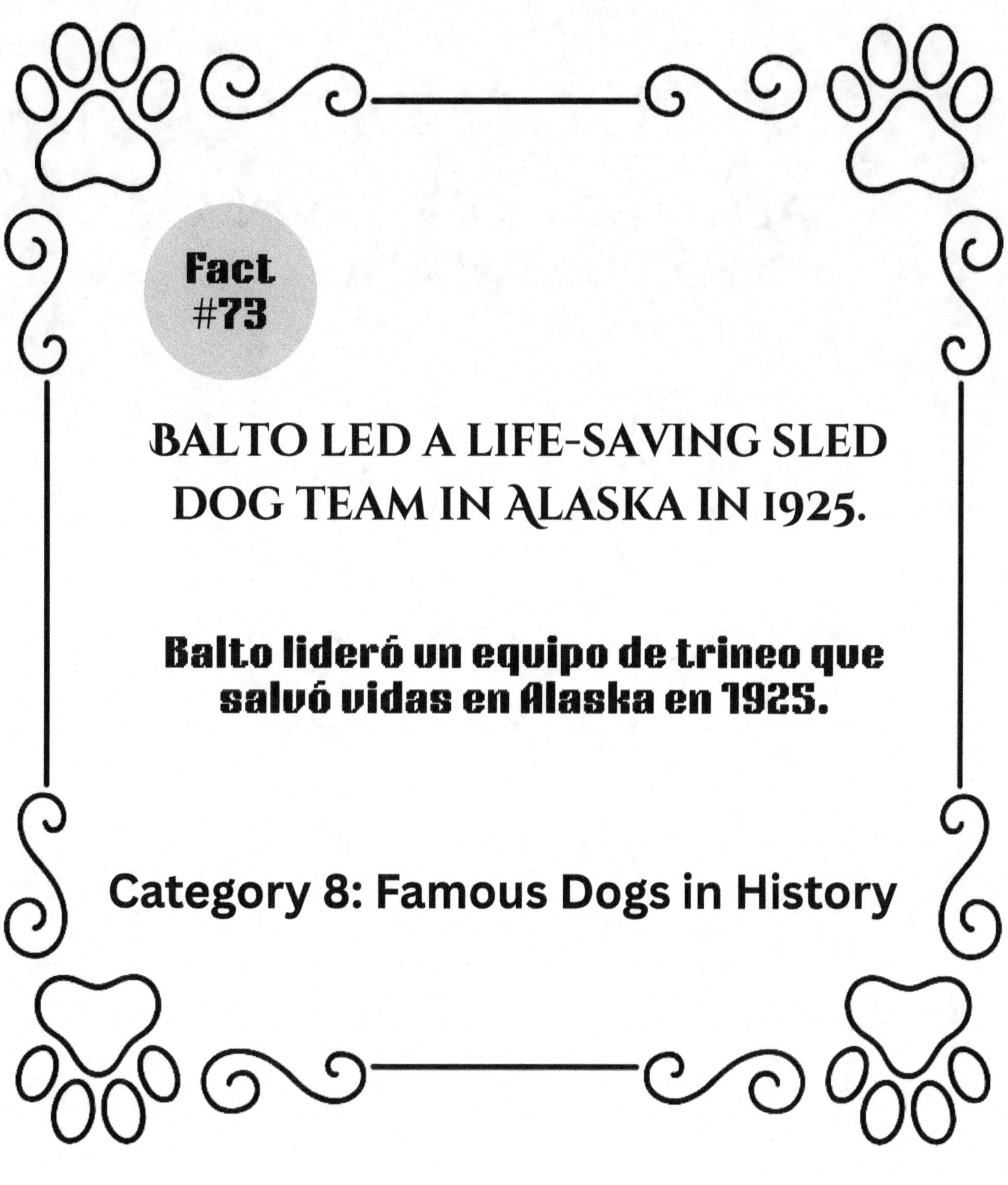

Fact #73

BALTO LED A LIFE-SAVING SLED DOG TEAM IN ALASKA IN 1925.

Balto lideró un equipo de trineo que salvó vidas en Alaska en 1925.

Category 8: Famous Dogs in History

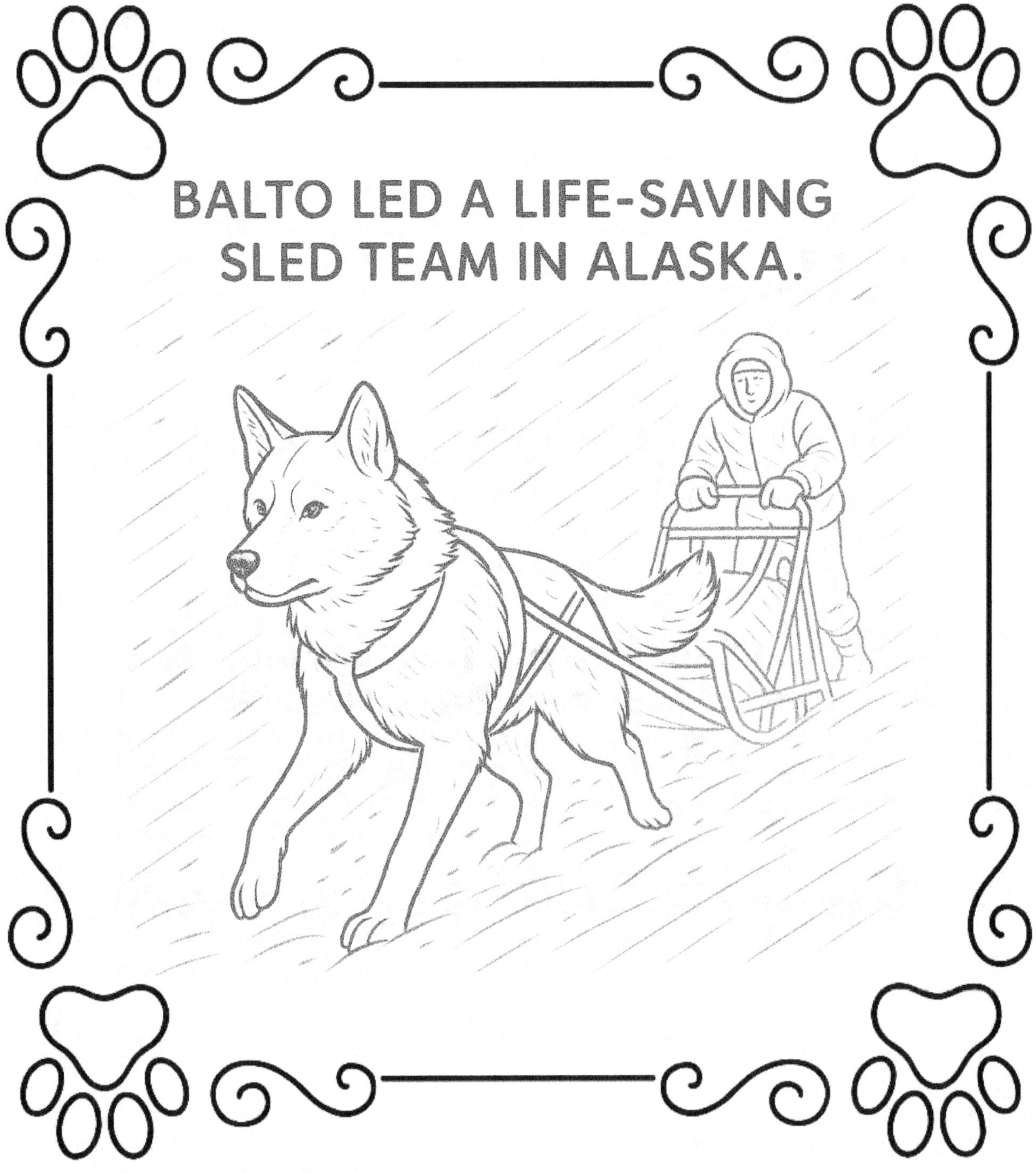
BALTO LED A LIFE-SAVING
SLED TEAM IN ALASKA.

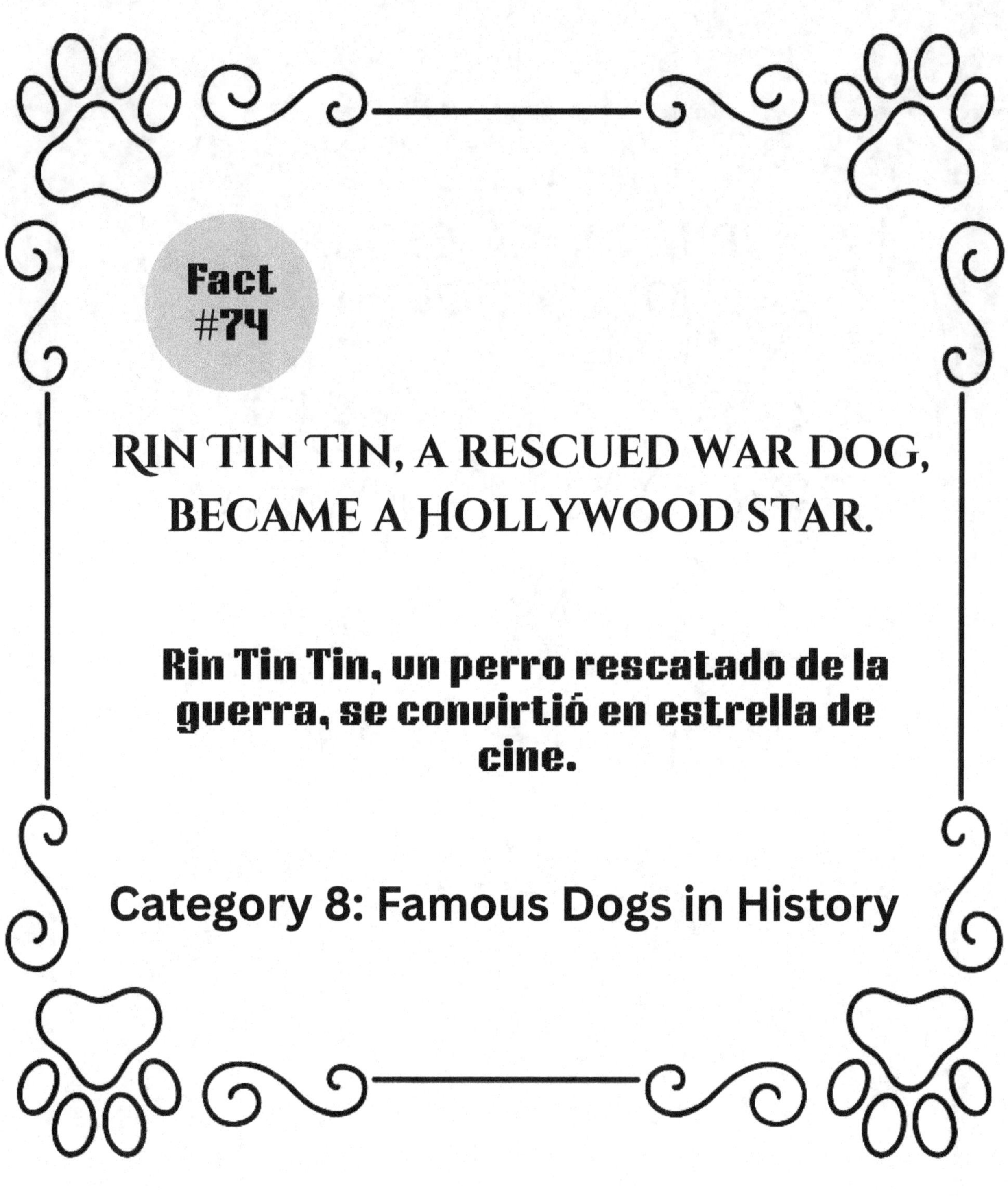

Fact #74

RIN TIN TIN, A RESCUED WAR DOG, BECAME A HOLLYWOOD STAR.

Rin Tin Tin, un perro rescatado de la guerra, se convirtió en estrella de cine.

Category 8: Famous Dogs in History

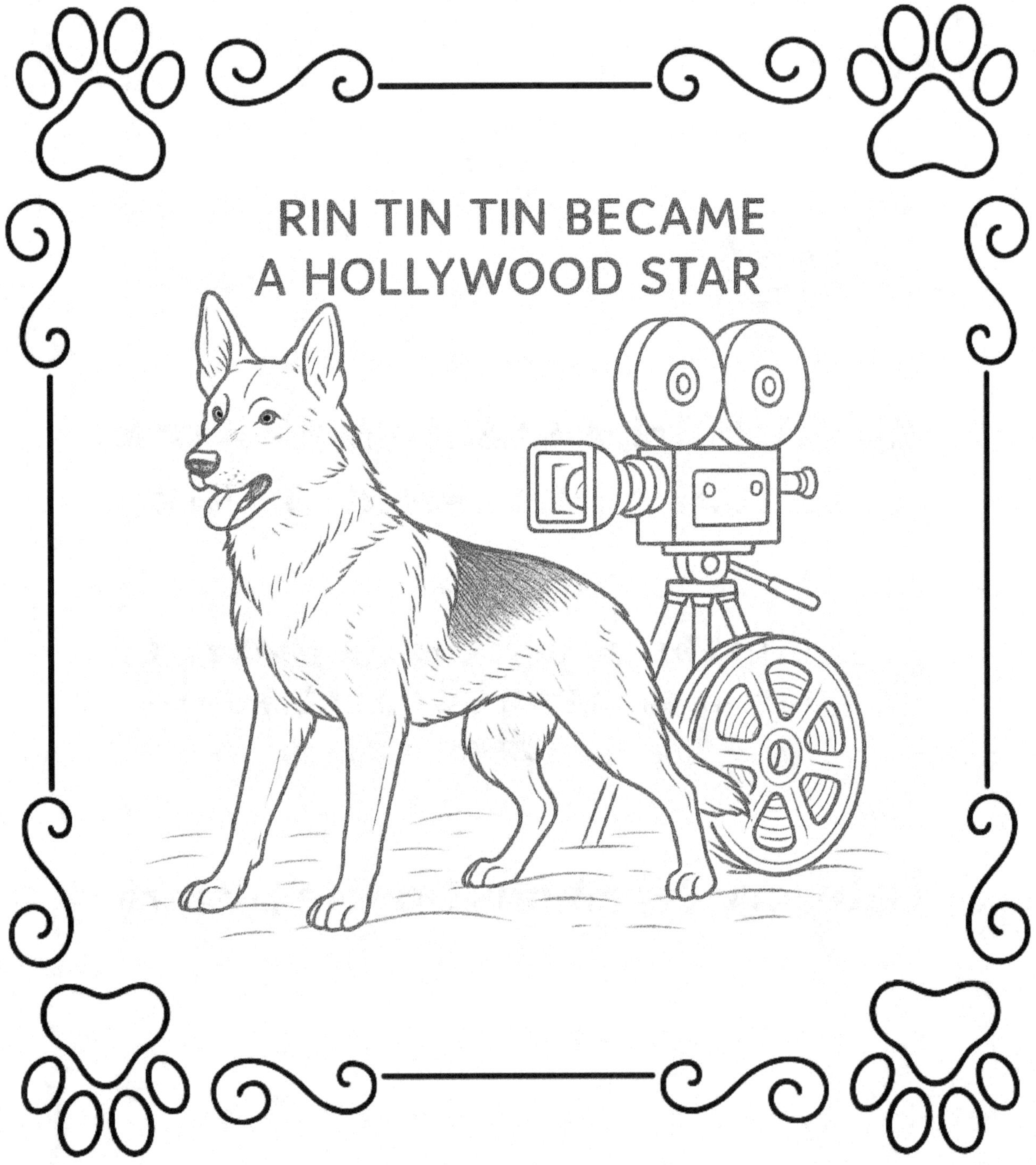
RIN TIN TIN BECAME
A HOLLYWOOD STAR

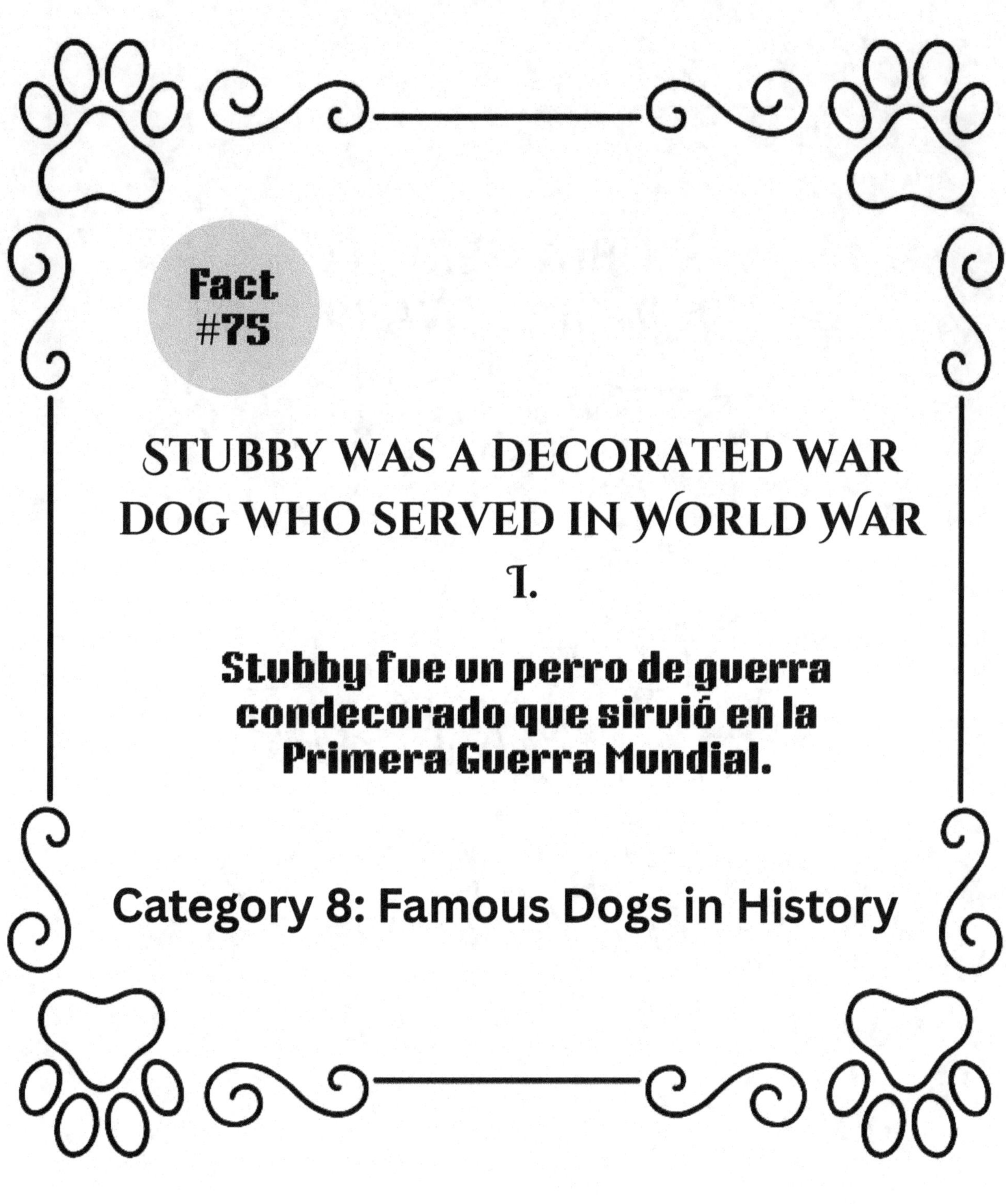

STUBBY WAS A DECORATED WAR DOG WHO SERVED IN WORLD WAR 1.

Stubby fue un perro de guerra condecorado que sirvió en la Primera Guerra Mundial.

Category 8: Famous Dogs in History

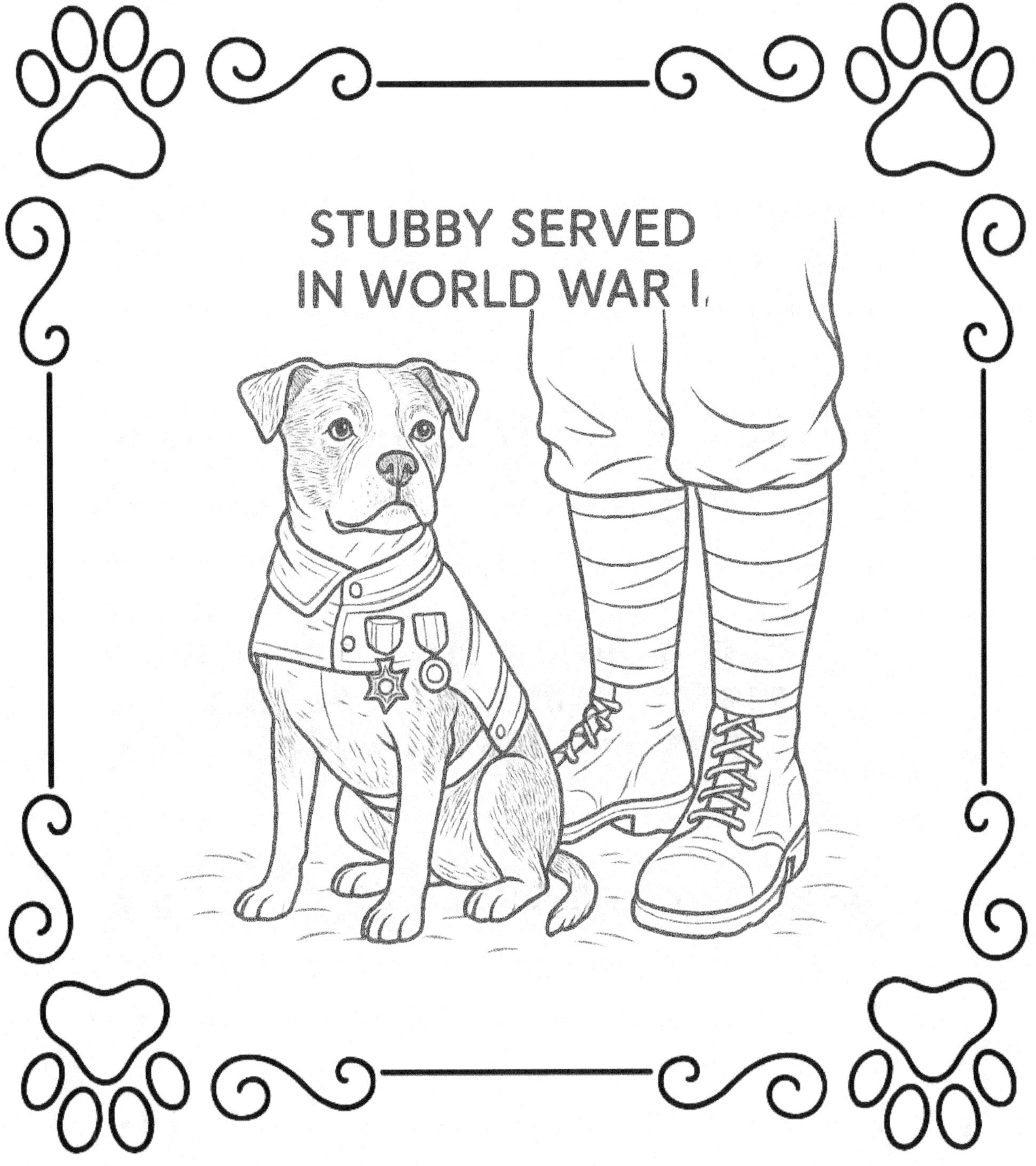

STUBBY SERVED
IN WORLD WAR I.

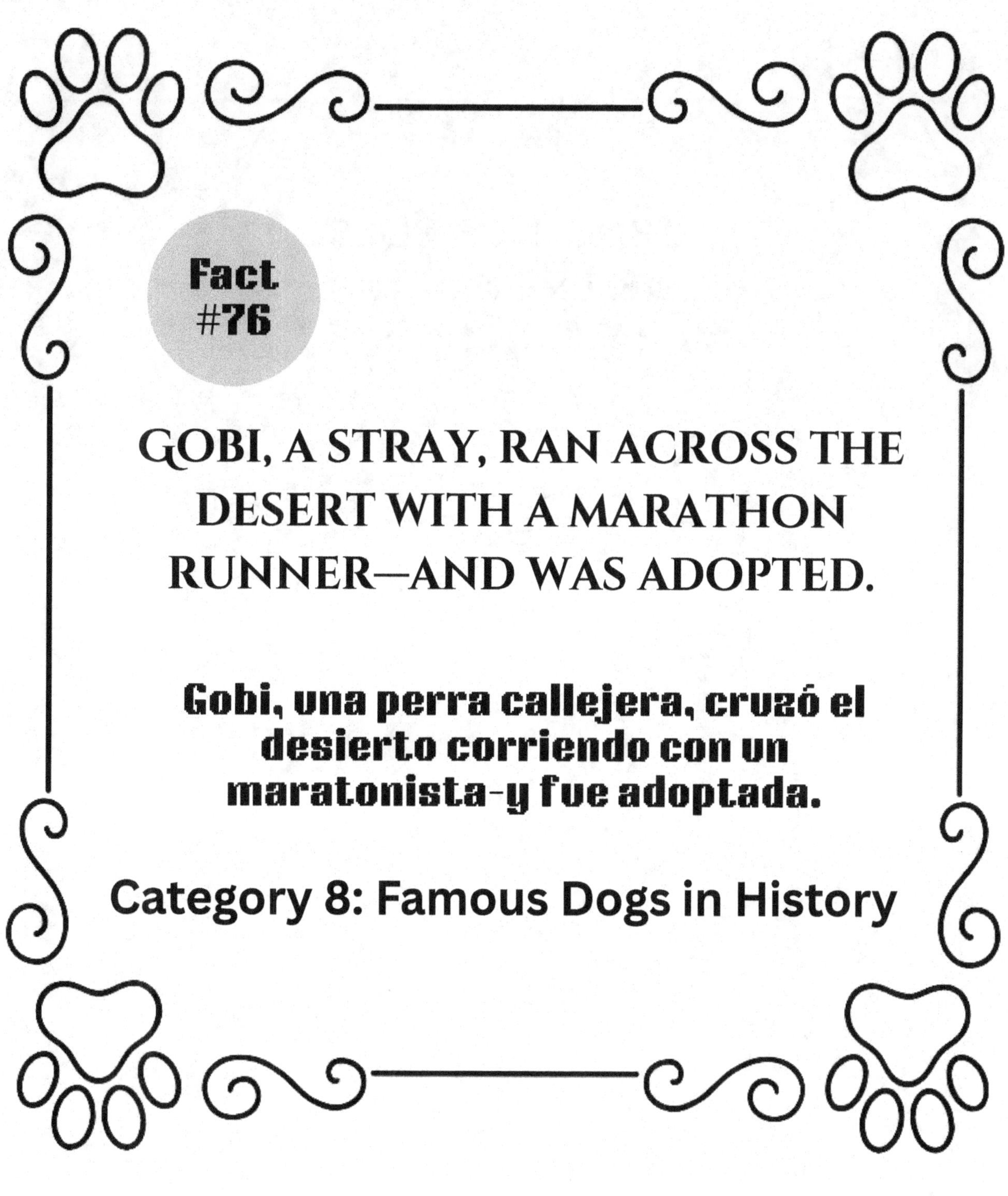

Fact
#76

GOBI, A STRAY, RAN ACROSS THE DESERT WITH A MARATHON RUNNER—AND WAS ADOPTED.

Gobi, una perra callejera, cruzó el desierto corriendo con un maratonista-y fue adoptada.

Category 8: Famous Dogs in History

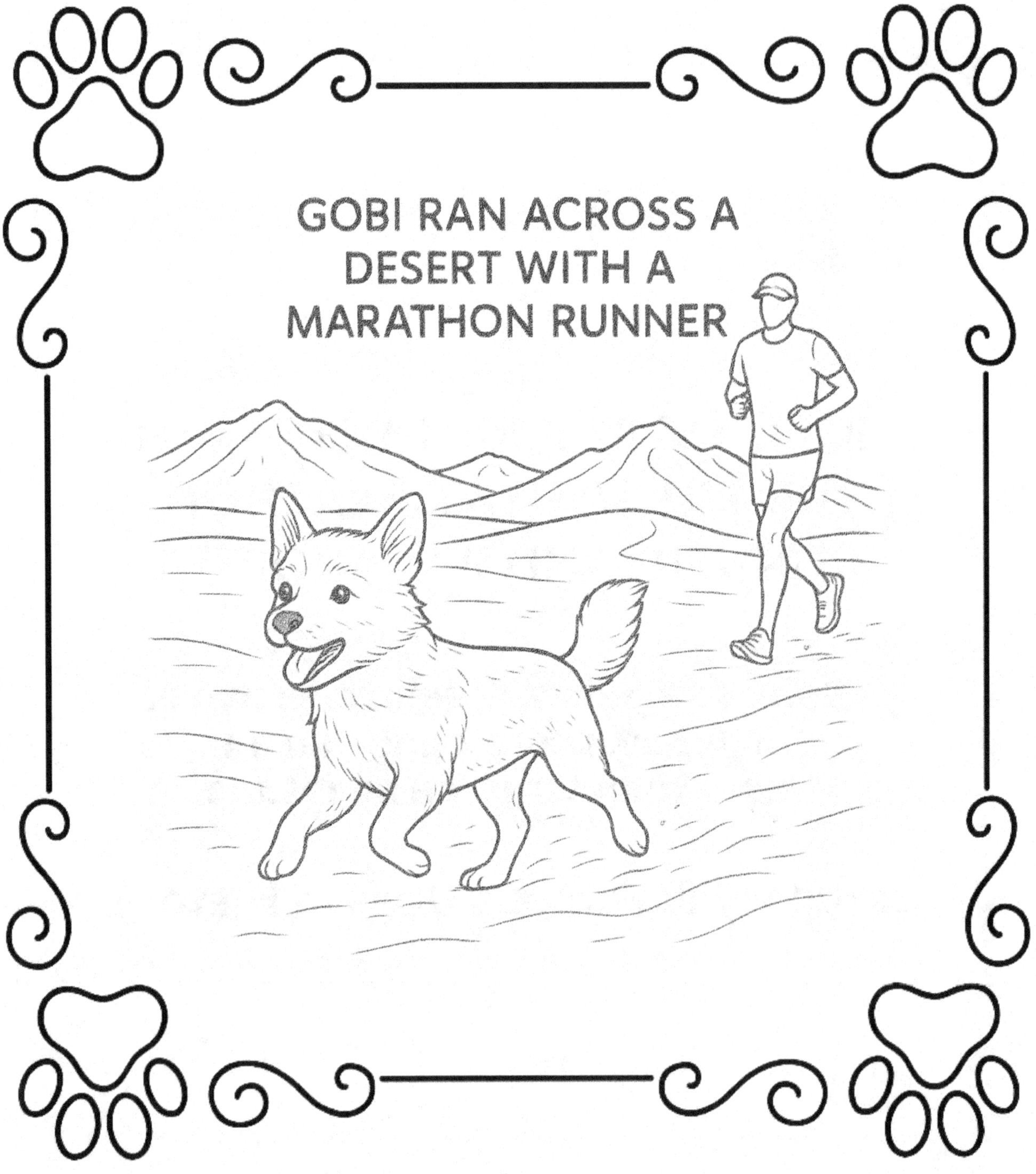
GOBI RAN ACROSS A
DESERT WITH A
MARATHON RUNNER

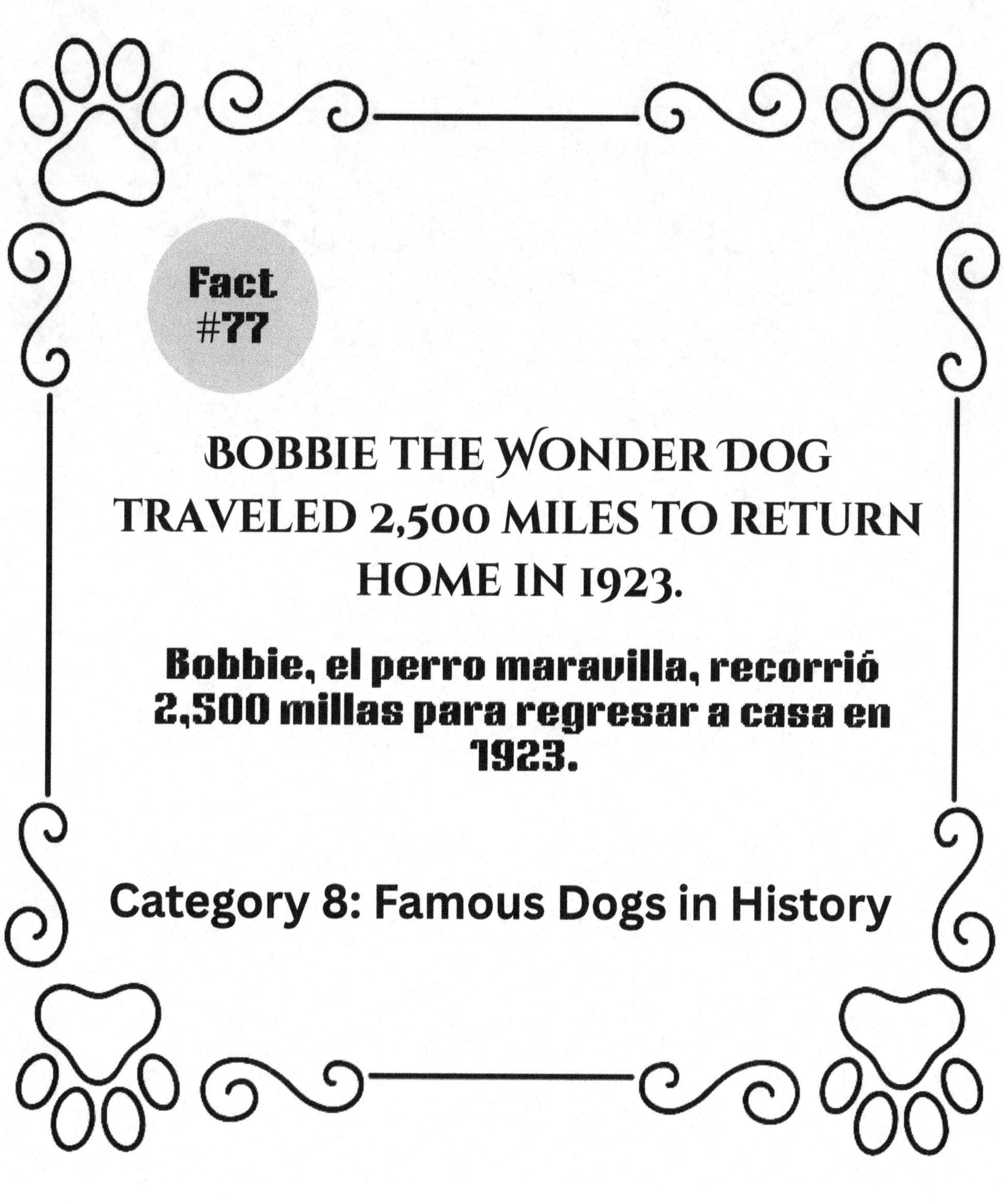

Fact
#77

BOBBIE THE WONDER DOG
TRAVELED 2,500 MILES TO RETURN
HOME IN 1923.

Bobbie, el perro maravilla, recorrió
2,500 millas para regresar a casa en
1923.

Category 8: Famous Dogs in History

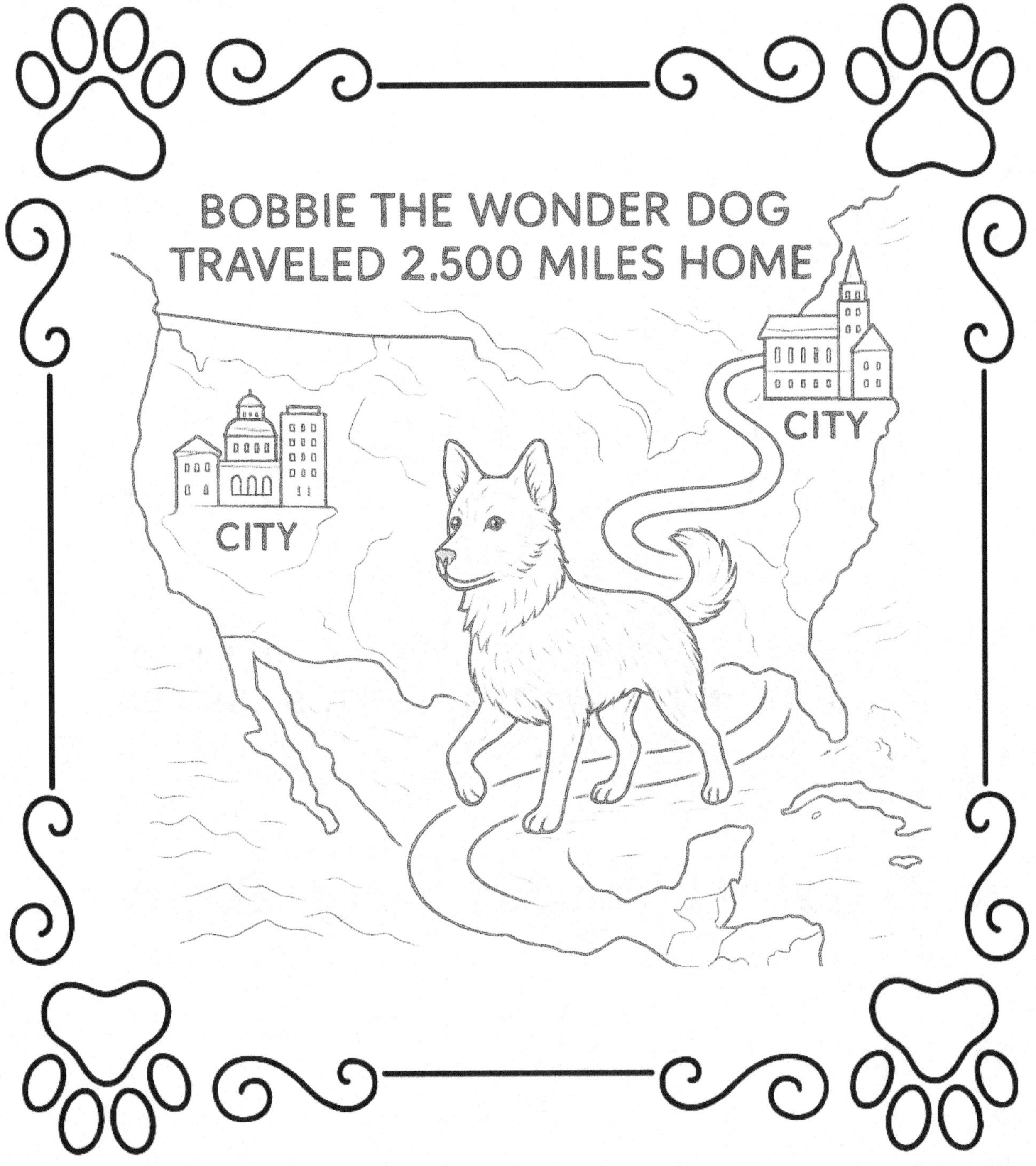
BOBBIE THE WONDER DOG
TRAVELED 2,500 MILES HOME
CITY
CITY

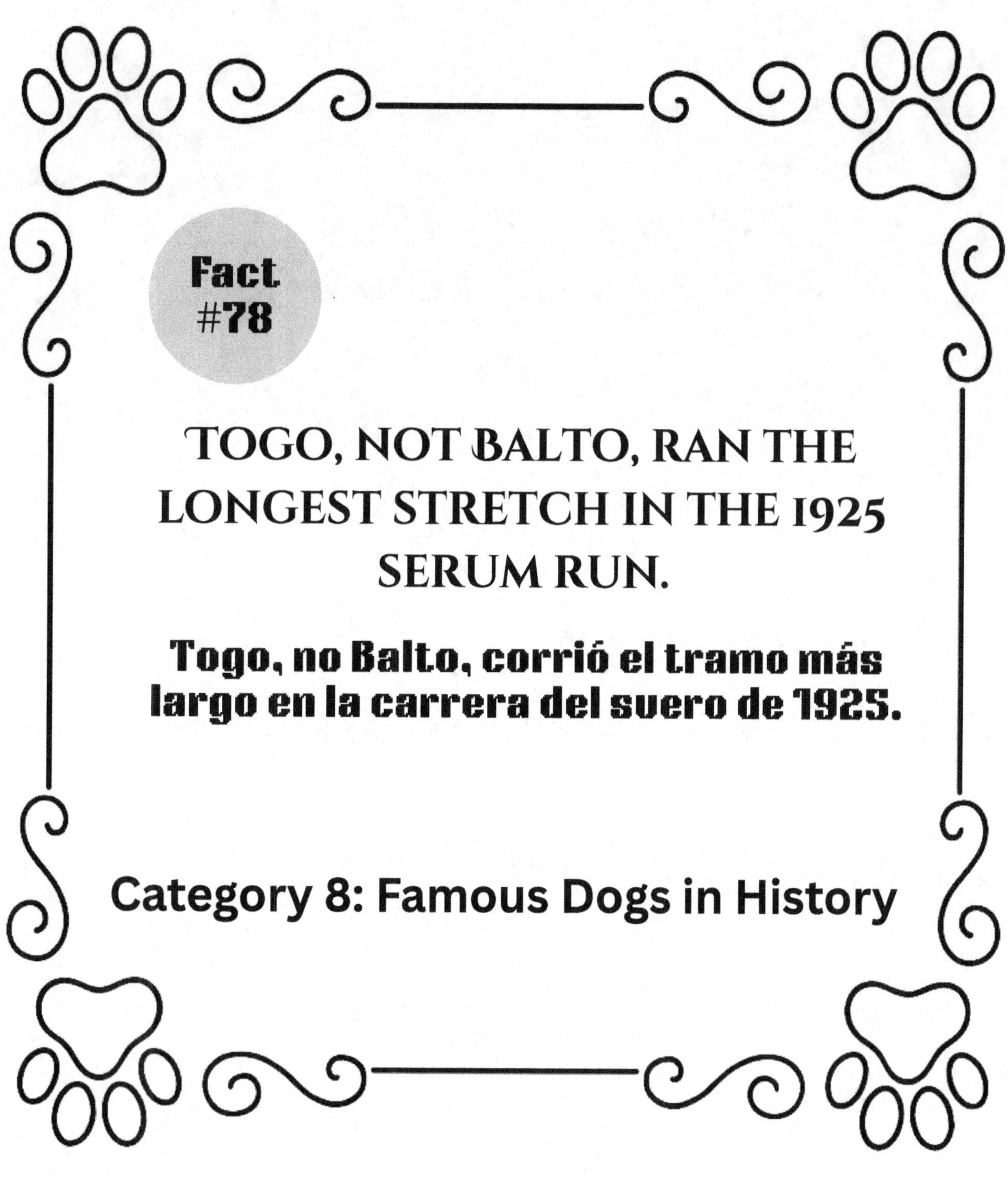

Fact #78

TOGO, NOT BALTO, RAN THE LONGEST STRETCH IN THE 1925 SERUM RUN.

Togo, no Balto, corrió el tramo más largo en la carrera del suero de 1925.

Category 8: Famous Dogs in History

TOGO RAN THE LONGEST STRETCH IN THE SERUM RUN

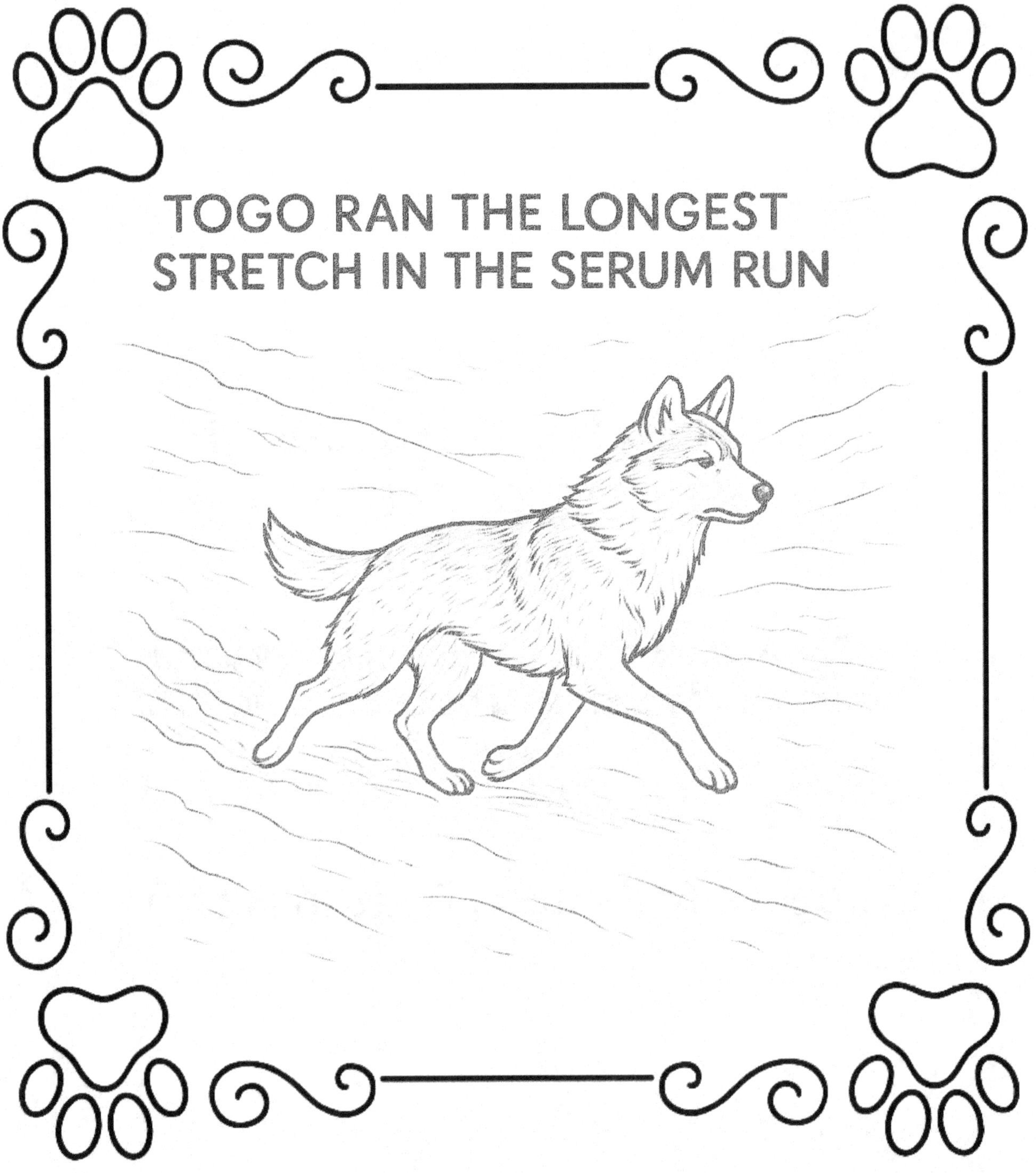

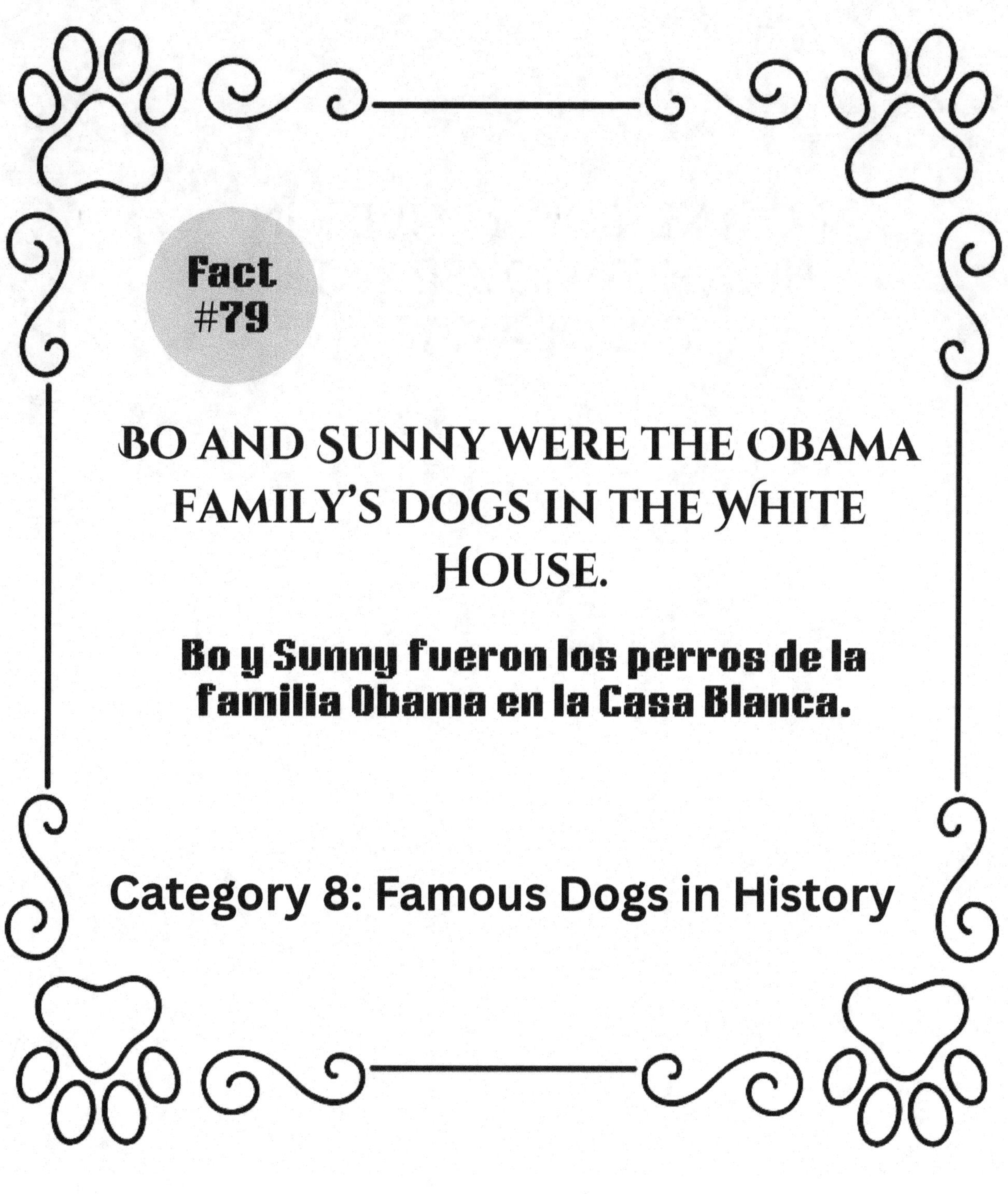

BO AND SUNNY WERE THE OBAMA FAMILY'S DOGS IN THE WHITE HOUSE.

Bo y Sunny fueron los perros de la familia Obama en la Casa Blanca.

Category 8: Famous Dogs in History

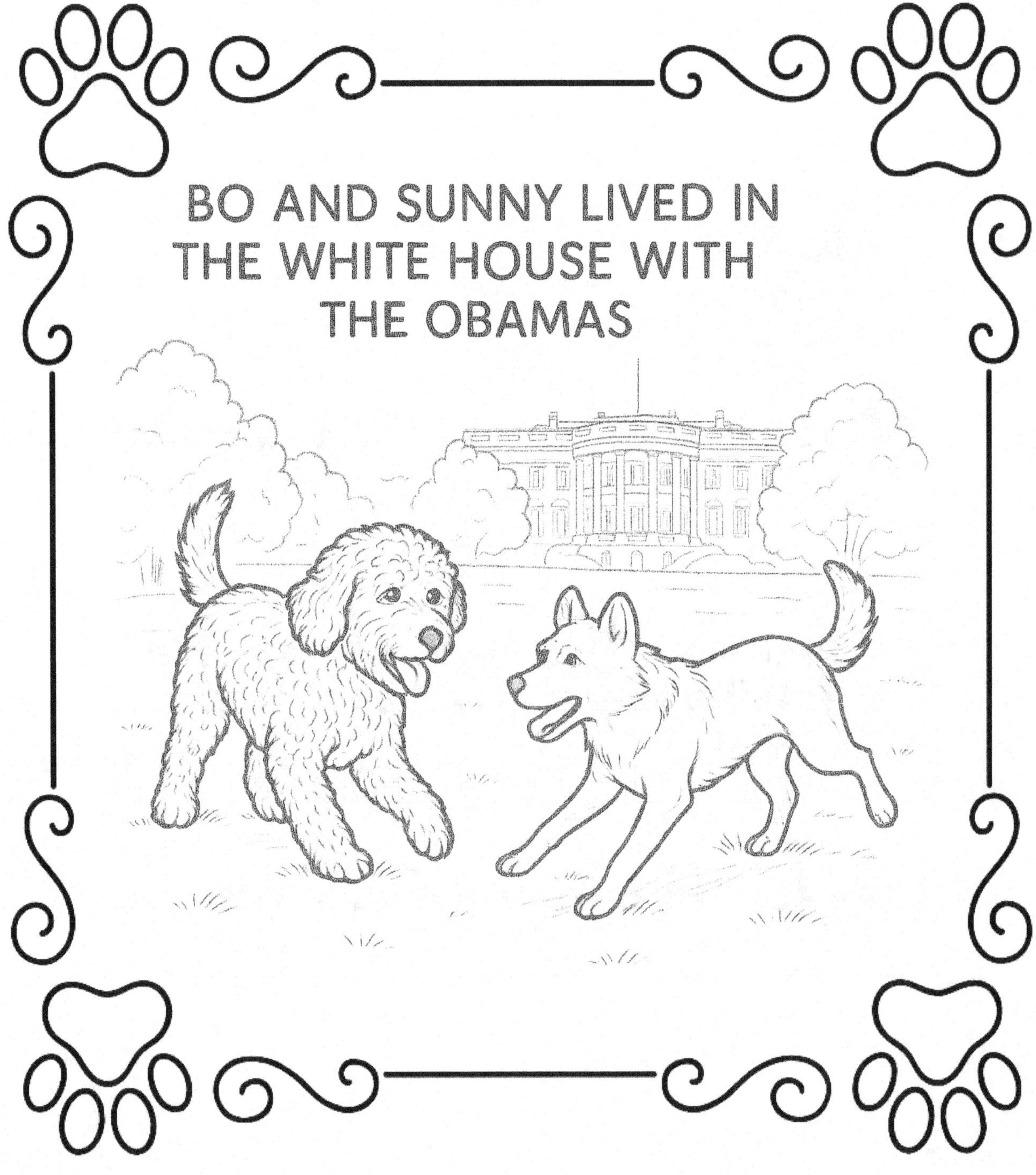

BO AND SUNNY LIVED IN
THE WHITE HOUSE WITH
THE OBAMAS

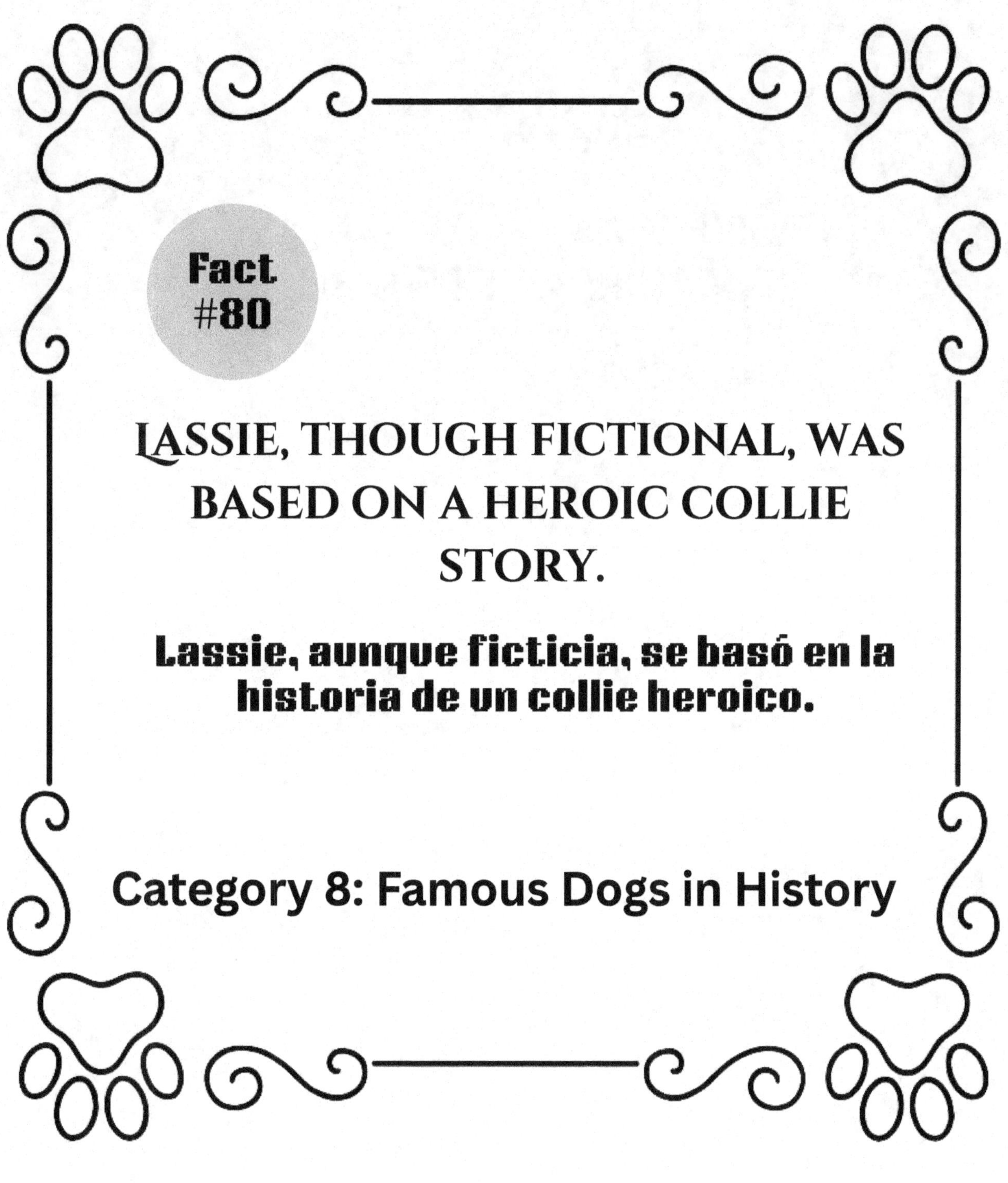

LASSIE, THOUGH FICTIONAL, WAS BASED ON A HEROIC COLLIE STORY.

Lassie, aunque ficticia, se basó en la historia de un collie heroico.

Category 8: Famous Dogs in History

LASSIE WAS BASED ON A HEROIC REAL-LIFE COLLIE

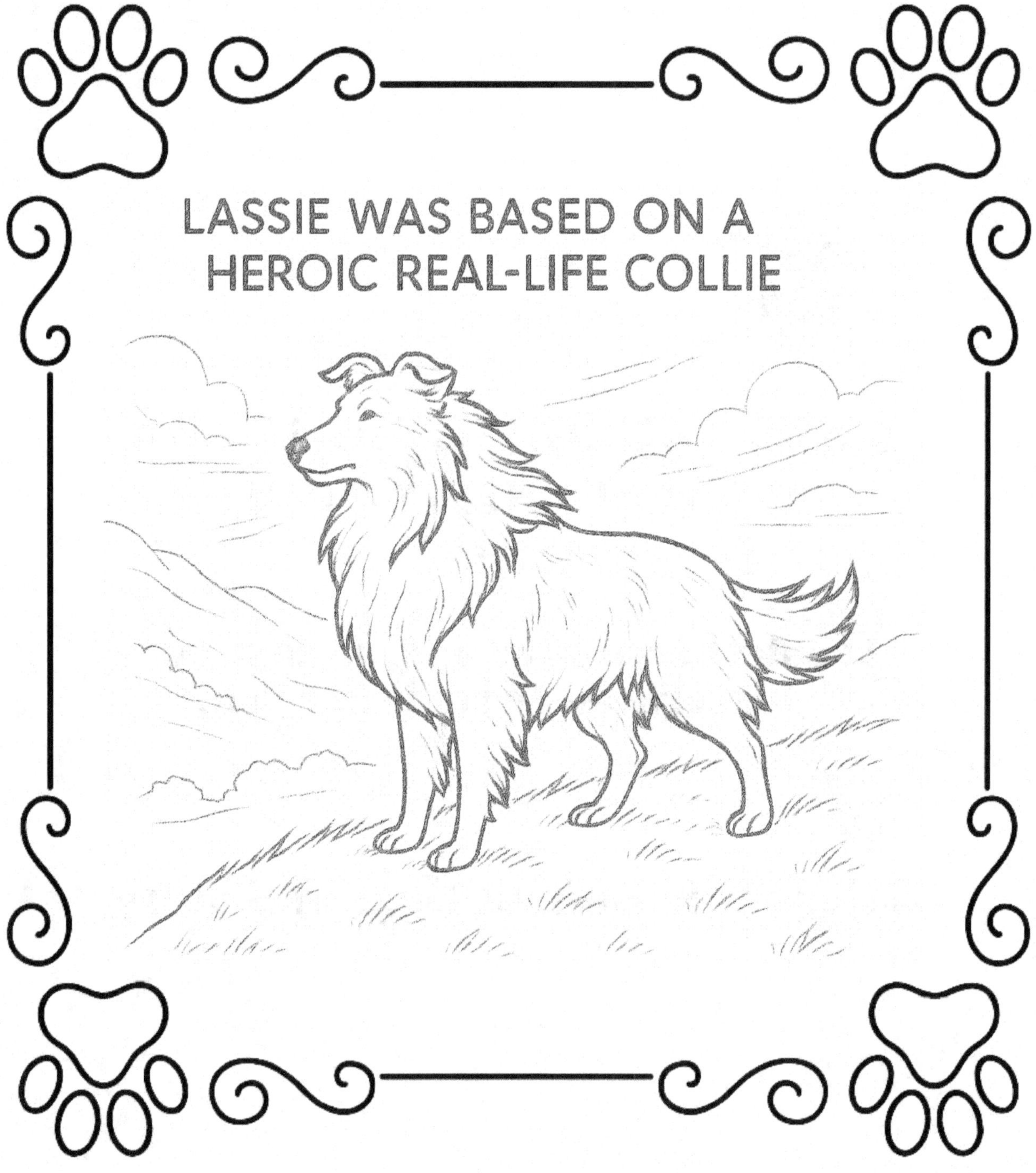

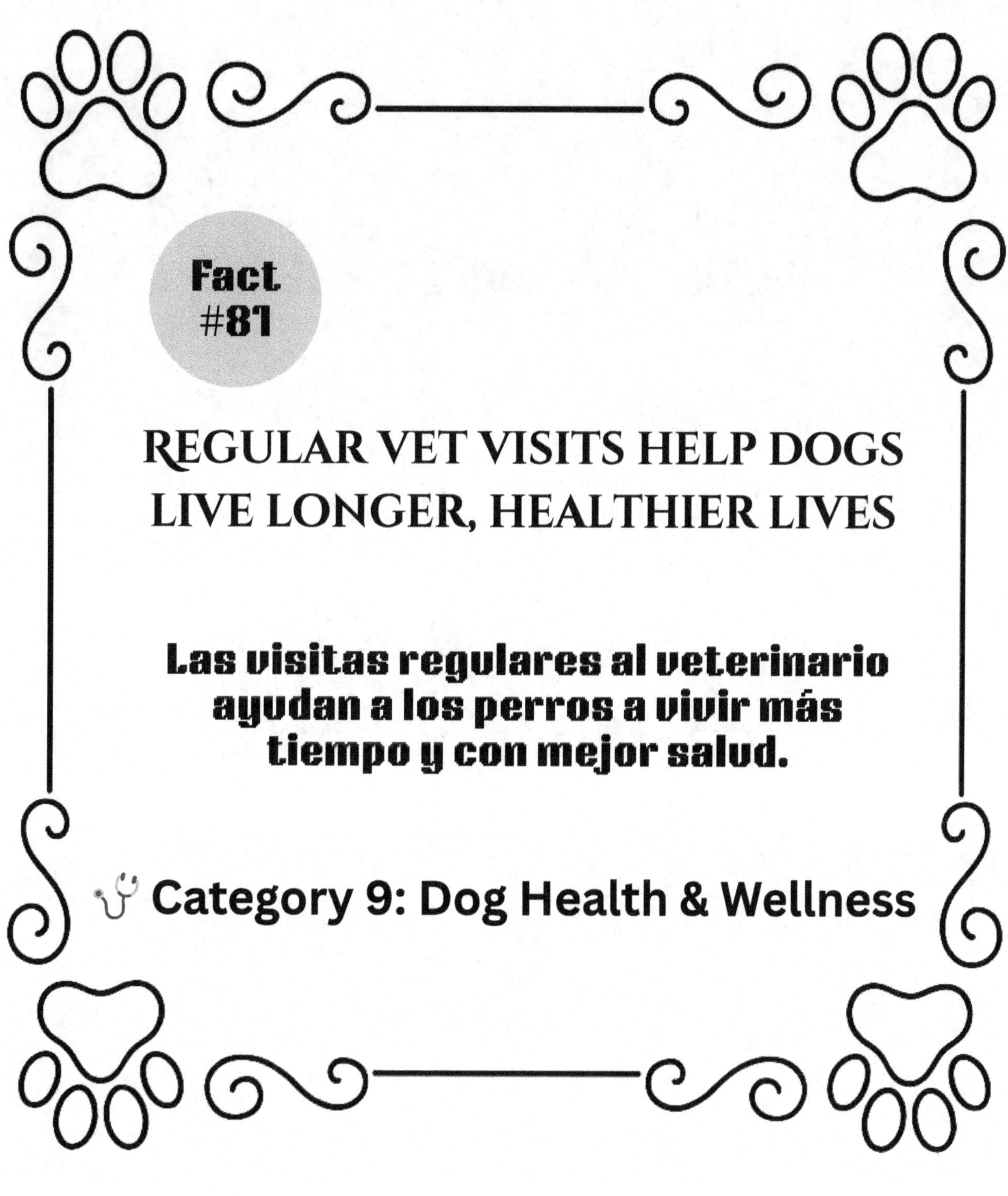

Fact #81
REGULAR VET VISITS HELP DOGS LIVE LONGER, HEALTHIER LIVES
Las visitas regulares al veterinario ayudan a los perros a vivir más tiempo y con mejor salud.
Category 9: Dog Health & Wellness

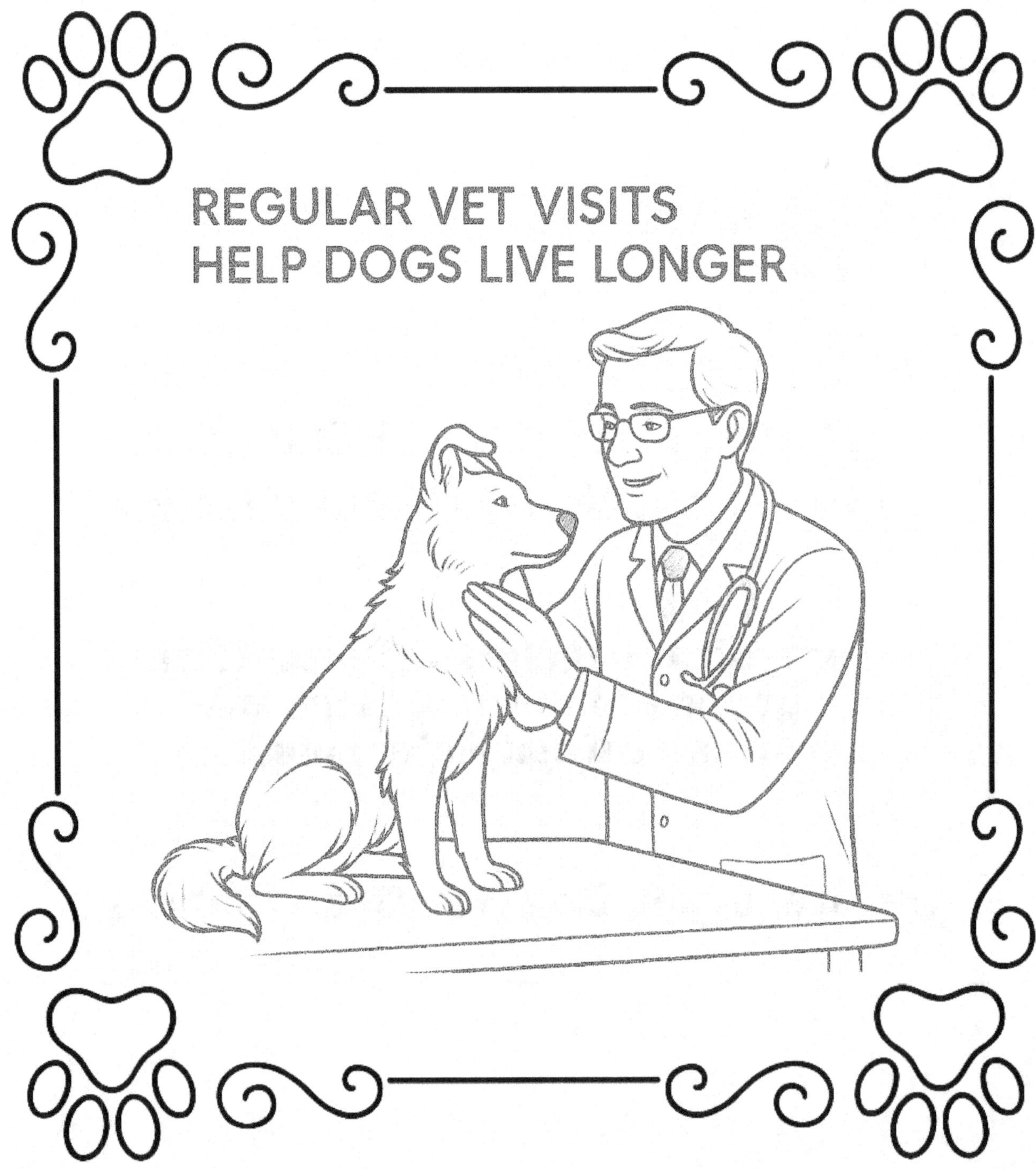
REGULAR VET VISITS
HELP DOGS LIVE LONGER

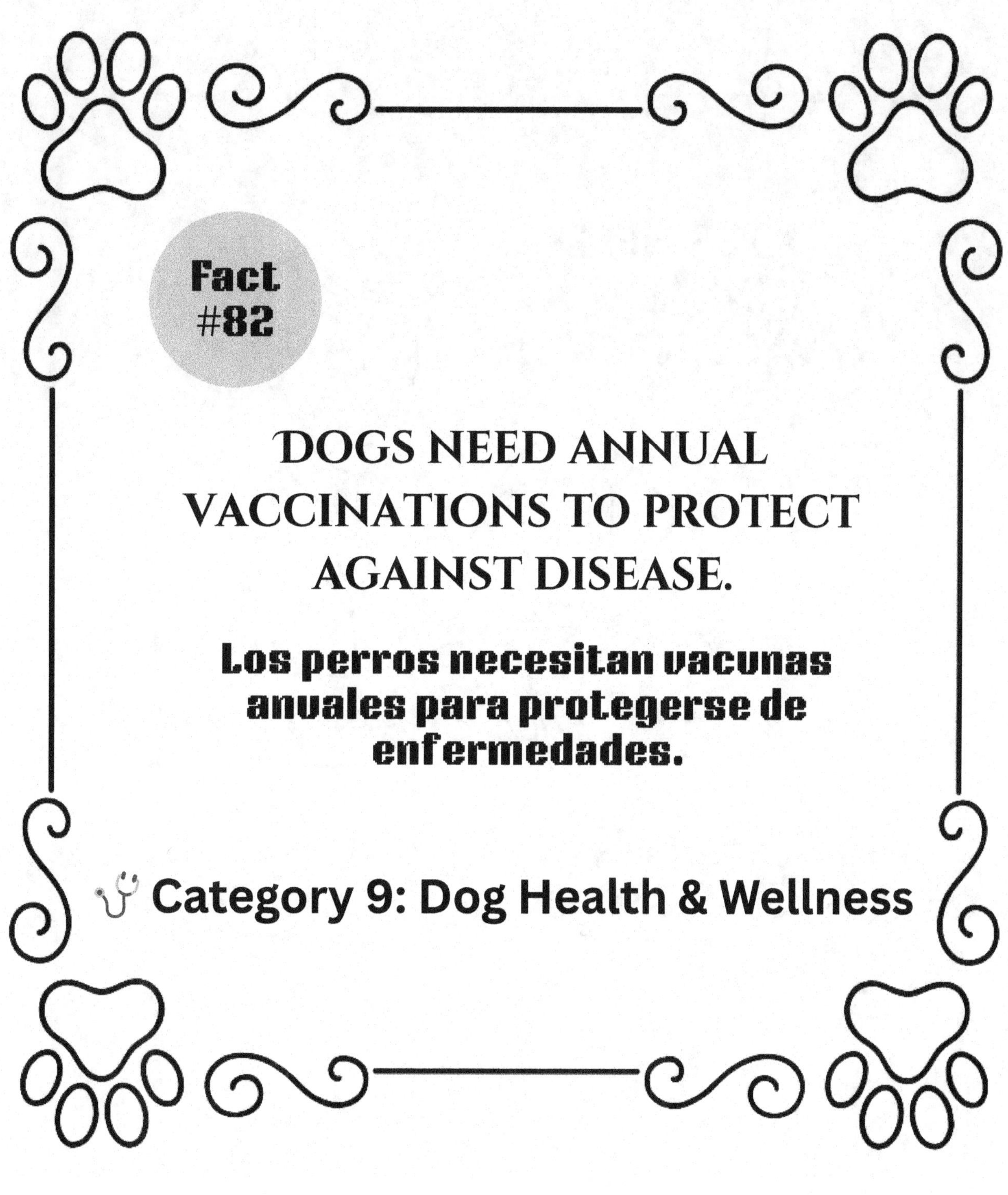

Fact #82

DOGS NEED ANNUAL VACCINATIONS TO PROTECT AGAINST DISEASE.

Los perros necesitan vacunas anuales para protegerse de enfermedades.

Category 9: Dog Health & Wellness

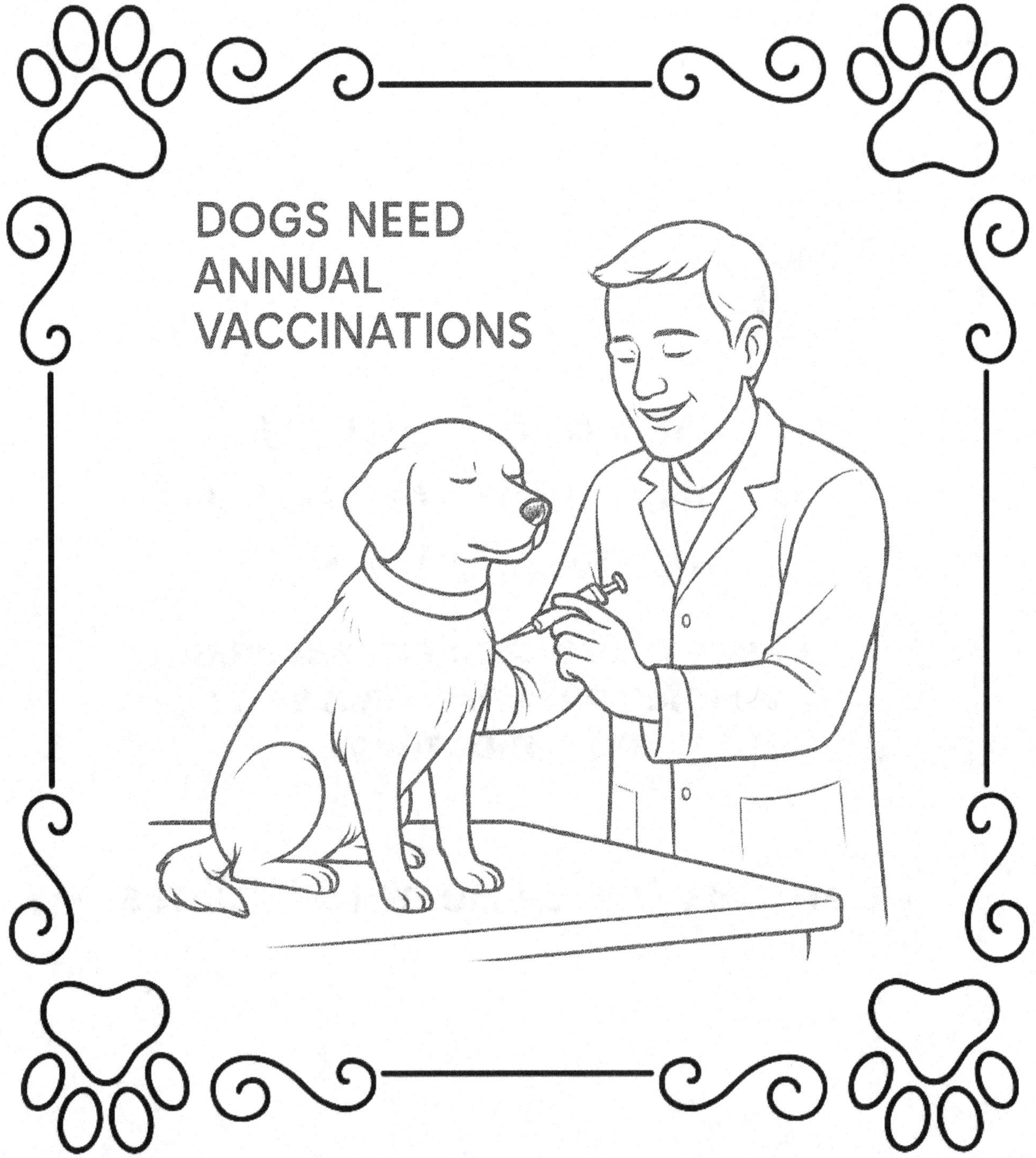
DOGS NEED
ANNUAL
VACCINATIONS

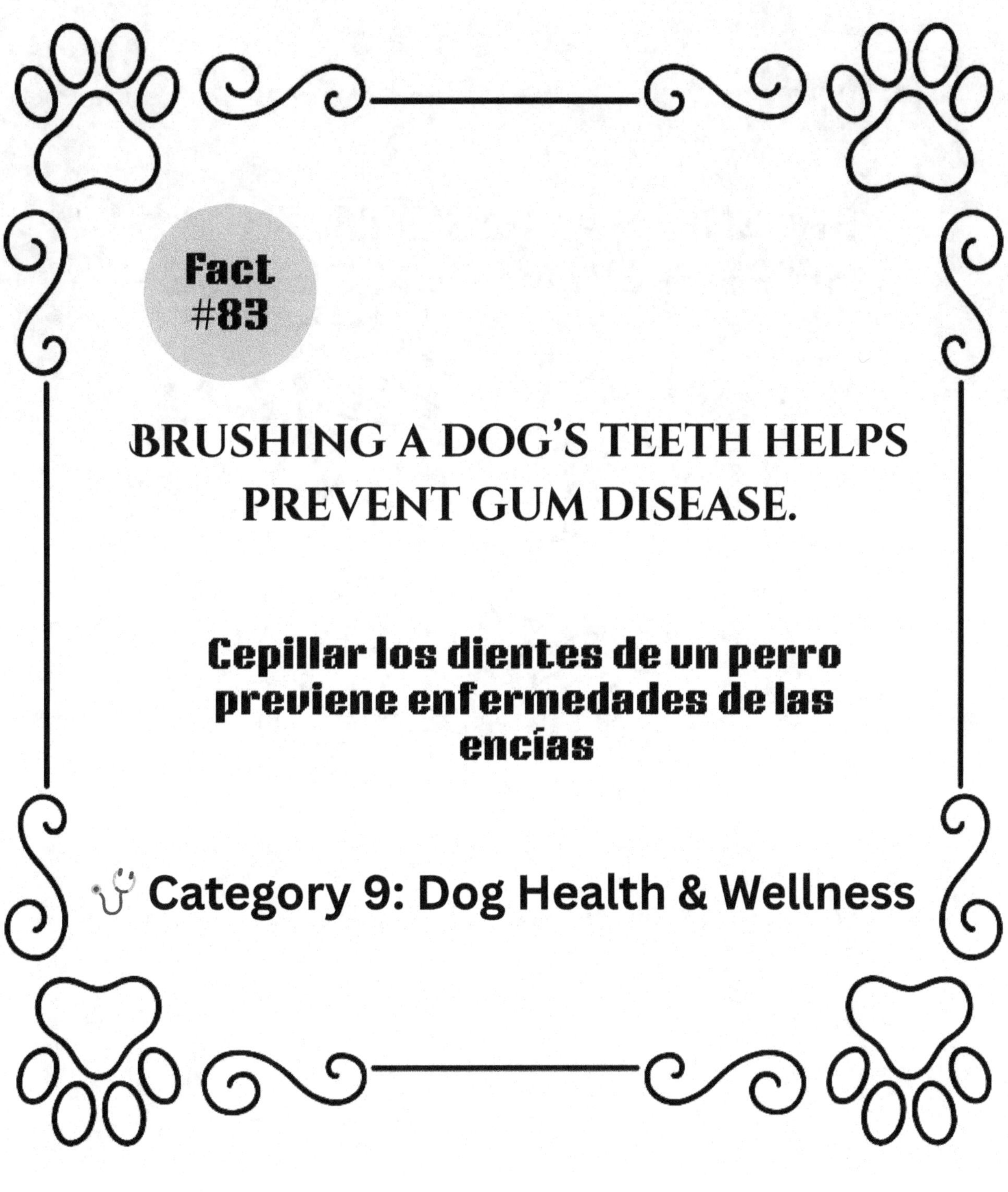

Fact #83

BRUSHING A DOG'S TEETH HELPS PREVENT GUM DISEASE.

Cepillar los dientes de un perro previene enfermedades de las encías

Category 9: Dog Health & Wellness

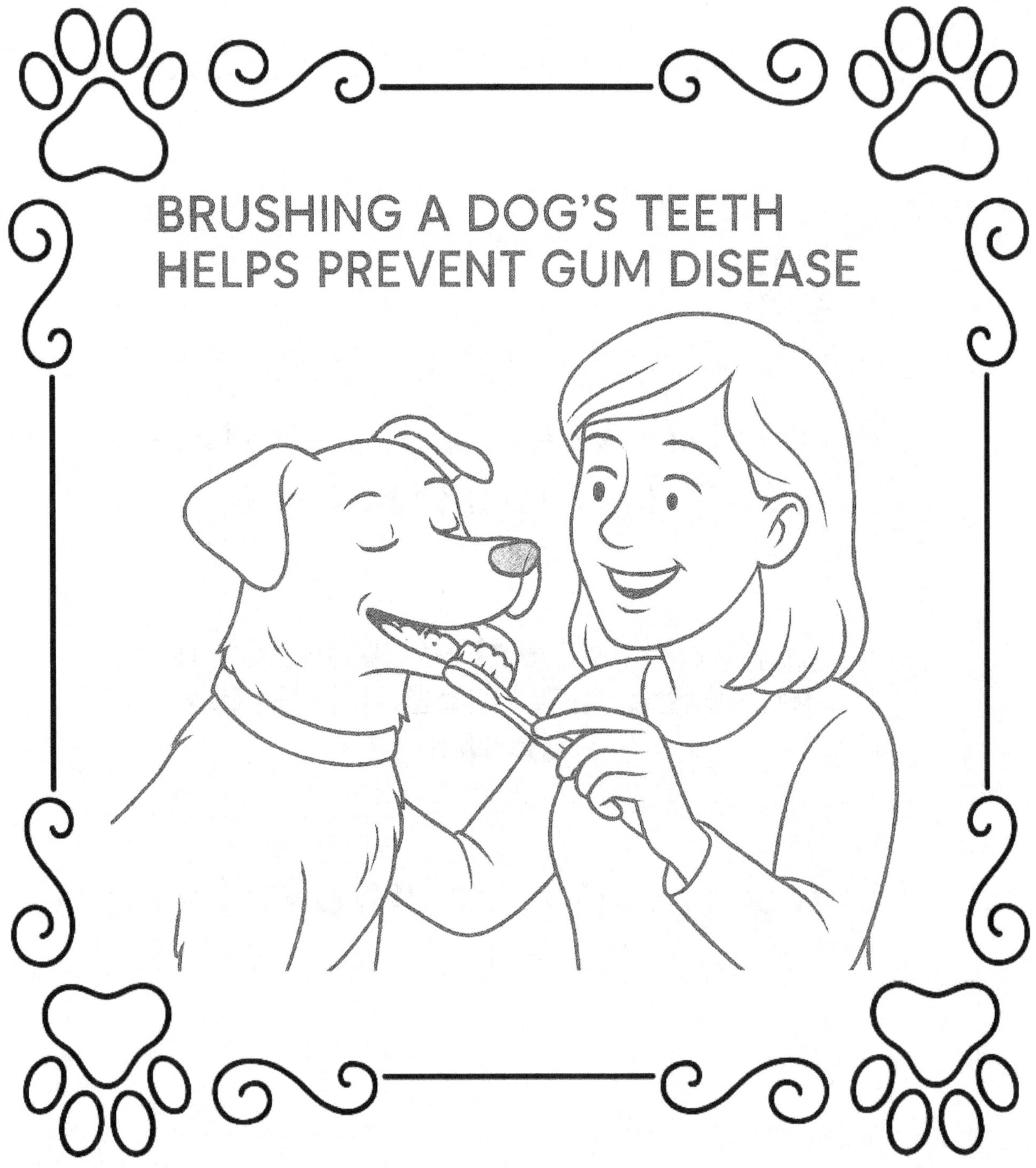
BRUSHING A DOG'S TEETH
HELPS PREVENT GUM DISEASE

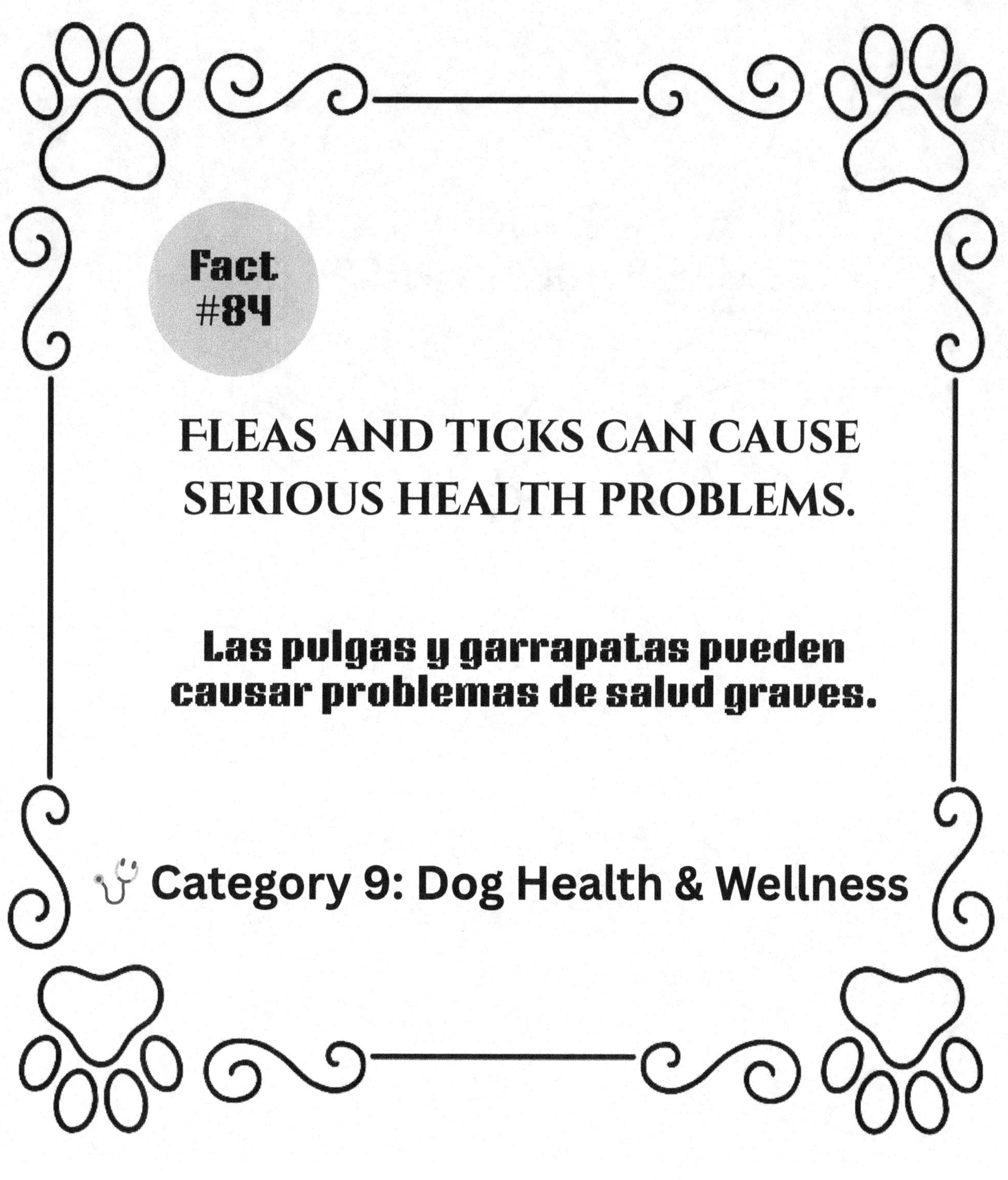
Fact #84

FLEAS AND TICKS CAN CAUSE SERIOUS HEALTH PROBLEMS.

Las pulgas y garrapatas pueden causar problemas de salud graves.

Category 9: Dog Health & Wellness

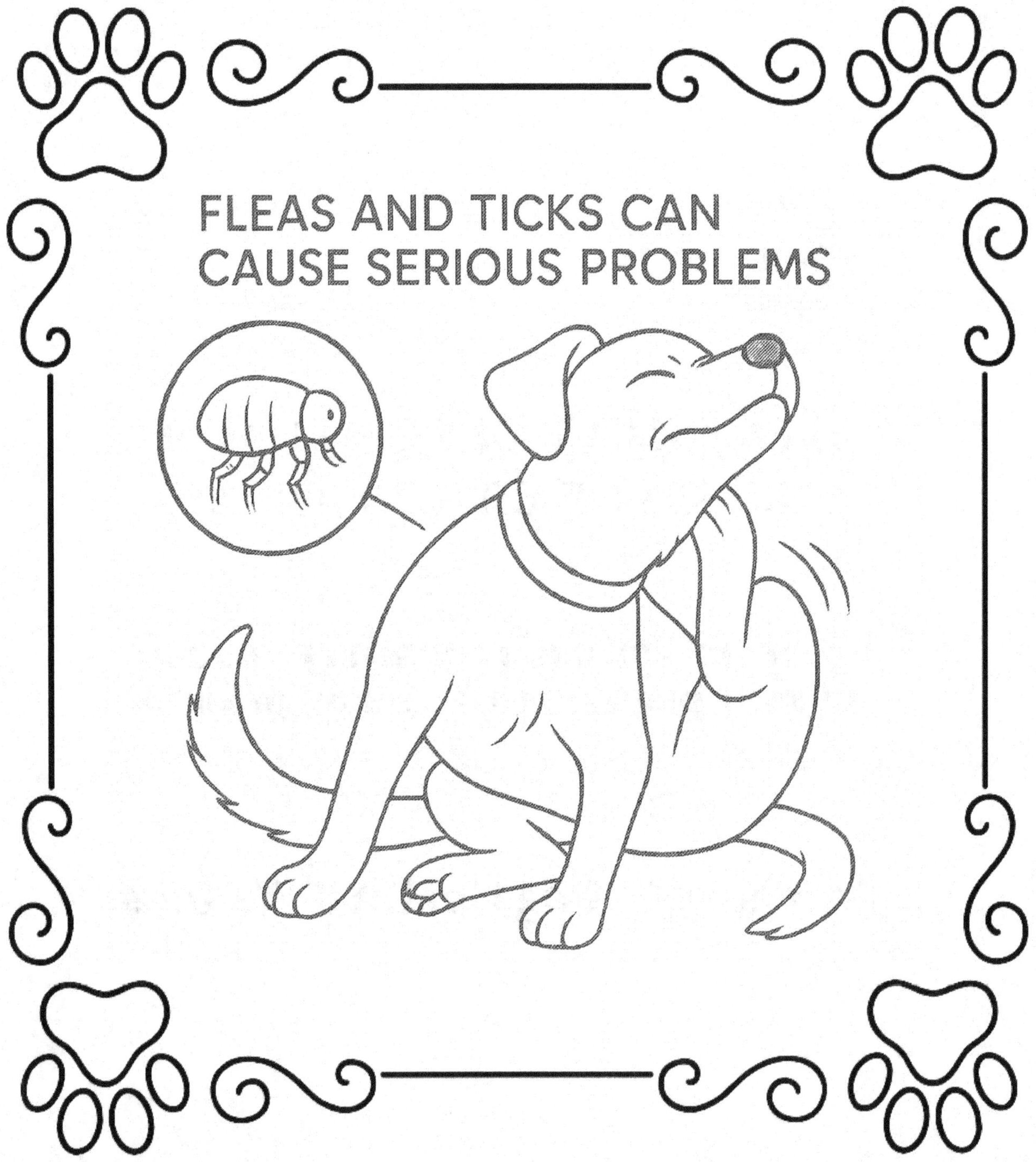
FLEAS AND TICKS CAN
CAUSE SERIOUS PROBLEMS

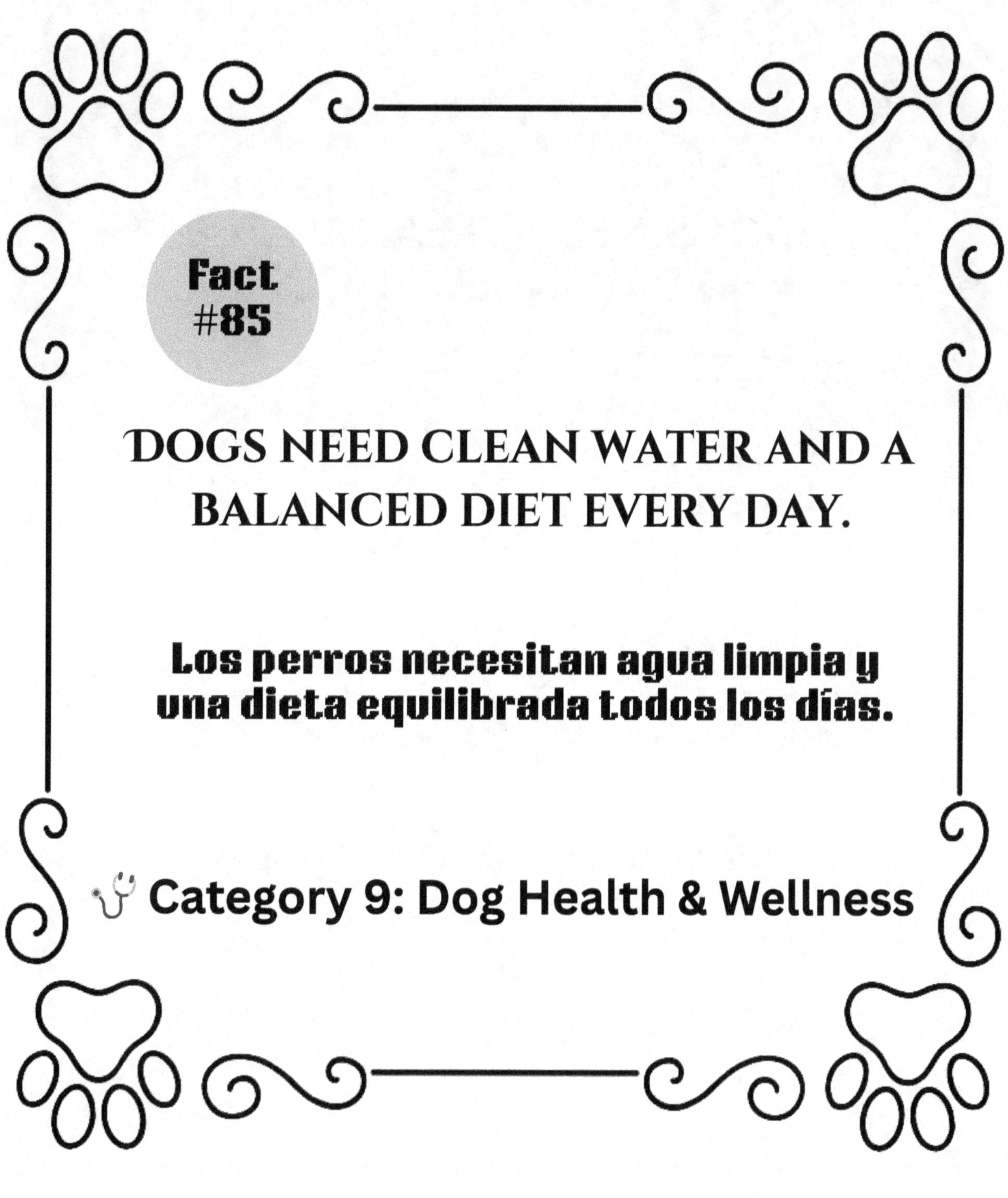

Fact
#85

DOGS NEED CLEAN WATER AND A
BALANCED DIET EVERY DAY.

Los perros necesitan agua limpia y
una dieta equilibrada todos los días.

Category 9: Dog Health & Wellness

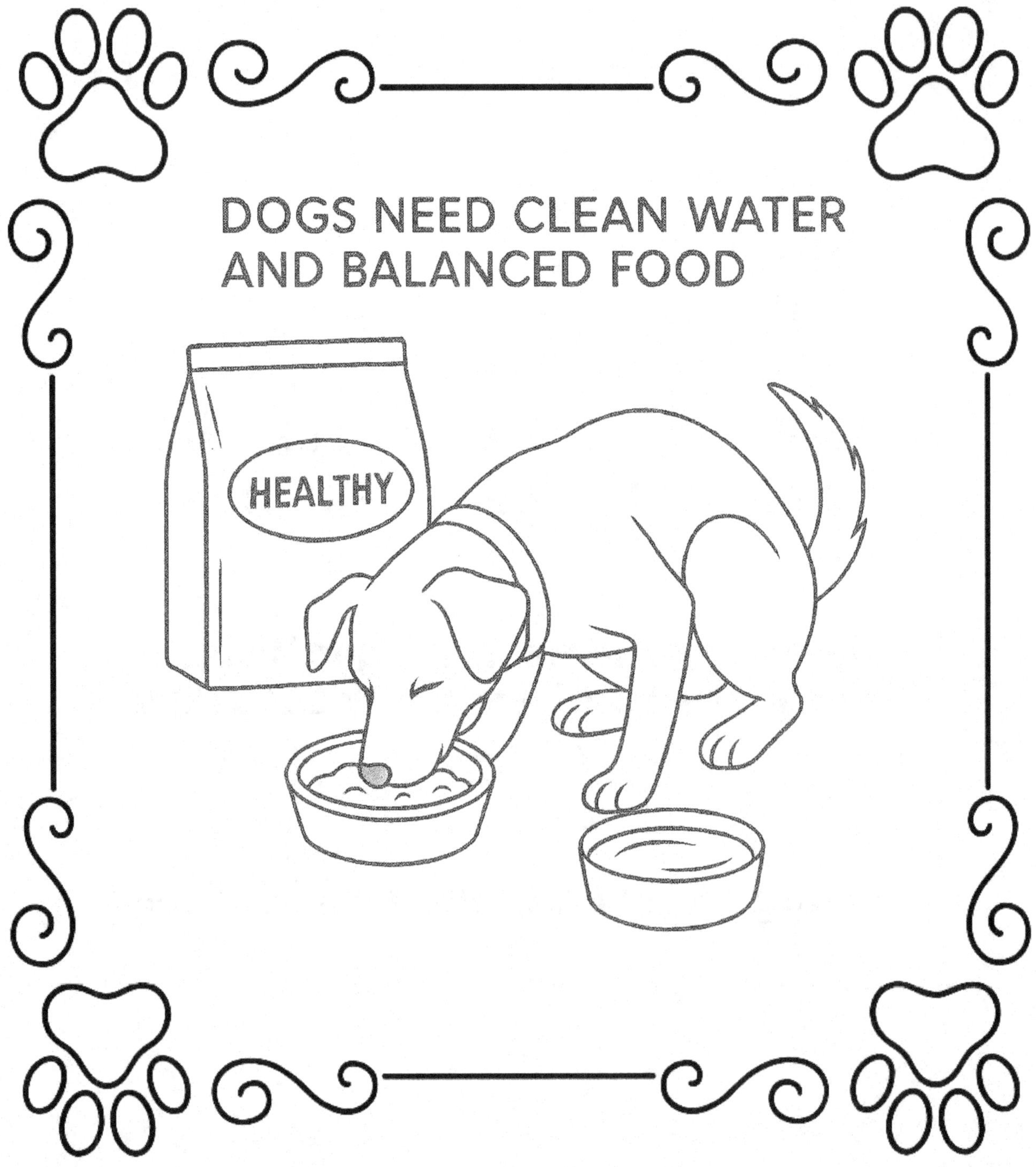

DOGS NEED CLEAN WATER
AND BALANCED FOOD
HEALTHY

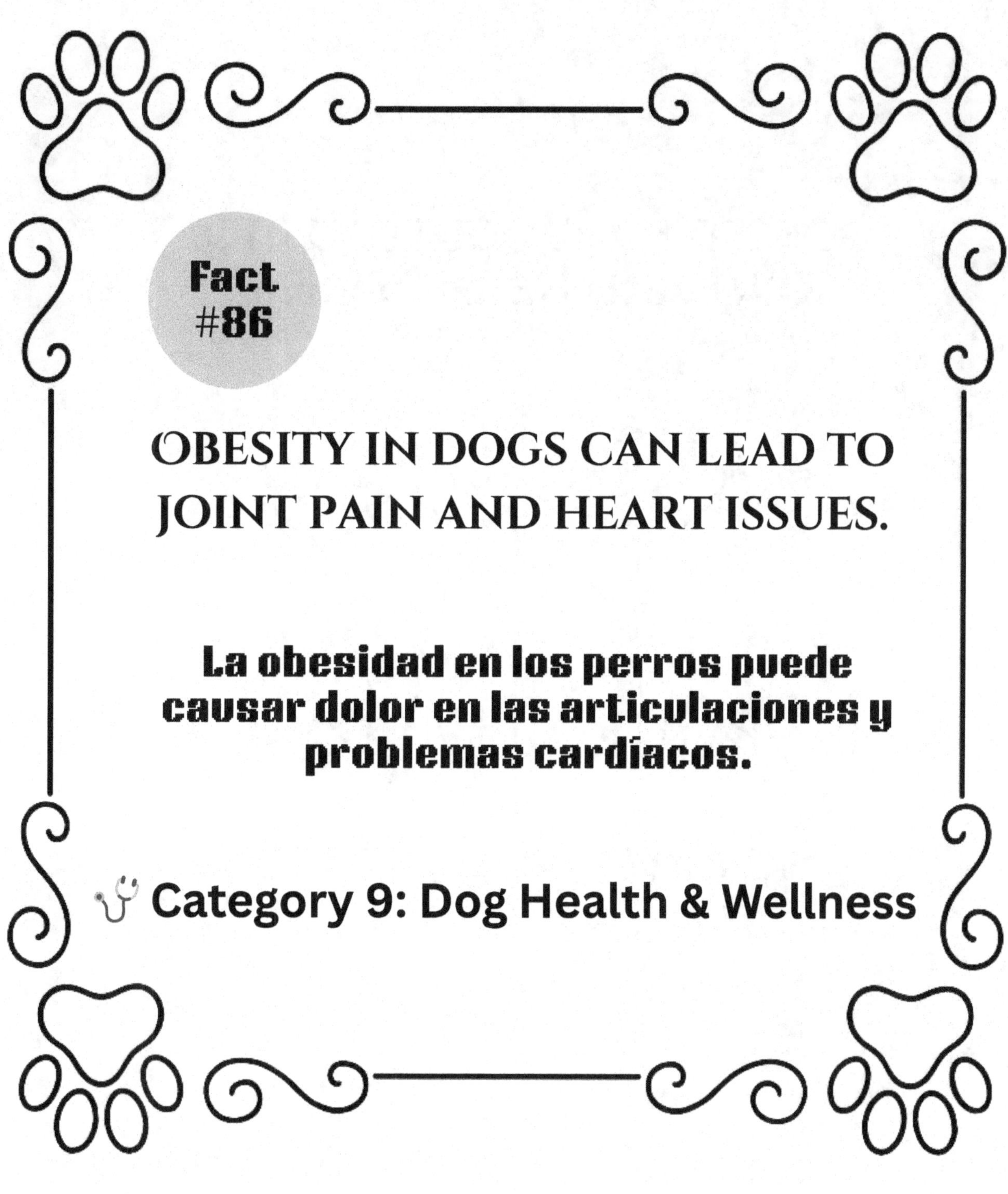

Fact #86

OBESITY IN DOGS CAN LEAD TO JOINT PAIN AND HEART ISSUES.

La obesidad en los perros puede causar dolor en las articulaciones y problemas cardíacos.

Category 9: Dog Health & Wellness

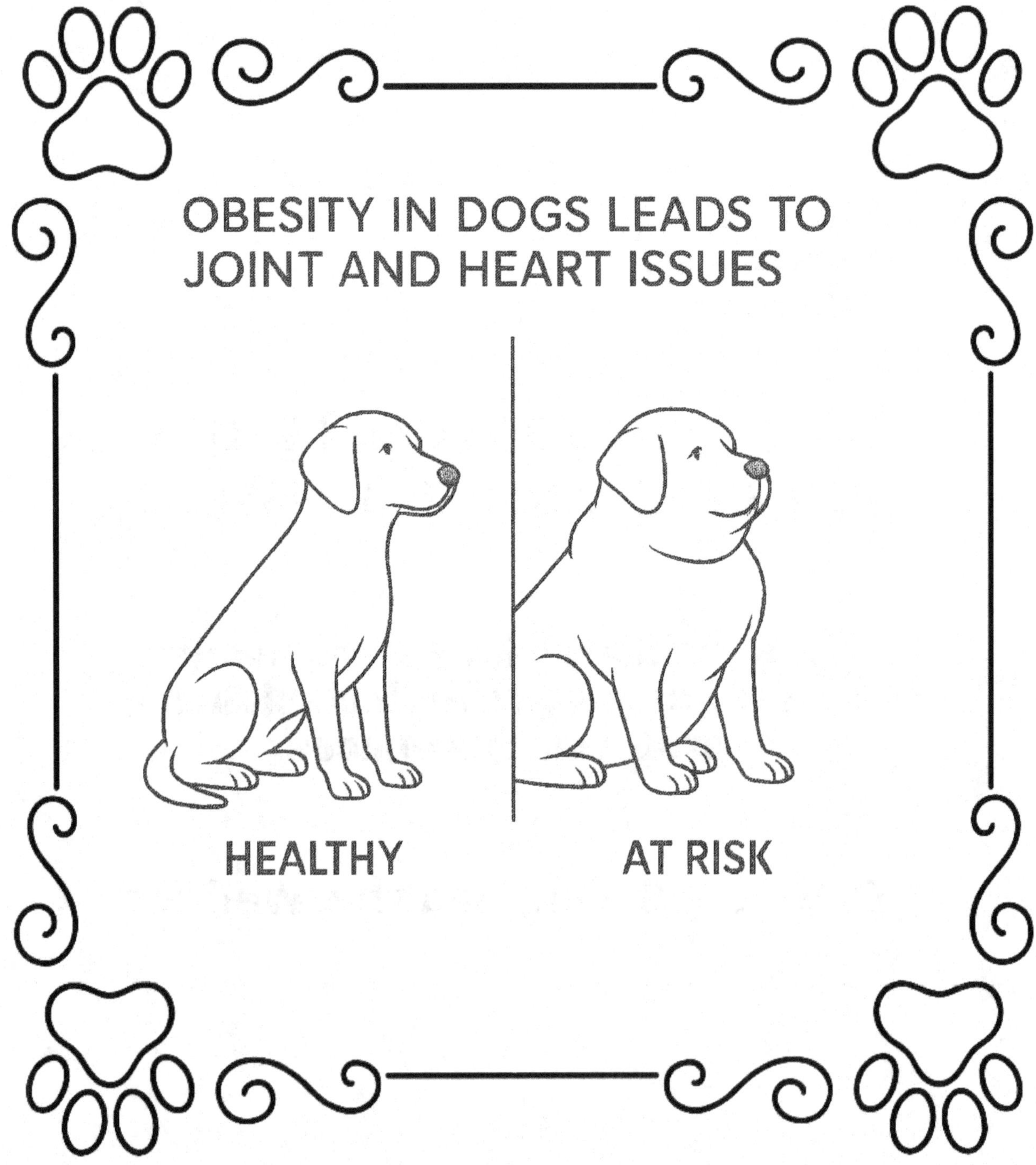

OBESITY IN DOGS LEADS TO
JOINT AND HEART ISSUES
HEALTHY
AT RISK

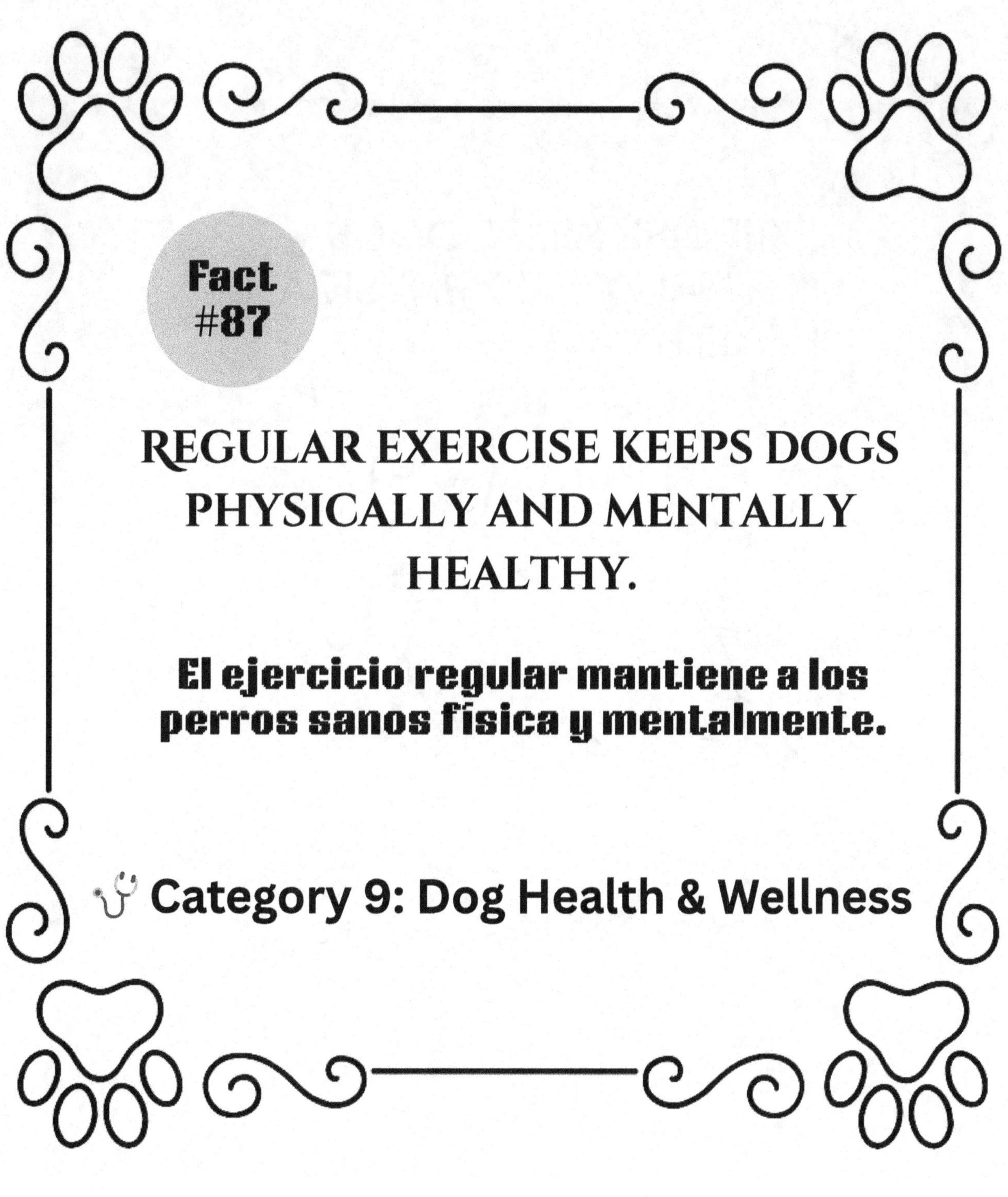

Fact #87

REGULAR EXERCISE KEEPS DOGS PHYSICALLY AND MENTALLY HEALTHY.

El ejercicio regular mantiene a los perros sanos física y mentalmente.

Category 9: Dog Health & Wellness

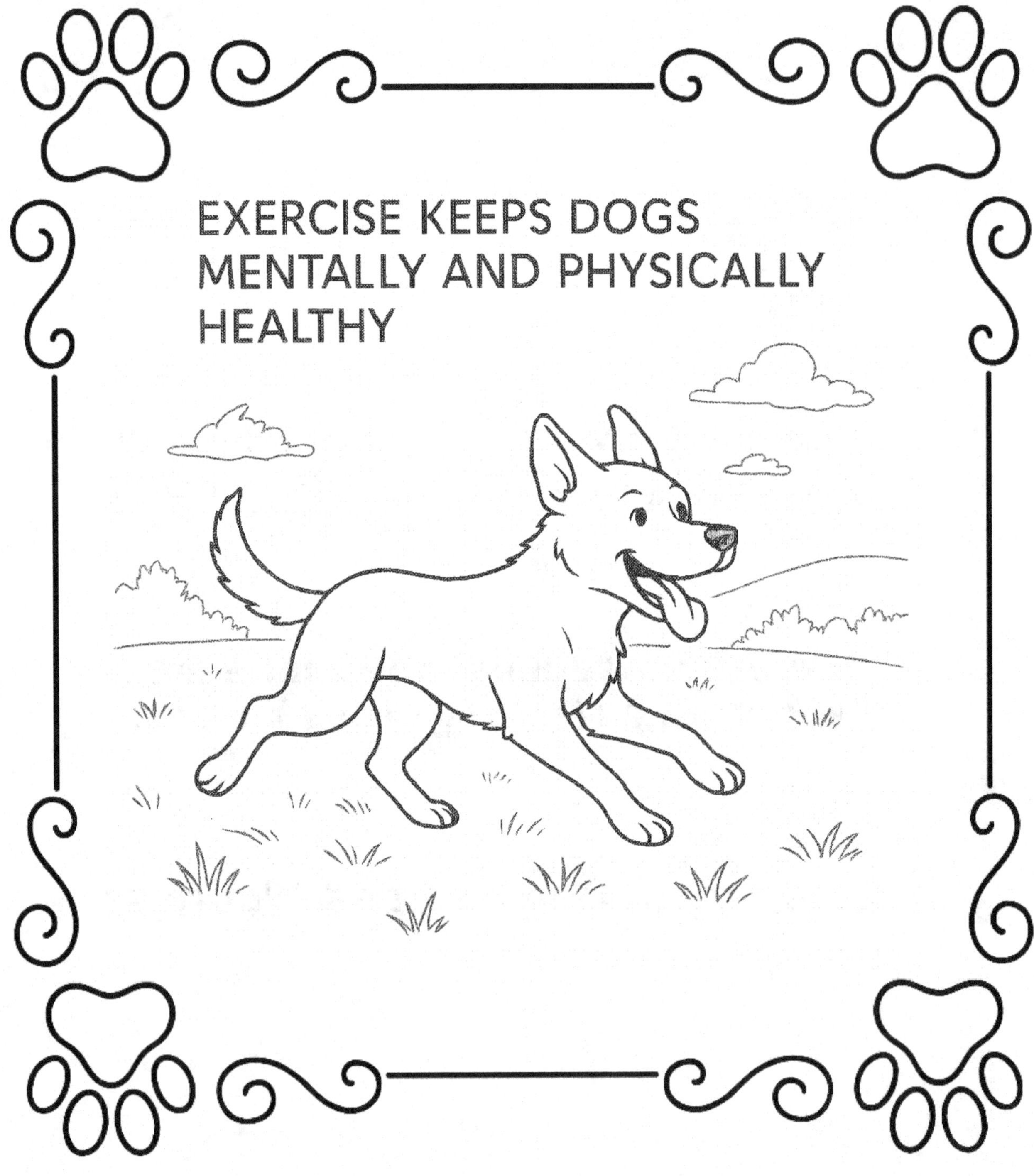

EXERCISE KEEPS DOGS
MENTALLY AND PHYSICALLY
HEALTHY

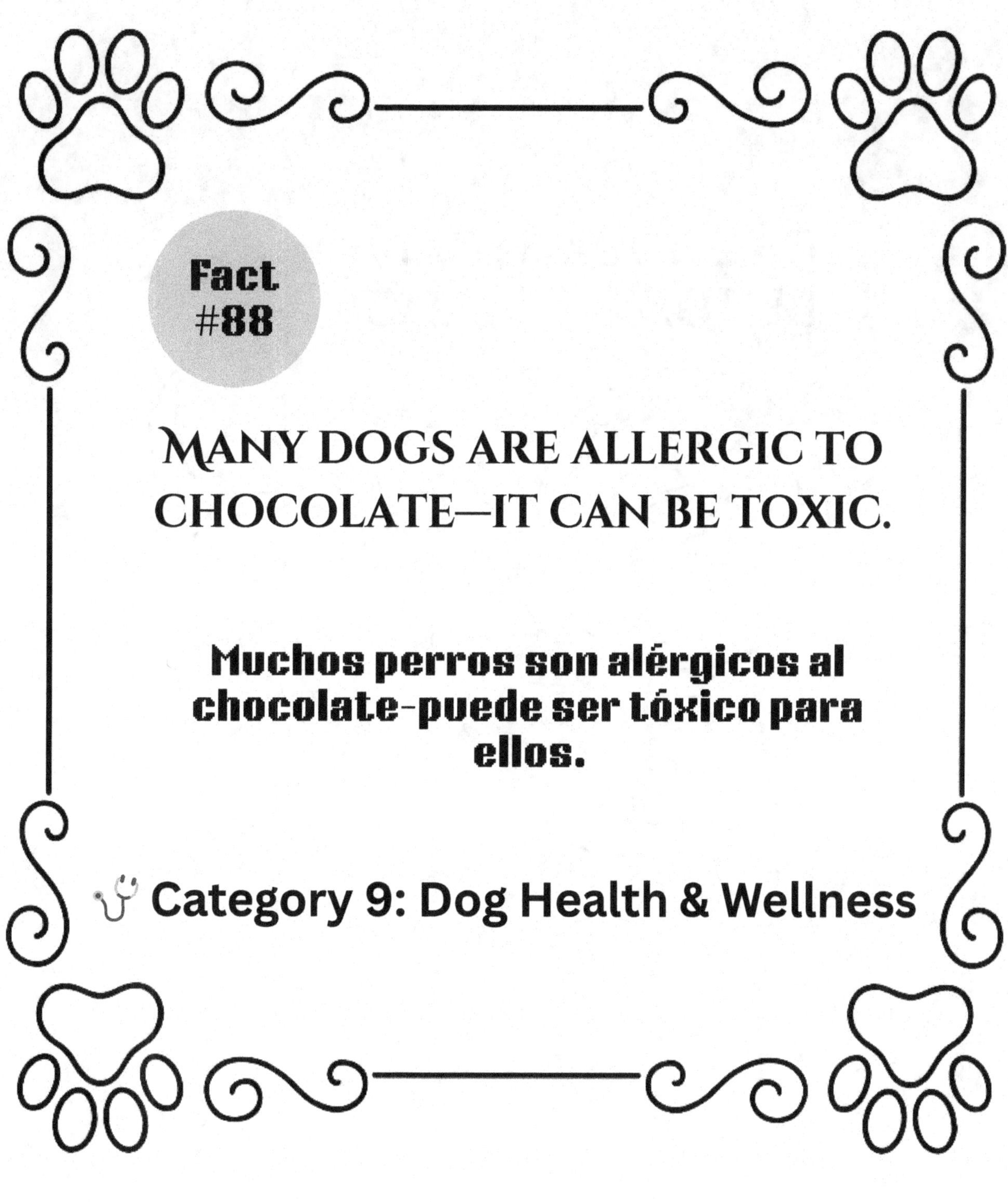
Fact #88

MANY DOGS ARE ALLERGIC TO CHOCOLATE—IT CAN BE TOXIC.

Muchos perros son alérgicos al chocolate-puede ser tóxico para ellos.

Category 9: Dog Health & Wellness

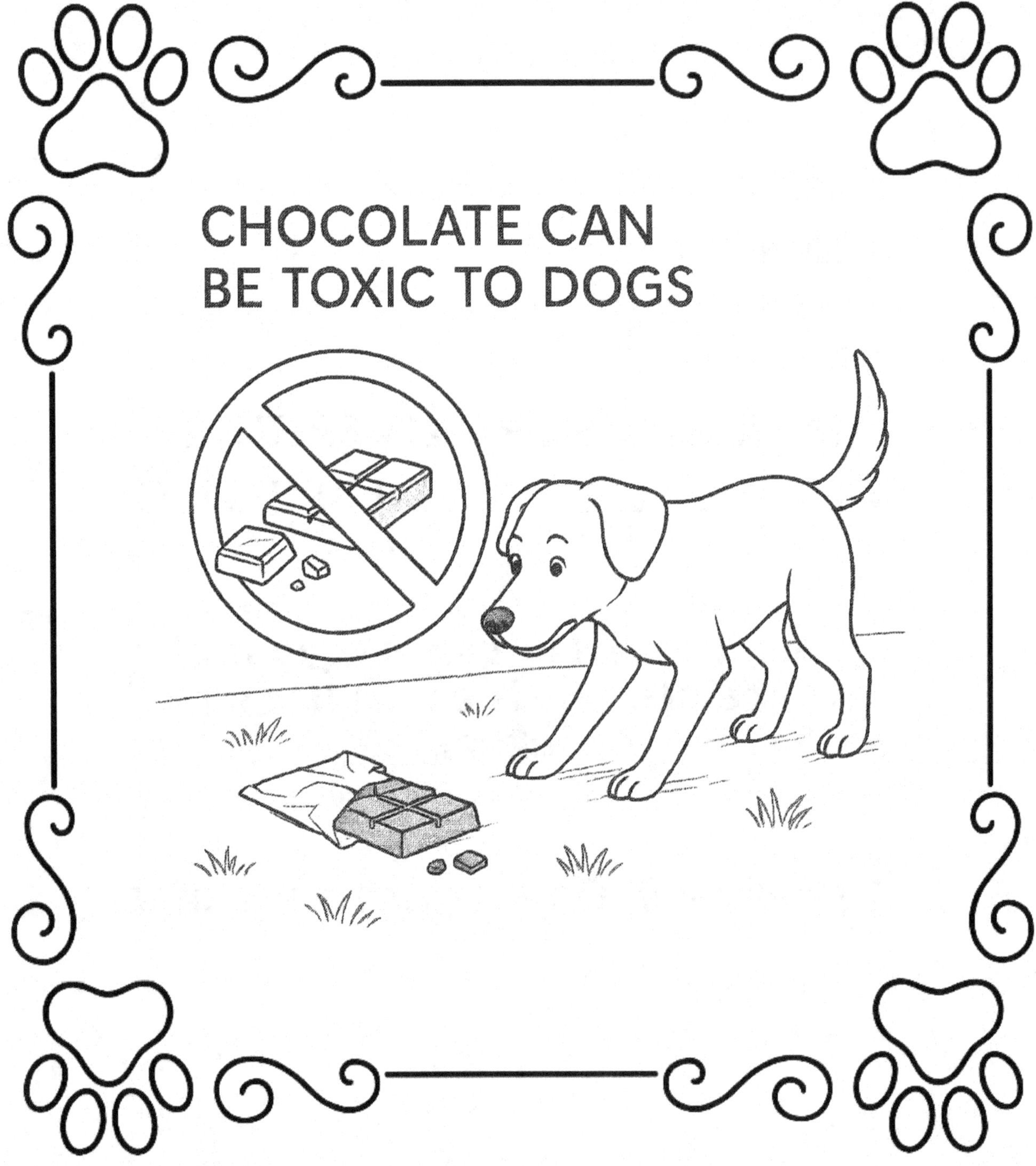

CHOCOLATE CAN
BE TOXIC TO DOGS

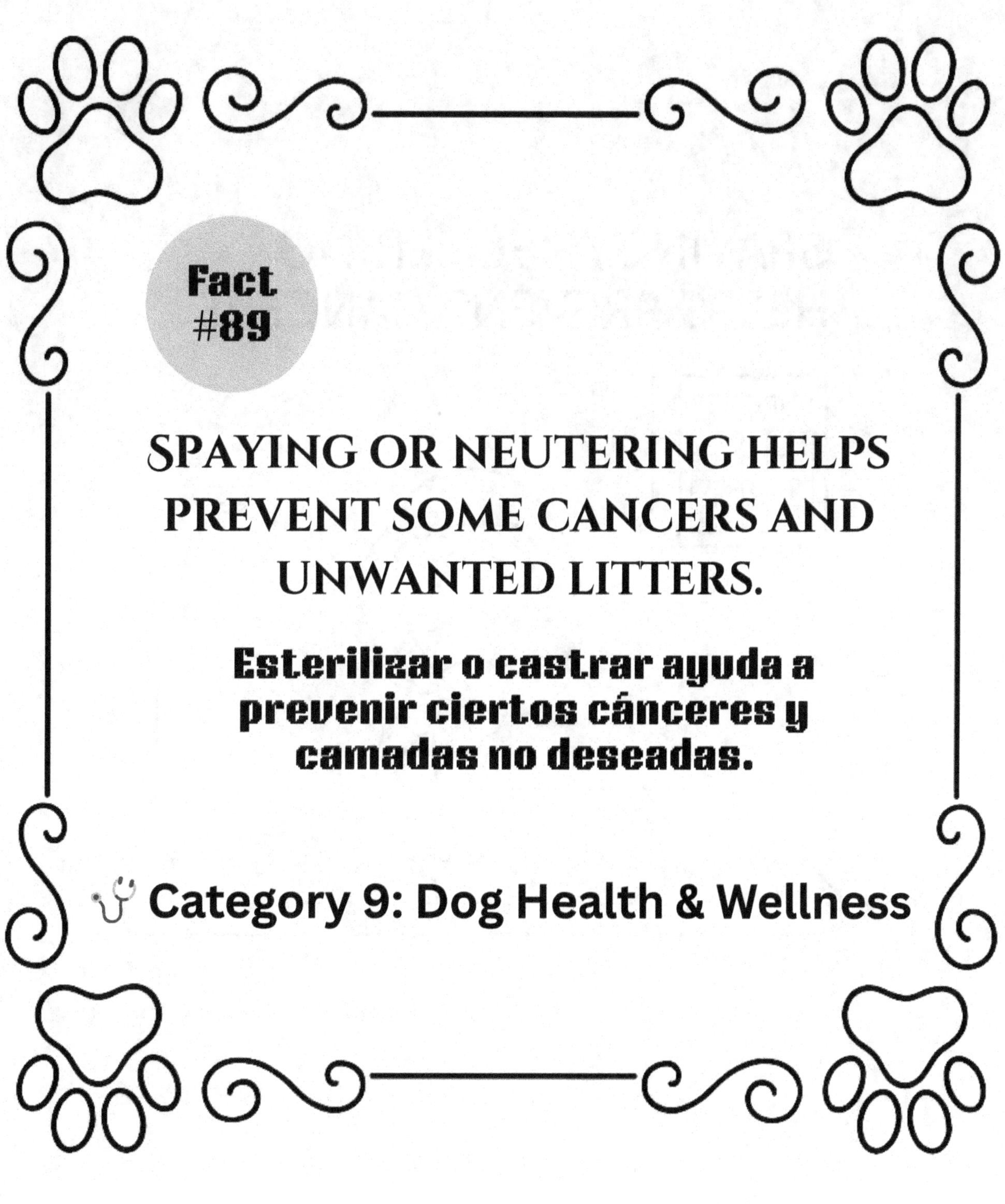

Fact #89

SPAYING OR NEUTERING HELPS PREVENT SOME CANCERS AND UNWANTED LITTERS.

Esterilizar o castrar ayuda a prevenir ciertos cánceres y camadas no deseadas.

Category 9: Dog Health & Wellness

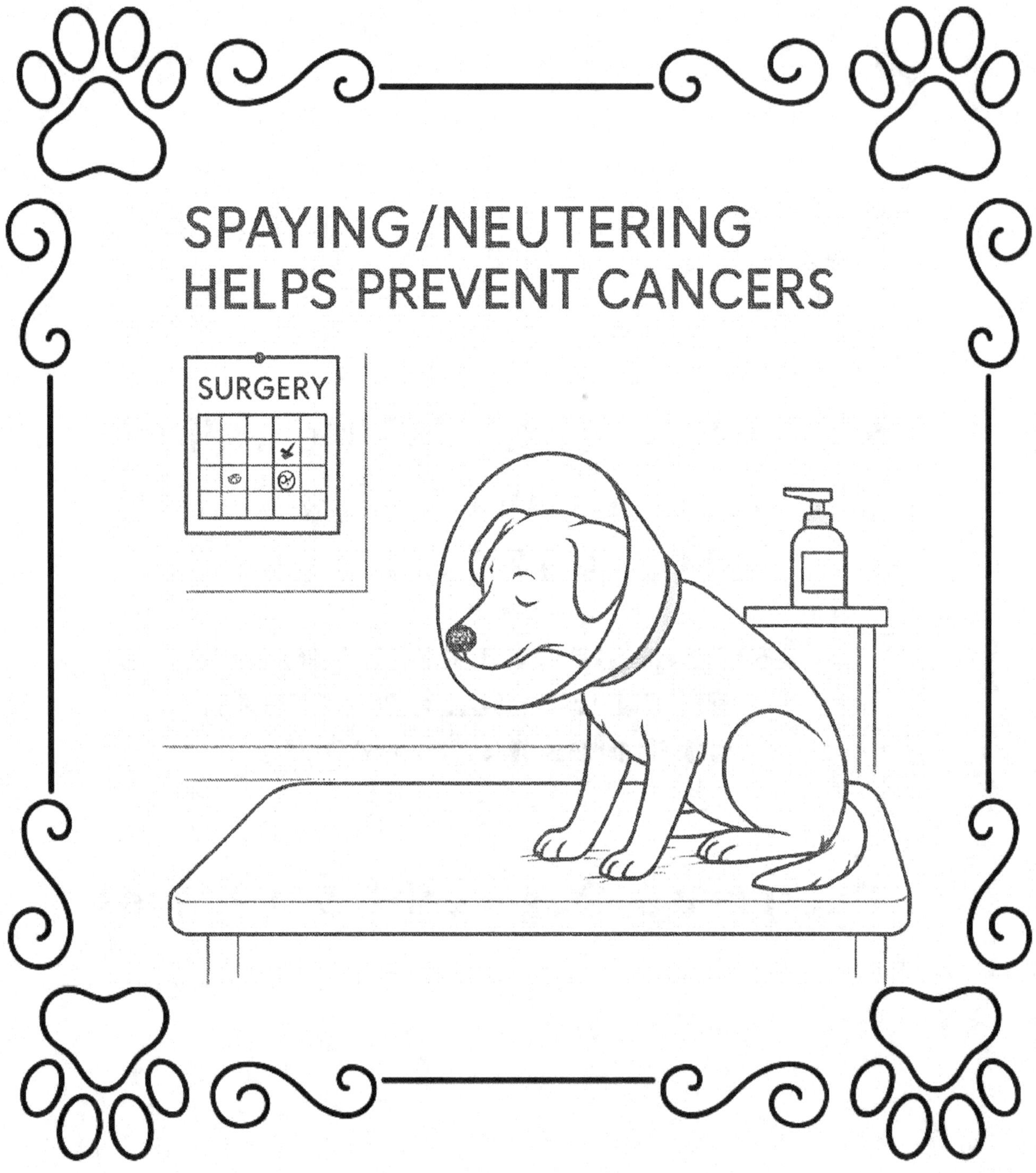

SPAYING/NEUTERING
HELPS PREVENT CANCERS
SURGERY

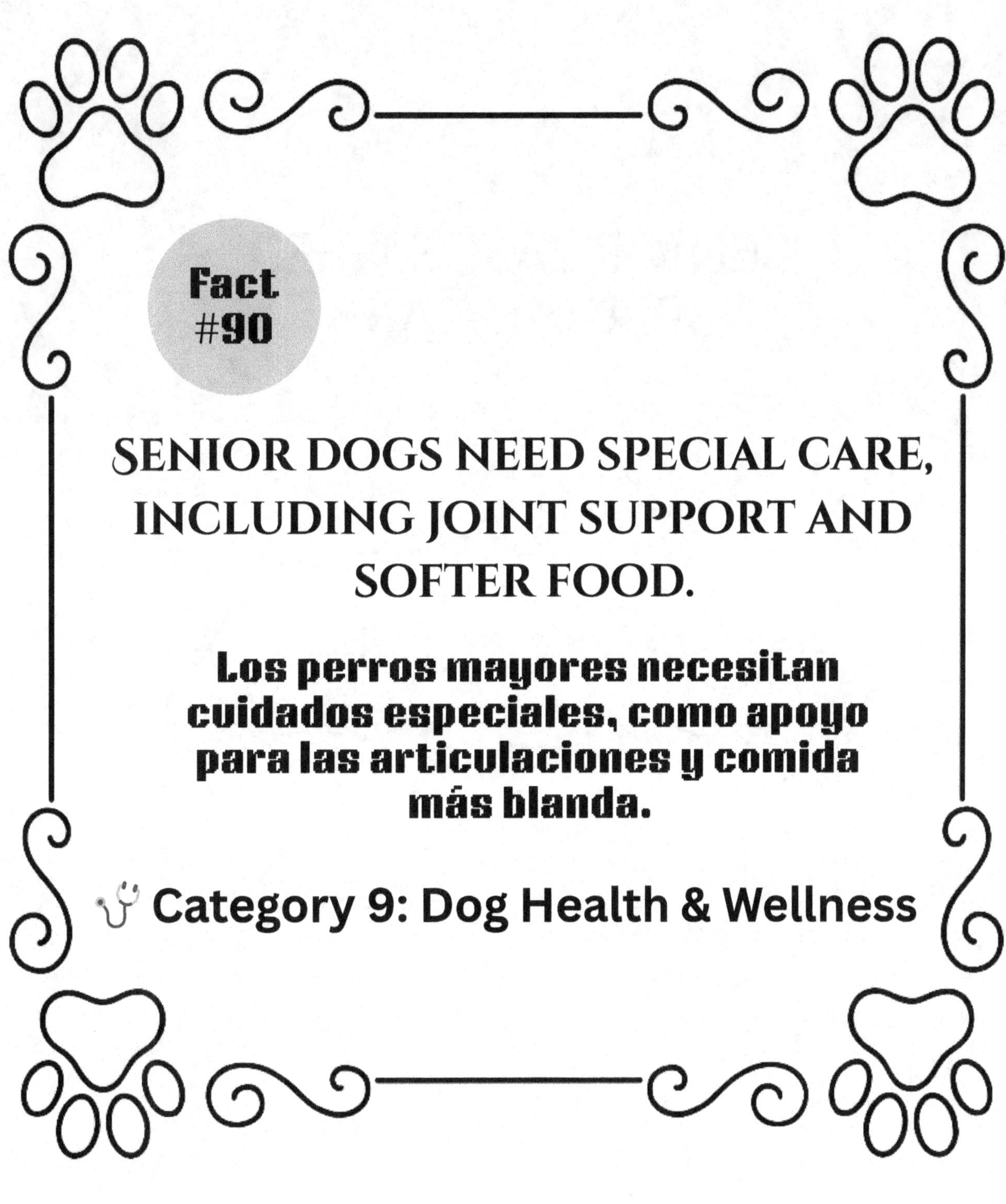

Fact #90

SENIOR DOGS NEED SPECIAL CARE, INCLUDING JOINT SUPPORT AND SOFTER FOOD.

Los perros mayores necesitan cuidados especiales, como apoyo para las articulaciones y comida más blanda.

Category 9: Dog Health & Wellness

SENIOR DOGS NEED SPECIAL CARE

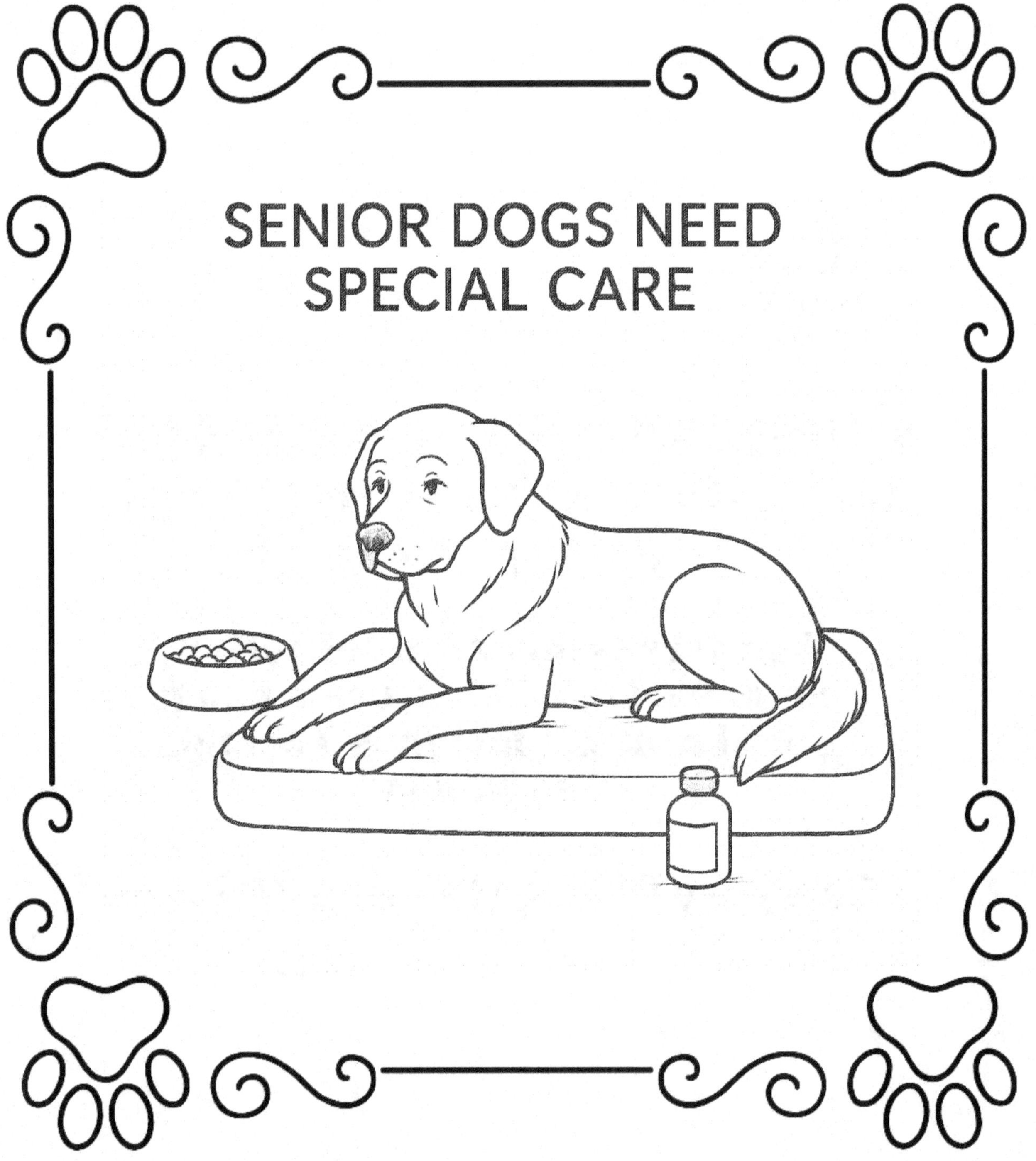

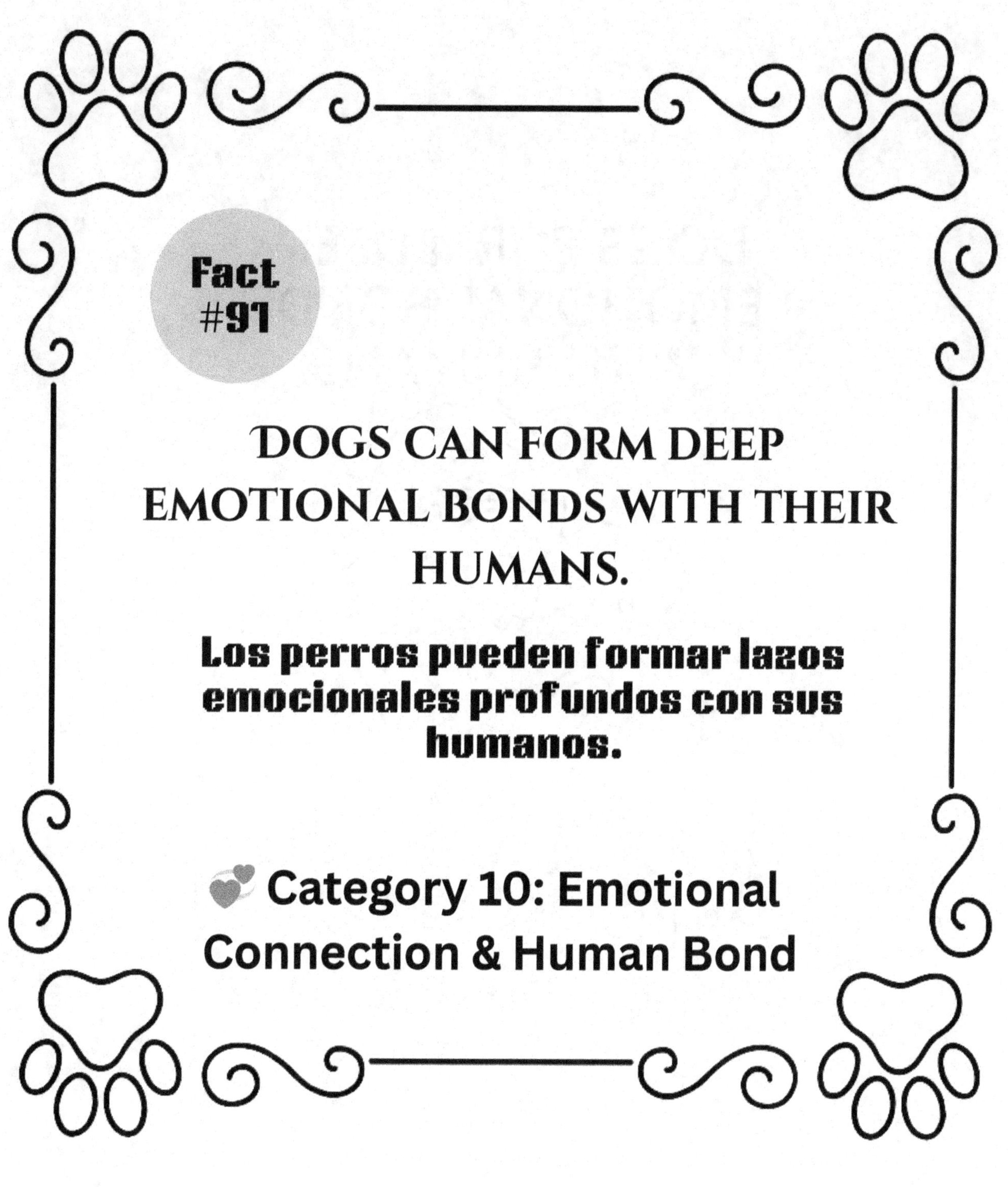

Fact #91

DOGS CAN FORM DEEP EMOTIONAL BONDS WITH THEIR HUMANS.

Los perros pueden formar lazos emocionales profundos con sus humanos.

Category 10: Emotional Connection & Human Bond

DOGS FORM DEEP EMOTIONAL BONDS WITH HUMANS

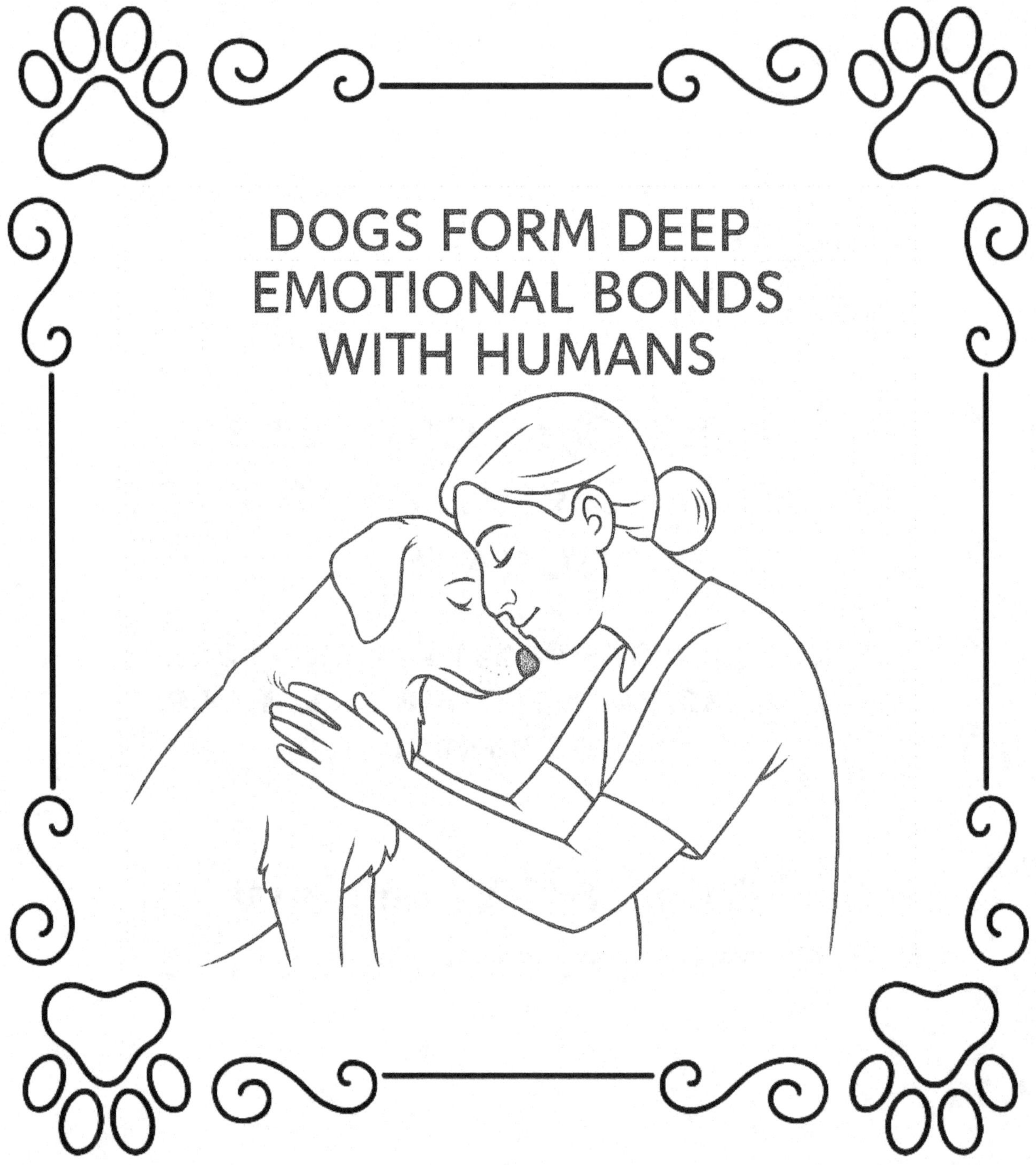

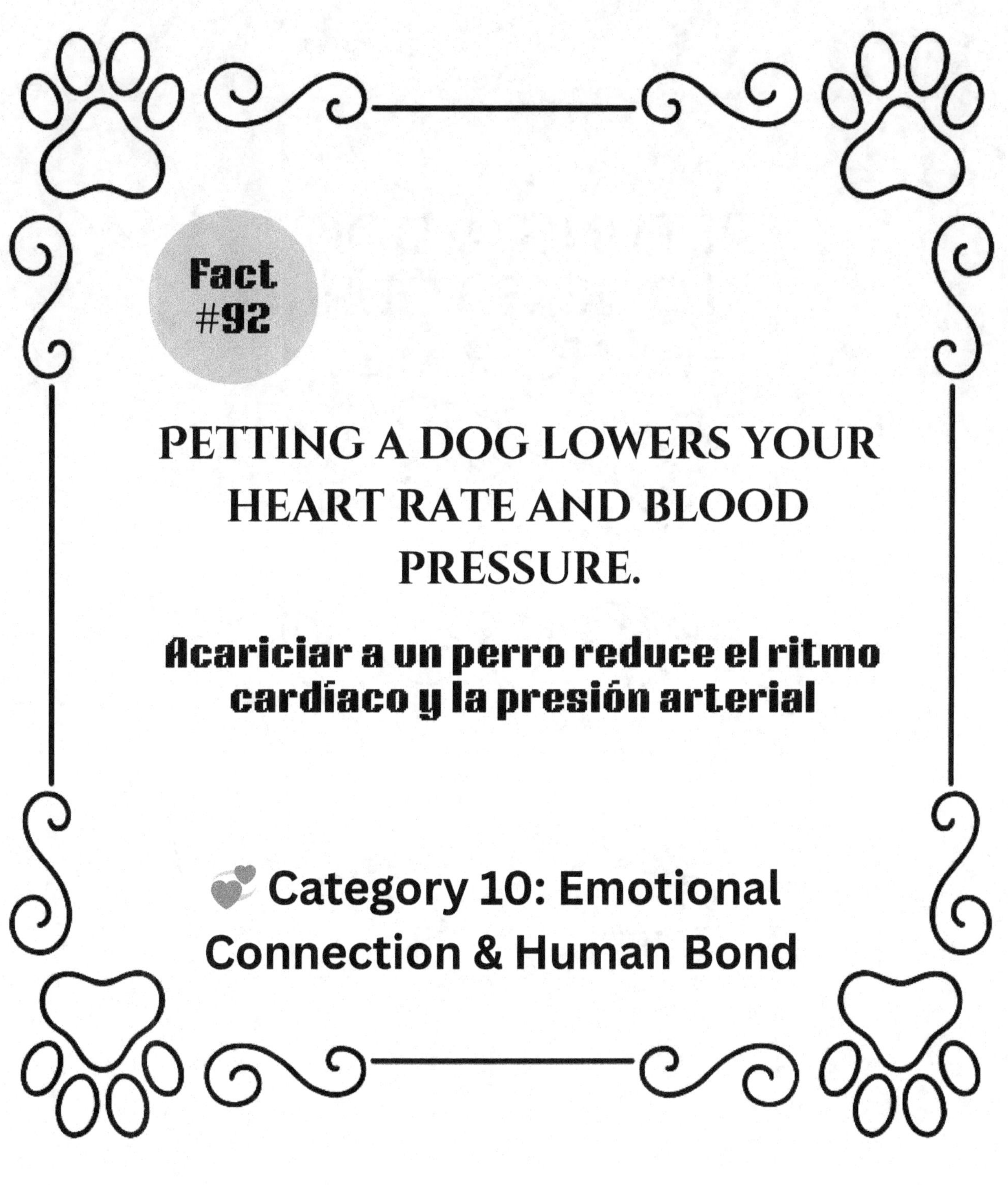

Fact #92

PETTING A DOG LOWERS YOUR HEART RATE AND BLOOD PRESSURE.

Acariciar a un perro reduce el ritmo cardíaco y la presión arterial

Category 10: Emotional Connection & Human Bond

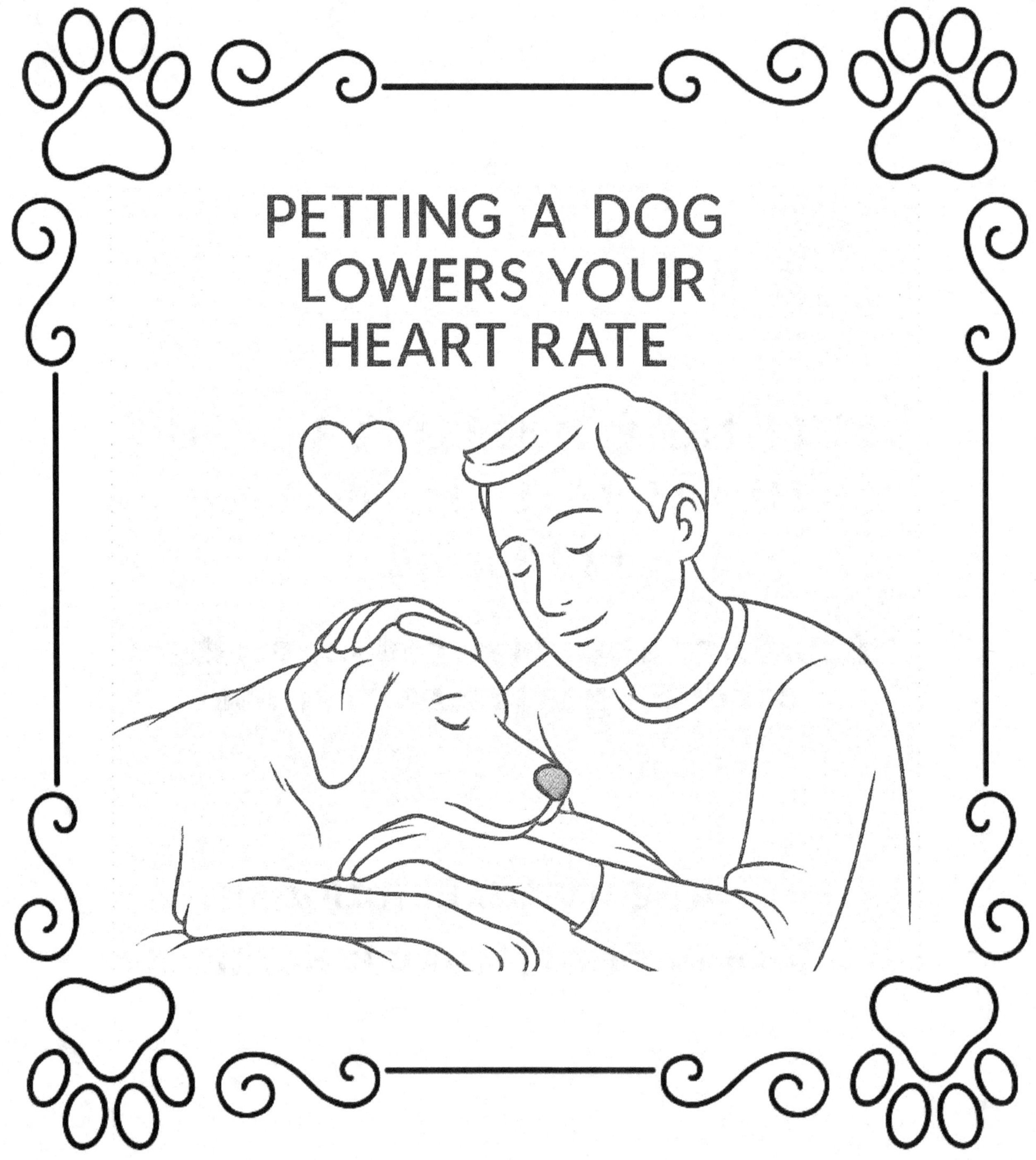
PETTING A DOG
LOWERS YOUR
HEART RATE

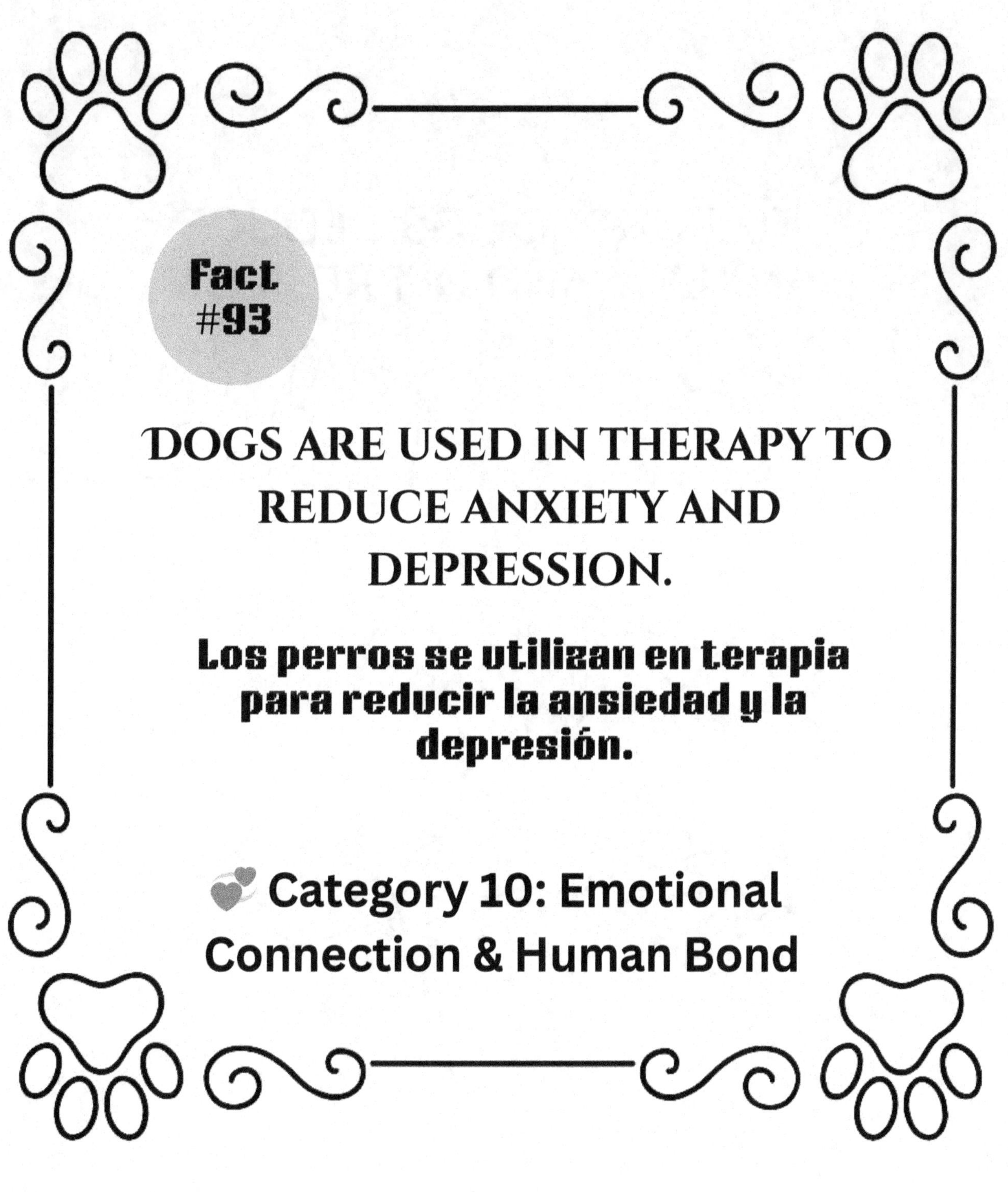

Fact #93

DOGS ARE USED IN THERAPY TO REDUCE ANXIETY AND DEPRESSION.

Los perros se utilizan en terapia para reducir la ansiedad y la depresión.

Category 10: Emotional Connection & Human Bond

THERAPY DOGS REDUCE ANXIETY AND DEPRESSION

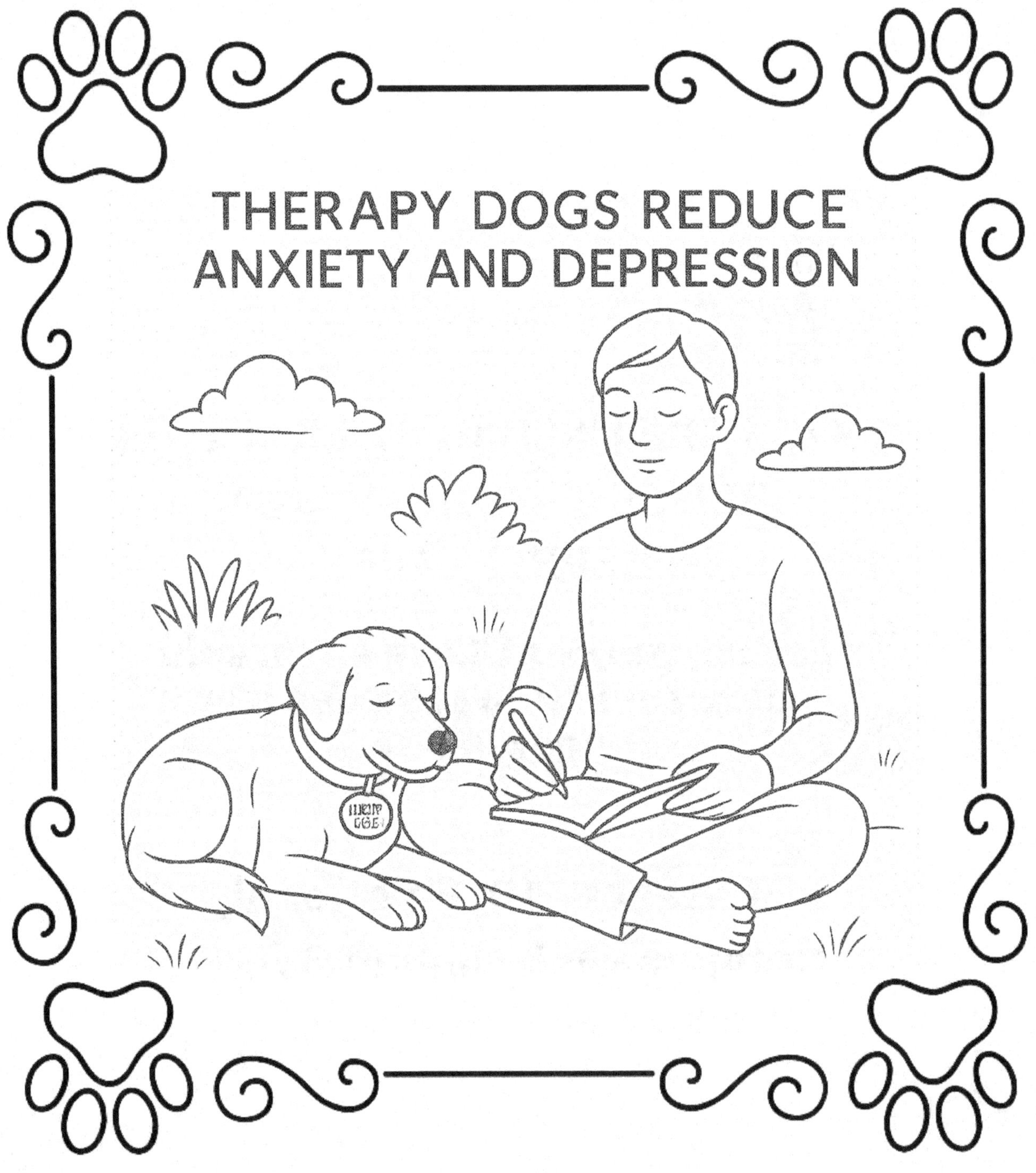

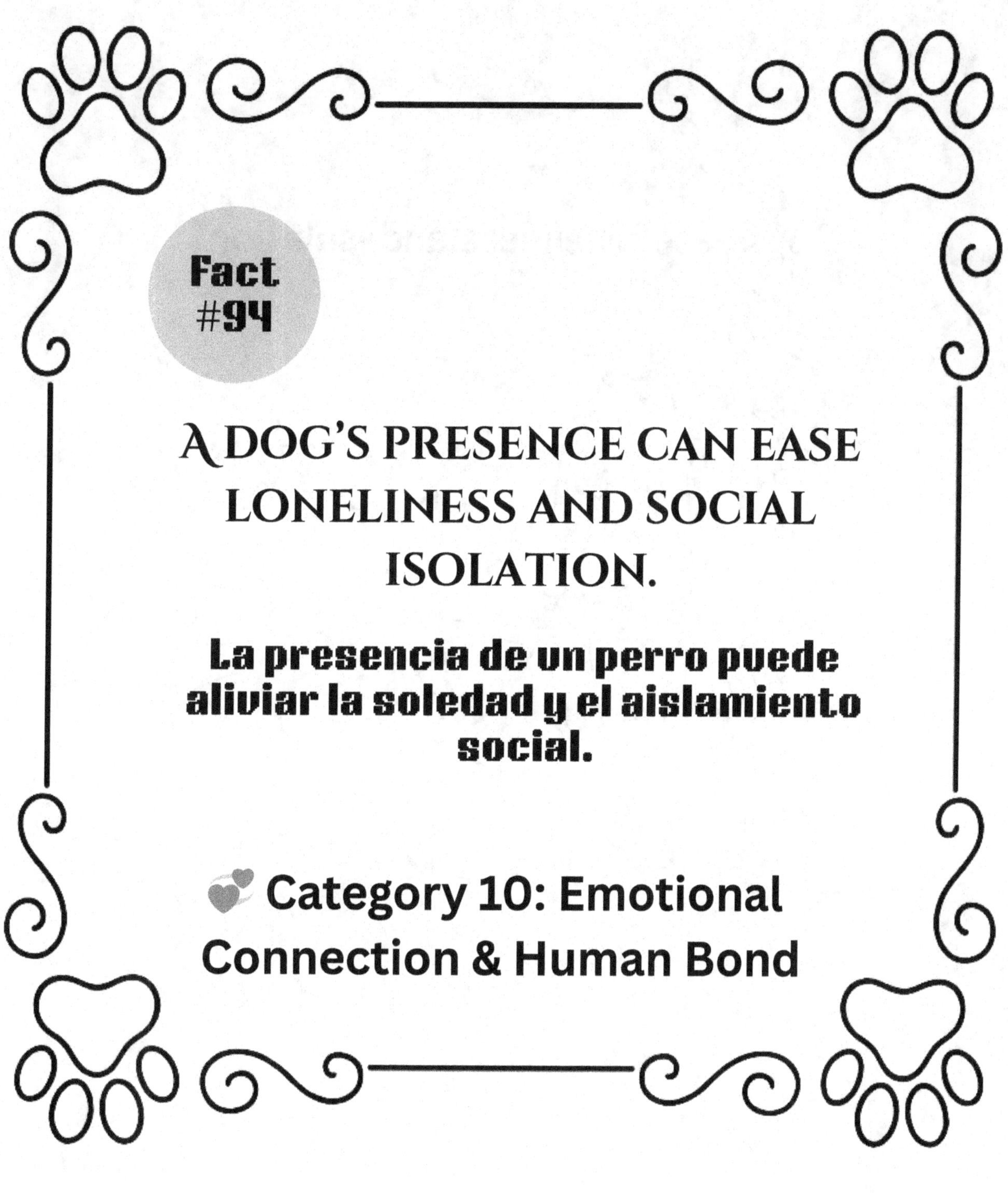

Fact #94

A DOG'S PRESENCE CAN EASE LONELINESS AND SOCIAL ISOLATION.

La presencia de un perro puede aliviar la soledad y el aislamiento social.

Category 10: Emotional Connection & Human Bond

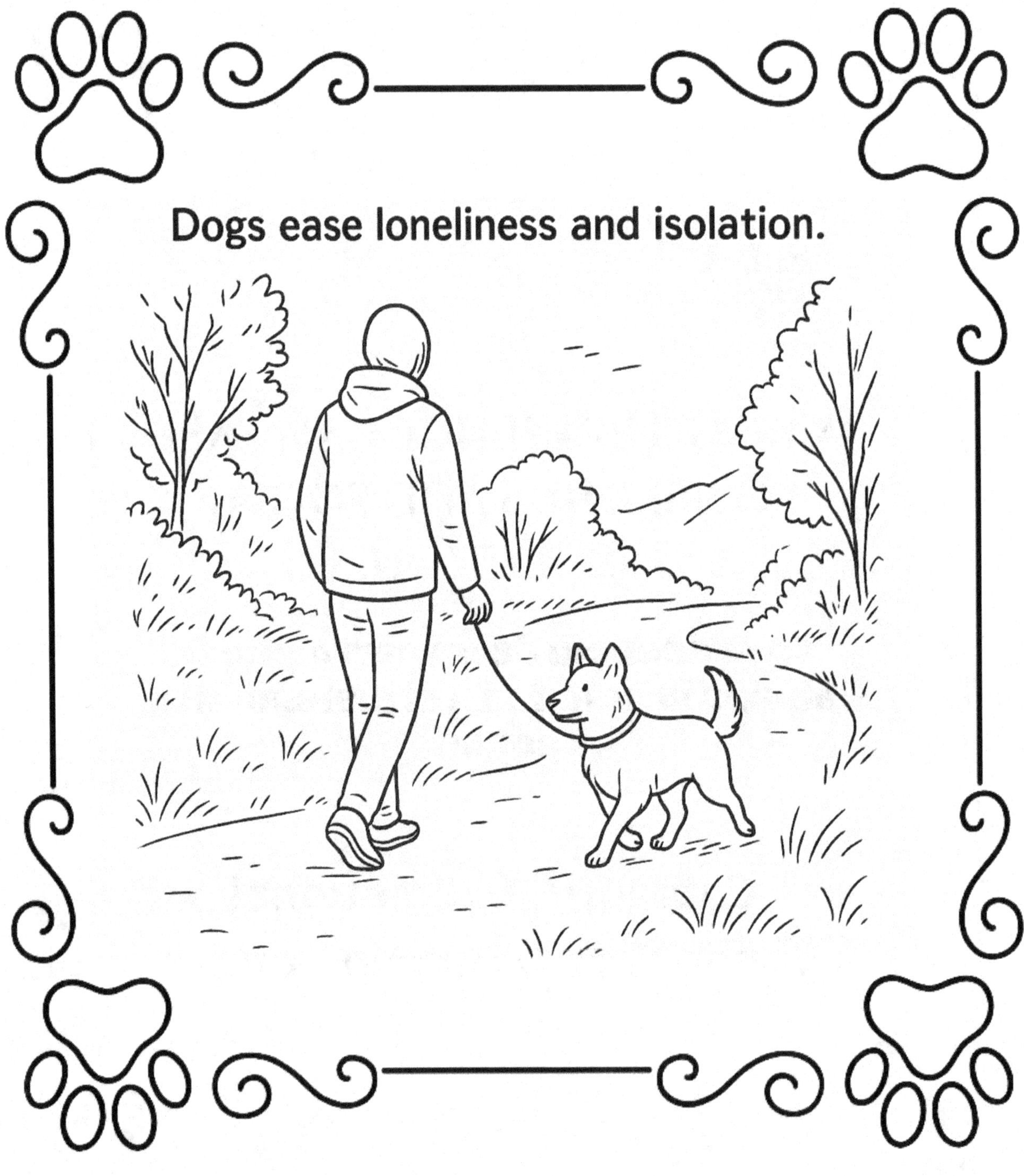

Dogs ease loneliness and isolation.

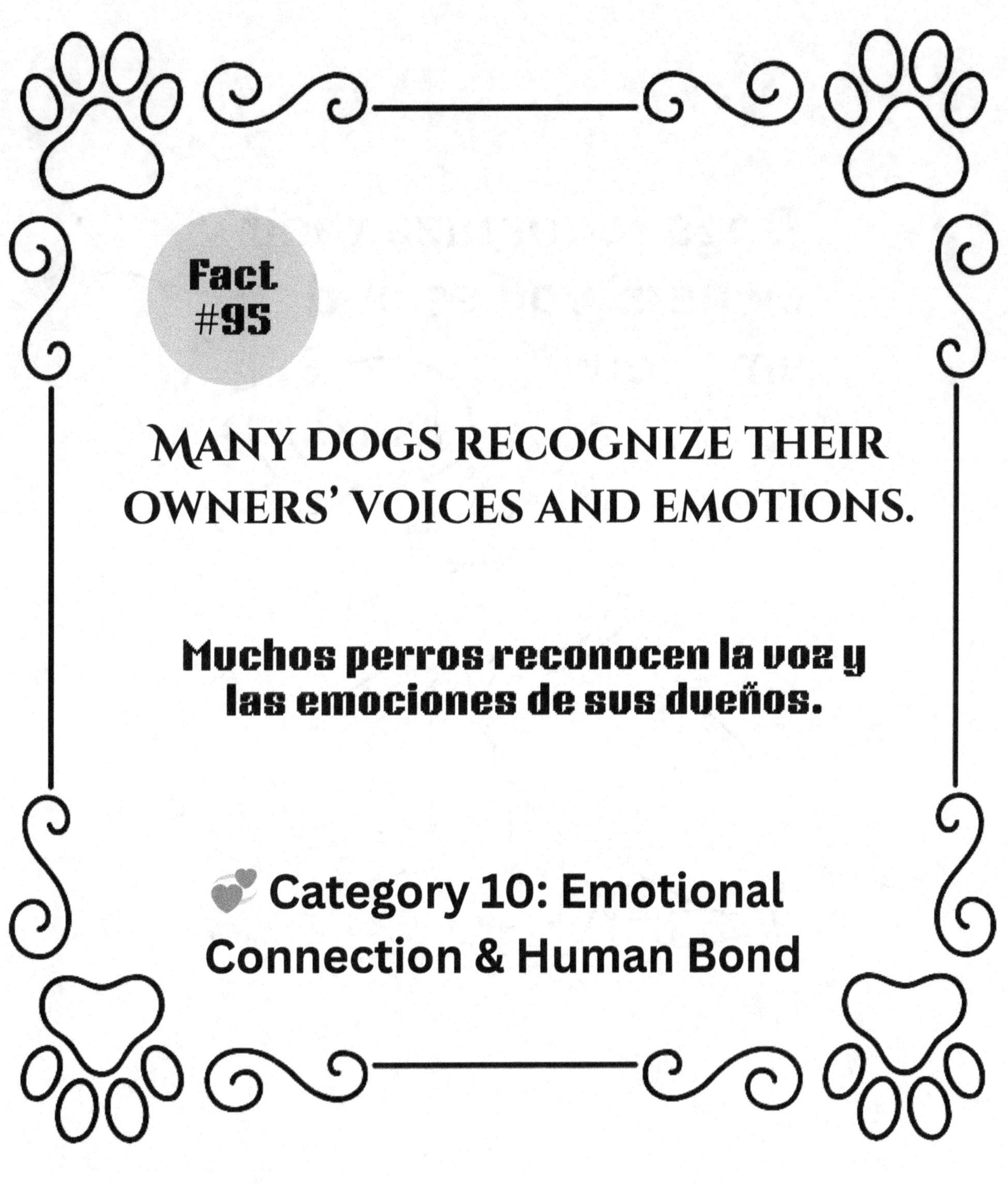

Fact #95

MANY DOGS RECOGNIZE THEIR OWNERS' VOICES AND EMOTIONS.

Muchos perros reconocen la voz y las emociones de sus dueños.

Category 10: Emotional Connection & Human Bond

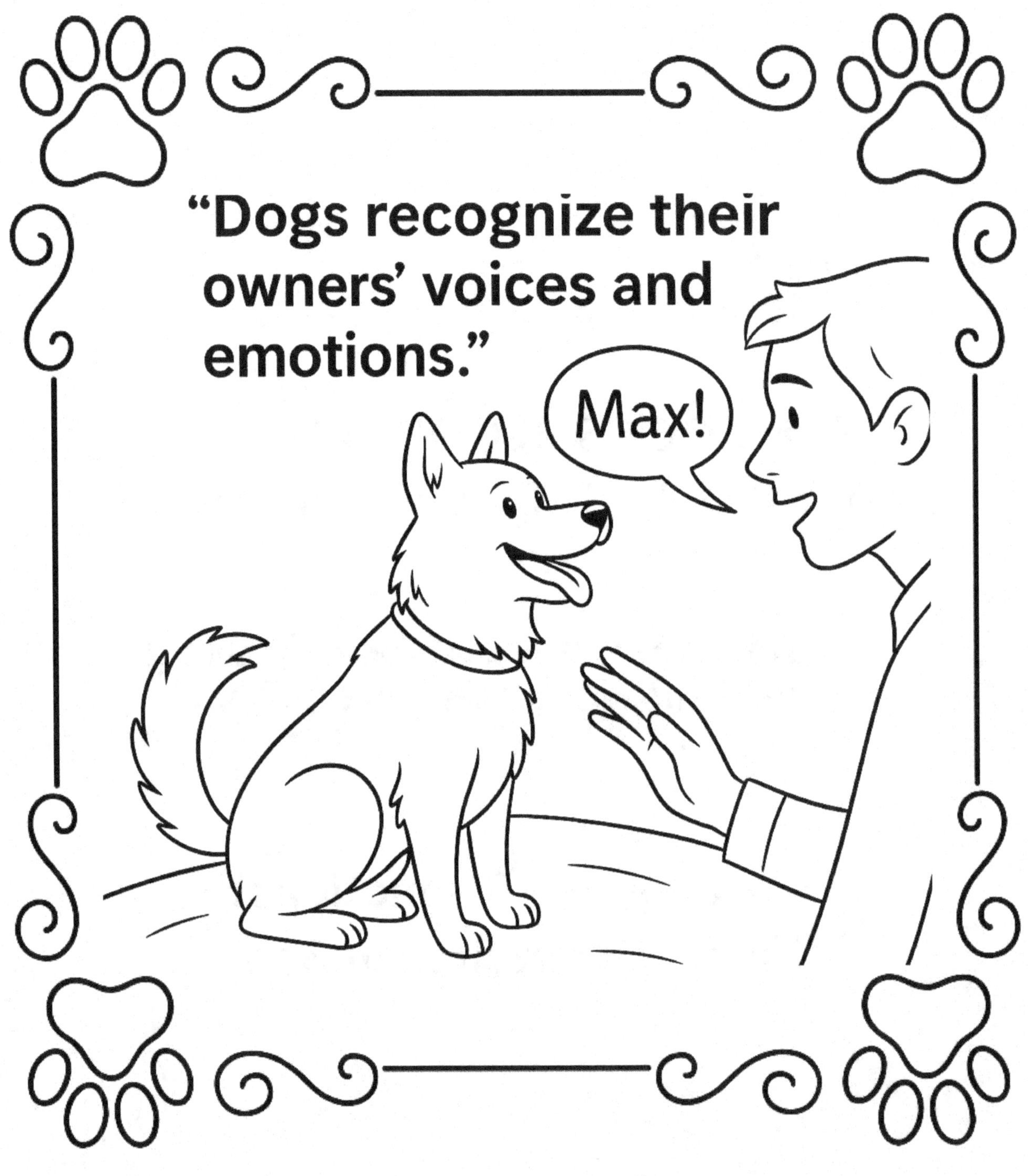

"Dogs recognize their owners' voices and emotions."
Max!

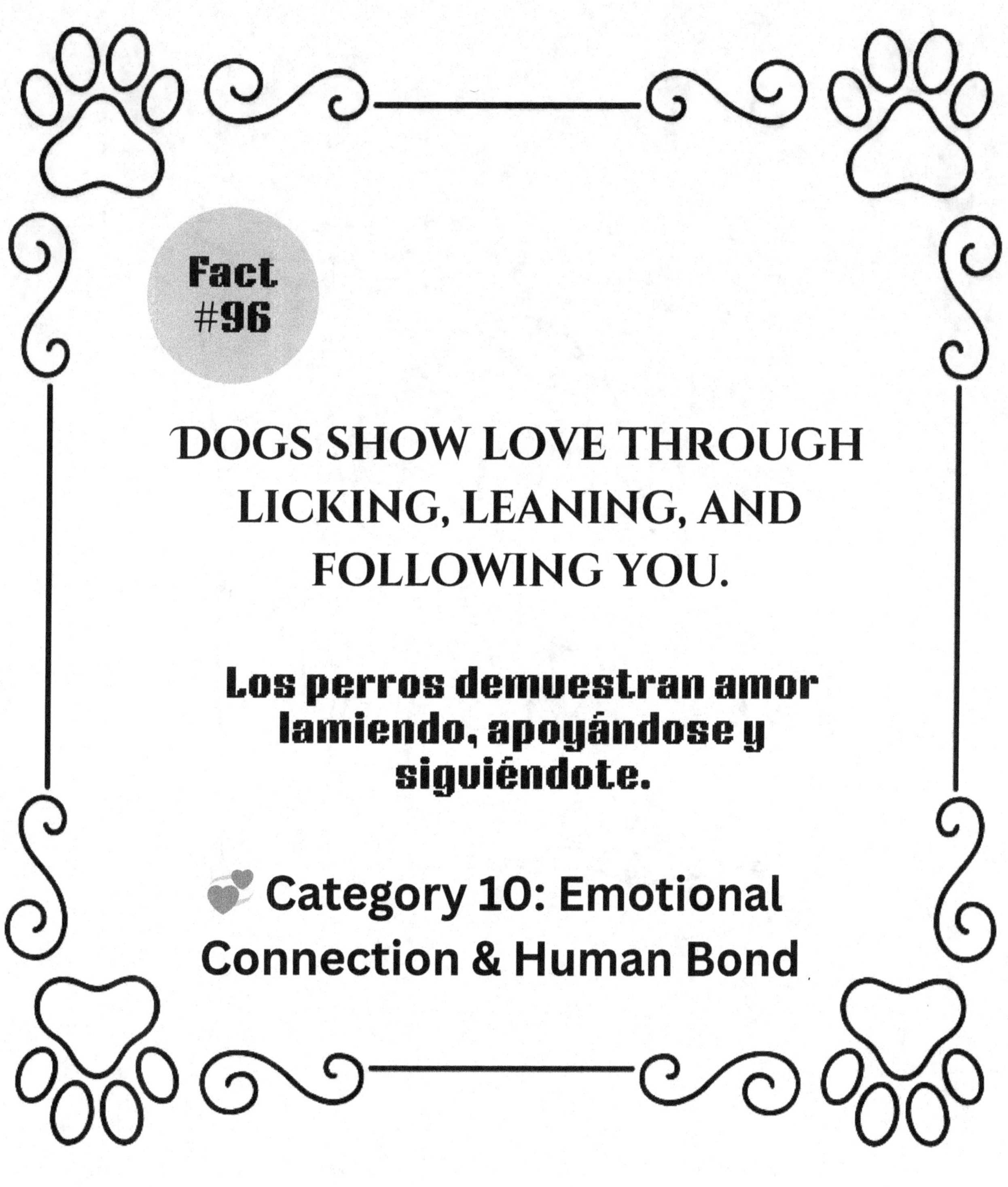

Fact #96

DOGS SHOW LOVE THROUGH LICKING, LEANING, AND FOLLOWING YOU.

Los perros demuestran amor lamiendo, apoyándose y siguiéndote.

Category 10: Emotional Connection & Human Bond

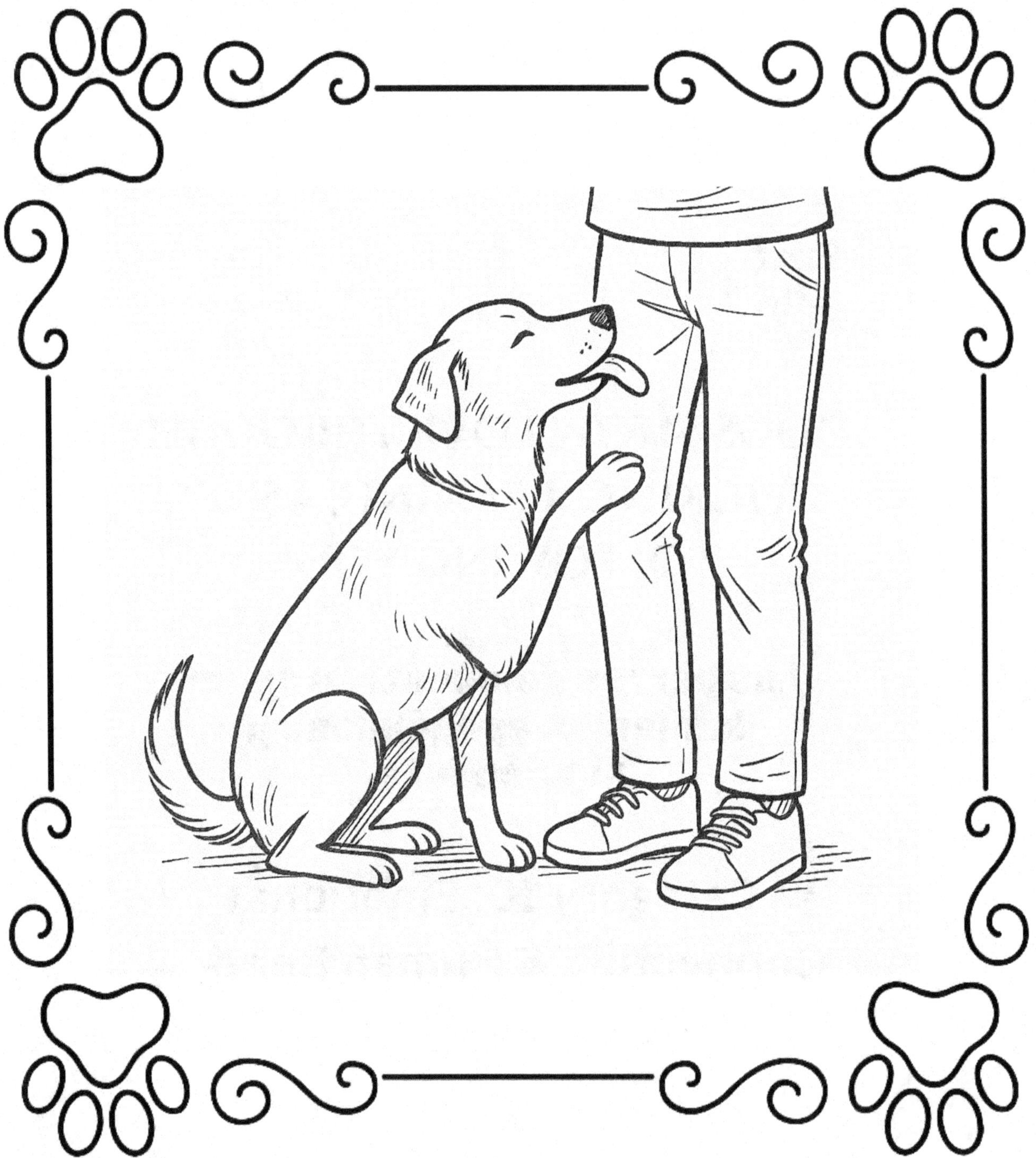

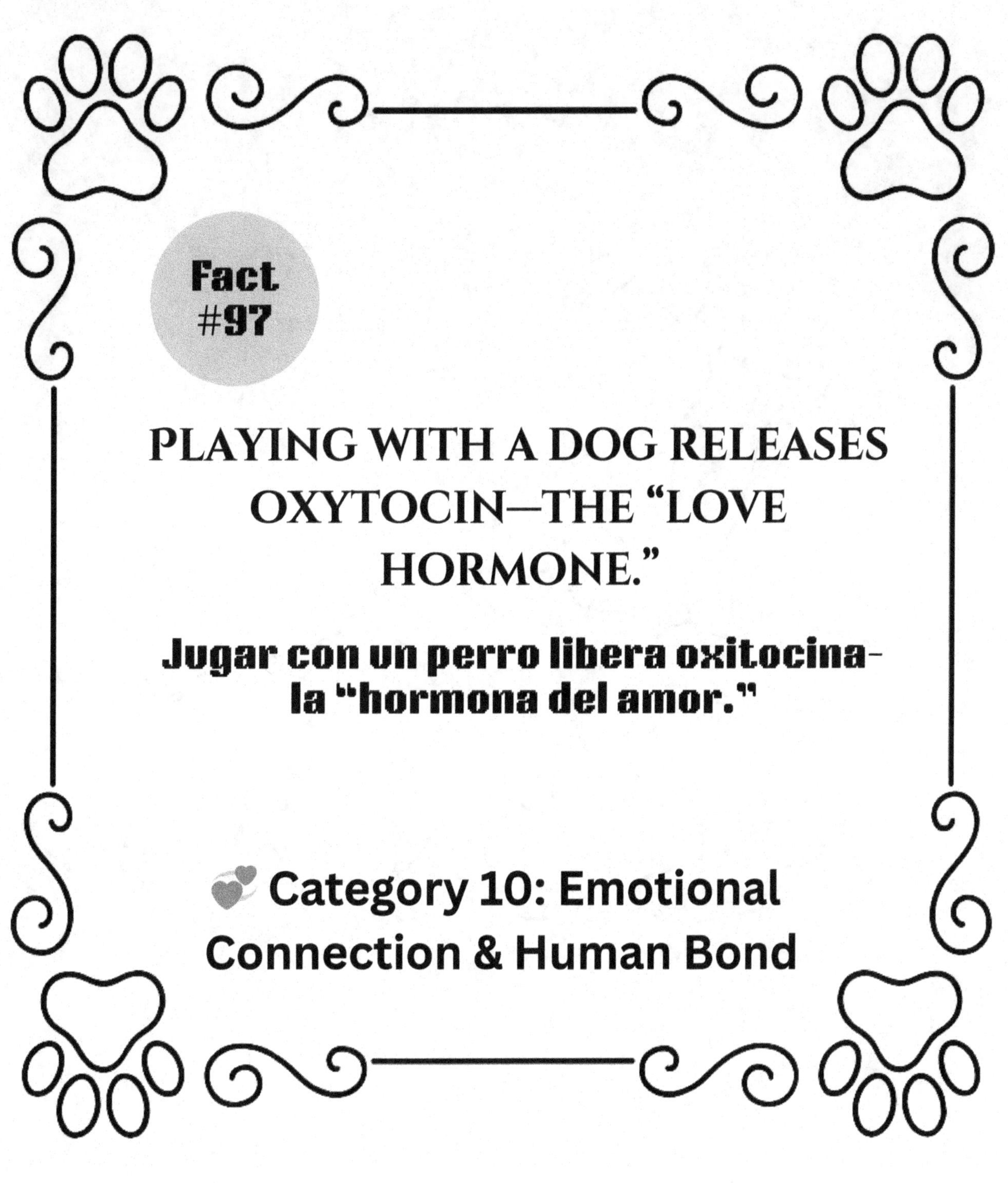

PLAYING WITH A DOG RELEASES OXYTOCIN—THE "LOVE HORMONE."

Jugar con un perro libera oxitocina— la "hormona del amor."

Category 10: Emotional Connection & Human Bond

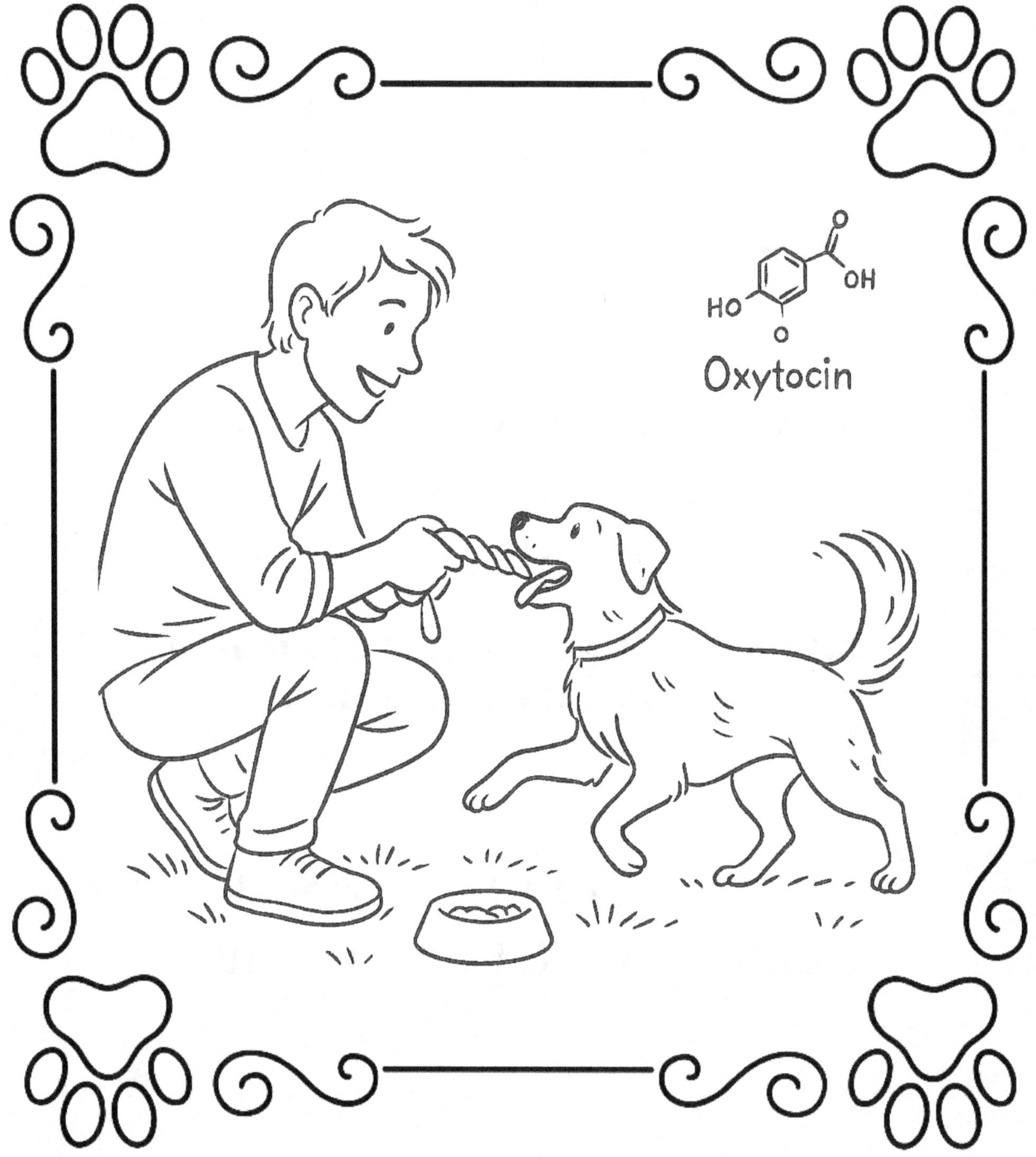

HO
OH
O
Oxytocin

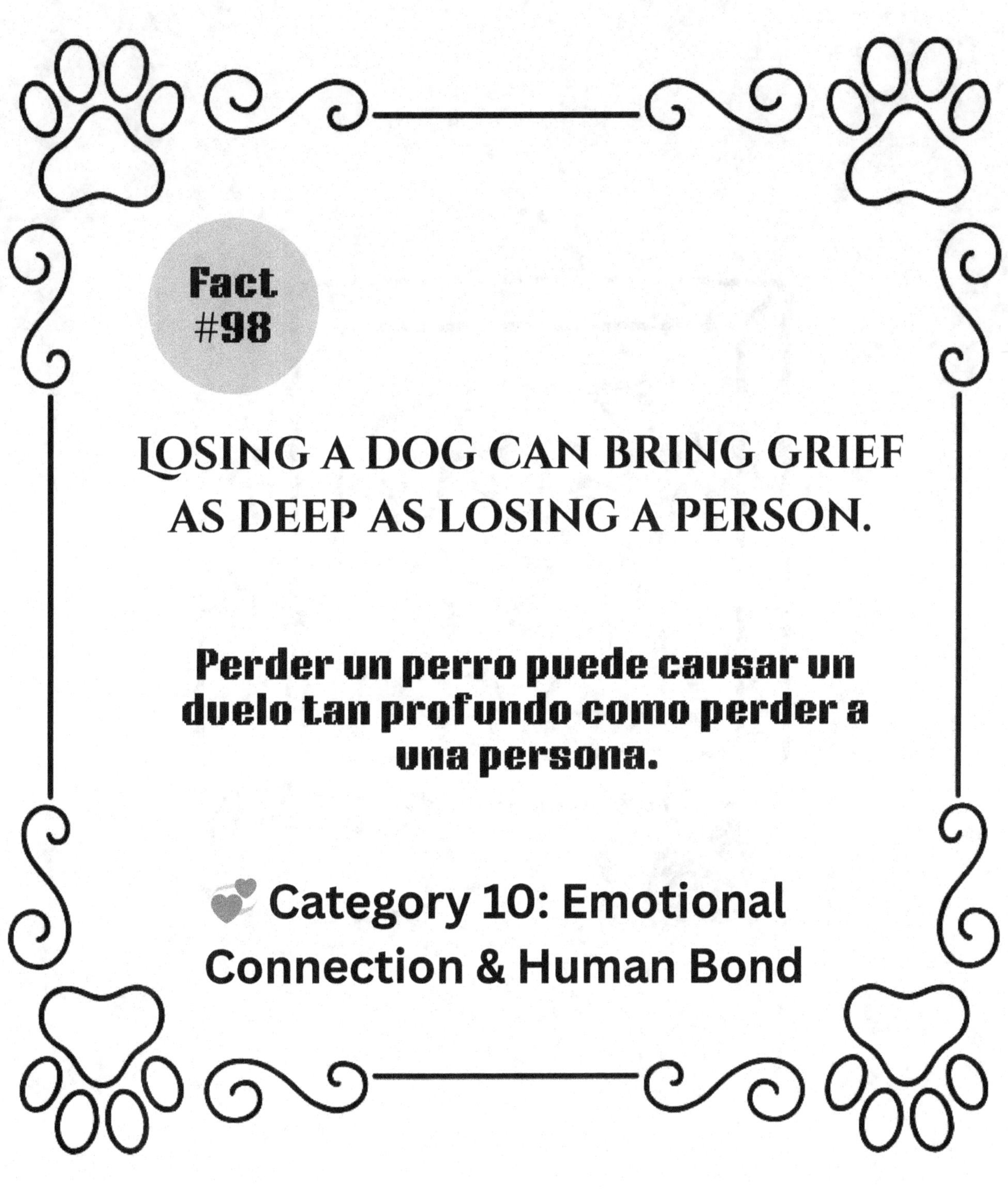

Fact #98

LOSING A DOG CAN BRING GRIEF AS DEEP AS LOSING A PERSON.

Perder un perro puede causar un duelo tan profundo como perder a una persona.

Category 10: Emotional Connection & Human Bond

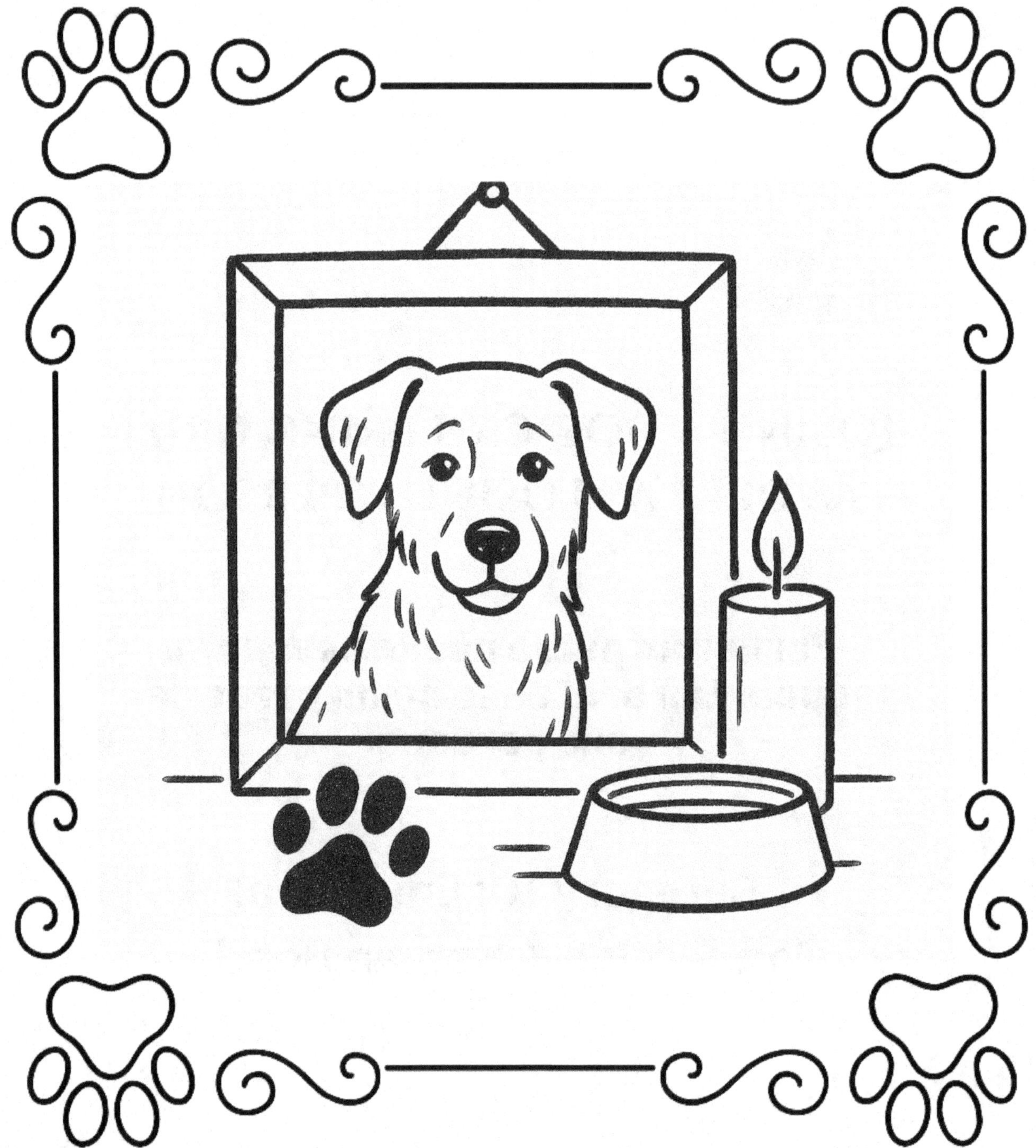

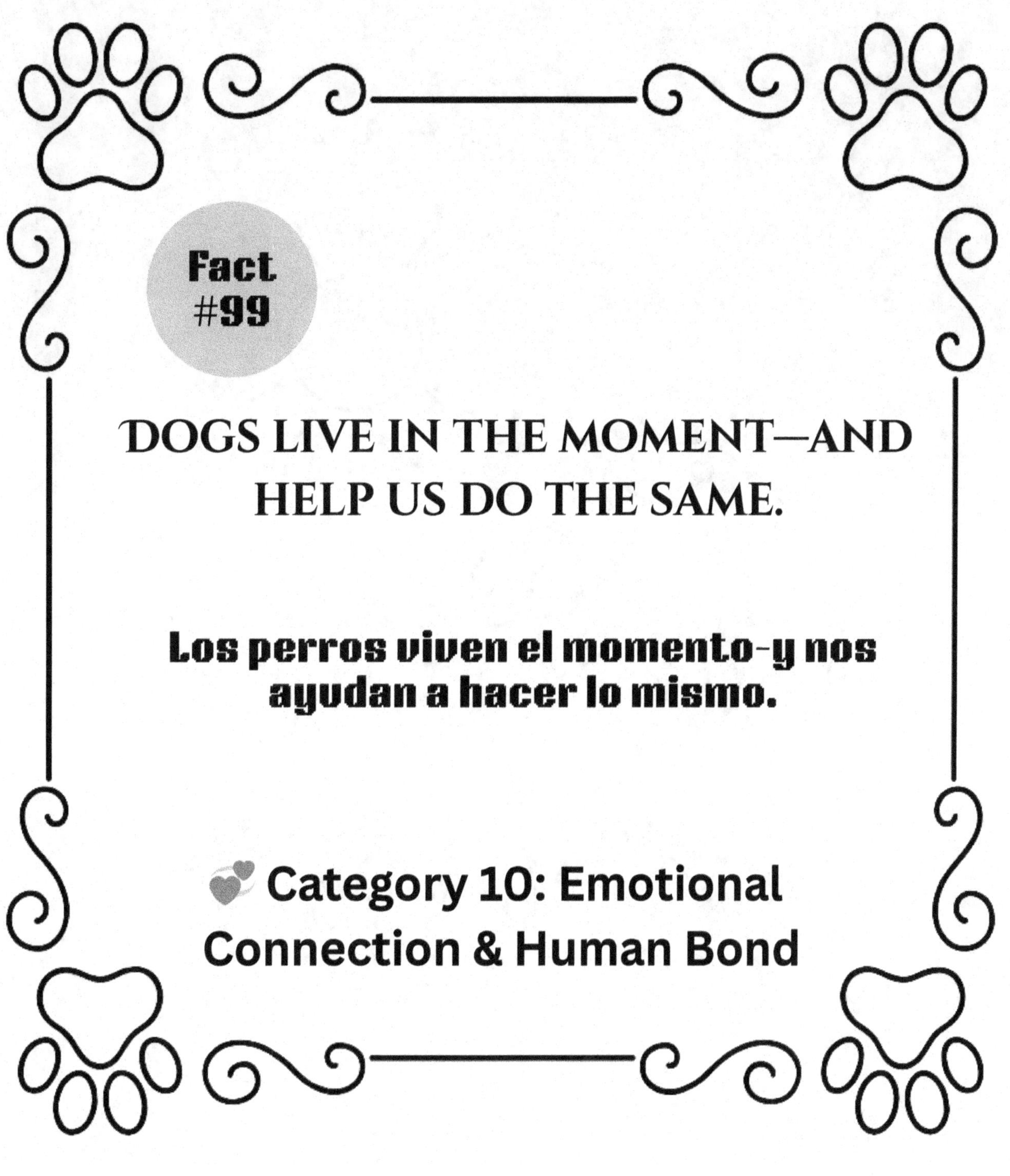

Fact #99

DOGS LIVE IN THE MOMENT—AND HELP US DO THE SAME.

Los perros viven el momento-y nos ayudan a hacer lo mismo.

Category 10: Emotional Connection & Human Bond

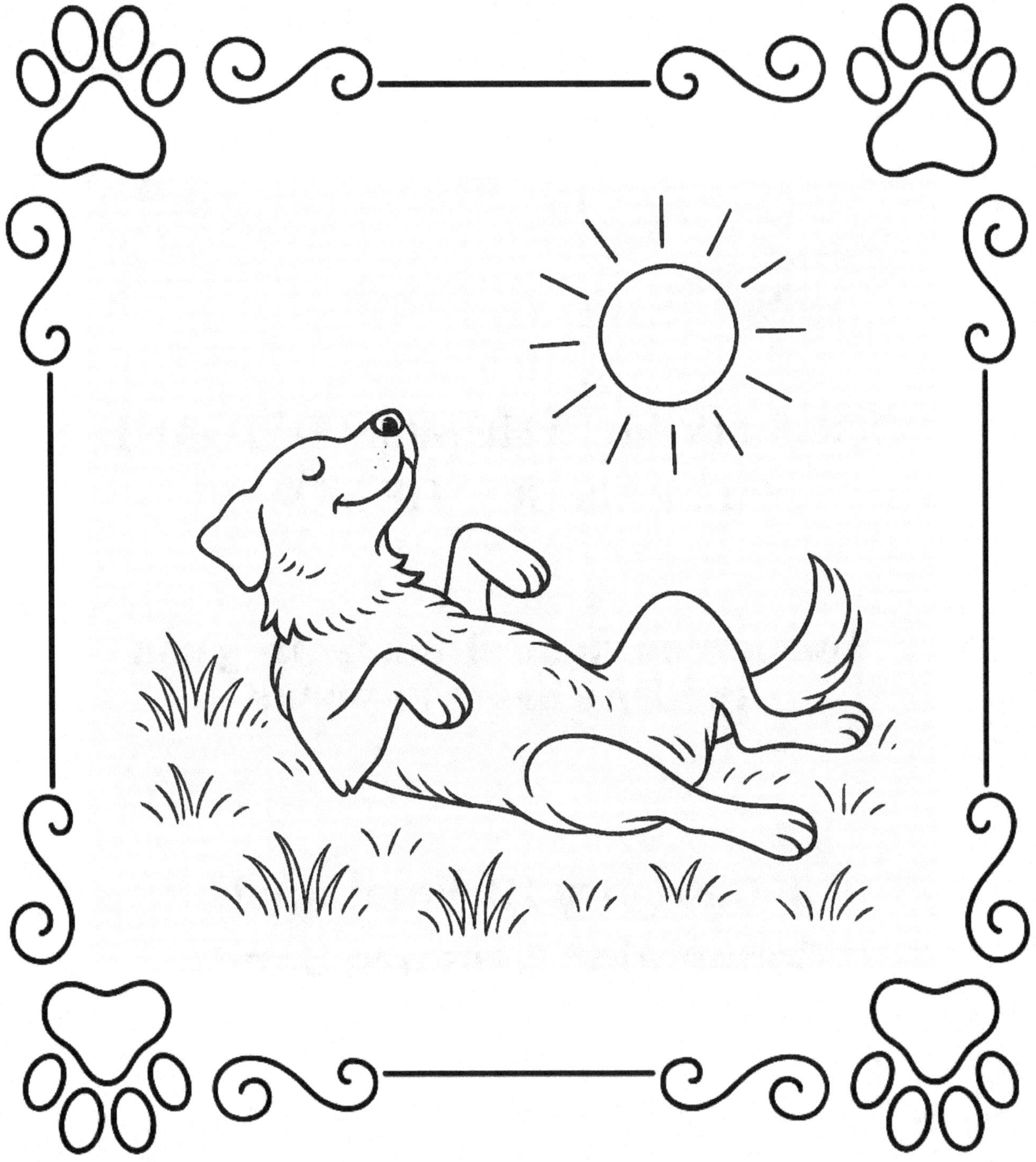

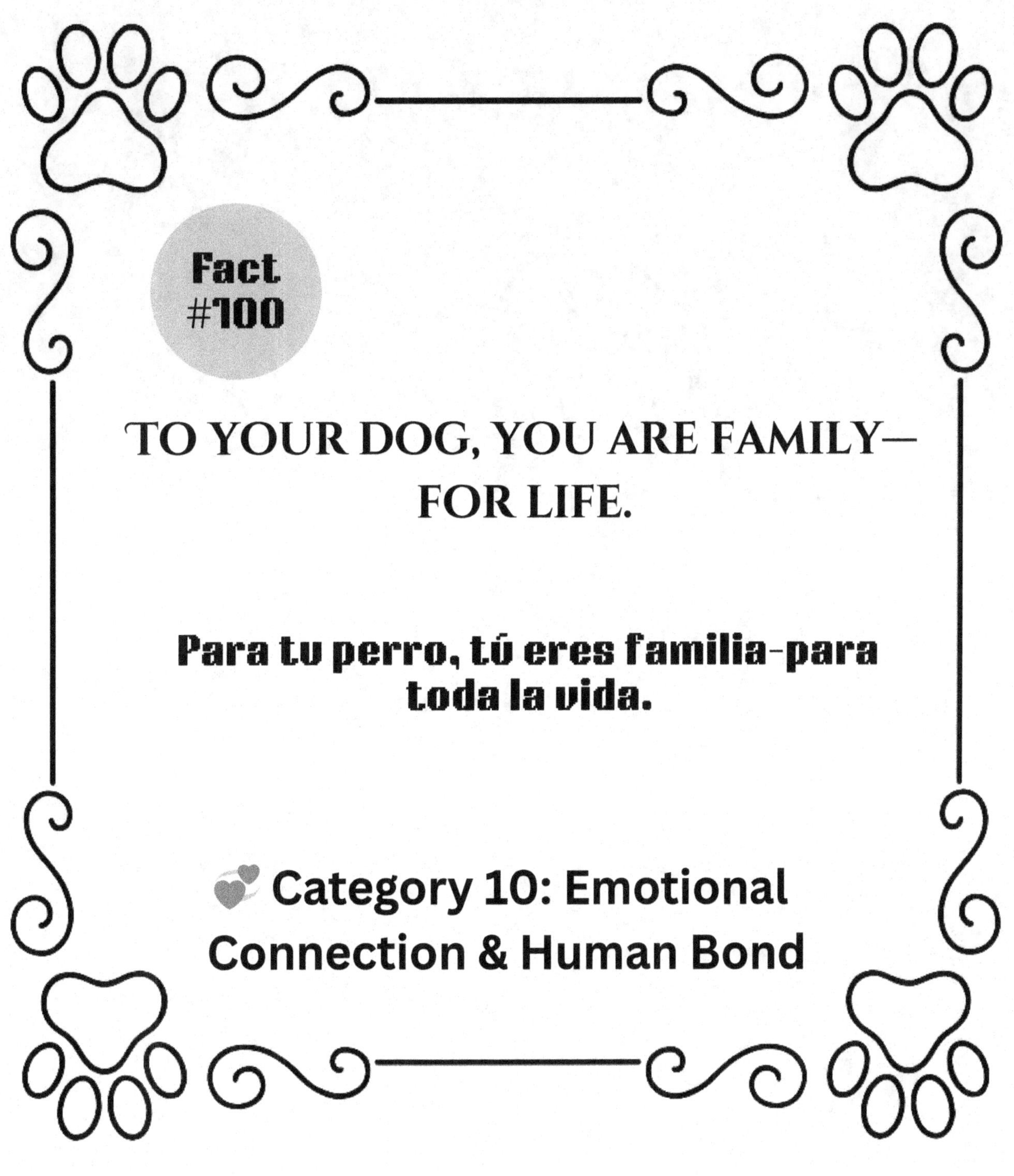

Fact #100

TO YOUR DOG, YOU ARE FAMILY—
FOR LIFE.

Para tu perro, tú eres familia-para
toda la vida.

Category 10: Emotional
Connection & Human Bond

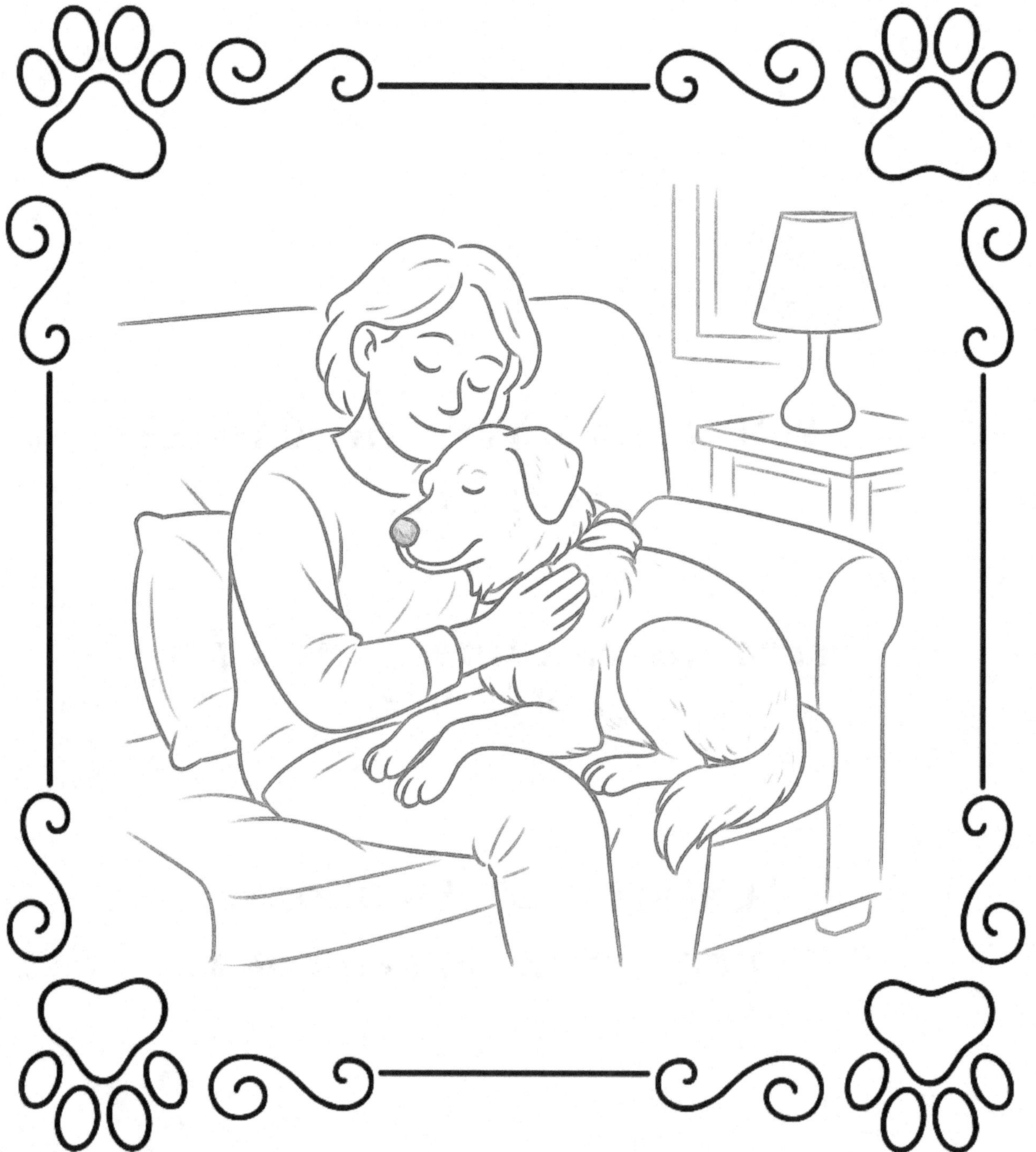

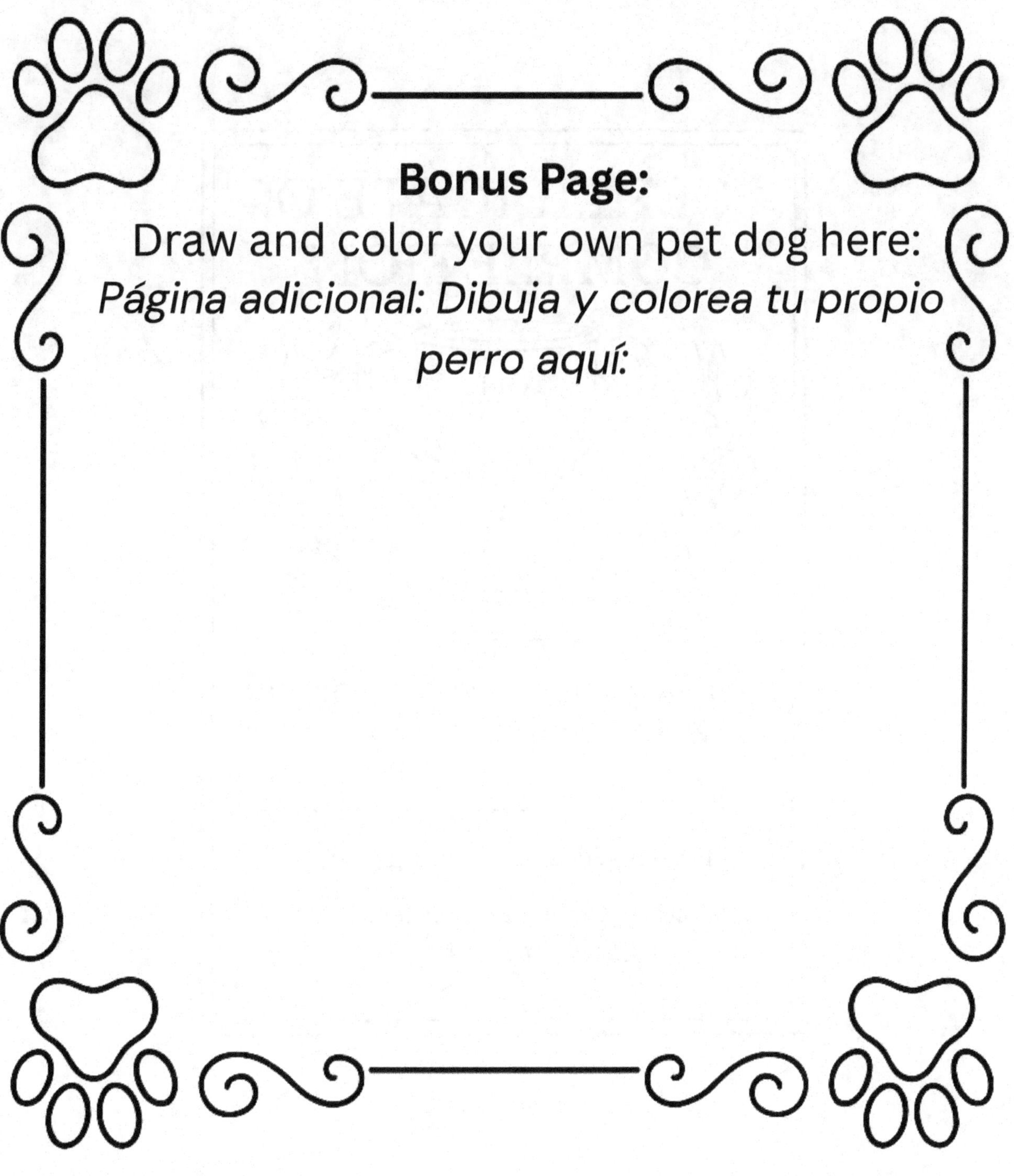

Bonus Page:

Draw and color your own pet dog here:

Página adicional: Dibuja y colorea tu propio perro aquí:

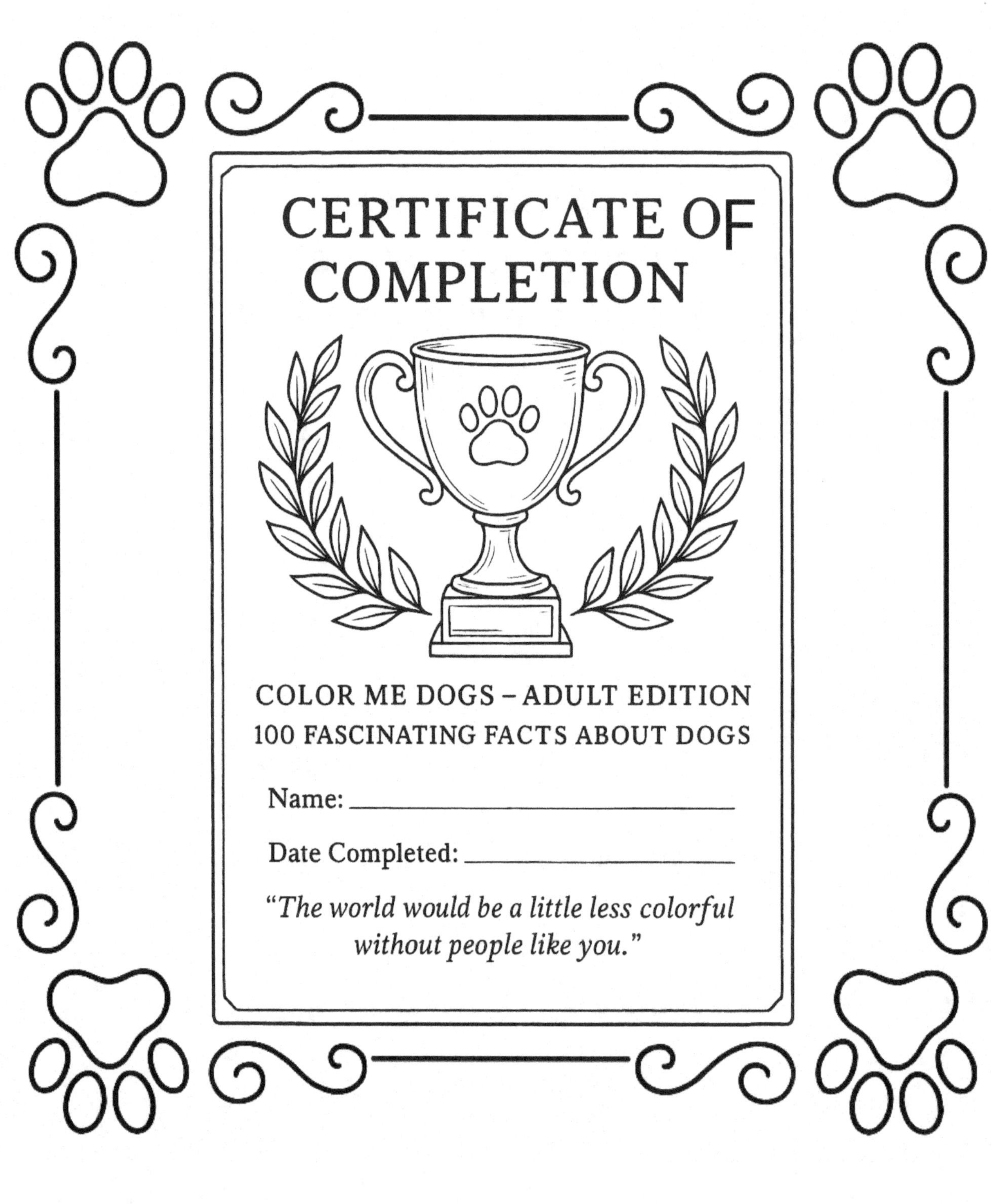

CERTIFICATE OF COMPLETION
COLOR ME DOGS – ADULT EDITION
100 FASCINATING FACTS ABOUT DOGS
Name:
Date Completed:
"The world would be a little less colorful without people like you."

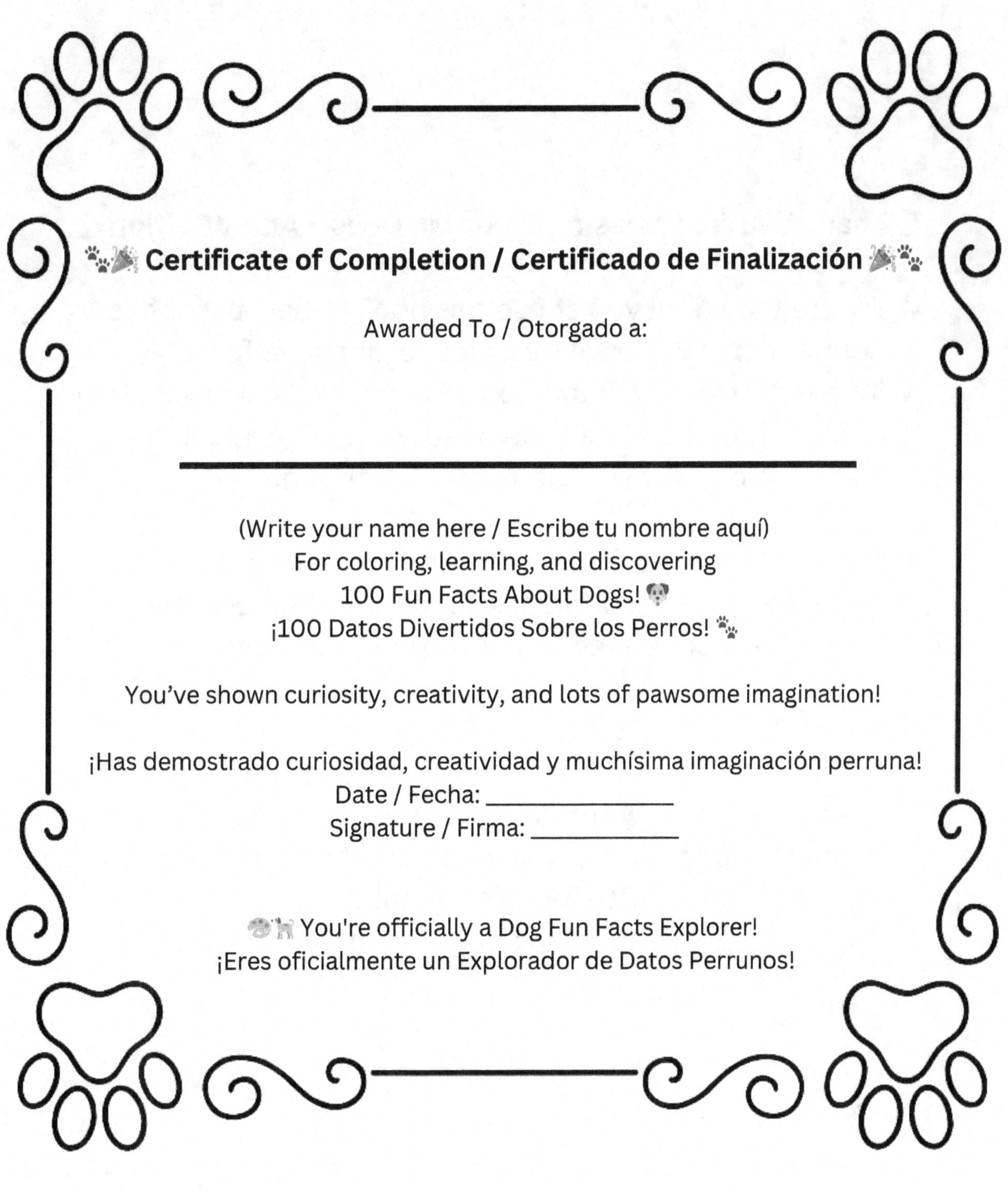

🎉🎊 **Certificate of Completion / Certificado de Finalización** 🎉🎊

Awarded To / Otorgado a:

____

(Write your name here / Escribe tu nombre aquí)
For coloring, learning, and discovering
100 Fun Facts About Dogs! 🐶
¡100 Datos Divertidos Sobre los Perros! 🐾

You've shown curiosity, creativity, and lots of pawsome imagination!

¡Has demostrado curiosidad, creatividad y muchísima imaginación perruna!
Date / Fecha: ________________
Signature / Firma: ____________

🎨🐕 You're officially a Dog Fun Facts Explorer!
¡Eres oficialmente un Explorador de Datos Perrunos!

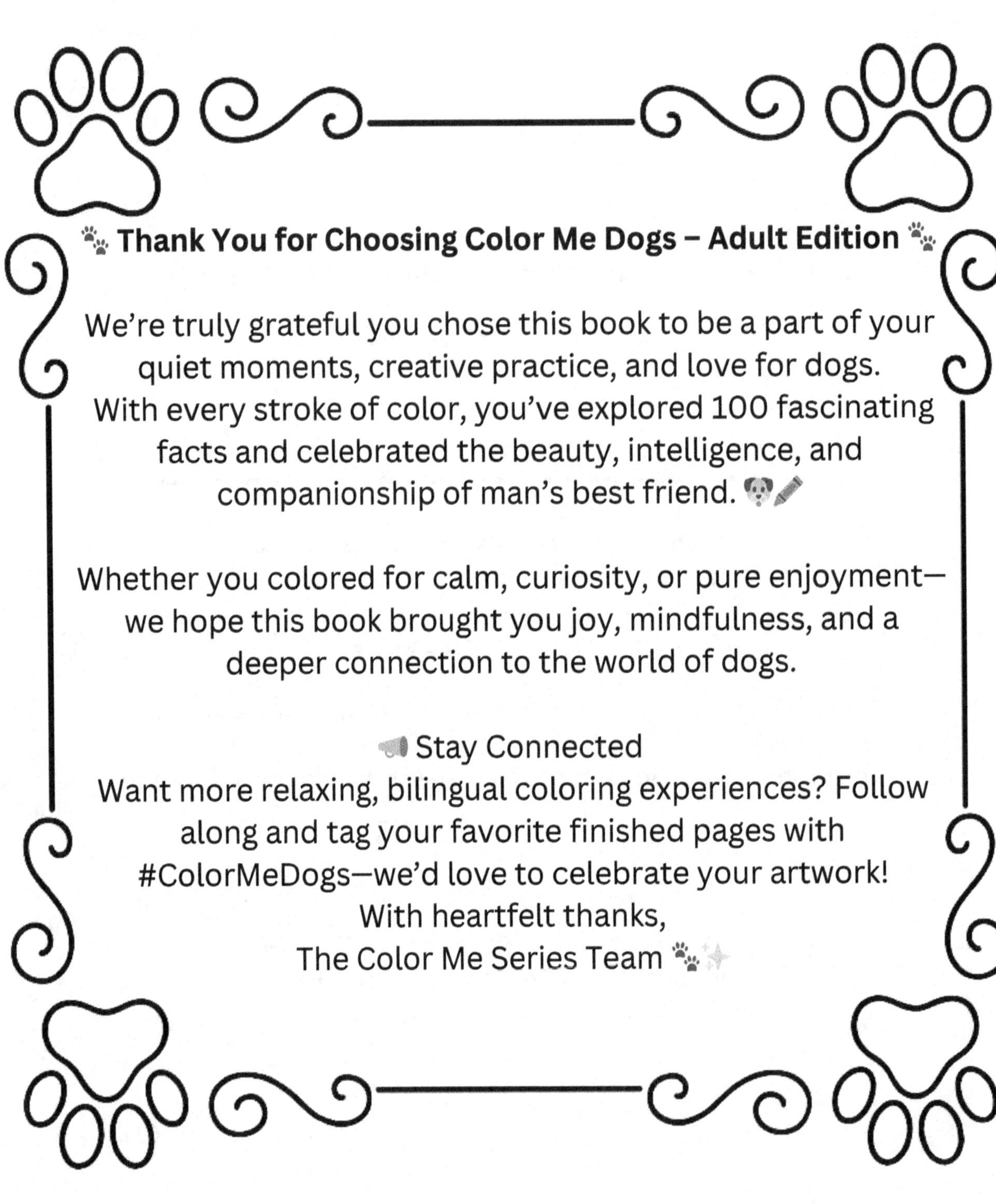

🐾 **Thank You for Choosing Color Me Dogs – Adult Edition** 🐾

We're truly grateful you chose this book to be a part of your quiet moments, creative practice, and love for dogs.
With every stroke of color, you've explored 100 fascinating facts and celebrated the beauty, intelligence, and companionship of man's best friend. 🐶🖍️

Whether you colored for calm, curiosity, or pure enjoyment—we hope this book brought you joy, mindfulness, and a deeper connection to the world of dogs.

📣 Stay Connected
Want more relaxing, bilingual coloring experiences? Follow along and tag your favorite finished pages with #ColorMeDogs—we'd love to celebrate your artwork!
With heartfelt thanks,
The Color Me Series Team 🐾✨

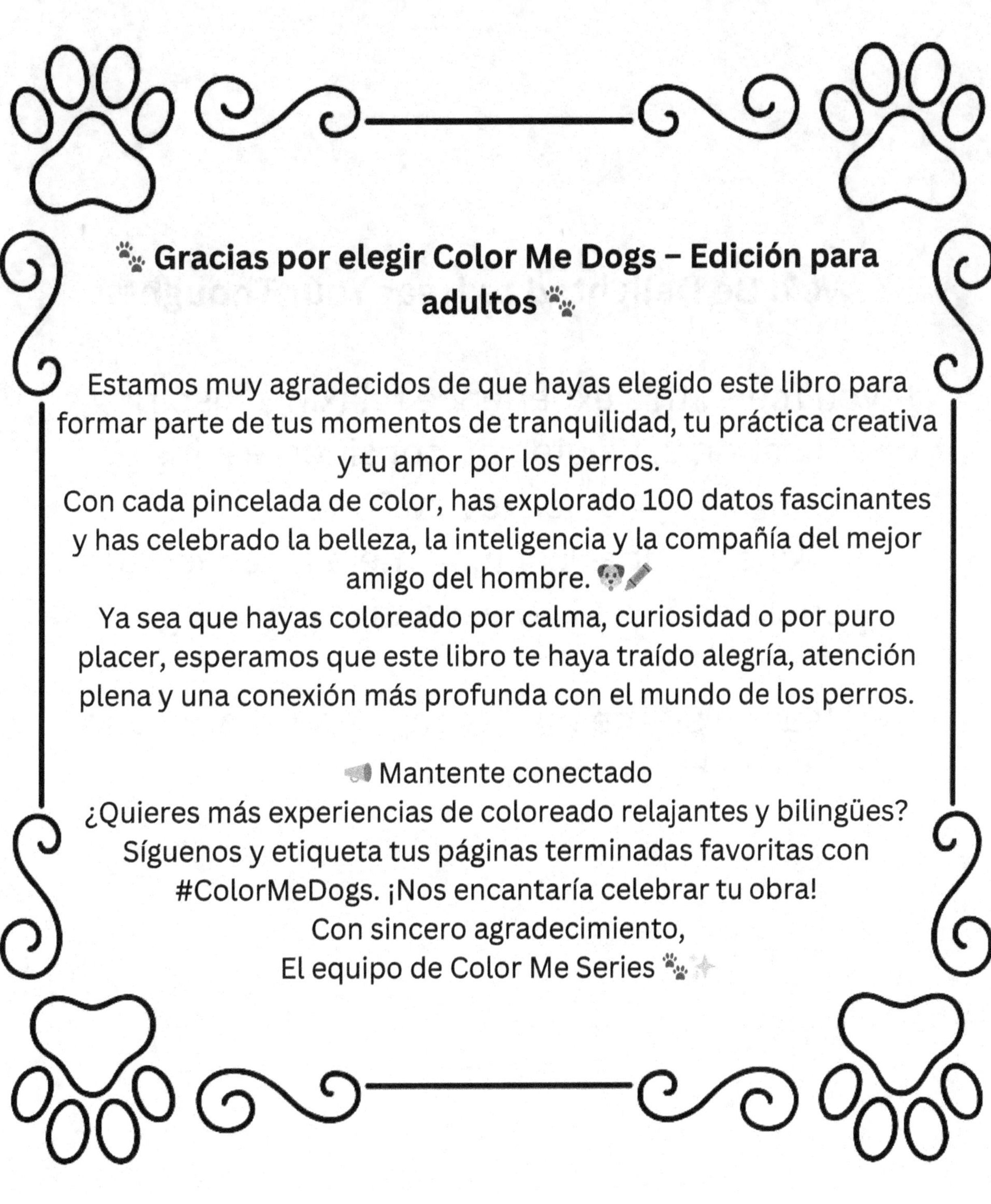

🐾 Gracias por elegir Color Me Dogs – Edición para adultos 🐾

Estamos muy agradecidos de que hayas elegido este libro para formar parte de tus momentos de tranquilidad, tu práctica creativa y tu amor por los perros.

Con cada pincelada de color, has explorado 100 datos fascinantes y has celebrado la belleza, la inteligencia y la compañía del mejor amigo del hombre. 🐶✏️

Ya sea que hayas coloreado por calma, curiosidad o por puro placer, esperamos que este libro te haya traído alegría, atención plena y una conexión más profunda con el mundo de los perros.

📣 Mantente conectado

¿Quieres más experiencias de coloreado relajantes y bilingües? Síguenos y etiqueta tus páginas terminadas favoritas con #ColorMeDogs. ¡Nos encantaría celebrar tu obra!

Con sincero agradecimiento,

El equipo de Color Me Series 🐾✨

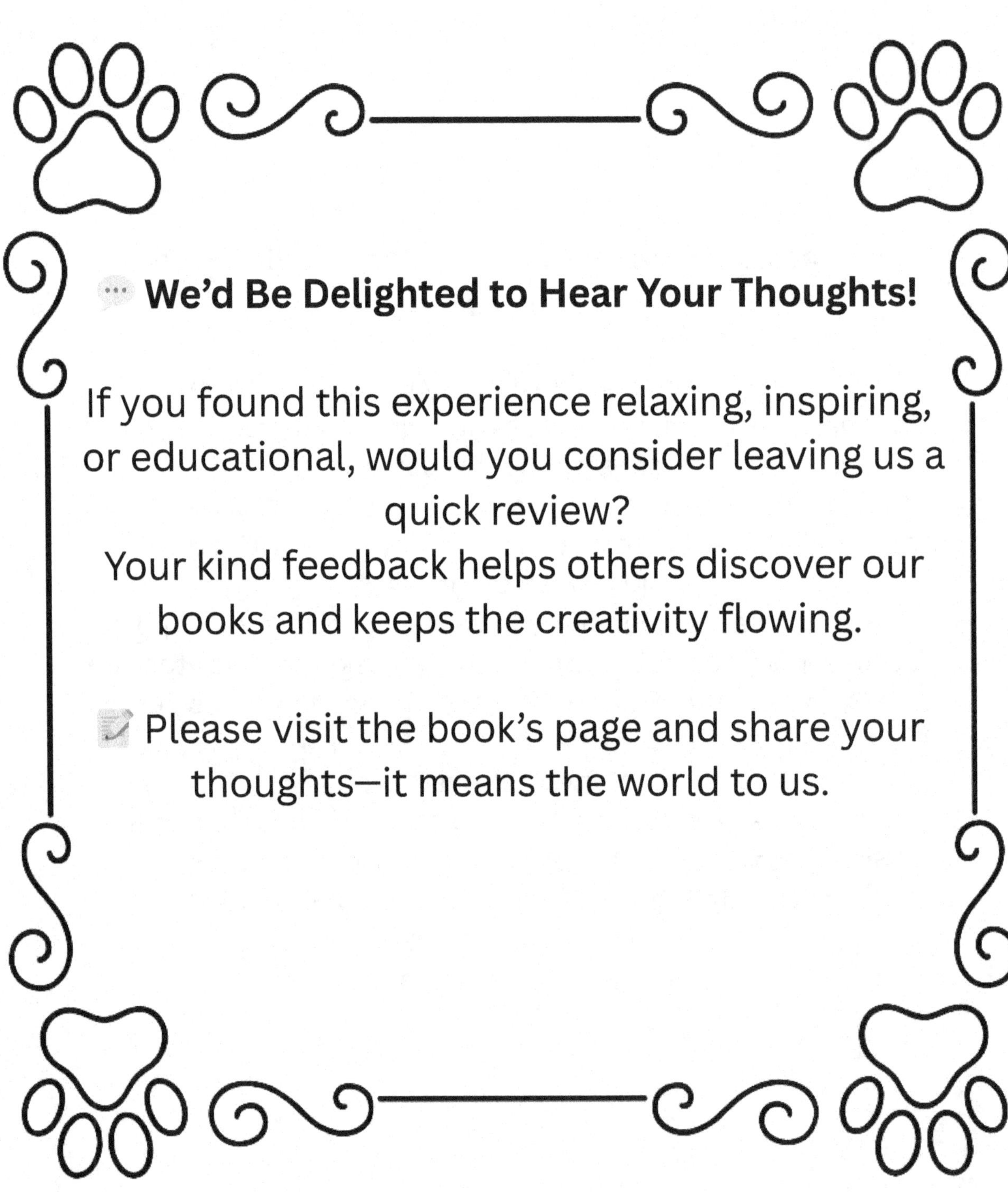

💬 We'd Be Delighted to Hear Your Thoughts!

If you found this experience relaxing, inspiring, or educational, would you consider leaving us a quick review?

Your kind feedback helps others discover our books and keeps the creativity flowing.

📝 Please visit the book's page and share your thoughts—it means the world to us.

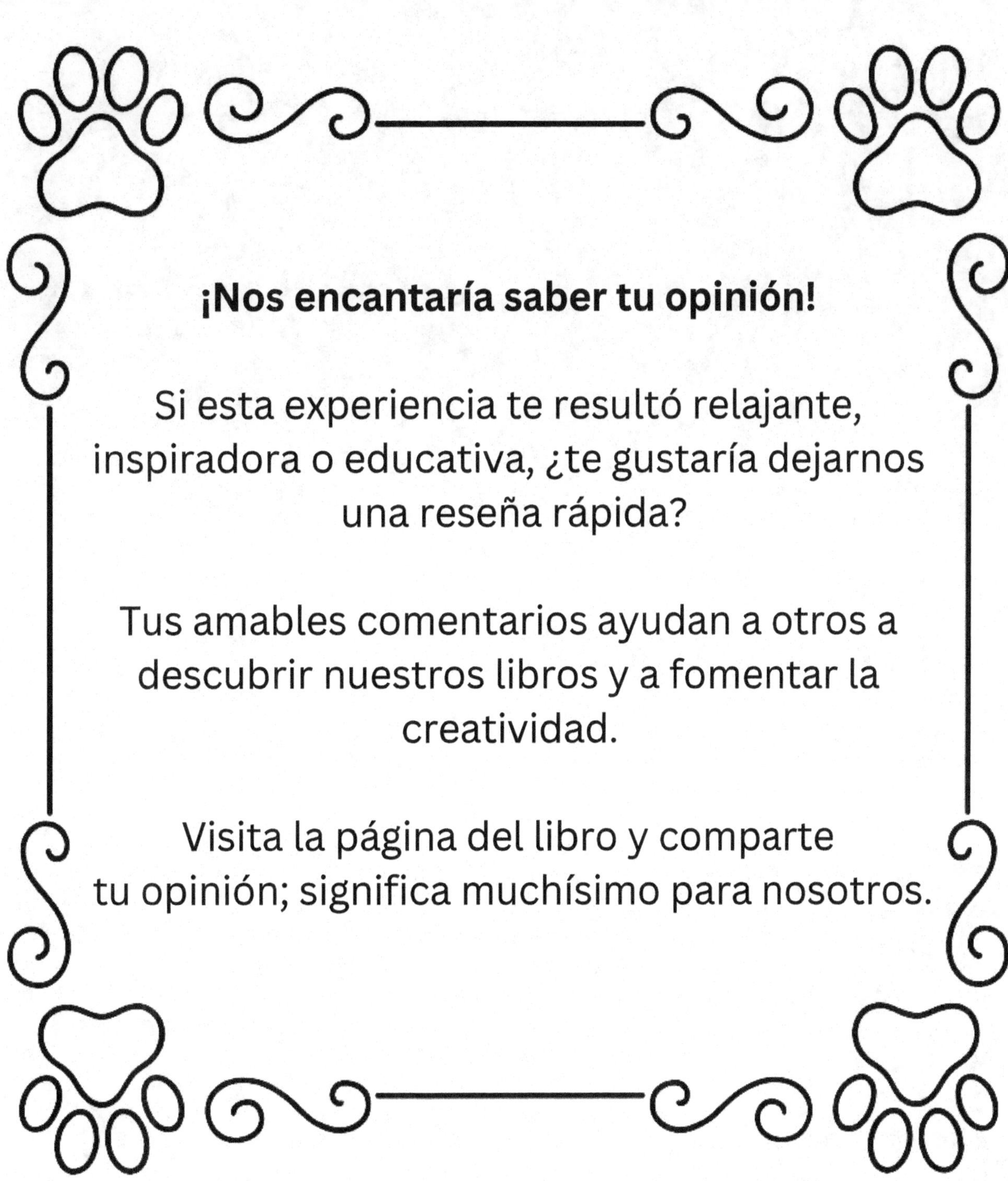

¡Nos encantaría saber tu opinión!

Si esta experiencia te resultó relajante,
inspiradora o educativa, ¿te gustaría dejarnos
una reseña rápida?

Tus amables comentarios ayudan a otros a
descubrir nuestros libros y a fomentar la
creatividad.

Visita la página del libro y comparte
tu opinión; significa muchísimo para nosotros.